Book 2

Language Arts

Lesson Guide

Book Staff and Contributors

Kristen Kinney *Director, Primary Literacy*
Alane Gernon-Paulsen *Content Specialist*
Anna Day *Senior Instructional Designer*
Miriam Greenwald, Michelle Iwaszuk, Jennifer Marrewa, David Shireman *Instructional Designers*
Karen Ingebretsen *Text Editor*
Suzanne Montazer *Creative Director, Print and ePublishing*
Sasha Blanton *Senior Print Visual Designer*
Carol Leigh *Print Visual Designer*
Stephanie Williams *Cover Designer*
Amy Eward *Senior Manager, Writers*
Susan Raley *Senior Manager, Editors*
Julie Cacal *Project Coordinator*
Colleen Line *Senior Project Manager*

Maria Szalay *Senior Vice President, Product Development*
John Holdren *Senior Vice President, Content and Curriculum*
David Pelizzari *Vice President, Content and Curriculum*
Kim Barcas *Vice President, Creative*
Laura Seuschek *Vice President, Instructional Design and Evaluation & Research*
Aaron Hall *Vice President, Program Management*

Lisa Dimaio Iekel *Senior Production Manager*

About K12 Inc.

K12 Inc., a technology-based education company, is the nation's leading provider of proprietary curriculum and online education programs to students in grades K–12. K[12] provides its curriculum and academic services to online schools, traditional classrooms, blended school programs, and directly to families. K12 Inc. also operates the K[12] International Academy, an accredited, diploma-granting online private school serving students worldwide. K[12]'s mission is to provide any child the curriculum and tools to maximize success in life, regardless of geographic, financial, or demographic circumstances. K12 Inc. is accredited by CITA. More information can be found at www.K12.com.

978-1-60153-142-1
Printed by Quad Graphics, Versailles, KY, USA, March 2012, Lot 032012

Contents

Language Skills

Comparison, Emotions, and Poems

Position, Opposites, and Poems

Opposites and Poems

Writing, Manners, and Poems

Manners, Traffic, and Poems

Ordinals, Sequences, and Poems

Sequences, Growing, and Poems

Adults & Babies, Homographs, and Poems

Review and Poems

Literature & Comprehension

Amazing Tales

A Visit to Australia

Creature Features

Listen to Learn

Out of the Mouths

Tiny People

Help Yourself and Others

Three

Hot and Cold

K[12] Language Arts Blue

General Program Overview and Structure

The K[12] Language Arts Blue program lays a strong foundation for beginning readers and writers. A well-balanced Language Arts program provides instruction on getting words off the page (reading) as well as on the page (writing). According to the National Reading Panel, a comprehensive reading program covers phonemic awareness, phonics, fluency, vocabulary, and text comprehension—all of which are covered in the following four programs:

Program	Daily Lesson Time (approximate)	Online/Offline
K[12] Language Arts PhonicsWorks	50 minutes	30 minutes offline/ 20 minutes online

Big Ideas

- Readers must understand that print carries meaning and there is a connection between letters and sounds.
- Fluent readers blend sounds represented by letters into words.
- Breaking words into syllables helps us read and spell unfamiliar words.
- Good readers practice reading grade-level text with fluency.
- Reading sight words helps young readers read complete sentences and short stories.

Program	Daily Lesson Time (approximate)	Online/Offline
K[12] Language Arts Language Skills	30 minutes	15 minutes offline/ 15 minutes online

Big Ideas

- Vocabulary words are words we need to know in order to communicate and understand.
- A *speaking vocabulary* includes the words we know and can use when speaking.
- A *reading vocabulary* includes the words we know and can read with understanding.
- A *listening vocabulary* includes the words we know and understand when we hear them.
- A *writing vocabulary* includes the words we know and understand when we write.
- The more we read, the more our vocabulary grows.
- Early learners acquire vocabulary through active exposure (by talking and listening, being read to, and receiving explicit instruction).

Program	Daily Lesson Time (approximate)	Online/Offline
K[12] Language Arts Literature & Comprehension	30 minutes	All offline

Big Ideas

- Comprehension is the reason for reading.
- Comprehension entails having and knowing a purpose for reading.
- Comprehension entails actively thinking about what is being read.
- Comprehension requires the reader to self-monitor understanding.
- Comprehension requires the reader to self-correct errors made while reading by using a wide variety of strategies.
- Comprehension requires an understanding of story structure.
- Comprehension entails asking and answering questions about the text.
- Comprehension strategies can be taught through explicit instruction.
- Connecting new information to previously learned information facilitates comprehension.
- Readers who visualize, or form mental pictures, when they read have better recall of text than those who do not.
- Reading strategies are conscious plans that readers apply and adapt to make sense of text.
- An understanding of physical presentation (headings, subheads, graphics, and other features) facilitates comprehension.
- Comprehension entails an understanding of the organizational patterns of text.
- Comprehension is enhanced when information is presented through more than one learning modality; learning modalities are visual (seeing), auditory (hearing), and kinesthetic (touching).
- Verbalizing their thoughts while modeling a reading strategy allows students to see what occurs in an effective reader's head; it makes visible the normally hidden process of comprehending text.
- Self-questioning improves comprehension and ensures that reading is an interactive process.
- Rereading texts helps students improve memory, listening skills, and comprehension.

Program	Daily Lesson Time (approximate)	Online/Offline
K[12] Language Arts Handwriting	10 minutes	All offline

Big Ideas

- Instruction in posture, pencil grip, and letter formation improves students' handwriting skills.
- Proper modeling of letter formation is imperative for developing handwriting skills.
- Students who have formal instruction in handwriting are more engaged in composition writing.

The PhonicsWorks, Language Skills, Literature & Comprehension, and Handwriting programs are independent courses that work together to give students a complete, well-balanced education in Language Arts. Some programs try to fit these four major components into one large "supercourse" that requires all students to move at the same pace through a very structured and ultimately confusing or limited program. By having students complete PhonicsWorks independently of Literature & Comprehension, K^{12} ensures they do not develop and reinforce misconceptions about letter–sound knowledge. Keeping Language Skills separate from Literature & Comprehension allows students to increase their speaking vocabularies and listening vocabularies while developing their comprehension skills, rather than mastering one at the expense of another.

Suggested Order of Lessons

K^{12} highly recommends that students complete the Language Arts lessons in the following order:

1. PhonicsWorks
2. Language Skills
3. Literature & Comprehension
4. Handwriting

A key aspect of K^{12} courses is the flexibility they offer students. Doing things that work best for them is vital to students' mastery. If students benefit from completing the Handwriting lesson first thing in the morning and closing the day with Literature & Comprehension, that is acceptable.

How to Work Through a Lesson

Types of Activities

The K[12] Language Arts programs contain both offline and online activities as well as assessments.

Offline Activities Offline activities take place away from the computer and are described in detail in the lesson plans within the Lesson Guide. During offline activities, you will work closely with students. (**Safety note:** When students are working with scissors, please supervise them to make sure they use their scissors safely and stay seated.)

Online Activities Online activities take place at the computer. At first, you may need to help students learn how to navigate and use the online activities. You may also need to provide support when activities cover new or challenging content. Eventually students will complete online activities with minimal support from you.

Assessments Students will complete online assessments, called Unit Checkpoints, in the Language Skills program. Because these assessments are all online, the computer will score them for you. You do not need to enter assessment scores in the Online School.

Where to Begin?

There is more than one way to begin a lesson; either way will get you where you need to go.

Beginning Online If you begin from the online lesson, the lesson screens will walk you through what you need to do, including gathering materials and moving offline if necessary. If the lesson begins with online activities, students will need to come to the computer and complete them. If the lesson begins with offline activities, gather the materials listed and begin the activities described in the lesson plan with students when you're ready.

Beginning Offline You may choose to begin a lesson by first checking the lesson plan for the day in the Lesson Guide. The table on the first page of the lesson plan will indicate whether the lesson begins with online or offline activities. If the lesson begins with online activities, students will need to move to the computer and complete them. If the lesson begins with offline activities, gather the materials listed and begin the activities described in the lesson plan with students when you're ready.

After you've completed a unit or two in a particular course, you'll be familiar with the pattern of the units and lessons and you'll know exactly where and how to begin.

How to Use This Book

The *K*[12] *Language Arts Lesson Guide* contains overviews for the Language Skills, Literature & Comprehension, and Handwriting programs and lesson plans for the Language Skills and Literature & Comprehension programs. Lesson plans for the PhonicsWorks and Handwriting programs appear in separate books.

The overviews on the following pages provide information on instructional philosophies, program content, and structure.

Each lesson plan gives you detailed instructions for completing the lesson. The first page of each lesson plan contains some or all of the following elements, depending on the program and lesson. (The sample on this page is from a Literature & Comprehension lesson.)

Program Name
This banner identifies the section of the book. Each program has its own banner color, so you can easily flip to a section if you know the color.

Lesson Title
The title indicates the lesson topic.

Unit Overview
The first lesson of each unit describes the content covered in the unit.

Lesson Overview Table
This table provides an overview of the lesson's activities, their approximate times, and whether they take place offline or online.

Advance Preparation
This section calls out what you need to prepare before beginning the lesson.

Big Ideas
These points are the major organizing ideas in Language Arts students will work toward.

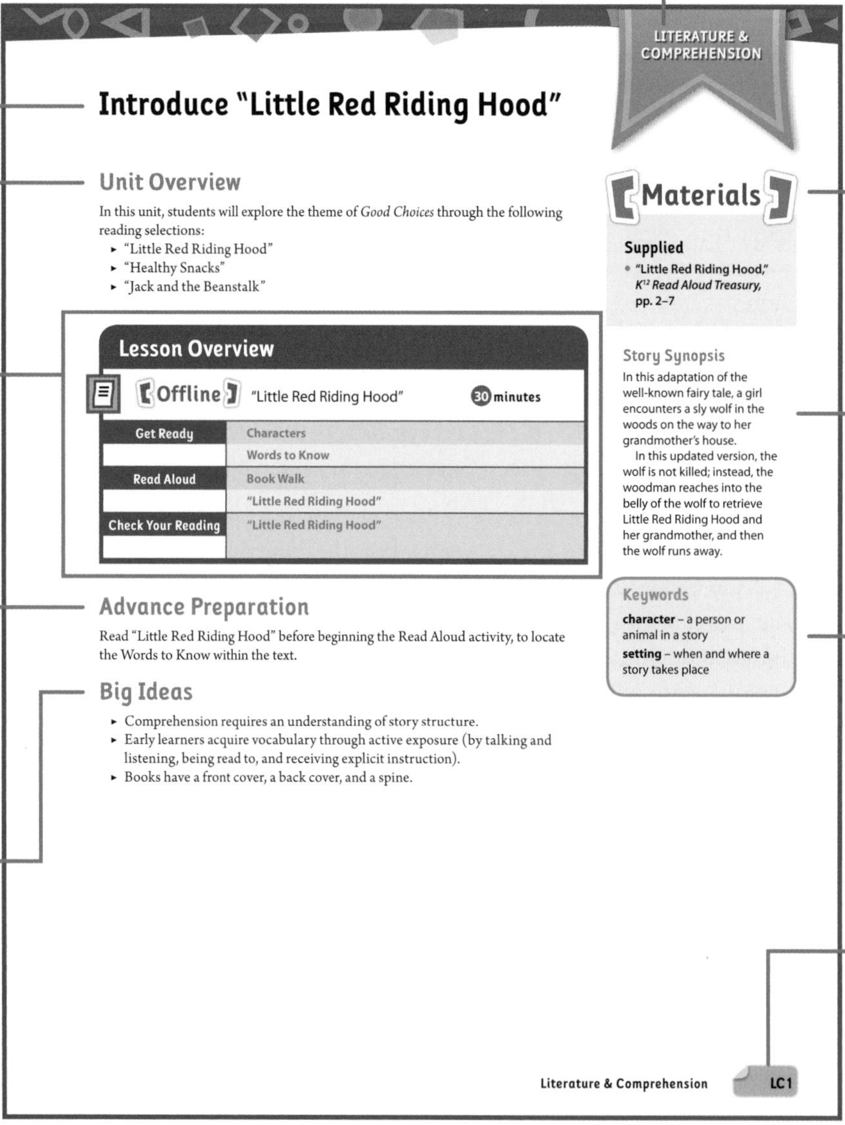
LITERATURE & COMPREHENSION

Introduce "Little Red Riding Hood"

Unit Overview

In this unit, students will explore the theme of *Good Choices* through the following reading selections:

- "Little Red Riding Hood"
- "Healthy Snacks"
- "Jack and the Beanstalk"

Lesson Overview

Offline — "Little Red Riding Hood" — 30 minutes

Get Ready	Characters
	Words to Know
Read Aloud	Book Walk
	"Little Red Riding Hood"
Check Your Reading	"Little Red Riding Hood"

Advance Preparation

Read "Little Red Riding Hood" before beginning the Read Aloud activity, to locate the Words to Know within the text.

Big Ideas

- Comprehension requires an understanding of story structure.
- Early learners acquire vocabulary through active exposure (by talking and listening, being read to, and receiving explicit instruction).
- Books have a front cover, a back cover, and a spine.

Materials

Supplied

- "Little Red Riding Hood," *K*[12] *Read Aloud Treasury*, pp. 2–7

Story Synopsis

In this adaptation of the well-known fairy tale, a girl encounters a sly wolf in the woods on the way to her grandmother's house.

In this updated version, the wolf is not killed; instead, the woodman reaches into the belly of the wolf to retrieve Little Red Riding Hood and her grandmother, and then the wolf runs away.

Keywords

character – a person or animal in a story

setting – when and where a story takes place

Literature & Comprehension LC1

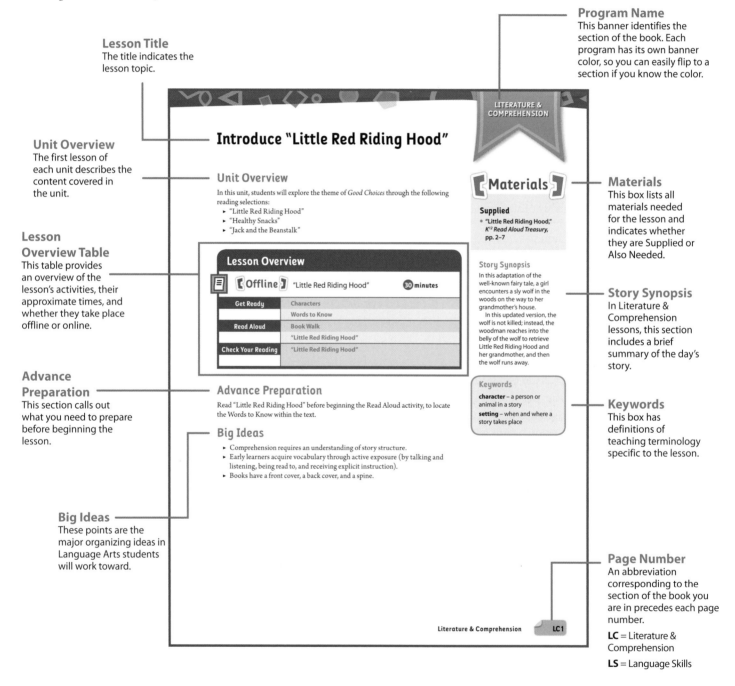

Materials
This box lists all materials needed for the lesson and indicates whether they are Supplied or Also Needed.

Story Synopsis
In Literature & Comprehension lessons, this section includes a brief summary of the day's story.

Keywords
This box has definitions of teaching terminology specific to the lesson.

Page Number
An abbreviation corresponding to the section of the book you are in precedes each page number.

LC = Literature & Comprehension

LS = Language Skills

My Accomplishments Chart

Research shows that rewarding students for quality work can increase their motivation. To help you reward students, you will receive a My Accomplishments chart and sticker sheet for use throughout the Language Arts program. This chart gives students a tangible record of their progress and accomplishments throughout the Language Skills, Literature & Comprehension, and PhonicsWorks programs. Help students proudly display and share their accomplishments with others by placing the chart somewhere visible, such as on the refrigerator or wall.

Throughout the online lessons, look for the reward icon, which indicates when and where students should place a sticker on the chart. Encourage students to set goals and watch their stickers accumulate. Praise them to help them understand the connection between their own growing skill set and the My Accomplishments chart. By the end of all programs, students should have filled up the entire chart.

For specific information about how to use the chart in each program, see the My Accomplishments Chart section in the following individual program overviews.

Noodleverse

Do your students have a favorite online activity? Do you wish you could find a favorite activity or practice a problem skill without hunting through lessons? If so, you and your students will love exploring Noodleverse—K[12]'s fun, engaging portal to many of the review and practice activities in the Language Arts program. The online lessons contain links to Noodleverse, where students can create a "buddy" to help them explore, navigate to fun locations to browse activities, and mark activities as favorites for quick access later. You'll be able to pull up a site map listing every activity, organized by course and topic.

Here are some of the Language Arts items that can be found in Noodleverse:

- Phonics practice activities
- Vocabulary practice activities
- Audio recordings of stories and poems from the *K[12] Read Aloud Treasury*
- Book browser for choosing books in Literature & Comprehension
- Letter Train activities for Handwriting

Student Portfolios

As students progress through each program, K[12] recommends keeping a student portfolio as a record of their progress. Students will write in the *K[12] Language Arts Activity Book* and *K[12] All About Me*, so place the Activity Book pages and the entire *K[12] All About Me* in the portfolio (a simple folder, large envelope, or three-ring binder would work) along with handwriting samples. Look back through the portfolio monthly and at the end of the program with students and celebrate their progress and achievements.

K¹² Language Arts PhonicsWorks Program Overview

K¹² provides the PhonicsWorks materials separately from the Language Arts materials, so you will not find PhonicsWorks lesson plans or activity book pages in the *K¹² Language Arts Lesson Guide* or the *K¹² Language Arts Activity Book*. Please refer to the PhonicsWorks Kit for all phonics materials.

K¹² Language Arts Language Skills Program Overview

Program Philosophy

The K¹² Language Arts Language Skills program guides students through vocabulary, early composition work (here, called All About Me), and poetry.

Vocabulary

What Is It? People have various types of vocabulary. We have *speaking vocabulary* (words we use proficiently when talking with others), *listening vocabulary* (words we understand well when hearing others speak), *reading vocabulary* (words we can decode and comprehend), and *writing vocabulary* (words we can spell and comprehend). Students typically have larger speaking vocabularies than listening, reading, and writing vocabularies. National Reading Panel research shows that students learn most vocabulary indirectly (through daily speaking and listening in the home, listening to stories, reading stories, and so on), but some vocabulary must be learned directly (through instruction on specific words, meanings, and proper uses).

Why We Do It Vocabulary includes the words we need to know in order to communicate. To write or read something, we must have a strong vocabulary so we can communicate effectively. Students with a strong and varied vocabulary have an easier time comprehending and composing written material. Researchers Margaret McKeown and Isabel Beck concluded that robust vocabulary instruction involving active learning, prior knowledge, and frequent encounters with vocabulary words is more powerful and effective.

The Vocabulary component of the K¹² Language Skills program gives students direct instruction on word meanings through a wide variety of words grouped in conceptually related sets, such as colors or jobs. You will introduce the words in each word set to students offline. They will then spend time online reviewing and practicing the words.

All About Me

What Is It? The All About Me activities in the K12 Language Skills program are designed to help students develop basic composition skills, including brainstorming, drafting, writing, revising, and publishing, in a developmentally and age-appropriate manner. Each All About Me activity is offline and most span two lessons. Each activity includes guiding discussion questions to help students develop a habit of talking through ideas to brainstorm about a topic.

You will do most of the basic writing for students, who will then illustrate sentences based on the discussion and written sentences. Some students may benefit from or truly enjoy doing the small amount of required writing on their own. In those cases, K12 encourages you to simply help them spell the words properly.

Most of students' work involves illustrating a topic in *K12 All About Me*. If time allows, students should begin their drawing typically on the first day, immediately following the discussion time. Typicaly on the second day, students should spend most of their time completing their illustration and adding supporting details.

Why We Do It As you do when assigning a written composition, encourage students to review their work and add more details to their picture. Developing this habit helps students get used to revising their writing, which becomes increasingly important in subsequent grades. In the All About Me activities, they share their illustration with others. Whether they show their work to 1 person or 20 people, students should use complete sentences and a wide variety of vocabulary. This simple task lays the groundwork for sharing written compositions and public speaking activities in subsequent grades.

Poetry

What Is It? The Poetry activities in the K12 Language Skills program are all offline and use one of three sources for the poems: *K12 Read Aloud Treasury, The Rooster Crows*, and *Tomie DePaolo's Rhyme Time*. Traditional nursery rhymes from Mother Goose, songs, and classic poems from Dorothy Aldis, Robert Louis Stevenson, and Christina Rosseti round out the Poetry lessons. The Lesson Guide gives you a plan for discussing the poems and their language, rhythm, and rhyme.

Why We Do It The K12 Language Skills program includes Poetry for two main reasons. First poetry is a fun and engaging way to expose students to a wider variety of language they may not hear in a traditional literature or phonics program. Second poetry's rhythm and rhyming nature make it easy to memorize and repeat—thereby providing opportunities for public speaking practice.

Overview of Language Skills Lessons

Materials

The following books are supplied for the Language Skills program:

K12 Language Arts Lesson Guide

K12 Language Arts Activity Book

K12 All About Me

K12 Read Aloud Treasury

The Rooster Crows and *Tomie DePaolo's Rhyme Time* are also supplied.

(Keep in mind that students will write in and tear pages out of the Activity Book and *K12 All About Me*; you may want to store loose Activity Book pages in a three-ring binder. Remember to build students' portfolios with completed work from these books.)

You will also need the following general materials to complete the Activity Book pages and optional flash card activities:

- 3½ x 5-inch index cards
- crayons or colored pencils
- scissors (**Safety note:** When students are working with scissors, please supervise them to make sure they use their scissors safely and stay seated.)
- glue stick

Lesson Structure

The K[12] Language Skills program consists of 18 ten-day units that follow a set, repeated pattern. In each unit, students rotate through Vocabulary, All About Me, and Poetry lessons. The following chart is an overview of how lessons are organized in each unit.

Day	Offline (15 minutes)	Online (15 minutes)
1	Vocabulary: Introduce Word Set 1 Create Flash Cards (optional)	Skills Update (except first unit) Learn: Introduce Word Set 1
2	All About Me	Practice: Word Set 1
3	Poetry	Practice: Word Set 1
4	Vocabulary: Introduce Word Set 2 Create Flash Cards (optional)	Skills Update (except first unit) Learn: Introduce Word Set 2
5	All About Me	Practice: Word Set 2
6	Poetry	Practice: Word Set 2
7	Vocabulary: Introduce Word Set 3 Create Flash Cards (optional)	Skills Update (except first unit) Learn: Introduce Word Set 3
8	All About Me	Practice: Word Set 3
9	Poetry	Unit Review
10	Unit Checkpoint (Online—30 minutes)	

Lesson Activities

Lesson plans in the Language Skills section of this Lesson Guide include detailed descriptions or instructions for each activity. Language Skills lesson plans include the following elements:

Activity Description

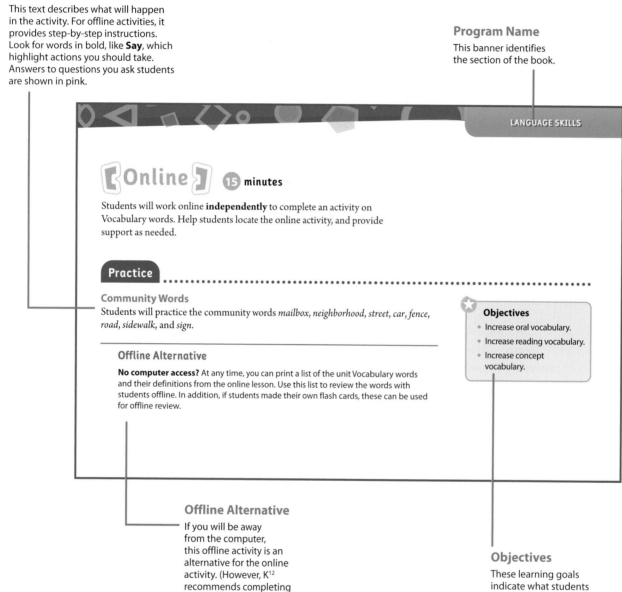

This text describes what will happen in the activity. For offline activities, it provides step-by-step instructions. Look for words in bold, like **Say**, which highlight actions you should take. Answers to questions you ask students are shown in pink.

Program Name

This banner identifies the section of the book.

LANGUAGE SKILLS

Online 15 **minutes**

Students will work online **independently** to complete an activity on Vocabulary words. Help students locate the online activity, and provide support as needed.

Practice

Community Words

Students will practice the community words *mailbox, neighborhood, street, car, fence, road, sidewalk,* and *sign.*

Objectives

- Increase oral vocabulary.
- Increase reading vocabulary.
- Increase concept vocabulary.

Offline Alternative

No computer access? At any time, you can print a list of the unit Vocabulary words and their definitions from the online lesson. Use this list to review the words with students offline. In addition, if students made their own flash cards, these can be used for offline review.

Offline Alternative

If you will be away from the computer, this offline activity is an alternative for the online activity. (However, K[12] recommends completing the online activity whenever possible.)

Objectives

These learning goals indicate what students should be able to do as a result of the lesson.

Language Skills activity types include the following:

- **Vocabulary (Offline)** You will introduce students to one of three sets of words covered in the unit. In addition, as an optional activity, encourage students who are reading and writing and who would benefit from the use of flash cards to write each vocabulary word on an index card and to write their own definition of that word on the back of the card. Students may study the cards during the course of the unit.
- **All About Me (Offline)** Students will work with you to complete an All About Me activity designed to engage them in drawing, writing, and oral language.
- **Poetry (Offline)** Students will work with you to explore a wide variety of poems, rhymes, and songs. Encourage students to repeat the poems, songs, and rhymes often. If they are assigned an Activity Book page, have them practice reciting the poem while coloring the page. Give students opportunities to recite poems from memory while standing erect and enunciating clearly. These small tasks provide a solid foundation for future public speaking activities.
- **Skills Update (Online)** The first day of each unit (after the first unit) contains a Skills Update. Students will refresh their knowledge of vocabulary words from previous units with this online assessment.
- **Learn (Online)** Students will become more familiar with one of three sets of words covered in the unit. The activity typically focuses on each word to give students a strong grounding in that word.
- **Practice (Online)** Students will review and practice one of three sets of words covered in the unit. This activity reinforces the meaning and use of the words and focuses on any vocabulary skills particular to the word set being studied, such as sorting or using context clues.
- **Unit Review (Online)** Students will work independently to review all vocabulary words from the unit in preparation for the Unit Checkpoint. They do the review by playing the online Boat Adventure game.
- **Unit Checkpoint (Online)** Students will work independently to complete an online Unit Checkpoint. This assessment covers all vocabulary words from the unit.

My Accomplishments Chart

Rewards in Language Skills are tied to completing Unit Checkpoints. Each time students score 80 percent or higher on a Unit Checkpoint, have them add a sticker for that unit to the My Accomplishments chart. If students score lower than 80 percent, review each Checkpoint exercise with them and work with them to correct any exercises they missed. Although students may retake the Unit Checkpoint anytime, K^{12} recommends that they wait until the next day.

K12 Language Arts Literature & Comprehension Program Overview

Program Philosophy

The K12 Language Arts Literature & Comprehension program includes four effective, instructional approaches to reading: Read Aloud, Shared Reading, Guided Reading, and Independent Reading. Each approach contributes to students' skill level and ability to apply specific reading strategies.

Read Aloud

What Is It? A proficient reader (in this case, you) reads aloud to students carefully selected texts from various genres. The texts have features that lend themselves to modeling what good readers do.

Why We Do It Reading aloud engages students in an enjoyable experience that promotes a love of reading. It is an opportunity to share quality literature that is too challenging for students to read independently. Listening to stories helps students build vocabulary knowledge and develop a sense of story structure. While reading aloud, you will model the following behaviors for students: fluent, expressive reading; what good readers think about as they read; and how good readers use strategies to understand text.

Shared Reading

What Is It? In Shared Reading, students join in reading text while guided by a proficient reader (in this case, you). Shared Reading is introduced in K12 Language Arts Green.

Guided Reading

What Is It? In Guided Reading, students read books specifically selected to challenge them and give them problem-solving opportunities. They become familiar with each new book through instruction that supports and enables them to read the text themselves. Guided Reading is introduced in K12 Language Arts Green.

Independent Reading

What Is It? When they do Independent Reading, students often choose their own books from a wide range of reading materials and read on their own for an extended block of time. During Independent Reading, they need to read books at a level just right for them, called their *independent level*. Independent Reading is introduced in K12 Language Arts Orange.

Overview of Literature & Comprehension Lessons

Materials

The following books are supplied for the Literature & Comprehension program:

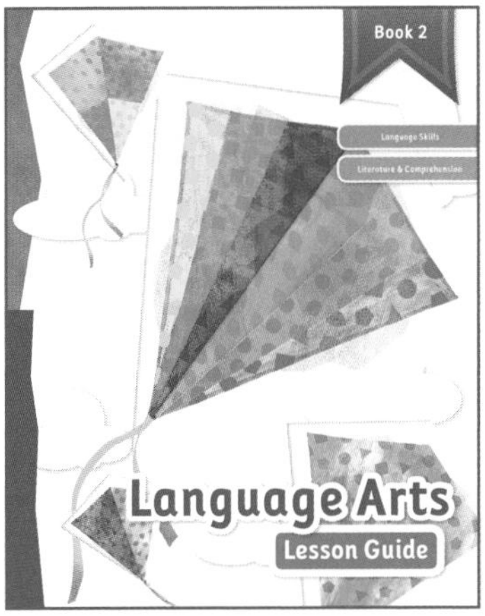

K^{12} Language Arts Lesson Guide

K^{12} Language Arts Activity Book

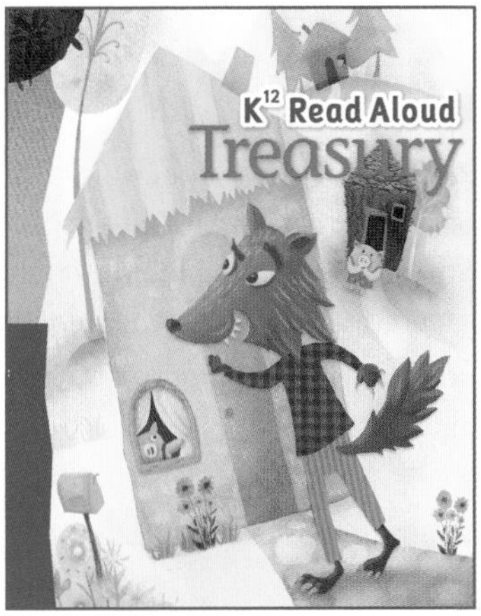

K^{12} Read Aloud Treasury

Nonfiction Magazine: ***Taking Care of Ourselves and Our Earth***

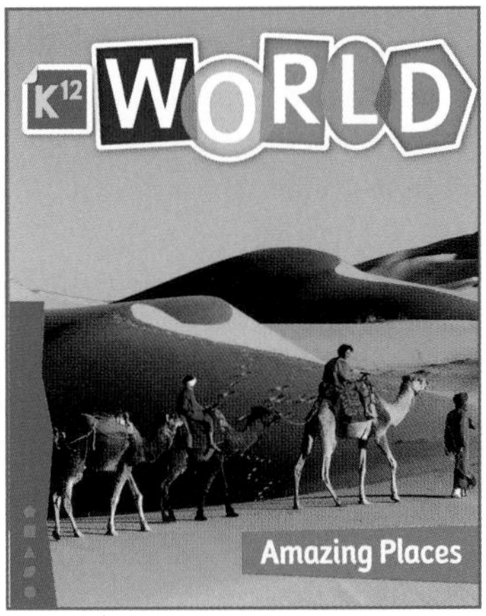

Nonfiction Magazine: ***Amazing Places***

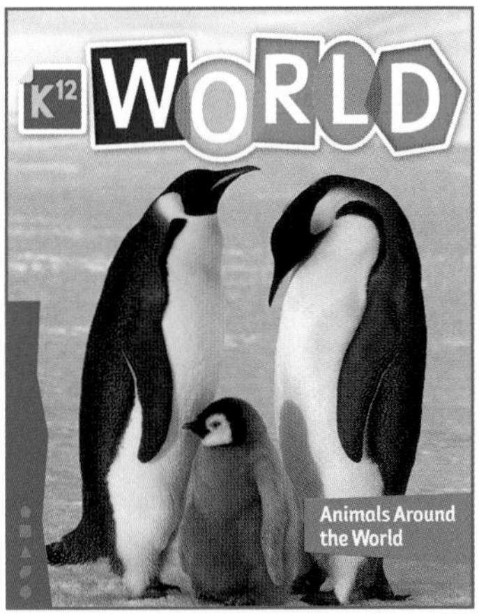

Nonfiction Magazine: ***Animals Around the World***

Nonfiction Magazine: ***Our Busy Bodies***

The following trade books are also supplied:

- *A Chair for My Mother*
- *Mike Mulligan and His Steam Shovel*
- *Caps for Sale*
- *Make Way for Ducklings*
- *A Story, A Story*
- *Tikki Tikki Tembo*
- *The Complete Adventures of Peter Rabbit*
- *The Snowy Day*

(Keep in mind that students will write in and tear pages out of the Activity Book; you may want to store loose Activity Book pages in a three-ring binder. Remember to build students' portfolios with completed Activity Book pages.)

You will also need the following general materials to complete Activity Book pages:

- crayons or colored pencils
- scissors (**Safety note:** When students are working with scissors, please supervise them to make sure they use their scissors safely and stay seated.)
- glue stick

Lesson Structure

The K[12] Literature & Comprehension program consists of 23 entirely offline units with reading selections from the *K[12] Read Aloud Treasury*, nonfiction magazines, and trade books. The daily 30-minute lessons build in a sequence designed to meet new readers' needs and are developmentally appropriate for a kindergarten reader's growing comprehension abilities. The following chart is an overview of how most lessons, which follow a three-day pattern, are organized for each reading selection.

Day	Offline (15 minutes)
1	**Get Ready** **Read Aloud** **Check Your Reading**
2	**Get Ready** **Read Aloud** **Check Your Reading** **Reading for Meaning**
3	**Get Ready** **Reading for Meaning** **Making Connections** **Beyond the Lesson (optional)**

Research on reading comprehension indicates that rereading improves memory and accuracy in comprehension. As such, each reading selection is read aloud to students in two consecutive lessons—first in the Introduce lesson and again in the Explore lesson. Typically the first reading focuses on the story, Words to Know, and comprehension, while the second reading focuses on the story, a specific feature of the text, and additional, deeper comprehension. Some students may benefit from a third reading of the text. In the Review lesson, the schedule includes time for **Reread or Retell**. Many students will have improved performance on the Reading for Meaning and/or Making Connections activities because of this third and final rereading.

Lesson Activities

Lesson plans in the Literature & Comprehension section of this Lesson Guide include detailed descriptions or instructions for each activity. Literature & Comprehension lesson plans include the following elements:

Program Name
This banner identifies the section of the book.

Activity Description
This text describes what will happen in the activity. For offline activities, it provides step-by-step instructions. Look for words in bold, like **Say**, which highlight actions you should take. Answers to questions you ask students are shown in pink.

LITERATURE & COMPREHENSION

Offline 30 minutes

"Sleeping Beauty"

Work **together** with students to complete offline Get Ready, Read Aloud, Check Your Reading, and Reading for Meaning activities.

Get Ready

What Is a Fairy Tale?
Tell students that "Sleeping Beauty" is a fairy tale. A **fairy tale** is a folk story with magical parts, such as a fairy godmother who can turn a pumpkin into a carriage with her wand. Magical characters don't exist in real life. Tell students to listen for parts of the story that could not happen in real life.

Objectives
- Identify genre.
- Build vocabulary through listening, reading, and discussion.
- Use new vocabulary in written and spoken sentences.

Words to Know
Before reading "Sleeping Beauty,"

1. Have students say each word aloud.
2. Ask students if they know what each word means.
   - If students know a word's meaning, have them define it and use it in a sentence.
   - If students don't know a word's meaning, read them the definition and discuss the word with them.

canopy – a cover above a bed
feast – a large, fancy meal attended by many people
hedge – a thick row of bushes
passage – a long, thin space that you can use to get from one place to another
prick – to poke a small hole with something sharp like a pin
spindle – the round stick on a spinning wheel that holds and winds the thread

Objectives
These learning goals indicate what students should be able to do as a result of the lesson.

Literature & Comprehension activity types include the following:

- **Get Ready** Every lesson begins with a Get Ready activity, which include detailed instructions on how to prepare students for the reading selection and lesson. You will provide instruction to help students understand the reading selection and develop knowledge of comprehension strategies. You will then complete steps for introducing Words to Know, which are words from the selection that students should become familiar with.
- **Read Aloud** You will read aloud all texts in the Literature & Comprehension lessons to students. The Read Aloud activities begin with a Book Walk. This activity is a structured introduction to the reading selection that familiarizes students with the content, and helps them recall related background knowledge and make predictions. After the Book Walk, you will read the selection aloud, following any directions related to the lesson focus. For example, you may be asked to emphasize the Words to Know, or you may be directed to pause at certain points in the selection and ask students to make predictions. K^{12} recommends that you preview the questions you will ask students before reading the selection. (Note that audio versions of the stories and poems you read aloud from the *K^{12} Read Aloud Treasury* can be found in Noodleverse. If students enjoy a particular reading selection, they might like to later listen to the audio version while following along in the book.)
- **Check Your Reading** You will ask students to demonstrate general comprehension of the reading selection by retelling what happens and answering basic comprehension questions. In most cases, answers to Check Your Reading questions are stated directly in the reading selection.
- **Reading for Meaning** You will work with students to develop a deeper understanding of the reading selection through Reading for Meaning activities. The main focus of these activities is comprehension strategies and analysis of the reading selection.
- **Making Connections** Students will apply information and strategies learned from lessons to the reading selection. This activity often involves connecting the reading selection to students' lives and the larger world, often through Activity Book pages.
- **Beyond the Lesson (Optional)** These activities are for students who have extra time and interest in exploring the reading selection further. These activities are *not required* and can be skipped.

My Accomplishments Chart

Rewards in the Literature & Comprehension program are tied to completing units. When students complete a unit, have them add a sticker for that unit to the My Accomplishments chart.

Reader's Choice Units

Throughout the K[12] Language Arts Literature & Comprehension program, Planning and Progress in the Online School will alert you to an approaching Reader's Choice Unit. These units are designed to give students an opportunity to self-select texts while fine-tuning their comprehension skills. Research indicates that providing opportunities for choice enhances performance and motivates early readers. Titles range from the classic to the contemporary and include fiction, folktales, and nonfiction.

In the six Reader's Choice Units spread across the program, you will have a bank of 18 texts to choose from. K[12] suggests you discuss the possible texts with students to guarantee that they will engage with texts that interest them. Like the regular Literature units, these Choice units are also three lessons each. There are two important differences:

1. **You will need to acquire these texts on your own, through a library or bookstore.** To help you choose a text for a Reader's Choice Unit, K[12] includes a brief synopsis of the story and information about grade and interest level.
2. Once you have selected the text, you will be prompted to ***print*** the accompanying lesson guide and activity pages. **You must print these pages because they are not provided in this Lesson Guide or the Activity Book.**

K^{12} Language Arts Handwriting Program Overview

Program Philosophy

K^{12} supplies the proven Handwriting Without Tears program for students in kindergarten through grade 3. This gentle, multisensory approach focuses on careful practice at a pace that suits students' fine motor skills development.

Overview of Handwriting Lessons

Materials

The following books and materials are supplied for the Handwriting program:

- *Handwriting Without Tears Pre-K Teacher's Guide* and *Kindergarten Teacher's Guide*
- *Handwriting Without Tears Get Set for School*
- *Handwriting Without Tears Letters and Numbers for Me*
- Slate chalkboard
- One package of specially lined writing paper for Handwriting Without Tears
  If you need more of this paper, the following options are available:
  - Online lesson openers provide a handwriting sheet that you can print and photocopy.
  - You can order more wide double-line notebook paper directly from Handwriting Without Tears at http://www.hwtears.com/hwt.

These materials are *separate* from the *K^{12} Language Arts Lesson Guide* and *K^{12} Language Arts Activity Book.*

Lesson Structure

The K[12] Handwriting program is entirely offline and uses the supplied Handwriting Without Tears materials. Before beginning the program, become familiar with the *Handwriting Without Tears Teacher's Guide*. The guide includes a Teaching Guidelines chart to help you plan students' handwriting lessons. In each lesson, you will work with students for 10 minutes. (You may want to set a timer for 10 minutes; most students enjoy the Handwriting program, so it's easy to lose track of time and do too much in one day.)

Students should complete as many workbook pages as they can, picking up where they left off during the previous Handwriting lesson and continuing from there. They are not expected to complete a set number of pages during the 10-minute lessons. Be sure to monitor students' writing time so you can help them develop good letter formation habits.

The following chart is an overview of the workbooks used in each semester.

Semester	Offline (10 minutes)
1	*Get Set for School*
2	*Letters and Numbers for Me*

Depending on students' pace, each workbook should take 8 to 12 weeks of instruction. Move as fast or slowly as students need. When they have completed the workbooks, have students use the packaged lined writing paper from Handwriting Without Tears to practice their handwriting.

The Handwriting Without Tears website (www.hwtears.com) is full of helpful tips, demonstration videos, and other resources. Use the passcode found on the cover of the Handwriting Without Tears Teacher's Guide to create an account and gain access to A Click Away. There you will be able to use the Digital Teaching Tools, A+ Worksheet Maker, and Screener of Handwriting Proficiency. In addition, visit www.hwtwears.com/k12 for information on ordering supplemental materials and teaching aids.

K[12] Language Arts Blue Keywords

author – a writer

autobiography – the story of a person's life written by that person

biography – the story of a person's life written by another person

brainstorming – an early step in writing that helps a writer come up with as many ideas about a topic as possible

caption – writing under a picture that describes a picture

cause – the reason why something happens

character – a person or animal in a story

compare – to explain how two or more things are alike

comprehension – understanding

connection – a link readers make between themselves, information in text, and the world around them

context – the parts of a sentence or passage surrounding a word

context clue – a word or phrase in a text that helps you figure out the meaning of an unknown word

contrast – to explain how two or more things are different

detail – a piece of information in a text

dialogue – the words that characters say in a written work

draft – an early effort at a piece of writing; not the finished work

drama – another word for *play*

draw a conclusion – to make a decision about something not stated directly in a text by considering information provided and what you know from past experience

effect – the result of a cause

environmental print – words and symbols found in the world around us, such as those on signs, ads, and labels

fable – a story that teaches a lesson and may contain animal characters

fact – something that can be proven true

fairy tale – a folktale with magical elements

fantasy – a story with characters, settings, or other elements that could not really exist

fiction – make-believe stories

first-person point of view – the telling of a story by a character in that story, using pronouns such as *I*, *me*, and *we*

folktale – a story passed down through a culture for many years that may have human, animal, or magical characters

genre – a category for classifying literary works

glossary – a list of important terms and their meanings that is usually found in the back of a book

graphic organizer – a visual tool used to show relationships between key concepts; formats include webs, diagrams, and charts

illustration – a drawing

illustrator – the person who draws the pictures that go with a story

imagery – language that helps readers imagine how something looks, sounds, smells, feels, or tastes

infer – to use clues and what you already know to make a guess

inference – a guess you make using the clues in a text and what you already know

informational text – text written to explain and give information about a topic

legend – a story that is passed down for many years to teach the values of a culture; the story may or may not contain some true events or people

line – a row of words in a poem

listening vocabulary – the words you can hear and understand

literal level – a reference to text information that is directly stated

literal recall – the ability to describe information stated directly in a text

literature – made-up stories, true stories, poems, and plays

main idea – the most important idea in a paragraph or text

moral – the lesson of a story, particularly a fable

multiple-meaning word – a word that has more than one meaning

narrative – a text genre that tells a story; a narrative usually includes characters, setting, and plot

narrator – the teller of a story

nonfiction – writings about true things

plot – what happens in a story

point of view – the perspective a story is told from

predictable text – text written with rhyme, rhythm, and repetition

prediction – a guess about what might happen that is based on information in a story and what you already know

prior knowledge – things you already know from past experience

problem – an issue a character must solve in a story

realistic fiction – a made-up story that has no magical elements

retelling – using your own words to tell a story that you have listened to or read

rhyme – when two or more words have the same ending sounds; for example, *cat* and *hat* rhyme

rhythm – a pattern of accented and unaccented syllables; a distinctive beat

self-monitor – to notice if you do or do not understand what you are reading

sensory language – language that appeals to the five senses

sequence – order

setting – when and where a story takes place

solution – how a character solves a problem in a story

speaking vocabulary – the words you can say and use correctly

stanza – a group of lines in a poem

story events – the things that happen in a story; the plot

story structure elements – components of a story; they include character, setting, plot, problem, and solution

summarize – to tell the most important ideas or events of a text

summary – a short retelling that includes only the most important ideas or events of a text

supporting detail – a detail that gives more information about a main idea

table of contents – a list at the start of a book that gives the titles of the book's stories, poems, articles, chapters, or nonfiction pieces and the pages where they appear

text feature – part of a text that helps a reader locate information and determine what is most important; examples include the title, table of contents, headings, pictures, and glossary

theme – the author's message or big idea

tone – the author's feelings toward the subject and/or characters of a text

topic – the subject of a text

vocabulary – the words we know and use to communicate

Language Arts

Lesson Guide

Language Skills

Comparison Words (B)

Unit Overview

In this unit, students will

- Learn vocabulary words for comparisons and feelings.
- Complete the *All About Me* pages *My Best Friend* and *My Emotions.*
- Explore the poems "The Caterpillar," "Little Miss Muffet," and "Humpty Dumpty."

Lesson Overview

Offline	15 minutes
Vocabulary	Introduce Comparison Words
	OPTIONAL: Make Your Own Flash Cards
Online	15 minutes
Skills Update	Review Color Words
Learn	Introduce Comparison Words

Materials

Supplied

- There are no supplied materials to gather for this lesson.

Also Needed

- index cards (6) (optional)
- household objects – items of graduated sizes (6)

Advance Preparation

Gather three household objects of different sizes, such as a paper clip, a pencil, and a loaf of bread, to represent small items. Gather three household objects of different sizes, such as a small waste basket, a chair, and a laundry basket, to represent large items.

Offline 15 minutes

Work **together** with students to complete an offline Vocabulary activity.

Vocabulary

Introduce Comparison Words

Introduce students to the following comparison words:

large	**largest**	**smaller**
larger	**small**	**smallest**

1. Gather the six household objects. Place the three small objects next to each other. Do the same for the three large objects.
2. Tell students that you are going to compare the sizes of the items.
   - Point to the small item.
     Say: This [item] is small compared to this [larger item].
   - Point to the smaller item.
     Say: This [item] is smaller than this [small item].
   - Point to the smallest item.
     Say: This [item] is the smallest of all three items.
   - Point to the large item.
     Say: This [item] is large compared to this [smaller item].
   - Point to the larger item.
     Say: This [item] is larger than this [large item].
   - Point to the largest item.
     Say: This [item] is the largest of all three items.
3. If time permits, have students gather three additional items of various sizes. Have students describe each item using the vocabulary words.

Objectives

- Increase oral vocabulary.
- Increase reading vocabulary.
- Increase concept vocabulary.

OPTIONAL: Make Your Own Flash Cards

This activity is intended for students who have extra time and would benefit from practicing vocabulary words with flash cards. Feel free to skip this activity.

Gather six index cards. Have students create flash cards by writing each vocabulary word on the front of an index card and illustrating each word on the back. For each word, draw three shapes of different sizes. Have students circle the shape that corresponds to the word on the front of the card. Help students with spelling and drawings as necessary.

TIP If students are not ready to read and write on their own, skip this optional activity.

Online 15 minutes

Students will work online **independently** to complete activities on Vocabulary words. Help students locate the online activities, and provide support as needed.

Skills Update

Review Color Words

Students will answer a few questions to refresh their Vocabulary knowledge.

Objectives

- Increase oral vocabulary.
- Increase concept vocabulary.

Learn

Introduce Comparison Words

Students will be introduced to the comparison words *small, smaller, smallest, large, larger,* and *largest.*

Objectives

- Increase oral vocabulary.
- Increase reading vocabulary.
- Increase concept vocabulary.

My Best Friend and Comparison Words (B)

Lesson Overview

Offline	15 minutes
All About Me	My Best Friend

Online	15 minutes
Practice	Comparison Words

Materials

Supplied

- K^{12} *All About Me*, p. 19

Also Needed

- crayons

Offline 15 minutes

Work **together** with students to complete an offline All About Me activity.

All About Me

My Best Friend

Students will discuss a drawing of their best friend to practice vocabulary.

1. Help students complete page 19 in K^{12} *All About Me.*
2. Have students finalize and explain their drawing of themself with their best friend. Encourage students to use their best friend's name, explain what the two are doing in the drawing, and tell why this is a favorite activity.
3. If time permits, have students describe other activities they like to do with their best friend.

Objectives

- Dictate or write simple sentences describing experiences, stories, people, objects, or events.
- Add supporting details to written or drawn work.
- Discuss own drawing.
- Share finished written and drawn works.

Online 15 minutes

Students will work online **independently** to complete activities on Vocabulary words. Help students locate the online activities and provide support as needed.

Practice

Comparison Words

Students will practice the comparison words *small, smaller, smallest, large, larger,* and *largest.*

Offline Alternative

No computer access? At any time, you can print a list of the unit Vocabulary words and their definitions from the online lesson. Use this list to review the words with students offline. In addition, if students made their own flash cards, these can be used for offline review.

Objectives

- Increase oral vocabulary.
- Increase reading vocabulary.
- Increase concept vocabulary.
- Use suffixes.

"The Caterpillar" and Comparison Words

Lesson Overview

Offline	15 minutes
Poetry	"The Caterpillar"
Online	**15 minutes**
Practice	Comparison Words

Materials

Supplied
- *Tomie dePaola's Rhyme Time*
- *K[12] Language Arts Activity Book*, p. LS 37

Also Needed
- crayons

Advance Preparation

Before reading today's poem, you will need to find the poem in the book *Tomie dePaola's Rhyme Time*. If your book has page numbers, turn to page 23. Otherwise, you will need to use a pencil to number the pages in the book. Mark the title page as page 1.

Offline 15 minutes

Work **together** with students to complete an offline Poetry activity.

Poetry

"The Caterpillar"

It's time to read "The Caterpillar" from *Tomie dePaola's Rhyme Time*.

1. Have students touch something soft and furry—a pet or a stuffed animal, for example. Tell them that one creature they might not expect to have soft hair is a caterpillar.
2. Have students tell you what they know about caterpillars. As necessary, tell them that caterpillars are small wormlike animals that eat plants. Then tell students that caterpillars do something amazing, and the poem they are about to hear will tell them what it is.

Objectives
- Listen to and discuss poetry.
- Respond to text through art, writing, and/or drama.
- Identify rhyme and rhythm in poetry.
- Describe character(s).

3. Read "The Caterpillar." Have students sit next to you so they can see the picture and words while you read the poem aloud. **Read aloud the entire poem**, and then ask:
   - What color does the poem say the caterpillars are? brown
   - What word tells you how it feels to touch a caterpillar? *furry*
   - Which two words from the poem rhyme—*shady* and *stalk*, *walk* and *stalk*, or *which* and *what*? *walk* and *stalk*
4. Tell students that caterpillars do not actually die and live again as butterflies. Rather, they turn into butterflies.
   Say: Caterpillars become butterflies when they grow up, just as children become adults.
5. Explain that caterpillars change after they wrap themselves up in a cocoon, which is like a case. Answers to questions may vary.
   - Did you know that caterpillars turn into butterflies?
   - If you were a caterpillar, would you be happy to turn into a butterfly? Why or why not?
6. Have students gather their crayons, and turn to page LS 37 in *K*[12] *Language Arts Activity Book*. Tell students that the pictures show the three steps of a caterpillar's life cycle. Point out the leaves the caterpillar eats, the cocoon it spins, and the butterfly's wings. Have students color the pictures.

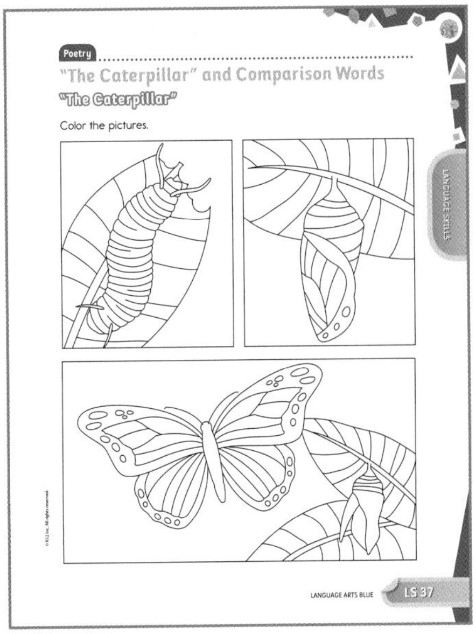

Online 15 minutes

Students will work online **independently** to complete activities on Vocabulary words. Help students locate the online activities, and provide support as needed.

Practice

Comparison Words

Students will practice the comparison words *small, smaller, smallest, large, larger,* and *largest.*

Offline Alternative

No computer access? At any time, you can print a list of the unit Vocabulary words and their definitions from the online lesson. Use this list to review the words with students offline. In addition, if students made their own flash cards, these can be used for offline review.

Objectives
- Increase oral vocabulary.
- Increase reading vocabulary.
- Increase concept vocabulary.

Feeling Words (A)

Lesson Overview

Offline	15 minutes
Vocabulary	Introduce Feeling Words
	OPTIONAL: Make Your Own Flash Cards

Online	15 minutes
Skills Update	Review Body Part Words
Learn	Introduce Feeling Words

Materials

Supplied

- *K[12] Language Arts Activity Book*, p. LS 38

Also Needed

- index cards (6) (optional)

Offline 15 minutes

Work **together** with students to complete an offline Vocabulary activity.

Vocabulary

Introduce Feeling Words

Introduce students to the following feeling words and how they are related:

bored	**curious**	**sad**
calm	**happy**	**surprised**

1. Tell students that they are going to learn some words related to feelings.
2. Read each word aloud. After reading each word, provide a facial expression that represents that word. For example, say "happy," and then smile.
3. Turn to page LS 38 in *K¹² Language Arts Activity Book.* Have students circle the face that matches each word.

Objectives

- Increase oral vocabulary.
- Increase reading vocabulary.
- Increase concept vocabulary.

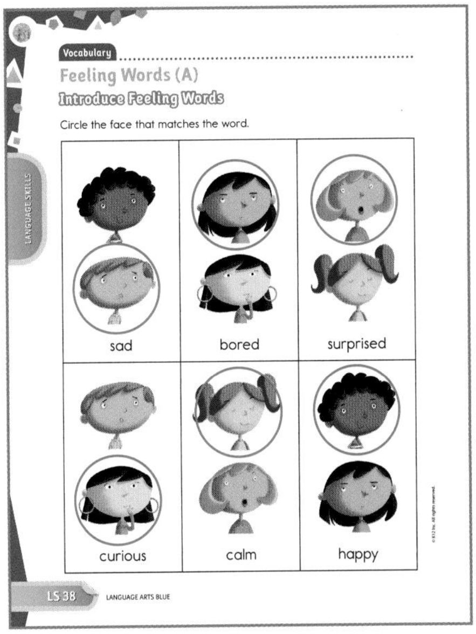

Vocabulary
Feeling Words (A)
Introduce Feeling Words
Circle the face that matches the word.
LANGUAGE SKILLS
sad
bored
surprised
curious
calm
happy
LS 38
LANGUAGE ARTS BLUE

⊕ OPTIONAL: Make Your Own Flash Cards

This activity is intended for students who have extra time and would benefit from practicing their vocabulary words with flash cards. Feel free to skip this activity.

Gather six index cards. Have students create flash cards by writing each vocabulary word on the front of an index card and their own definition for each word on the back. Help students with spelling as necessary.

Online 15 minutes

Students will work online **independently** to complete activities on Vocabulary words. Help students locate the online activities, and provide support as needed.

Skills Update

Review Body Part Words

Students will answer a few questions to refresh their Vocabulary knowledge.

Objectives

- Increase reading vocabulary.
- Increase concept vocabulary.

Learn

Introduce Feeling Words

Students will be introduced to the feeling words *happy, sad, curious, bored, surprised,* and *calm*.

Objectives

- Increase oral vocabulary.
- Increase reading vocabulary.
- Increase concept vocabulary.
- Identify and use picture clues to define words.

Emotions and Feeling Words (A)

Lesson Overview

Offline		15 minutes
All About Me	My Emotions	
Online		15 minutes
Practice	Feeling Words	

Materials

Supplied

- *K[12] All About Me*, pp. 20–21

Also Needed

- crayons

Offline 15 minutes

Work **together** with students to complete an offline All About Me activity.

All About Me

My Emotions

Students will begin pages 20 and 21 in *K[12] All About Me*; they will complete these pages over two lessons.

1. Read aloud the first incomplete sentence to students, pointing to each word as you read. Have students repeat the first part of the sentence and tell you the answer to write in the blank space. Read the complete sentence to students, pointing to each word.
2. Have students repeat the complete sentence and point to the word *happy*.
3. Repeat Steps 1 and 2 with the remaining sentences.
4. Ask students to choose two emotions to illustrate. Discuss with students a time when they felt those emotions. If time permits, have them begin drawing pictures of these events.

Objectives

- Dictate or write simple sentences describing experiences, stories, people, objects, or events.
- Write and/or draw narrative text.
- Describe people, places, things, locations, actions, events, and/or feelings.

Online 15 minutes

Students will work online **independently** to complete an activity on Vocabulary words. Help students locate the online activity, and provide support as needed.

Practice

Feeling Words

Students will practice the feeling words *happy, sad, curious, bored, surprised,* and *calm.*

Offline Alternative

No computer access? At any time, you can print a list of the unit Vocabulary words and their definitions from the online lesson. Use this list to review the words with students offline. In addition, if students made their own flash cards, these can be used for offline review.

Objectives

- Increase oral vocabulary.
- Increase reading vocabulary.
- Increase concept vocabulary.
- Identify and use picture clues to define words.

"Little Miss Muffet" and Feeling Words

Lesson Overview

Offline	15 minutes
Poetry	"Little Miss Muffet"
Online	**15 minutes**
Practice	Feeling Words

Materials

Supplied
- *The Rooster Crows*
- *K[12] Language Arts Activity Book*, p. LS 39

Also Needed
- household objects – bowl, spoon, low stool or chair

Advance Preparation

Before reading today's poem, you will need to find the poem in the book *The Rooster Crows*. If your book has page numbers, turn to page 24. Otherwise, you will need to use a pencil to number the pages in the book. Mark the title page as page 1.

Offline 15 minutes

Work **together** with students to complete an offline Poetry activity.

Poetry

"Little Miss Muffet"

It's time to read "Little Miss Muffet" from *The Rooster Crows*. Gather a bowl, a spoon, and a low stool or chair.

1. Remind students that when we come across a word we do not know in a poem, we can use the other words to help us figure out what it means. Tell them that, in today's poem, they will hear the word *tuffet* and the phrase *curds and whey*.
   Answers to questions may vary.
   - What do you think *tuffet* means?
   - What do you think *curds and whey* is?

Objectives
- Listen to and discuss poetry.
- Identify and use context clues to define words.
- Respond to text through art, writing, and/or drama.
- Identify rhyme and rhythm in poetry.
- Describe character(s).

2. Have students sit next to you so they can see the picture and words while you **read the poem aloud**, and then ask:
   - What is Little Miss Muffet doing at the start of the poem? Sitting and eating her curds and whey.
   - What rhymes with *spider* in line 3? *beside her*
   - How does Miss Muffet feel when she sees the spider? scared
3. Tell students to think again about what *tuffet* means and what *curds and whey* might be.
   - What is Little Miss Muffet doing on a tuffet? sitting
4. Tell students that the word *sitting* helps us know that a *tuffet* is something to sit on; a *tuffet* is a seat. Then remind students that Little Miss Muffet is eating *curds and whey* as she sits on her seat.
   - Since Little Miss Muffet is eating, what do we know about curds and whey? Answers will vary, but students should understand that we know that *curds and whey* is a type of food.
5. Turn to page LS 39 in K[12] *Language Arts Activity Book*. Have students cut out the spider and then act out the poem, using the bowl, spoon, and stool or chair.

Poetry
"Little Miss Muffet" and Feeling Words
"Little Miss Muffet"
Cut out the spider. Then, act out what happens in "Little Miss Muffet."
LANGUAGE ARTS BLUE
LS 39

TIP *Curds and whey* is more commonly known today as cottage cheese.

Online 15 minutes

Students will work online **independently** to complete activities on Vocabulary words. Help students locate the online activities, and provide support as needed.

Practice

Feeling Words

Students will practice the feeling words *happy, sad, curious, bored, surprised,* and *calm.*

Offline Alternative

No computer access? At any time, you can print a list of the unit Vocabulary words and their definitions from the online lesson. Use this list to review the words with students offline. In addition, if students made their own flash cards, these can be used for offline review.

Objectives

- Increase oral vocabulary.
- Increase reading vocabulary.
- Increase concept vocabulary.
- Identify and use picture clues to define words.

Feeling Words (B)

Lesson Overview

Offline	15 minutes
Vocabulary	Feeling Words
	OPTIONAL: Make Your Own Flash Cards
Online	**15 minutes**
Skills Update	Review Subject Words
Learn	Feeling Words

Materials

Supplied
- There are no supplied materials to gather for this lesson.

Also Needed
- index cards (6) (optional)

Offline 15 minutes

Work **together** with students to complete an offline Vocabulary activity.

Vocabulary

Feeling Words

Introduce students to the following feeling words:

angry	**puzzled**	**stubborn**
excited	**scared**	**thoughtful**

1. Tell students that they are going to learn some words related to feelings.
2. Read each word aloud. After reading each word, provide a facial expression that represents that word. For example, say "scared," and then widen your eyes, raise your shoulders, and open your mouth like you want to scream.
3. Ask students to give examples of when they were scared, excited, puzzled, angry, stubborn, and thoughtful. For example, "I was angry when I lost my favorite game."
4. If time permits, have students show a facial expression for each feeling word and have others guess the correct word.

Objectives
- Increase oral vocabulary.
- Increase reading vocabulary.
- Increase concept vocabulary.
- Identify and use context clues to define words.

⊕ OPTIONAL: Make Your Own Flash Cards

This activity is intended for students who have extra time and would benefit from practicing their vocabulary words with flash cards. Feel free to skip this activity.

Gather six index cards. Have students create flash cards by writing each vocabulary word on the front of an index card and their own definition for each word on the back. Help students with spelling as necessary.

Online 15 minutes

Students will work online **independently** to complete activities on Vocabulary words. Help students locate the online activities, and provide support as needed.

Skills Update

Review Subject Words

Students will answer a few questions to refresh their Vocabulary knowledge.

Objectives

- Increase oral vocabulary.
- Increase concept vocabulary.

Learn

Feeling Words

Students will be introduced to the feeling words *angry, scared, excited, stubborn, thoughtful,* and *puzzled.*

Objectives

- Increase oral vocabulary.
- Increase reading vocabulary.
- Increase concept vocabulary.
- Identify and use context clues to define words.

Emotions and Feeling Words (B)

Lesson Overview

Offline	15 minutes
All About Me	My Emotions

Online	15 minutes
Practice	Feeling Words

Materials

Supplied

- *K*[12] *All About Me*, pp. 20–21

Also Needed

- crayons

Offline 15 minutes

Work **together** with students to complete an offline All About Me activity.

All About Me

My Emotions

Students will complete pages 20 and 21 in *K*[12] *All About Me* and discuss their emotions to practice vocabulary.

1. Have students finalize and explain their drawings. Encourage students to describe their pictures using as much detail as possible.
2. Read each sentence aloud. Have students point to the words *happy, sad, excited,* and *scared* in the sentences.
3. Have students explain why each activity or situation they chose makes them feel the emotion described.

Objectives

- Write and/or draw narrative text.
- Describe people, places, things, locations, actions, events, and/or feelings.
- Add supporting details to written or drawn work.
- Discuss own drawing.

Online 15 minutes

Students will work online **independently** to complete activities on Vocabulary words. Help students locate the online activities, and provide support as needed.

Practice

Feeling Words

Students will practice the feeling words *angry, scared, excited, stubborn, thoughtful,* and *puzzled.*

Offline Alternative

No computer access? At any time, you can print a list of the unit Vocabulary words and their definitions from the online lesson. Use this list to review the words with students offline. In addition, if students made their own flash cards, these can be used for offline review.

Objectives

- Increase oral vocabulary.
- Increase reading vocabulary.
- Increase concept vocabulary.
- Identify and use context clues to define words.

"Humpty Dumpty" and Vocabulary Unit Review

Lesson Overview

Offline	15 minutes
Poetry	"Humpty Dumpty"
	OPTIONAL: Draw a Character
Online	**15 minutes**
Unit Review	Comparison and Feeling Words

Materials

Supplied
- *K¹² Read Aloud Treasury*, p. 99

Also Needed
- crayons (optional)
- paper, drawing (optional)

Offline 15 minutes

Work **together** with students to complete an offline Poetry activity.

Poetry

Objectives
- Listen to and discuss poetry.
- Identify rhyme and rhythm in poetry.

"Humpty Dumpty"

It's time to read "Humpty Dumpty" from *K¹² Read Aloud Treasury*.

1. Ask students what they think of when they hear the words *Humpty Dumpty*. Answers will vary.
2. Remind students that many poems have a steady **rhythm**. Rhythm is a repeated pattern of beats or sounds. **Read this poem aloud**, clapping with each beat to demonstrate rhythm:

   Ring around the rosie,
   A pocket full of posies.
   Ashes, ashes,
   We all fall down.

3. Have students sit next to you so they can see the picture and words while you **read aloud the entire poem**, and then ask:
   - Where is Humpty Dumpty when the poem begins? on a wall
   - What happens to Humpty Dumpty in line 2? He falls.
   - Who tries to put Humpty Dumpty together again? all the king's horses and all the king's men
   - What word in the poem rhymes with *men*—*horses, king's,* or *again*? again

4. Discuss rhythm with students.
   - Could you hear the rhythm of the poem? Answers will vary.
5. Read the poem again, this time clapping and stressing the bold syllables. Encourage students to clap along with you so that they can feel the rhythm.

   Hump**-ty **Dump**-ty **sat** on a **wall.
   Hump**-ty **Dump**-ty **had** a great **fall.
   ***All** the king's **hor**-ses*
   *And **all** the king's **men***
   ***Could**-n't put **Hump**-ty to-**geth**-er a-**gain**.*

OPTIONAL: Draw a Character

This activity is optional. It is intended for students who have extra time and would benefit from using art to connect to the text.

Have students gather crayons and paper, and draw a character from the poem—Humpty Dumpty, one of the king's horses, or one of the king's men.

Online 15 minutes

Students will work online **independently** to complete an activity on Vocabulary words. Help students locate the online activity, and provide support as needed.

Unit Review

Comparison and Feeling Words

Students will review all words from the unit to prepare for the Unit Checkpoint.

Objectives
- Increase oral vocabulary.
- Increase reading vocabulary.
- Increase concept vocabulary.
- Identify and use context clues to define words.

Offline Alternative

No computer access? At any time, you can print a list of the unit Vocabulary words and their definitions from the online lesson. Use this list to review the words with students offline. In addition, if students made their own flash cards, these can be used for offline review.

Unit Checkpoint

Lesson Overview

Online	15 minutes
Unit Checkpoint	Comparison and Feeling Words

Materials

There are no materials to gather for this lesson.

Online 15 minutes

Students will work online to complete the Unit Checkpoint. Help students locate the Unit Checkpoint, and provide support as needed.

Unit Checkpoint

Comparison and Feeling Words

Explain that students are going to show what they have learned about vocabulary words for comparisons and feelings.

Objectives

- Increase oral vocabulary.
- Increase reading vocabulary.
- Increase concept vocabulary.
- Identify and use context clues to define words.
- Use suffixes.
- Identify and use picture clues to define words.

Position Words (A)

Unit Overview

In this unit, students will

- Learn position and opposite vocabulary words.
- Complete the *All About Me* pages *Playing Inside and Outside* and *Loud and Quiet.*
- Explore the poems "Yankee Doodle," "from The Island," and "Little Bo Peep."

Lesson Overview

Offline	15 minutes
Vocabulary	Introduce Position Words
	OPTIONAL: Make Your Own Flash Cards
Online	**15 minutes**
Skills Update	Review Body Part Words
Learn	Introduce Position Words

Materials

Supplied

- There are no supplied materials to gather for this lesson.

Also Needed

- index cards (7) (optional)
- household objects – small stuffed animal or toy, pillow

Advance Preparation

Gather a small stuffed animal or toy and a pillow.

Offline 15 minutes

Work **together** with students to complete an offline Vocabulary activity.

Vocabulary

Introduce Position Words

Introduce students to the following position words:

above	**beside**	**outside**
around	**between**	
below	**inside**	

Objectives

- Increase oral vocabulary.
- Increase concept vocabulary.

1. Gather the small toy or stuffed animal and the pillow. Hold the stuffed animal over the pillow, and tell students that the stuffed animal is *above* the pillow.
2. Demonstrate the words *below* and *beside* the same way.
3. Demonstrate the word *around* by wrapping the pillow around the stuffed animal.
4. Demonstrate the word *between* by putting the stuffed animal between the pillow and yourself.
5. Demonstrate the words *inside* and *outside* by putting the stuffed animal inside and outside the pillow if you can. If you can't open the pillow to put something inside, you can demonstrate *inside* and *outside* by using a drawer or cupboard.
6. If time allows, have students demonstrate the position words back to you. Make sure they say a sentence that describes the position of the stuffed animal using the correct position word. For example, "The animal is *below* the pillow."

OPTIONAL: Make Your Own Flash Cards

This activity is intended for students who have extra time and would benefit from practicing their vocabulary words with flash cards. Feel free to skip this activity.

Gather seven index cards. Have students create flash cards by writing each vocabulary word on the front of an index card and their own definition for each word on the back. Help students with spelling as necessary.

TIP If students are not ready to read and write on their own, skip this optional activity.

Online 15 minutes

Students will work online **independently** to complete activities on Vocabulary words. Help students locate the online activities, and provide support as needed.

Skills Update

Review Body Part Words

Students will answer a few questions to refresh their Vocabulary knowledge.

Objectives

- Increase oral vocabulary.
- Increase concept vocabulary.

Learn

Introduce Position Words

Students will be introduced to the position words *inside, outside, above, below, beside, between,* and *around.*

Objectives

- Increase oral vocabulary.
- Increase reading vocabulary.
- Increase concept vocabulary.
- Identify and use picture clues to define words.

Playing Inside & Outside and Position Words (A)

Lesson Overview

Offline	15 minutes
All About Me	Playing Inside and Outside
Online	**15 minutes**
Practice	Position Words

Materials

Supplied

- *K*[12] *All About Me,* pp. 22–23

Also Needed

- crayons

Offline 15 minutes

Work **together** with students to complete an offline All About Me activity.

All About Me

Playing Inside and Outside

Students will begin pages 22 and 23 in *K*[12] *All About Me*; they will complete these pages over two lessons.

1. Discuss things students like to do in their free time. Answers to questions may vary.
   - When you play inside, what do you like to do?
   - When you play outside, what do you like to do?
2. Read aloud the first incomplete sentence to students, pointing to each word as you read. Have them repeat the first part of the sentence and tell you the answer to write in the blank space. Read the complete sentence to students, pointing to each word.
3. Have students repeat the complete sentence and point to the word *inside*.
4. Repeat Steps 2 and 3 with the remaining incomplete sentence, asking students to point to the word *outside*.
5. If time permits, have students begin to illustrate their sentences.

Objectives

- Dictate or write simple sentences describing experiences, stories, people, objects, or events.

Online 15 minutes

Students will work online **independently** to complete activities on Vocabulary words. Help students locate the online activities, and provide support as needed.

Practice

Position Words

Students will practice the position words *inside, outside, above, below, beside, between,* and *around.*

Offline Alternative

No computer access? At any time, you can print a list of the unit Vocabulary words and their definitions from the online lesson. Use this list to review the words with students offline. In addition, if students made their own flash cards, these can be used for offline review.

Objectives

- Increase oral vocabulary.
- Increase reading vocabulary.
- Increase concept vocabulary.
- Identify and use picture clues to define words.

"Yankee Doodle" and Position Words

Lesson Overview

Offline		15 minutes
Poetry	"Yankee Doodle"	
	OPTIONAL: Sing It Out	
Online		15 minutes
Practice	Position Words	

Materials

Supplied

- *The Rooster Crows*

Advance Preparation

Before reading today's poem, you will need to find the poem in the book *The Rooster Crows*. If your book has page numbers, turn to page 35. Otherwise, you will need to use a pencil to number the pages in the book. Mark the title page as page 1.

Offline 15 minutes

Work **together** with students to complete an offline Poetry activity.

Poetry

Objectives

- Listen to and discuss poetry.
- Recite short poems or rhymes.
- Identify rhyme and rhythm in poetry.
- Describe character(s).

"Yankee Doodle"

It's time to read "Yankee Doodle" from *The Rooster Crows.*

1. Remind students that many poems have a steady **rhythm**. Rhythm is a repeated pattern of beats or sounds.
2. Tell students that some poems with steady rhythms can be sung, such as today's poem, "Yankee Doodle."
3. Ask students if they know of other poems that can be sung. Answers will vary; may include "Twinkle, Twinkle, Little Star."

4. Have students sit next to you so they can see the picture and words while you **read aloud the entire poem**, and then ask:
   - Where does Yankee Doodle go in this poem? to town
   - How does Yankee Doodle get to town? He rides a pony.
   - Where does Yankee Doodle put the feather? in his hat
5. Show students the picture that accompanies this poem in *The Rooster Crows*.
   - Which person in the picture is Yankee Doodle? the grown-up with the feather in his hat
   - What do you think of when you hear the word *macaroni*? Answers will vary.
6. Tell students that when "Yankee Doodle" was written, *macaroni* meant "very stylish or cool." Explain that Yankee Doodle calls the feather in his hat *macaroni* because he thinks it makes him look cool.
   - Do you think the feather makes Yankee Doodle look cool, or is the poem a joke about how silly Yankee Doodle looks? Answers will vary.

OPTIONAL: Sing It Out

This activity is optional. It is intended for students who have extra time and would benefit from hearing the poem sung in order to feel its rhythm.

Have students sing "Yankee Doodle" with you and clap along with the rhythm. There will be four claps per line.

Online 15 minutes

Students will work online **independently** to complete activities on Vocabulary words. Help students locate the online activities, and provide support as needed.

Practice

Position Words

Students will practice the position words *inside, outside, above, below, beside, between,* and *around.*

Objectives
- Increase oral vocabulary.
- Increase reading vocabulary.
- Increase concept vocabulary.
- Identify and use picture clues to define words.

Offline Alternative

No computer access? At any time, you can print a list of the unit Vocabulary words and their definitions from the online lesson. Use this list to review the words with students offline. In addition, if students made their own flash cards, these can be used for offline review.

Position Words (B)

Lesson Overview

Offline		15 minutes
Vocabulary	Introduce Position Words	
	OPTIONAL: Make Your Own Flash Cards	
Online		15 minutes
Skills Update	Review Reading Words	
Learn	Introduce Position Words	

Materials

Supplied
- There are no supplied materials to gather for this lesson.

Also Needed
- index cards (6) (optional)

Offline 15 minutes

Work **together** with students to complete an offline Vocabulary activity.

Vocabulary

Introduce Position Words

Introduce the following position words:

away	**near**	**off**
far	**on**	**toward**

1. If the weather permits, go outside to demonstrate the position words. If not, you can demonstrate the words in a large room.
2. Demonstrate the pair of words *near* and *far* by asking students to stand *near* you and then moving across the yard or room to show *far*. Say sentences using the words. For example, "Now you are *near* me . . . and now you are *far* from me."
3. Repeat Step 2 to demonstrate the following pairs of words:
   - *on* and *off*
   - *toward* and *away*
4. Ask students to demonstrate the pairs of words again, mixing up the order. Remind them to use the words in complete sentences.

Objectives
- Increase oral vocabulary.
- Increase concept vocabulary.

⊕ OPTIONAL: Make Your Own Flash Cards

This activity is intended for students who have extra time and would benefit from practicing their vocabulary words with flash cards. Feel free to skip this activity.

Gather six index cards. Have students create flash cards by writing each vocabulary word on the front of an index card and their own definition for each word on the back. Help students with spelling as necessary.

Online 15 minutes

Students will work online **independently** to complete activities on Vocabulary words. Help students locate the online activities, and provide support as needed.

Skills Update

Review Reading Words

Students will answer a few questions to refresh their Vocabulary knowledge.

Objectives

- Increase oral vocabulary.
- Increase reading vocabulary.
- Increase concept vocabulary.

Learn

Introduce Position Words

Students will be introduced to the position words *near, far, on, off, toward,* and *away*.

Objectives

- Increase oral vocabulary.
- Increase reading vocabulary.
- Increase concept vocabulary.
- Identify and use picture clues to define words.

Playing Inside & Outside and Position Words (B)

Lesson Overview

Offline	15 minutes
All About Me	Playing Inside and Outside

Online	15 minutes
Practice	Position Words

Materials

Supplied
- K^{12} *All About Me*, pp. 22–23

Also Needed
- crayons

Offline 15 minutes

Work **together** with students to complete an offline All About Me activity.

All About Me

Playing Inside and Outside

Students will complete pages 22 and 23 in K^{12} *All About Me* and discuss favorite activities they do or games they play inside and outside.

1. Have students finalize and explain their drawings. Encourage them to describe their pictures using as much detail as possible.
2. Read aloud the complete sentences to students, pointing to each word as you read. If students are ready, have them take a turn reading aloud their completed sentences.

TIP If time permits, have students tell you more activities they like to do inside and outside.

Objectives
- Write and/or draw narrative text.
- Draw and label pictures.
- Add supporting details to written or drawn work.
- Discuss own drawing.
- Share finished written and drawn works.

Online 15 minutes

Students will work online **independently** to complete activities on Vocabulary words. Help students locate the online activities, and provide support as needed.

Practice

Position Words

Students will practice the position words *near, far, on, off, toward,* and *away.*

Offline Alternative

No computer access? At any time, you can print a list of the unit Vocabulary words and their definitions from the online lesson. Use this list to review the words with students offline. In addition, if students made their own flash cards, these can be used for offline review.

Objectives

- Increase oral vocabulary.
- Increase reading vocabulary.
- Increase concept vocabulary.
- Identify and use picture clues to define words.

"from The Island" and Position Words

Lesson Overview

Offline		15 minutes
Poetry	"from The Island"	
Online		**15 minutes**
Practice	Position Words	

Materials

Supplied

- *Tomie dePaola's Rhyme Time*

Advance Preparation

Before reading today's poem, you will need to find the poem in the book *Tomie dePaola's Rhyme Time.* If your book has page numbers, turn to page 5. Otherwise, you will need to use a pencil to number the pages in the book. Mark the title page as page 1.

Offline 15 minutes

Work **together** with students to complete an offline Poetry activity.

Poetry

"from The Island"

It's time to read "from The Island" from *Tomie dePaola's Rhyme Time.*

1. Tell students that the poem they are about to hear is about one child's special place to play. Answers to questions may vary.
   - Do you have a special place where you like to play?
   - What is your special place like?
2. Remind students that some poems contain words we don't know. However, we can use other words in the poem to help us learn those words.

Objectives

- Listen to and discuss poetry.
- Make connections with text: text-to-text, text-to-self, text-to-world.
- Identify and use context clues to define words.
- Identify words that create mental imagery.

3. Have students sit next to you so they can see the picture and words while you **read aloud the entire poem**, and then ask:
   - What do the children in the poem do at the island? play
   - What color is the island? green
   - What are the two animals that are named in the poem? bees and butterflies
4. Read the first line of the poem again.
   - What do you think a *meadow* is? Answers will vary.
5. Tell students that we can figure out what a *meadow* is by looking at other words in the poem. Point out that the poem says that people *mowed* the meadow.
   - What do people usually *mow*? grass
6. Point out that the poem says that the people who mowed the meadow left a *grassy* island.
   Say: A meadow must be a place with grass.
7. Continue the investigation by reading the first line of the second stanza again, stressing the word *field*.
   - Do you think a meadow might be a grass field? Yes
8. Ask students if there are any other clues that show students that a meadow is a grass field. Answers will vary but may include the word *green* or the word *clover*, or even the word *butterflies*.

Online 15 minutes

Students will work online **independently** to complete activities on Vocabulary words. Help students locate the online activities, and provide support as needed.

Practice

Position Words

Students will practice the position words *near*, *far*, *on*, *off*, *toward*, and *away*.

Objectives

- Increase oral vocabulary.
- Increase reading vocabulary.
- Increase concept vocabulary.
- Identify and use picture clues to define words.

Offline Alternative

No computer access? At any time, you can print a list of the unit Vocabulary words and their definitions from the online lesson. Use this list to review the words with students offline. In addition, if students made their own flash cards, these can be used for offline review.

Opposite Words (A)

Lesson Overview

Offline		15 minutes
Vocabulary	Introduce Opposite Words OPTIONAL: Make Your Own Flash Cards	
Online		15 minutes
Skills Update	Review Food Words	
Learn	Introduce Opposite Words	

Materials

Supplied

- *K¹² Language Arts Activity Book*, p. LS 41

Also Needed

- index cards (3) (optional)

Offline 15 minutes

Work **together** with students to complete an offline Vocabulary activity.

Vocabulary

Introduce Opposite Words

Introduce the following opposite words:

back	**front**
bottom	**top**
down	**up**

1. Tell students that they may already know some opposites, such as *near* and *far*, and *on* and *off*.
2. Read aloud each word in the left column and its opposite in the right column.

Objectives

- Increase oral vocabulary.
- Increase reading vocabulary.
- Increase concept vocabulary.
- Use antonyms.

3. Have students complete page LS 41 in *K[12] Language Arts Activity Book*. They should match the words and pictures with their opposites on the right. Provide support as needed.

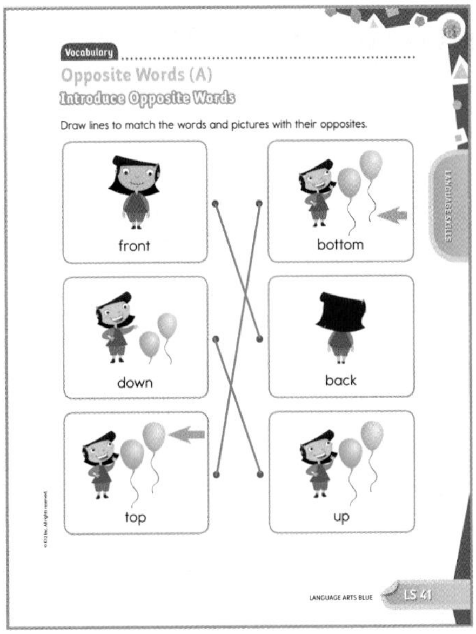

⊕ OPTIONAL: Make Your Own Flash Cards

This activity is intended for students who have extra time and would benefit from practicing their vocabulary words with flash cards. Feel free to skip this activity.

Gather three index cards. Have students create flash cards by writing each word on the front of an index card and its opposite on the back. Help students with spelling as necessary

Online 15 minutes

Students will work online **independently** to complete activities on Vocabulary words. Help students locate the online activities, and provide support as needed.

Skills Update

Review Food Words

Students will answer a few questions to refresh their Vocabulary knowledge.

Objectives
- Increase oral vocabulary.
- Increase concept vocabulary.

Learn

Introduce Opposite Words

Students will be introduced to the opposite words *up, down, back, front, top,* and *bottom.*

Objectives
- Increase oral vocabulary.
- Increase reading vocabulary.
- Increase concept vocabulary.
- Use antonyms.

Loud & Quiet and Opposite Words (A)

Lesson Overview

Offline	15 minutes
All About Me	Loud and Quiet
Online	**15 minutes**
Practice	Opposite Words

Materials

Supplied

- K^{12} *All About Me*, pp. 24–25

Also Needed

- crayons

Offline 15 minutes

Work **together** with students to complete an offline All About Me activity.

All About Me

Loud and Quiet

Students will begin pages 24 and 25 in K^{12} *All About Me*; they will complete these pages over two lessons.

1. Discuss with students times when it's fun (and acceptable) to be very loud. Then talk about times when it's important to be very quiet.
2. Read aloud the first incomplete sentence to students, pointing to each word as you read. Have students repeat the first part of the sentence and tell you the answer to write in the blank space. Read the complete sentence to students, pointing to each word.
3. Have students repeat the complete sentence and point to the word *loud*.
4. Repeat Steps 2 and 3 with the remaining sentence, asking students to point to the word *quiet*.
5. If time permits, have students begin their illustrations.

Objectives

- Dictate or write simple sentences describing experiences, stories, people, objects, or events.

Online 15 minutes

Students will work online **independently** to complete activities on Vocabulary words. Help students locate the online activities, and provide support as needed.

Practice

Opposite Words

Students will practice the opposite words *up, down, back, front, top,* and *bottom.*

Offline Alternative

No computer access? At any time, you can print a list of the unit Vocabulary words and their definitions from the online lesson. Use this list to review the words with students offline. In addition, if students made their own flash cards, these can be used for offline review.

Objectives

- Increase oral vocabulary.
- Increase reading vocabulary.
- Increase concept vocabulary.
- Use antonyms.

"Little Bo Peep" and Vocabulary Unit Review

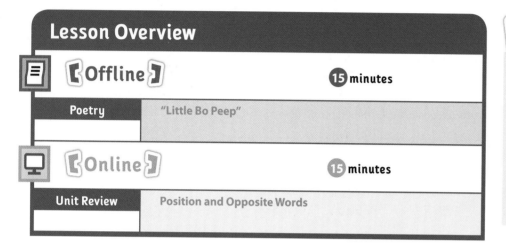

Lesson Overview

Offline	15 minutes
Poetry	"Little Bo Peep"
Online	**15 minutes**
Unit Review	Position and Opposite Words

Materials

Supplied

- *K*[12] *Read Aloud Treasury*, p. 104
- *K*[12] *Language Arts Activity Book*, p. LS 42

Also Needed

- crayons

Offline 15 minutes

Work **together** with students to complete an offline Poetry activity.

Poetry

"Little Bo Peep"

It's time to read "Little Bo Peep" from *K*[12] *Read Aloud Treasury*.

Objectives

- Listen to and discuss poetry.
- Respond to text through art, writing, and/or drama.
- Identify rhyme and rhythm in poetry.
- Describe character(s).

1. Have students tell you about a time when they lost something. Answers to questions may vary.
   - What did you lose?
   - How did you feel?
   - Did you ever find what you lost? If so, how did you feel then?
2. Remind students that rhyming words in poems may come at the ends of different lines or within the same line. In some poems, there are rhymes both at the ends of lines and within lines. Tell students that this is the case with "Little Bo Peep."

3. Have students sit next to you so they can see the picture and words while you **read aloud the entire poem**, and then ask:
   - What is Little Bo Peep's problem? She lost her sheep.
   - What two words rhyme in the third line? *alone* and *home*
   - What are the sheep doing in the fourth line? wagging their tails behind them
4. Tell students that in the poem, Little Bo Peep gets advice. The poem says to leave the sheep alone and they will come home. Ask students to think again about a time when they lost something. Then have them give their own advice to Little Bo Peep. Answers to questions may vary.
   - What would you tell Little Bo Peep to do about her sheep?
   - Do you agree with what the poem says—to leave the sheep alone? Why or why not?
5. Have students gather their crayons and turn to page LS 42 in K^{12} *Language Arts Activity Book*. As students color the picture, discuss possible reasons why Little Bo Peep lost her sheep.

Poetry
"Little Bo Peep" and Vocabulary Unit Review
"Little Bo Peep"
Color the picture.
LANGUAGE SKILLS
LS 42
LANGUAGE ARTS BLUE

Online 15 minutes

Students will work online **independently** to complete an activity on Vocabulary words. Help students locate the online activity, and provide support as needed.

Unit Review

Position and Opposite Words

Students will review all words from the unit to prepare for the Unit Checkpoint.

Objectives

- Increase oral vocabulary.
- Increase reading vocabulary.
- Increase concept vocabulary.
- Identify and use picture clues to define words.
- Use antonyms.

Offline Alternative

No computer access? At any time, you can print a list of the unit Vocabulary words and their definitions from the online lesson. Use this list to review the words with students offline. In addition, if students made their own flash cards, these can be used for offline review.

Unit Checkpoint

Lesson Overview

Online 30 minutes

Unit Checkpoint	Position and Opposite Words

Materials

There are no materials to gather for this lesson.

Online 30 minutes

Students will work online to complete the Unit Checkpoint. Help students locate the Unit Checkpoint, and provide support as needed.

Unit Checkpoint

Position and Opposite Words

Explain that students are going to show what they have learned about vocabulary words for position and opposites.

Objectives

- Increase oral vocabulary.
- Increase reading vocabulary.
- Increase concept vocabulary.
- Identify and use picture clues to define words.
- Use antonyms.

Opposite Words (B)

Unit Overview

In this unit, students will

- Learn vocabulary words for opposites.
- Complete the *All About Me* pages *Loud and Quiet* and *Hot and Cold.*
- Explore the poems "Lady Bug, Lady Bug," "Little Boy Blue," and "Sing a Song of Sixpence."

Materials

Supplied

- There are no supplied materials to gather for this lesson.

Also Needed

- index cards (3) (optional)

Lesson Overview

Offline	15 minutes
Vocabulary	Introduce Opposite Words OPTIONAL: Make Your Own Flash Cards
Online	**15 minutes**
Skills Update	Review Travel Words
Learn	Introduce Opposite Words

Offline — 15 minutes

Work **together** with students to complete an offline Vocabulary activity.

Vocabulary

Introduce Opposite Words

Introduce the following opposite words:

young	**old**
wide	**narrow**
push	**pull**

1. Read aloud each word in the left column and its opposite in the right column.
2. Tell students that they may already know some opposites, such as *up* and *down,* and *back* and *front.*
3. Play a game to practice the words for opposites. Act out *old,* and ask students to guess which word you are acting out.

Objectives

- Increase oral vocabulary.
- Increase concept vocabulary.
- Use antonyms.

4. Once students guess the word, ask them for the opposite of that word. *young*
5. Follow the same procedure to act out *narrow,* and then ask for its opposite. *wide*
6. Follow the same procedure to act out *push,* and then ask for its opposite. *pull*
7. If time permits, switch roles and ask students to act out the words while you identify their opposites.

OPTIONAL: Make Your Own Flash Cards

This activity is intended for students who have extra time and would benefit from practicing their vocabulary words with flash cards. Feel free to skip this activity.

Gather three index cards. Have students create flash cards by writing each word on the front of an index card and its opposite on the back. Help students with spelling as necessary.

TIP If students are not ready to read and write on their own, skip this optional activity.

Online 15 minutes

Students will work online **independently** to complete activities on Vocabulary words. Help students locate the online activities, and provide support as needed.

Skills Update

Review Travel Words

Students will answer a few questions to refresh their Vocabulary knowledge.

Objectives

- Increase oral vocabulary.
- Increase concept vocabulary.

Learn

Introduce Opposite Words

Students will be introduced to the opposite words *young, old, wide, narrow, push,* and *pull.*

Objectives

- Increase oral vocabulary.
- Increase reading vocabulary.
- Increase concept vocabulary.
- Use antonyms.

Loud & Quiet and Opposite Words (B)

Lesson Overview

Offline	15 minutes
All About Me	Loud and Quiet
Online	**15 minutes**
Practice	Opposite Words

Materials

Supplied
- *K[12] All About Me,* pp. 24–25

Also Needed
- crayons

Offline 15 minutes

Work **together** with students to complete an offline All About Me activity.

All About Me

Loud and Quiet

Students will complete pages 24 and 25 in *K[12] All About Me.*

1. Have students finalize and explain their drawings. Encourage them to describe their pictures using as much detail as possible.
2. Read aloud the complete sentences to students, pointing to each word as you read. If students are ready, have them take a turn reading aloud their completed sentences.

TIP If time permits, have students tell you more situations when they can be loud and when they should be quiet.

Objectives
- Write and/or draw narrative text.
- Draw and label pictures.
- Add supporting details to written or drawn work.
- Discuss own drawing.
- Share finished written and drawn works.

Online 15 minutes

Students will work online **independently** to complete activities on Vocabulary words. Help students locate the online activities, and provide support as needed.

Practice

Opposite Words

Students will practice the words *young, old, wide, narrow, push,* and *pull.*

Objectives

- Increase oral vocabulary.
- Increase reading vocabulary.
- Increase concept vocabulary.
- Use antonyms.

Offline Alternative

No computer access? At any time, you can print a list of the unit Vocabulary words and their definitions from the online lesson. Use this list to review the words with students offline. In addition, if students made their own flash cards, these can be used for offline review.

"Lady Bug, Lady Bug" and Opposite Words

Lesson Overview

Offline	15 minutes
Poetry	"Lady Bug, Lady Bug"
Online	**15 minutes**
Practice	Opposite Words

Materials

Supplied
- *The Rooster Crows*
- *K[12] Language Arts Activity Book,* p. LS 43

Also Needed
- crayons
- scissors, round-end safety

Advance Preparation

Before reading today's poem, you will need to find the poem in the book *The Rooster Crows.* If your book has page numbers, turn to page 14. Otherwise, you will need to use a pencil to number the pages in the book. Mark the title page as page 1.

Offline 15 minutes

Work **together** with students to complete an offline Poetry activity.

Poetry

"Lady Bug, Lady Bug"
It's time to read "Lady Bug, Lady Bug" from *The Rooster Crows.*

1. Have students tell you when or if they have seen a ladybug. Answers to questions will vary.
   - Have you ever heard that it's good luck to let a ladybug crawl across your hand?
   - Would you let a ladybug crawl across your hand for luck? Why or why not?
2. Tell students that many people like ladybugs because of how they look—red or orange or yellow with black dots on their backs. Ladybugs do not usually cause damage to crops the way other bugs might, so they are not thought of as pests.

Objectives
- Listen to and discuss poetry.
- Use visual text features to aid understanding of text.
- Respond to text through art, writing, and/or drama.
- Identify rhyme and rhythm in poetry.

3. Have students sit next to you so they can see the picture and words while you **read aloud the entire poem**, and then ask:
   - What does the poem tell the ladybug to do? fly away home
   - Why must the ladybug fly away home? Her house is on fire.
   - Which of the ladybug's children is still at home? Anne
   - What word in the poem rhymes with *Anne—name, under,* or *pan*? pan

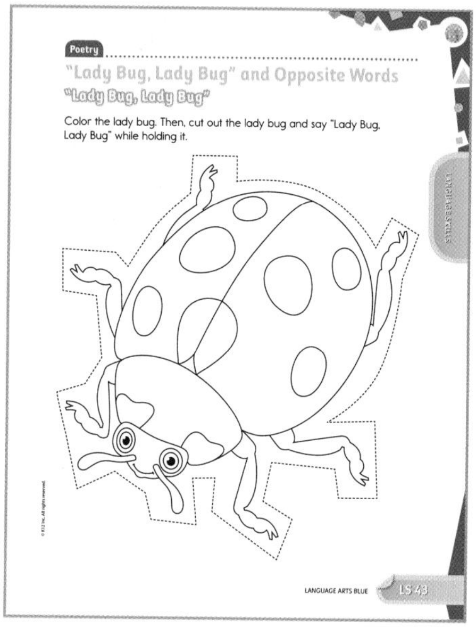

4. Tell students that people say this poem when they catch or see a ladybug outside. Then point to the picture above the poem in *The Rooster Crows*.
   - Where is the ladybug in this picture? on the finger of the girl in the middle
   - Do the other children in the picture look scared? No
   - Why do you think the other children look more interested than scared? Answers will vary.
   - How do you think you would act if a ladybug landed on your finger? Answers will vary.
5. Have students gather their crayons and scissors, and turn to page LS 43 in *K[12] Language Arts Activity Book*. Students should color the ladybug picture and then cut it out. Have students practice reciting the poem with their ladybug.

Online 15 minutes

Students will work online **independently** to complete activities on Vocabulary words. Help students locate the online activities, and provide support as needed.

Practice

Opposite Words

Students will practice the opposite words *young, old, wide, narrow, push,* and *pull.*

Objectives
- Increase oral vocabulary.
- Increase reading vocabulary.
- Increase concept vocabulary.
- Use antonyms.

Offline Alternative

No computer access? At any time, you can print a list of the unit Vocabulary words and their definitions from the online lesson. Use this list to review the words with students offline. In addition, if students made their own flash cards, these can be used for offline review.

Opposite Words (C)

Lesson Overview

Offline		15 minutes
Vocabulary	Introduce Opposite Words OPTIONAL: Make Your Own Flash Cards	
Online		15 minutes
Skills Update	Review Animal Words	
Learn	Introduce Opposite Words	

Materials

Supplied

- *K[12] Language Arts Activity Book,* p. LS 45

Also Needed

- index cards (3) (optional)
- scissors, round-end safety

Offline 15 minutes

Work **together** with students to complete an offline Vocabulary activity.

Vocabulary

Introduce Opposite Words

Have students play a memory game to learn words for opposites. Introduce the following words for opposites:

loud	**quiet**
sweet	**sour**
hot	**cold**

1. Read aloud each word in the left column and its opposite in the right column.
2. Turn to page LS 45 in *K[12] Language Arts Activity Book*, and help students cut out the opposite cards.
3. Lay the cards face down on the table in random order. Ask students to turn over two cards. If the cards are not opposite, turn them both face down again.

Objectives

- Increase oral vocabulary.
- Increase reading vocabulary.
- Increase concept vocabulary.
- Use antonyms.

4. Repeat until students find two cards that are opposites. Put those cards in a separate pile. Continue until students find all the pairs of opposites.
5. If time permits, play the card game again.

OPTIONAL: Make Your Own Flash Cards

This activity is intended for students who have extra time and would benefit from practicing their vocabulary words with flash cards. Feel free to skip this activity.

Gather three index cards. Have students create flash cards by writing each word on the front of an index card and its opposite on the back. Help students with spelling as necessary.

Online 15 minutes

Students will work online **independently** to complete activities on Vocabulary words. Help students locate the online activities, and provide support as needed.

Skills Update

Review Animal Words

Students will answer a few questions to refresh their Vocabulary knowledge.

Objectives
- Increase oral vocabulary.
- Increase concept vocabulary.

Learn

Introduce Opposite Words

Students will be introduced to the opposite words *loud, quiet, sweet, sour, hot,* and *cold.*

Objectives
- Increase oral vocabulary.
- Increase reading vocabulary.
- Increase concept vocabulary.
- Use antonyms.

Hot & Cold and Opposite Words (A)

Lesson Overview

Offline		15 minutes
All About Me	Hot and Cold	
Online		15 minutes
Practice	Opposite Words	

Materials

Supplied

- *K[12] All About Me,* pp. 26–27

Also Needed

- crayons

Offline 15 minutes

Work **together** with students to complete an offline All About Me activity.

All About Me

Hot and Cold

Students will begin pages 26 and 27 in *K[12] All About Me*; they will complete these pages over two lessons.

1. Discuss with students what they like to do and what they wear when the weather is hot and when it is cold.
2. Read aloud the first incomplete sentence to students, pointing to each word as you read. Have students tell you the answer to write in the blank space. Read the complete sentence to them, pointing to each word. Repeat with the second incomplete sentence.
3. If time permits, have students begin their illustrations.

Objectives

- Dictate or write simple sentences describing experiences, stories, people, objects, or events.

Online 15 minutes

Students will work online **independently** to complete activities on Vocabulary words. Help students locate the online activities, and provide support as needed.

Practice

Opposite Words

Students will practice the words *loud, quiet, sweet, sour, hot,* and *cold.*

Objectives

- Increase oral vocabulary.
- Increase reading vocabulary.
- Increase concept vocabulary.
- Use antonyms.

Offline Alternative

No computer access? At any time, you can print a list of the unit Vocabulary words and their definitions from the online lesson. Use this list to review the words with students offline. In addition, if students made their own flash cards, these can be used for offline review.

"Little Boy Blue" and Opposite Words

Lesson Overview

Offline	15 minutes
Poetry	"Little Boy Blue"

Online	15 minutes
Practice	Opposite Words

Materials

Supplied
- *K*[12] *Read Aloud Treasury,* p. 105
- *K*[12] *Language Arts Activity Book,* p. LS 47

Also Needed
- crayons
- scissors, round-end safety

Offline 15 minutes

Work **together** with students to complete an offline Poetry activity.

Poetry

"Little Boy Blue"

It's time to read "Little Boy Blue" from *K*[12] *Read Aloud Treasury.*

1. Remind students that nursery rhymes are poems that almost everyone hears when they are very young. Tell them that they will hear the nursery rhyme "Little Boy Blue." If students know this poem already, have them recite it to you.
2. Also remind students that they may have already learned the word *meadow.*
   - What is a meadow? a grassy field
3. As necessary, help students remember the meaning of the word *meadow.* Then tell them that the poem contains the word *meadow.*

Objectives
- Listen to and discuss poetry.
- Create illustrations that represent personal connections to text.
- Identify rhyme and rhythm in poetry.
- Describe character(s).

4. Have students sit next to you so they can see the picture and words while you **read aloud the entire poem**, and then ask:
   - What is Little Boy Blue supposed to do? blow his horn
   - What animal is in the corn? the cow
   - Where is Little Boy Blue? under the haystack, asleep
   - Which word in the poem rhymes with *asleep—haystack, sheep,* or *wake*? *sheep*
   - What does the poem say might happen if anyone wakes up Little Boy Blue? He will cry.
5. Help students gather their crayons and scissors. Turn to page LS 47 in *K[12] Language Arts Activity Book*. Have students color the pictures of Little Boy Blue and the haystack, and then cut them out. Reread the poem. Have students hold Little Boy Blue *under* the haystack. Then practice position words by having students hold Little Boy Blue *over* the haystack, *next to* it, and so on.

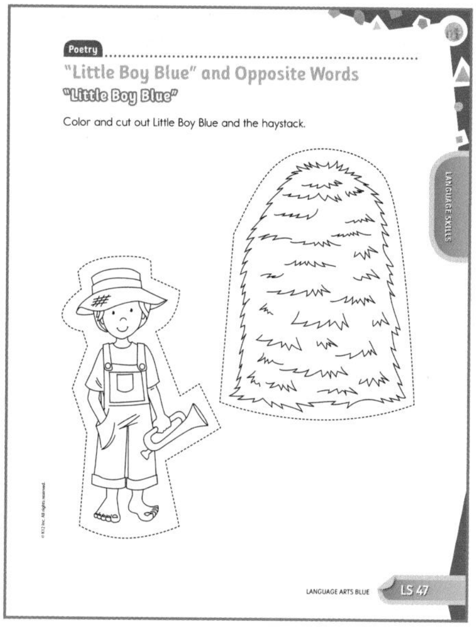

Online 15 minutes

Students will work online **independently** to complete activities on Vocabulary words. Help students locate the online activities, and provide support as needed.

Practice

Opposite Words

Students will practice the opposite words *loud, quiet, sweet, sour, hot,* and *cold.*

Offline Alternative

No computer access? At any time, you can print a list of the unit Vocabulary words and their definitions from the online lesson. Use this list to review the words with students offline. In addition, if students made their own flash cards, these can be used for offline review.

Objectives

- Increase oral vocabulary.
- Increase reading vocabulary.
- Increase concept vocabulary.
- Use antonyms.

Opposite Words (D)

Lesson Overview

Offline	15 minutes
Vocabulary	Introduce Opposite Words
	OPTIONAL: Make Your Own Flash Cards
Online	**15 minutes**
Skills Update	Review Job Words
Learn	Introduce Opposite Words

Materials

Supplied
- There are no supplied materials to gather for this activity.

Also Needed
- index cards (up to 6)
- index cards (3) (optional)
- tape, masking
- crayons

Offline 15 minutes

Work **together** with students to complete an offline Vocabulary activity.

Vocabulary

Introduce Opposite Words
Introduce the following opposite words and have students practice those words:

hard	**soft**
clean	**dirty**
fast	**slow**

1. Walk around the room or the building, and gather items that can be described as *hard, soft, clean, dirty, fast,* and *slow.* If you can't find items for some of the words, have students use index cards and crayons to draw items. For example, if you can't find something for *slow,* students can draw a turtle.
2. Assist students in writing labels on index cards for each item and taping them to the items. If students have drawn a picture to represent an item, help them write the label on the index card.
3. Ask students to arrange the items or cards with their opposites. For example, a rock labeled *hard* should be next to a pillow labeled *soft.*
4. If time permits, mix up the items and let students pair the opposites again.

Objectives
- Increase oral vocabulary.
- Increase reading vocabulary.
- Increase concept vocabulary.
- Use antonyms.

OPTIONAL: Make Your Own Flash Cards

This activity is intended for students who have extra time and would benefit from practicing their vocabulary words with flash cards. Feel free to skip this activity.

Gather three index cards. Have students create flash cards by writing each word on the front of an index card and its opposite on the back. Help students with spelling as necessary.

Online 15 minutes

Students will work online **independently** to complete activities on Vocabulary words. Help students locate the online activities, and provide support as needed.

Skills Update

Review Job Words

Students will answer a few questions to refresh their Vocabulary knowledge.

Objectives

- Increase oral vocabulary.
- Increase concept vocabulary.

Learn

Introduce Opposite Words

Students will be introduced to the opposite words *hard, soft, dirty, clean, fast,* and *slow*.

Objectives

- Increase oral vocabulary.
- Increase reading vocabulary.
- Increase concept vocabulary.
- Use antonyms.

Hot & Cold and Opposite Words (B)

Lesson Overview

Offline	15 minutes
All About Me	Hot and Cold
Online	**15 minutes**
Practice	Opposite Words

Materials

Supplied

- *K¹² All About Me*, pp. 26–27

Also Needed

- crayons

Offline 15 minutes

Work **together** with students to complete an offline All About Me activity.

All About Me

Hot and Cold

Students will complete pages 26 and 27 in *K¹² All About Me*.

1. Have students finalize and explain their drawings. Encourage them to describe their drawings using as much detail as possible.
2. Read aloud the complete sentences to students, pointing to each word as you read. If students are ready, have them take a turn reading aloud their completed sentences.

TIP If time permits, have students tell you more pieces of clothing they like to wear when they are hot and cold.

Objectives

- Write and/or draw narrative text.
- Draw and label pictures.

Online 15 minutes

Students will work online **independently** to complete activities on Vocabulary words. Help students locate the online activities, and provide support as needed.

Practice

Opposite Words

Students will practice the opposite words *hard, soft, dirty, clean, fast,* and *slow.*

Offline Alternative

No computer access? At any time, you can print a list of the unit Vocabulary words and their definitions from the online lesson. Use this list to review the words with students offline. In addition, if students made their own flash cards, these can be used for offline review.

Objectives

- Increase oral vocabulary.
- Increase reading vocabulary.
- Increase concept vocabulary.
- Use antonyms.

"Sing a Song of Sixpence" and Vocabulary Unit Review

Lesson Overview

Offline	15 minutes
Poetry	"Sing a Song of Sixpence"
	OPTIONAL: Play the Parts
Online	**15 minutes**
Unit Review	Opposite Words

Materials

Supplied

- *K[12] Read Aloud Treasury,* pp. 110–111

Offline 15 minutes

Work **together** with students to complete an offline Poetry activity.

Poetry

"Sing a Song of Sixpence"

It's time to read "Sing a Song of Sixpence" from *K[12] Read Aloud Treasury.*

1. Tell students that a **stanza** is a group of lines in a poem. Some poems have many stanzas. Explain that together you will count how many stanzas are in today's poem.
2. Tell students that today's poem is a nursery rhyme that is more than 100 years old, and that the word *sixpence* means "a small British coin worth six pennies."
3. Have students sit next to you so they can see the picture and words while you **read aloud the entire poem,** pointing to each stanza as you read, and then ask:
   - What is baked in the pie in this poem? blackbirds
   - Which word in the poem rhymes with *money—parlor, bread,* or *honey*? *honey*
   - Where is the queen? in the parlor
   - What is the maid doing in the garden? hanging out the clothes
   - How many stanzas are in this poem? four
   - How many lines are in each stanza? four

Objectives

- Listen to and discuss poetry.
- Build vocabulary through listening, reading, and discussion.
- Respond to text through art, writing, and/or drama.
- Identify rhyme and rhythm in poetry.
- Describe character(s).

4. Reread the first stanza now, stressing the rhyming words at the ends the second and fourth lines.
   Say: In every stanza, the second and fourth lines rhyme.

5. Read the second stanza.
   - Which words in this stanza rhyme? *sing* and *king*

   Show students that these words end the second and fourth lines of the stanza.

OPTIONAL: Play the Parts

This activity is optional. It is intended for students who have extra time and would benefit from acting out the descriptions of the characters in the poem.

Have students pretend to be the king, the queen, and the maid in the poem. Encourage students to mime what each character is doing as you read the poem aloud.

Online 15 minutes

Students will work online **independently** to complete an activity on Vocabulary words. Help students locate the online activity, and provide support as needed.

Unit Review

Opposite Words

Students will review all words from the unit to prepare for the Unit Checkpoint.

Objectives
- Increase oral vocabulary.
- Increase reading vocabulary.
- Increase concept vocabulary.
- Use antonyms.

Offline Alternative

No computer access? At any time, you can print a list of the unit Vocabulary words and their definitions from the online lesson. Use this list to review the words with students offline. In addition, if students made their own flash cards, these can be used for offline review.

Unit Checkpoint

Lesson Overview

Online — 30 minutes

Unit Checkpoint	Opposite Words

Materials

There are no materials to gather for this lesson.

Online — 30 minutes

Students will work online to complete the Unit Checkpoint. Help students locate the Unit Checkpoint, and provide support as needed.

Unit Checkpoint

Opposite Words

Explain that students are going to show what they have learned about vocabulary words for opposites.

Objectives

- Increase oral vocabulary.
- Increase reading vocabulary.
- Increase concept vocabulary.
- Use antonyms.

Writing Words (A)

Unit Overview

In this unit, students will

- Learn vocabulary words for writing and manners.
- Complete the *All About Me* pages *A Letter to My Friend* and *A Thank-You Note.*
- Explore the poems "Hushabye, Don't You Cry," "Bed in Summer," and "A Bear Went Over the Mountain."

Lesson Overview

Offline		15 minutes
Vocabulary	Introduce Writing Words	
	OPTIONAL: Make Your Own Flash Cards	
Online		15 minutes
Skills Update	Review Music Words	
Learn	Introduce Writing Words	

Materials

Supplied

- There are no supplied materials to gather for this lesson.

Also Needed

- index cards (6) (optional)
- crayon (1, any color)
- marker, coloring (1, any color)
- household objects – notebook, eraser

Advance Preparation

Gather the crayon, marker, notebook, and eraser. Also gather a pen and a pencil.

Offline 15 minutes

Work **together** with students to complete an offline Vocabulary activity.

Vocabulary

Introduce Writing Words

Introduce students to the following writing words:

crayon	**marker**	**pen**
eraser	**notebook**	**pencil**

1. Gather the crayon, eraser, marker, notebook, pen, and pencil. Tell students that you are going to play Twenty Questions.
2. Explain the rules of Twenty Questions.
   - One person chooses an object from the items you collected.
   - Everyone else gets to ask the person a yes or no question about the chosen object. For example: Is it made of wax? Does it hold paper? Does it erase?
   - Students may ask a total of twenty questions. Whoever guesses correctly gets to choose another object. If the tally of questions hits twenty, the person who chose the object wins.
3. If necessary, pare the questions down to ten.

Objectives

- Increase oral vocabulary.
- Increase reading vocabulary.
- Increase concept vocabulary.

OPTIONAL: Make Your Own Flash Cards

This activity is intended for students who have extra time and would benefit from practicing their vocabulary words with flash cards. Feel free to skip this activity.

Gather six index cards. Have students create flash cards by writing each vocabulary word on the front of an index card and their own definition for each word on the back. Help students with spelling as necessary.

Online 15 minutes

Students will work online **independently** to complete Vocabulary activities. Help students locate the online activities, and provide support as needed.

Skills Update

Review Music Words

Students will answer a few questions to refresh their Vocabulary knowledge.

Objectives

- Increase oral vocabulary.
- Increase concept vocabulary.

Learn

Introduce Writing Words

Students will be introduced to the writing words *crayon, eraser, marker, notebook, pen,* and *pencil.*

Objectives

- Increase oral vocabulary.
- Increase reading vocabulary.
- Increase concept vocabulary.

A Letter to My Friend and Writing Words (A)

Lesson Overview

Offline	15 minutes
All About Me	A Letter to My Friend
Online	**15 minutes**
Practice	Writing Words

Materials

Supplied

- *K[12] All About Me*, p. 28

Offline 15 minutes

Work **together** with students to complete an offline All About Me activity.

All About Me

A Letter to My Friend

Students will begin page 28 in *K[12] All About Me*; they will complete this page over two lessons.

1. Explain to students that sometimes we write letters to our friends. Whether we handwrite them or type them, letters always include a greeting, the body (made up of paragraphs), and a closing.
2. Have students think of a friend to whom they would like to write a friendly letter. Discuss with students what the letter will be about.
3. Discuss with students what their greetings will be (for example, "Dear Jim," or "Hello, Amy!"). Help them as necessary.
4. Help students begin the body of their letter. Help them indent the first line, capitalize the first word of each sentence, end each sentence with the appropriate punctuation, and use proper spacing between words.

TIP The purpose of this activity is to introduce students to the process of writing in a fun and enjoyable way. If students are not ready to write on their own, allow them to dictate sentences to you. Point out the use of proper punctuation, capitalization, and spacing as your write.

Objectives

- Communicate in writing.
- Write and/or draw functional text.
- Generate ideas for writing and drawing through discussion.
- Use proper spacing between words.
- Reread own writing.

Online 15 minutes

Students will work online **independently** to complete activities on Vocabulary words. Help students locate the online activities, and provide support as needed.

Practice

Writing Words

Students will practice the writing words *crayon, eraser, marker, notebook, pen,* and *pencil.*

Offline Alternative

No computer access? At any time, you can print a list of the unit Vocabulary words and their definitions from the online lesson. Use this list to review the words with students offline. In addition, if students made their own flash cards, these can be used for offline review.

Objectives

- Increase oral vocabulary.
- Increase reading vocabulary.
- Increase concept vocabulary.

"Hushabye, Don't You Cry" and Writing Words

Lesson Overview

Offline	15 minutes
Poetry	"Hushabye, Don't You Cry"
Online	**15 minutes**
Practice	Writing Words

Materials

Supplied

- *The Rooster Crows*
- *K[12] Language Arts Activity Book*, p. LS 49

Also Needed

- crayons

Advance Preparation

Before reading today's poem, you will need to find the poem in the book *The Rooster Crows*. If your book has page numbers, turn to page 32. Otherwise, you will need to use a pencil to number the pages in the book. Mark the title page as page 1.

Offline 15 minutes

Work **together** with students to complete an offline Poetry activity.

Poetry

"Hushabye, Don't You Cry"

It's time to read "Hushabye, Don't You Cry" from *The Rooster Crows.*

1. Tell students that some poems are meant to be sung to help young children fall asleep. Explain that we call these poems lullabies.
   - Do you know any lullabies? Answers will vary.
2. If students know a lullaby, have them sing it to you. If not, sing a favorite lullaby of your own to them.
   - Do we sing lullabies loudly or softly? softly
   - Why do we sing lullabies softly? It is easier to fall asleep to soft music than loud music.

Objectives

- Listen to and discuss poetry.
- Identify words that create mental imagery.
- Identify rhyme and rhythm in poetry.
- Identify the purpose of a text.

3. Have students sit next to you so they can see the picture and words while you **read aloud the entire poem**, and then ask:
   - Which word in the poem rhymes with *wake*—*cry, cake,* or *when*? cake
   - What will be baby get when he or she wakes up? cake and lots of pretty horses
   - How many horses does the poem describe? three
4. Tell students that "Hushabye, Don't You Cry" is a lullaby.
   - How do you know that this poem is a lullaby? The line "Go to sleepy, little baby" is repeated.
   - At what time of day would you probably hear or say this poem? nighttime or bedtime
5. Explain that the poem contains color words to help readers imagine how the horses look.
   - What colors are the first two horses? red and blue
   - What color might "the color of Mammy's shoe" be? Answers will vary.
6. Have students gather their crayons and color the picture of the horses on page LS 49 in *K^12 Language Arts Activity Book*. As they work, remind them that one horse should be red, one should be blue, and one should be the color of their mother's shoe.

Poetry
"Hushabye, Don't You Cry" and Writing Words
"Hushabye, Don't You Cry"
Color the horses to match the ones in the poem.
LANGUAGE ARTS BLUE LS 49

Online 15 minutes

Students will work online **independently** to complete activities on Vocabulary words. Help students locate the online activities, and provide support as needed.

Practice

Writing Words

Students will practice the writing words *crayon, eraser, marker, notebook, pen,* and *pencil.*

Offline Alternative

No computer access? At any time, you can print a list of the unit Vocabulary words and their definitions from the online lesson. Use this list to review the words with students offline. In addition, if students made their own flash cards, these can be used for offline review.

Objectives
- Increase oral vocabulary.
- Increase reading vocabulary.
- Increase concept vocabulary.

Writing Words (B)

Lesson Overview

Offline	15 minutes
Vocabulary	Introduce Writing Words OPTIONAL: Make Your Own Flash Cards
Online	**15 minutes**
Skills Update	Review Family Words
Learn	Introduce Writing Words

Materials

Supplied

- *K[12] Language Arts Activity Book*, p. LS 50

Also Needed

- index cards (5) (optional)

Offline 15 minutes

Work **together** with students to complete an offline Vocabulary activity.

Vocabulary

Introduce Writing Words

Introduce students to the following writing words and how they are related:

address	**envelope**	**stamp**
card	**note**	

1. Ask students if any of them has received a letter. Ask them the following questions. Answers to questions may vary.
   - What was on the letter?
   - Who was it from?
   - How did you know?
   - How was it written?
   - What did it say?
2. Tell students that they are going to write and mail a letter to an author. Discuss with students their favorite books and the people who wrote them. You can get an author's mailing address by writing to the publishing company listed inside the book, or by visiting http://www.superkidz.com/authors.html.

Objectives

- Increase oral vocabulary.
- Increase reading vocabulary.
- Increase concept vocabulary.

3. Turn to page LS 50 in *K[12] Language Arts Activity Book*. Guide students through the template for completing the letter.
4. Have students fill out an envelope, including the author's address and the student's return address. Have them add a stamp.

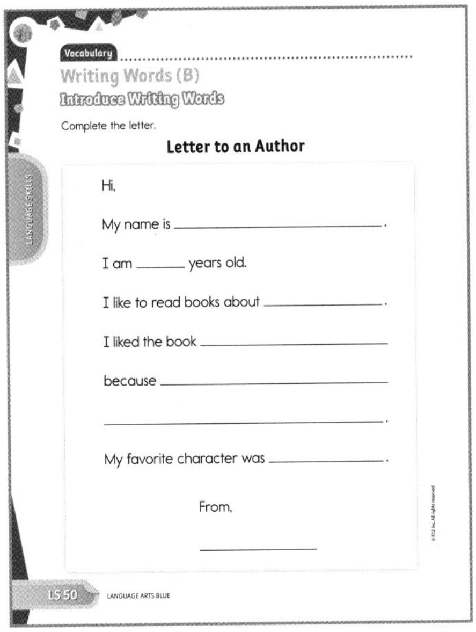
Vocabulary
Writing Words (B)
Introduce Writing Words
Complete the letter.
Letter to an Author
Hi,
My name is ______.
I am ____ years old.
I like to read books about ______.
I liked the book ______
because ______
______.
My favorite character was ______.
From,
______
LS 50 LANGUAGE ARTS BLUE

OPTIONAL: Make Your Own Flash Cards

This activity is intended for students who have extra time and would benefit from practicing their vocabulary words with flash cards. Feel free to skip this activity.

Gather five index cards. Have students create flash cards by writing each vocabulary word on the front of an index card and their own definition for each word on the back. Help students with spelling as necessary.

Online 15 minutes

Students will work online **independently** to complete activities on Vocabulary words. Help students locate the online activities, and provide support as needed.

Skills Update

Review Family Words

Students will answer a few questions to refresh their Vocabulary knowledge.

Objectives
- Increase reading vocabulary.
- Increase concept vocabulary.

Learn

Introduce Writing Words

Students will be introduced to the writing words *address, card, envelope, note,* and *stamp*.

Objectives
- Increase oral vocabulary.
- Increase reading vocabulary.
- Increase concept vocabulary.

A Letter to My Friend and Writing Words (B)

Lesson Overview

Offline	15 minutes
All About Me	A Letter to My Friend
Online	**15 minutes**
Practice	Writing Words

Materials

Supplied
- *K[12] All About Me*, p. 28

Offline 15 minutes

Work **together** with students to complete an offline All About Me activity.

All About Me

A Letter to My Friend

Students will complete page 28 in *K[12] All About Me.*

1. Review with students the parts of the letter they have written up to this point. Point out the remaining parts of the letter to complete.
2. Discuss again what the letter will be about, and help students complete the body of the letter. Help students with capitalization, punctuation, proper spacing, and spelling as needed.
3. Have students write the closing and their name.
4. Have students point to and name the different parts of their letter, and then read aloud the completed letter.

TIP If possible, help students address, stamp, and mail the letter.

Objectives
- Communicate in writing.
- Write and/or draw functional text.
- Generate ideas for writing and drawing through discussion.
- Use proper spacing between words.
- Reread own writing.
- Share finished written and drawn works.

[Online] 15 minutes

Students will work online **independently** to complete activities on Vocabulary words. Help students locate the online activities, and provide support as needed.

Practice

Writing Words

Students will practice the writing words *address, card, envelope, note,* and *stamp.*

Offline Alternative

No computer access? At any time, you can print a list of the unit Vocabulary words and their definitions from the online lesson. Use this list to review the words with students offline. In addition, if students made their own flash cards, these can be used for offline review.

Objectives

- Increase oral vocabulary.
- Increase reading vocabulary.
- Increase concept vocabulary.

"Bed in Summer" and Writing Words

Lesson Overview

Offline	15 minutes
Poetry	"Bed in Summer"
Online	**15 minutes**
Practice	Writing Words

Materials

Supplied

- *Tomie dePaola's Rhyme Time*

Advance Preparation

Before reading today's poem, you will need to find the poem in the book *Tomie dePaola's Rhyme Time*. If your book has page numbers, turn to page 7. Otherwise, you will need to use a pencil to number the pages in the book. Mark the title page as page 1.

Offline 15 minutes

Work **together** with students to complete an offline Poetry activity.

Poetry

"Bed in Summer"

It's time to read "Bed in Summer" from *Tomie dePaola's Rhyme Time.*

1. Remind students that poems are sometimes divided into groups of lines and that these groups of lines are called **stanzas**.
2. Tell students that some poems describe feelings that they might have had themselves.
   Say: When we read a poem about a feeling we have had, we often feel like we understand the poem better.
3. Remind students that there are more hours of daylight in summer than in winter.

Objectives

- Listen to and discuss poetry.
- Make connections with text: text-to-text, text-to-self, text-to-world.
- Identify author's use of sensory language.
- Identify rhyme and rhythm in poetry.

4. Have students sit next to you so they can see the picture and words while you **read aloud the entire poem**, and then ask:
   - What is it like outside when the person in the poem gets up in winter? It is still dark.
   - Which words rhyme with *see* and *feet* in the second stanza? *tree* and *street*
   - What is it like outside when the person in the poem goes to bed in summer? It is still light.
   - What does the person in the poem want to be doing when he goes to bed in the summer? playing
5. Tell students that the poem's language helps us understand what it is like to go to bed when it is still light outside. Point out that the second stanza does so by describing what the person in the poem sees and hears.
   - What does the person see? birds hopping on a tree
   - What does the person hear? the sound of people walking on the street
   - What words in the third stanza help us picture the evening sky in summer? *clear* and *blue*
6. Ask students the following questions. Answers to questions may vary.
   - Have you ever gone to bed when it is still light outside?
   - If so, how did you feel? If not, how do you think you would feel?
7. If time permits, reread the poem and have students chime in as they are able.

Online 15 minutes

Students will work online **independently** to complete activities on Vocabulary words. Help students locate the online activities, and provide support as needed.

Practice

Writing Words

Students will practice the writing words *address, card, envelope, note,* and *stamp*.

Offline Alternative

No computer access? At any time, you can print a list of the unit Vocabulary words and their definitions from the online lesson. Use this list to review the words with students offline. In addition, if students made their own flash cards, these can be used for offline review.

Objectives

- Increase oral vocabulary.
- Increase reading vocabulary.
- Increase concept vocabulary.

Manners Words (A)

Lesson Overview

Offline		15 minutes
Vocabulary	Introduce Manners Words OPTIONAL: Make Your Own Flash Cards	
Online		15 minutes
Skills Update	Review Feelings Words	
Learn	Introduce Manners Words	

Materials

Supplied
- There are no supplied materials to gather for this lesson.

Also Needed
- index cards (5) (optional)
- crayons
- paper, drawing

Offline 15 minutes

Work **together** with students to complete an offline Vocabulary activity.

Vocabulary

Introduce Manners Words

Introduce students to the following manners words:

excuse me	**please**	**thank you**
manners	**respect**	

1. Tell students that they are going to learn some words related to manners.
2. Read each word aloud and discuss its meaning. After reading each word, ask students if they have ever used one of these words. Have them explain why they used that word.
3. Explain to students that you are going to ask a few questions and they need to choose the word that would best answer the question.
   - If you want to get someone's attention, what words would you use? *excuse me*
   - If you want something from someone, you ask for it nicely. What word would you use? *please*
   - If someone gave you a present, what would you say to that person? *thank you*

Objectives
- Increase oral vocabulary.
- Increase reading vocabulary.
- Increase concept vocabulary.

4. Ask students the following questions. Answers to questions may vary.
    - Who are people you feel respect for? How do you show your respect?
    - What does it mean to have manners? What are good manners? What are bad manners?
5. If time permits, have students draw a picture of someone they respect or have them draw a picture showing good manners and one showing bad manners.

OPTIONAL: Make Your Own Flash Cards

This activity is intended for students who have extra time and would benefit from practicing their vocabulary words with flash cards. Feel free to skip this activity.

Gather five index cards. Have students create flash cards by writing each vocabulary word on the front of an index card and their own definition for each word on the back. Help students with spelling as necessary.

Online 15 minutes

Students will work online **independently** to complete activities on Vocabulary words. Help students locate the online activities, and provide support as needed.

Skills Update

Review Feeling Words

Students will answer a few questions to refresh their Vocabulary knowledge.

Objectives

- Increase oral vocabulary.
- Increase reading vocabulary.
- Increase concept vocabulary.

Learn

Introduce Manners Words

Students will be introduced to the manners words *excuse me, manners, please, respect,* and *thank you.*

Objectives

- Increase oral vocabulary.
- Increase reading vocabulary.
- Increase concept vocabulary.

A Thank-You Note and Manners Words (A)

Lesson Overview

Offline		15 minutes
All About Me	A Thank-You Note	
Online		**15 minutes**
Practice	Manners Words	

Materials

Supplied

- *K*[12] *All About Me*, p. 29

Offline 15 minutes

Work **together** with students to complete an offline All About Me activity.

All About Me

A Thank-You Note

Students will begin page 29 in *K*[12] *All About Me*; they will complete this page over two lessons.

1. Discuss with students the features of a thank-you note (greeting, body, closing, and so on).
2. Have students think of and describe a time when a friend or family member gave them something or did something for which they were thankful.
3. Have students fill in the greeting. Help them complete the body of their letter. Help them use proper capitalization, punctuation, spacing, and spelling as needed.
4. Remind students that they will have time to complete the letter on another day. Before stopping for the day, review the parts of the letter written to this point.

TIP If students are not ready to write on their own, allow them to dictate sentences to you. Point out the use of proper punctuation, capitalization, and spacing as your write.

Objectives

- Communicate in writing.
- Write and/or draw functional text.
- Generate ideas for writing and drawing through discussion.
- Use proper spacing between words.
- Reread own writing.
- Dictate or write simple sentences describing experiences, stories, people, objects, or events.

Online 15 minutes

Students will work online **independently** to complete activities on Vocabulary words. Help students locate the online activities, and provide support as needed.

Practice

Manners Words

Students will practice the manners words *excuse me, manners, please, respect,* and *thank you.*

Offline Alternative

No computer access? At any time, you can print a list of the unit Vocabulary words and their definitions from the online lesson. Use this list to review the words with students offline. In addition, if students made their own flash cards, these can be used for offline review.

Objectives

- Increase oral vocabulary.
- Increase reading vocabulary.
- Increase concept vocabulary.

"A Bear Went Over the Mountain" and Vocabulary Unit Review

Lesson Overview

Offline	15 minutes
Poetry	"A Bear Went Over the Mountain"
	OPTIONAL: Sing the Poem
Online	**15 minutes**
Unit Review	Writing and Manners Words

Materials

Supplied

- *The Rooster Crows*

Advance Preparation

Before reading today's poem, you will need to find the poem in the book *The Rooster Crows.* If your book has page numbers, turn to pages 16 and 17. Otherwise, you will need to use a pencil to number the pages in the book. Mark the title page as page 1.

Offline 15 minutes

Work **together** with students to complete an offline Poetry activity.

Poetry

"A Bear Went Over the Mountain"

It's time to read "A Bear Went Over the Mountain" from *The Rooster Crows.*

1. Ask students:
   - Have you ever heard the word *curious*? Answers will vary.
2. Have students tell you what it means to be curious. If students do not know the word, tell them that to be curious is to be eager to learn (or learn more) about things.
   - Are you a curious person? Answers will vary.

Objectives

- Listen to and discuss poetry.
- Use visual text features to aid understanding of text.
- Identify repetitive text.

3. Have students sit next to you so they can see the picture and words while you **read aloud the entire poem**, and then ask:
   - What words are repeated in the first stanza? *A bear went over the mountain.*
   - Why does the bear go over the mountain? to see what he could see
   - What does the bear see once he gets over the top of the mountain? only the other side of the mountain
4. Remind students of the word *curious*, and point to the picture above the first stanza of this poem. Answers to questions may vary.
   - Is the bear curious? Why or why not?
   - How do you think the bear feels when he gets to the other side of the mountain? Why?

OPTIONAL: Sing the Poem

This activity is optional. It is intended for students who have extra time and would benefit from further exploration of the poem.

Often this poem is sung to the tune of "For He's a Jolly Good Fellow." If time permits, sing the poem with students.

Online 15 minutes

Students will work online **independently** to complete an activity on Vocabulary words. Help students locate the online activity, and provide support as needed.

Unit Review

Writing and Manners Words

Students will review all words from the unit to prepare for the Unit Checkpoint.

Objectives
- Increase oral vocabulary.
- Increase reading vocabulary.
- Increase concept vocabulary.

Offline Alternative

No computer access? At any time, you can print a list of the unit Vocabulary words and their definitions from the online lesson. Use this list to review the words with students offline. In addition, if students made their own flash cards, these can be used for offline review.

Unit Checkpoint

Lesson Overview

Online	30 minutes
Unit Checkpoint	Writing and Manners Words

Materials

There are no materials to gather for this lesson.

Online 30 minutes

Students will work online to complete the Unit Checkpoint. Help students locate the Unit Checkpoint, and provide support as needed.

Unit Checkpoint

Writing and Manners Words

Explain that students are going to show what they have learned about vocabulary words for writing and manners.

Objectives

- Increase oral vocabulary.
- Increase reading vocabulary.
- Increase concept vocabulary.

Manners Words (B)

Unit Overview

In this unit, students will

- Learn vocabulary words for manners and traffic.
- Complete the *All About Me* pages *A Thank-You Note* and *Signs in My Neighborhood.*
- Explore haikus and the poems "Peter, Peter, Pumpkin Eater" and "Cat Kisses."

Materials

Supplied

- There are no supplied materials to gather for this lesson.

Also Needed

- index cards (5) (optional)
- crayons
- drawing paper

Lesson Overview

Offline	15 minutes
Vocabulary	Introduce Manners Words OPTIONAL: Make Your Own Flash Cards
Online	15 minutes
Skills Update	Review Family Words
Learn	Introduce Manners Words

Offline 15 minutes

Work **together** with students to complete an offline Vocabulary activity.

Vocabulary

Introduce Manners Words

Introduce students to the following manners words:

attitude	**kind**	**sportsmanship**
considerate	**rude**	

1. Tell students that they are going to learn some words related to manners.
2. Read each word aloud and discuss its meaning. After reading all the words, ask students if they have ever used one of these words. Have them explain why they used that word.
3. Tell students that you are going to ask a few questions and they need to choose which word would best answer the question. Answers to questions may vary.
   - What is it like to have a good attitude? A bad attitude?
   - Can you give an example of a time when you were considerate or kind?

Objectives

- Increase oral vocabulary.
- Increase concept vocabulary.
- Increase reading vocabulary.

- Can you give an example of when you saw someone showing good sportsmanship while playing a sport? How about someone showing bad sportsmanship? How did that make you feel?
- Have you ever had someone be rude to you? What did they do? How did it make you feel?

4. If time permits, have students draw a picture of someone showing good sportsmanship, being kind, being rude, being considerate, or showing a good attitude. Have them explain their drawing.

OPTIONAL: Make Your Own Flash Cards

This activity is intended for students who have extra time and would benefit from practicing vocabulary words with flash cards. Feel free to skip this activity.

Gather five index cards. Have students create flash cards by writing each vocabulary word on the front of an index card and their own definition for each word on the back. Help students with spelling as necessary.

TIP If students are not ready to read and write on their own, skip this optional activity.

Online 15 minutes

Students will work online **independently** to complete Vocabulary activities. Help students locate the online activities, and provide support as needed.

Skills Update

Review Family Words

Students will answer a few questions to refresh their Vocabulary knowledge.

Objectives
- Increase oral vocabulary.
- Increase concept vocabulary.

Learn

Introduce Manners Words

Students will be introduced to the manners words *attitude, considerate, kind, rude,* and *sportsmanship*.

Objectives
- Increase oral vocabulary.
- Increase reading vocabulary.
- Increase concept vocabulary.

A Thank-You Note and Manners Words (B)

Lesson Overview

Offline		15 minutes
All About Me	A Thank-You Note	
Online		15 minutes
Practice	Manners Words	

Materials

Supplied

- K^{12} *All About Me*, p. 29

Offline 15 minutes

Work **together** with students to complete an offline All About Me activity.

All About Me

A Thank-You Note

Students will complete page 29 in K^{12} *All About Me.*

1. Review with students the parts of the thank-you note written up to this point, and briefly discuss the remaining parts of the letter to complete.
2. Have students write or dictate additional sentences to include in the body paragraph, if necessary.
3. Have students write the closing and their name. Help them where necessary. Make sure students use proper spacing between words and capital letters where appropriate.
4. Have students point to and name the different parts of their thank-you note (greeting, body, closing, and so on). Work with them to read aloud the completed letter.
5. If possible, work with students to address, stamp, and mail an envelope with the letter in it.

Objectives

- Communicate in writing.
- Write and/or draw functional text.
- Generate ideas for writing and drawing through discussion.
- Use proper spacing between words.
- Dictate or write simple sentences describing experiences, stories, people, objects, or events.
- Capitalize proper names.
- Reread own writing.
- Shared finished written and drawn works.

Online 15 minutes

Students will work online **independently** to complete activities on Vocabulary words. Help students locate the online activities, and provide support as needed.

Practice

Manners Words

Students will practice the manners words *attitude, considerate, kind, rude,* and *sportsmanship*.

Objectives

- Increase oral vocabulary.
- Increase reading vocabulary.
- Increase concept vocabulary.

Offline Alternative

No computer access? At any time, you can print a list of the unit Vocabulary words and their definitions from the online lesson. Use this list to review the words with students offline. In addition, if students made their own flash cards, these can be used for offline review.

Haikus and Manners Words

Lesson Overview

Offline	15 minutes
Poetry	Haikus
	OPTIONAL: More Haikus

Online	15 minutes
Practice	Manners Words

Materials

Supplied

- *Tomie dePaola's Rhyme Time*

Keywords

syllable – a unit of spoken language; a syllable contains only one vowel sound

Advance Preparation

Before reading today's poem, you will need to find the poem in the book *Tomie dePaola's Rhyme Time.* If your book has page numbers, turn to page 22. Otherwise, you will need to use a pencil to number the pages in the book. Mark the title page as page 1.

Offline 15 minutes

Work **together** with students to complete an offline Poetry activity.

Poetry

Haikus

It's time to read two haikus about frogs from *Tomie dePaola's Rhyme Time.*

Objectives

- Listen to and discuss poetry.
- Identify words that create mental imagery.
- Listen and respond to texts representing a variety of cultures, time periods, and traditions.
- Describe character(s).

1. Tell students that **haikus** are poems that were first written in a place called Japan. Haikus always have just three lines. Since haikus are short, each word is very important.
2. Tell students that the first and third lines of a haiku each have five syllables, while the second line has seven syllables.
   Say: Each time we say a word, we use a puff of air. Each puff of air is a syllable. The word *good* has one syllable because it is made of one puff of air: good. The word *better* has two syllables: bet / ter.
3. Have students count the syllables in the following line by clapping with you as you say each syllable: I was working today. six: *I / was / work / ing / to / day*

4. Have students sit next to you so they can see the pictures and words while you **read aloud the two haikus**, and then ask:
   - What are both haikus about? frogs
   - What color are the frogs in these haikus? green
   - What two things in the first haiku seem to be splashed with green paint? the frog and the leaves
   - What is missing from the belly of the frog in the second haiku? a belly button
5. Reread the haikus and have students clap the syllables in each line.

OPTIONAL: More Haikus

This activity is optional. It is intended for students who have extra time and would benefit from further exposure to haikus.

Take a trip to the library or search the Internet for haikus for children. Read them to students, and have students clap out the syllables.

Online 15 minutes

Students will work online **independently** to complete activities on Vocabulary words. Help students locate the online activities, and provide support as needed.

Practice

Manners Words

Students will practice the manners words *attitude, considerate, kind, rude,* and *sportsmanship*.

Objectives
- Increase oral vocabulary.
- Increase reading vocabulary.
- Increase concept vocabulary.

Offline Alternative

No computer access? At any time, you can print a list of the unit Vocabulary words and their definitions from the online lesson. Use this list to review the words with students offline. In addition, if students made their own flash cards, these can be used for offline review.

Traffic Words (A)

Lesson Overview

Offline	15 minutes
Vocabulary	Introduce Traffic Words
	⊕ **OPTIONAL:** Make Your Own Flash Cards
Online	**15 minutes**
Skills Update	Review Location Words
Learn	Introduce Traffic Words

Materials

Supplied
- *K¹² Language Arts Activity Book*, p. LS 51

Also Needed
- index cards (5)
- index cards (5) (optional)
- household objects – hat or container

Advance Preparation

Write these words on index cards, one word per card: *crosswalk, intersection, signpost, traffic,* and *traffic light.*

Offline 15 minutes

Work **together** with students to complete an offline Vocabulary activity.

Vocabulary

Introduce Traffic Words

Introduce students to the following traffic words:

crosswalk	**signpost**	**traffic light**
intersection	**traffic**	

1. Tell students that they are going to play a game called Traffic Bingo.
2. Turn to page LS 51 in *K¹² Language Arts Activity Book*. Have students write each vocabulary word in a square. Repeat words as needed to fill all the squares. Help students write the words, if necessary.

Objectives
- Increase oral vocabulary.
- Increase reading vocabulary.
- Increase concept vocabulary.

3. Gather the prepared index cards. Place them in a hat or container.
4. Choose an index card and read the word aloud. Have students cross out the word on the Activity Book page.
5. Repeat Step 4 until students get "bingo" (three words in a row crossed out horizontally, vertically, or diagonally).

TIP Instead of using index cards, walk around the neighborhood or drive into town. Have students cross out a square for each item they see.

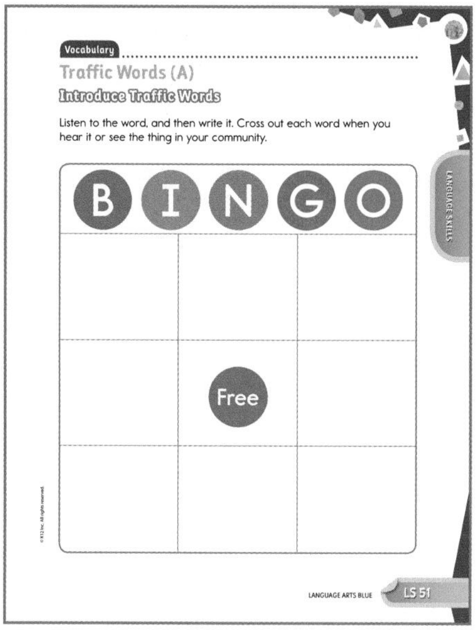

OPTIONAL: Make Your Own Flash Cards

This activity is intended for students who have extra time and would benefit from practicing their vocabulary words with flash cards. Feel free to skip this activity.

Gather five index cards. Have students create flash cards by writing each vocabulary word on the front of an index card and their own definition for each word on the back. Help students with spelling as necessary.

Online 15 minutes

Students will work online **independently** to complete activities on Vocabulary words. Help students locate the online activities, and provide support as needed.

Skills Update

Review Location Words

Students will answer a few questions to refresh their Vocabulary knowledge.

Objectives
- Increase oral vocabulary.
- Increase reading vocabulary.
- Increase concept vocabulary.

Learn

Introduce Traffic Words

Students will be introduced to the traffic words *crosswalk, intersection, signpost, traffic,* and *traffic light.*

Objectives
- Increase oral vocabulary.
- Increase reading vocabulary.
- Increase concept vocabulary.

Signs in My Neighborhood and Traffic Words (A)

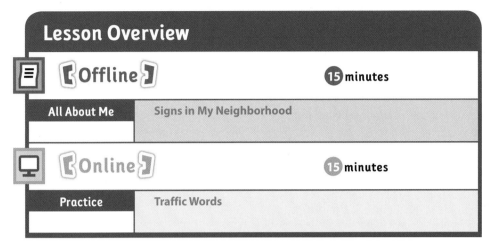

Lesson Overview

Offline	15 minutes
All About Me	Signs in My Neighborhood
Online	**15 minutes**
Practice	Traffic Words

Materials

Supplied

- *K^{12} All About Me*, p. 30

Also Needed

- crayons

Offline 15 minutes

Work **together** with students to complete an offline All About Me activity.

All About Me

Signs in My Neighborhood

Students will begin page 30 in *K^{12} All About Me*; they will complete this page over two lessons.

1. Have students think of and describe common signs they see around their neighborhood. Encourage students to think of indoor signs (enter, exit, caution) and outdoor signs (walk, stop, yield), and then discuss with students the purpose of the signs.
2. Have students write a list of all the signs you discussed. Help with the writing and spelling as necessary.
3. Review with students the list of signs they've written. Have them point to each word and read it aloud.
4. Place the list inside *K^{12} All About Me*, as it will be needed to complete the page.

Objectives

- Describe familiar and common objects and events.
- Reread own writing.

Online 15 minutes

Students will work online **independently** to complete activities on Vocabulary words. Help students locate the online activities, and provide support as needed.

Practice

Traffic Words

Students will practice the traffic words *crosswalk, intersection, signpost, traffic,* and *traffic light.*

Objectives

- Increase oral vocabulary.
- Increase reading vocabulary.
- Increase concept vocabulary.

Offline Alternative

No computer access? At any time, you can print a list of the unit Vocabulary words and their definitions from the online lesson. Use this list to review the words with students offline. In addition, if students made their own flash cards, these can be used for offline review.

"Peter, Peter, Pumpkin Eater" and Traffic Words

Lesson Overview

Offline	15 minutes
Poetry	"Peter, Peter, Pumpkin Eater"
Online	**15 minutes**
Practice	Traffic Words

Materials

Supplied
- *The Rooster Crows*
- *K¹² Language Arts Activity Book*, p. LS 52

Also Needed
- crayons

Advance Preparation

Before reading today's poem, you will need to find the poem in the book *The Rooster Crows*. If your book has page numbers, turn to page 24. Otherwise, you will need to use a pencil to number the pages in the book. Mark the title page as page 1.

Offline 15 minutes

Work **together** with students to complete an offline Poetry activity.

Poetry

"Peter, Peter, Pumpkin Eater"
It's time to read the nursery rhyme "Peter, Peter, Pumpkin Eater" from *The Rooster Crows.*

1. Remind students that nursery rhymes are poems that almost everyone hears when they are very young. Tell them that nursery rhymes do not always make sense. They can be silly or funny. Strange or amazing things can happen in nursery rhymes.
2. Have students recite a nursery rhyme they know. Answers to questions may vary.
   - What is silly or funny about that nursery rhyme?
   - Does anything strange or amazing happen? If so, what?

Objectives
- Listen to and discuss poetry.
- Respond to text through art, writing, and/or drama.
- Identify rhyme and rhythm in poetry.
- Describe character(s).

3. Have students sit next to you so they can see the picture and words while you **read aloud the entire poem**, and then ask:
   - What word rhymes with *Peter* in the poem—*pumpkin, eater,* or *wife*? *eater*
   - Who are the two characters in this poem? Peter and his wife
   - Where does Peter put his wife? in a pumpkin shell
4. Reread the poem and encourage students to repeat each line after you.
   - Could what happens in this poem really happen? No Why not? Answers will vary, but students should understand that no one is small enough to fit in a pumpkin shell.
5. Discuss with students why poems that are full of strange or amazing things are fun to read. Guide them to talk about the fun that comes from imagining silly or funny people and situations.
6. Gather crayons and turn to page LS 52 in *K[12] Language Arts Activity Book*. Have students illustrate the poem. Be sure students include Peter, his wife, and a pumpkin.
7. If time permits, have students share and explain their illustration.

Poetry
"Peter, Peter, Pumpkin Eater" and Traffic Words
"Peter, Peter, Pumpkin Eater"
Draw a picture of Peter, his wife, and the pumpkin.
LS 52 LANGUAGE ARTS BLUE

Online 15 minutes

Students will work online **independently** to complete activities on Vocabulary words. Help students locate the online activities, and provide support as needed.

Practice

Traffic Words

Students will practice the traffic words *crosswalk, intersection, signpost, traffic,* and *traffic light.*

Offline Alternative

No computer access? At any time, you can print a list of the unit Vocabulary words and their definitions from the online lesson. Use this list to review the words with students offline. In addition, if students made their own flash cards, these can be used for offline review.

Objectives
- Increase oral vocabulary.
- Increase reading vocabulary.
- Increase concept vocabulary.

Traffic Words (B)

Lesson Overview

Offline	15 minutes
Vocabulary	Introduce Traffic Words OPTIONAL: Make Your Own Flash Cards
Online	**15 minutes**
Skills Update	Review Comparison Words
Learn	Introduce Traffic Words

Materials

Supplied

- *K[12] Language Arts Activity Book*, p. LS 53

Also Needed

- index cards (6) (optional)

Offline 15 minutes

Work **together** with students to complete an offline Vocabulary activity.

Vocabulary

Introduce Traffic Words

Introduce students to the following traffic words:

arrow	**don't walk**	**stop**
caution	**school zone**	**walk**

1. Tell students that they are going to learn some words related to traffic signs.
2. Turn to page LS 53 in *K[12] Language Arts Activity Book*. Read the name of one of the signs. Then have students point to the correct sign. Continue until all signs have been discussed.
3. Ask students to explain why it is important to know what each sign means. If students don't know an answer, discuss it with them.
   - Why is it important for drivers to slow down in a school zone? because there are children in the area
   - Why is it important for people to follow the don't walk sign? because cars may be nearby and it is not safe to cross the street yet
   - Why is it important for drivers to follow the arrow sign? because it tells them which way the road turns

Objectives

- Increase oral vocabulary.
- Increase reading vocabulary.
- Increase concept vocabulary.

- Why is it important for drivers to slow down when they see a caution sign? because it tells them that they need to look around carefully
- Why is it important for drivers to understand what a stop sign means? because they need to come to a complete stop before continuing
- Why is it important for people to follow the walk sign? because it tells people when it is safe to cross the street

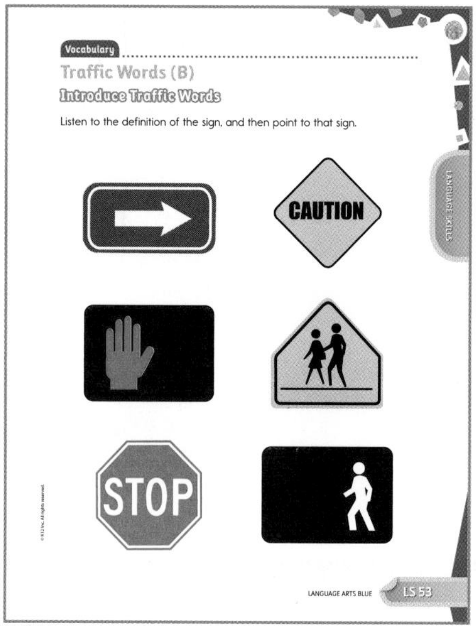

OPTIONAL: Make Your Own Flash Cards

This activity is intended for students who have extra time and would benefit from practicing their vocabulary words with flash cards. Feel free to skip this activity.

Gather six index cards. Have students create flash cards by writing each vocabulary word on the front of an index card and their own definition for each word on the back. Help students with spelling as necessary.

Online 15 minutes

Students will work online **independently** to complete activities on Vocabulary words. Help students locate the online activities, and provide support as needed.

Skills Update

Review Comparison Words

Students will answer a few questions to refresh their Vocabulary knowledge.

Objectives

- Increase oral vocabulary.
- Increase reading vocabulary.
- Increase concept vocabulary.

Learn

Introduce Traffic Words

Students will be introduced to the traffic words *stop, walk, don't walk, arrow, school zone,* and *caution.*

Objectives

- Increase oral vocabulary.
- Increase reading vocabulary.
- Increase concept vocabulary.

Signs in My Neighborhood and Traffic Words (B)

Lesson Overview

Offline	15 minutes
All About Me	Signs in My Neighborhood
Online	**15 minutes**
Practice	Traffic Words

Materials

Supplied
- *K*[12] *All About Me*, p. 30

Also Needed
- crayons

Offline 15 minutes

Work **together** with students to complete an offline All About Me activity.

All About Me

Signs in My Neighborhood
Students will complete page 30 in *K*[12] *All About Me.*

1. Review with students the list of signs. Have them point to each word, read it aloud, and describe the sign's purpose.
2. Have students select their five favorite signs from their brainstorming list. Tell them that they will use their best handwriting to complete page 30 in *K*[12] *All About Me.*
3. For each word, students should neatly write the word, and then draw the sign in the space provided.
4. When they have finished, ask students to point to each word and read it aloud.

Objectives
- Reread own writing.
- Share finished written and drawn works.

Online 15 minutes

Students will work online **independently** to complete activities on Vocabulary words. Help students locate the online activities and provide support as needed.

Practice

Traffic Words

Students will practice the traffic words *stop, walk, don't walk, arrow, school zone,* and *caution.*

Offline Alternative

No computer access? At any time, you can print a list of the unit Vocabulary words and their definitions from the online lesson. Use this list to review the words with students offline. In addition, if students made their own flash cards, these can be used for offline review.

Objectives

- Increase oral vocabulary.
- Increase concept vocabulary.
- Identify and use picture clues to define words.
- Identify purpose of environmental print.
- Identify and comprehend environmental print.

"Cat Kisses" and Vocabulary Unit Review

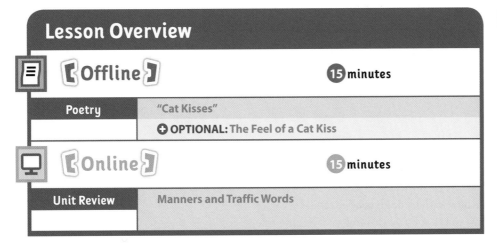

Lesson Overview

Offline	15 minutes
Poetry	"Cat Kisses"
	OPTIONAL: The Feel of a Cat Kiss
Online	**15 minutes**
Unit Review	Manners and Traffic Words

Materials

Supplied
- *Tomie dePaola's Rhyme Time*

Also Needed
- sandpaper (optional)

Advance Preparation

Before reading today's poem, you will need to find the poem in the book *Tomie dePaola's Rhyme Time*. If your book has page numbers, turn to page 15. Otherwise, you will need to use a pencil to number the pages in the book. Mark the title page as page 1.

Offline 15 minutes

Work **together** with students to complete an offline Poetry activity.

Poetry

"Cat Kisses"

It's time to read "Cat Kisses" from *Tomie dePaola's Rhyme Time.*

1. Remind students that some words are meant to capture a certain sound. A word like *boom*, for instance, captures the sound of a loud noise. Tell students that there are many words meant to capture the sounds made by different animals.
2. Have students tell you some of these words. As necessary, remind students of words like *woof*, *quack*, and *whoo*, and which animals make those sounds (a dog, a duck, and an owl).

Objectives
- Listen to and discuss poetry.
- Make connections with text: text-to-text, text-to-self, text-to-world.
- Identify author's use of sensory language.
- Identify rhyme and rhythm in poetry.

3. Have students sit next to you so they can see the picture and words while you **read the poem aloud**, and then ask:
   - Where does the boy in the poem like to be kissed? his cheek or his chin
   - When does everything in this poem happen—morning, afternoon, or evening? morning
   - What is the "alarm clock / that's covered with fur"? a cat
   - Why does the boy call the cat an "alarm clock"? Like an alarm clock, the cat wakes him up.
4. Reread the second stanza of the poem.
   - Which word captures the sound a cat makes? *purr*
5. Have students imitate a cat, making a purring noise.
   - Why are cat kisses called "sandpaper kisses" in the poem? Answers will vary.
     As necessary, explain that cats have rather rough tongues that feel somewhat like sandpaper. Point out that by describing a cat licking the boy's cheek or chin as a "sandpaper" kiss, the poem helps us imagine what the kiss *feels* like.

OPTIONAL: The Feel of a Cat Kiss

This activity is optional. It is intended for students who have extra time and would benefit from some hands-on exposure to what the poem describes.

Have students touch sandpaper and describe its texture. Discuss why cats may have rough tongues, and whether or not students would like a cat to be their alarm clock.

Online 15 minutes

Students will work online **independently** to complete an activity on Vocabulary words. Help students locate the online activity, and provide support as needed.

Unit Review

Manners and Traffic Words

In this activity, students will review all words from the unit to prepare for the Unit Checkpoint.

Objectives
- Increase oral vocabulary.
- Increase reading vocabulary.
- Increase concept vocabulary.

Offline Alternative

No computer access? At any time, you can print a list of the unit Vocabulary words and their definitions from the online lesson. Use this list to review the words with students offline. In addition, if students made their own flash cards, these can be used for offline review.

Unit Checkpoint

Lesson Overview

Online	30 minutes
Unit Checkpoint	Manners and Traffic Words

Materials

There are no materials to gather for this lesson.

Online 30 minutes

Students will work online to complete the Unit Checkpoint. Help students locate the Unit Checkpoint, and provide support as needed.

Unit Checkpoint

Manners and Traffic Words

Explain that students are going to show what they have learned about vocabulary words for manners and traffic.

Objectives

- Increase oral vocabulary.
- Increase reading vocabulary.
- Increase concept vocabulary.
- Identify and use picture clues to define words.
- Identify purpose of environmental print.
- Identify and comprehend environmental print.

Ordinal Words (A)

Unit Overview

In this unit, students will

- Learn vocabulary words for ordinals and sequences
- Complete the *All About Me* pages *A Race with My Friends* and *My Mornings*
- Explore the poems "Hickory, Dickory, Dock," "from Teddy Bear," and "Patty-Cake, Patty-Cake"

Materials

Supplied

- There are no supplied materials to gather for this lesson.

Also Needed

- household objects – any small or medium objects of the same type (5)
- index cards (6)
- tape, masking
- index cards (6) (optional)

Lesson Overview

Offline	15 minutes
Vocabulary	Introduce Ordinal Words OPTIONAL: Make Your Own Flash Cards
Online	15 minutes
Skills Update	Review Opposite Words
Learn	Introduce Ordinal Words

Advance Preparation

Gather five household objects of the same type, such as stuffed animals, toy cars, cups, or pencils.

Offline 15 minutes

Work **together** with students to complete an offline Vocabulary activity.

Vocabulary

Introduce Ordinal Words

Introduce students to the following ordinal words:

first	**third**	**fifth**
second	**fourth**	**last**

1. Gather the household objects.
2. Point out the ordinal vocabulary words to students.
3. Have students line up the items.
4. Ask students:
   - Which item is first?
   - Which item is second?
   - Which item is third?
   - Which item is fourth?
   - Which item is fifth?
   - Which item is last?
5. Help students use index cards to make labels for the items, using the ordinal words. Attach the labels to the objects with masking tape. Point out that the word "last" can be used in place of any number, as long as it's the one that comes at the very end and has nothing after it.
6. Ask students to close their eyes, and then mix up the items.
7. Ask students to reorder the items by their labels ("first," "second," "third," and so on).
8. If time permits, repeat Steps 6 and 7.

Objectives

- Increase oral vocabulary.
- Increase reading vocabulary.
- Increase concept vocabulary.

OPTIONAL: Make Your Own Flash Cards

This activity is intended for students who have extra time and would benefit from practicing their vocabulary words with flash cards. Feel free to skip this activity.

Gather six index cards, or use the index cards created in the previous activity. Have students create flash cards by writing each vocabulary word on the front of an index card and their own definition for each word on the back. Help students with spelling as necessary.

TIP If students are not ready to read and write on their own, skip this optional activity.

Online 15 minutes

Students will work online **independently** to complete activities on Vocabulary words. Help students locate the online activities, and provide support as needed.

Skills Update

Review Opposite Words

Students will answer a few questions to refresh their Vocabulary knowledge.

Objectives

- Increase oral vocabulary.
- Increase reading vocabulary.
- Increase concept vocabulary.

Learn

Introduce Ordinal Words

Students will be introduced to the ordinal words *first, second, third, fourth, fifth,* and *last.*

Objectives

- Increase oral vocabulary.
- Increase reading vocabulary.
- Increase concept vocabulary.

A Race with My Friends and Ordinal Words (A)

Lesson Overview

Offline	15 minutes
All About Me	A Race with My Friends
Online	**15 minutes**
Practice	Ordinal Words

Materials

Supplied
- *K*[12] *All About Me*, p. 31

Also Needed
- crayons

Offline 15 minutes

Work **together** with students to complete an offline All About Me activity.

All About Me

A Race with My Friends

Students will begin page 31 in *K*[12] *All About Me*; they will complete this page over two lessons.

1. Have students imagine running a race with two of their friends. Ask them to think about and discuss the order in which the runners would finish. Encourage students to use the terms *first*, *second*, and *third* in their description.
2. When discussing the race results, explain to students that since there are only three runners, third place would also be considered last place.
3. If time permits, have students begin to draw a picture of the race results.

Objectives
- Generate ideas for writing and drawing through discussion.
- Draw a picture or write about an idea generated through discussion.

Online 15 minutes

Students will work online **independently** to complete activities on Vocabulary words. Help students locate the online activities, and provide support as needed.

Practice

Ordinal Words

Students will practice the ordinal words *first, second, third, fourth, fifth,* and *last.*

Offline Alternative

No computer access? At any time, you can print a list of the unit Vocabulary words and their definitions from the online lesson. Use this list to review the words with students offline. In addition, if students made their own flash cards, these can be used for offline review.

Objectives

- Increase oral vocabulary.
- Increase reading vocabulary.
- Increase concept vocabulary.

"Hickory, Dickory, Dock" and Ordinal Words

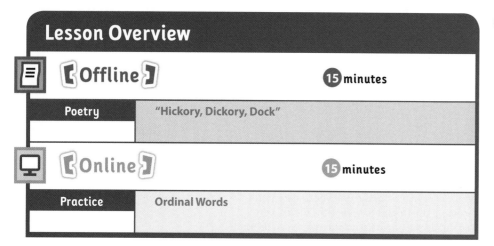

Lesson Overview

Offline		15 minutes
Poetry	"Hickory, Dickory, Dock"	
Online		15 minutes
Practice	Ordinal Words	

Materials

Supplied
- *K[12] Read Aloud Treasury*, p. 133
- *K[12] Language Arts Activity Book*, p. LS 55

Also Needed
- crayons

Offline 15 minutes

Work **together** with students to complete an offline Poetry activity.

Poetry

"Hickory, Dickory, Dock"

It's time to read "Hickory, Dickory, Dock" from *K[12] Read Aloud Treasury.*

Objectives
- Listen to and discuss poetry.
- Respond to text through art, writing, and/or drama.
- Identify rhyme and rhythm in poetry.
- Identify repetitive text.

1. Remind students that nursery rhymes, which are poems that almost everyone hears when they are very young, can be funny or silly. They do not have to make sense.
   - Have you ever seen a grandfather clock? If so, what does it look like? Answers will vary.
2. If students have not seen a grandfather clock, explain to them that it is a type of clock, often made of wood, which is quite tall and narrow.
   - What are some sounds that clocks make? Answers will vary.

   As necessary, tells students that clocks not only make a "tick-tock" sound, but also may sound a gong or chime at certain times.
3. Have students sit next to you so they can see the picture and words while you **read aloud the entire poem**, and then ask:
   - Which word from the poem rhymes with *clock*—*hickory, dickory,* or *dock*? *dock*
   - What time is it when the mouse runs down the clock? one o'clock
   - What words are repeated in this poem? *Hickory, dickory, dock*

4. Have students imagine that they are the mouse in the poem. Answers to questions will vary.
   - Why do you think the mouse runs up the clock?
   - Why do you think the mouse runs down the clock?
5. Turn to page LS 55 in *K¹² Language Arts Activity Book*. Help students read the time on each grandfather clock. Have students color the clock that shows the time in the poem—one o'clock. Help them recite the poem as they color the clock.

Poetry
"Hickory, Dickory, Dock" and Ordinal Words
"Hickory, Dickory, Dock"
Color that clock that shows one o'clock.
LANGUAGE ARTS BLUE LS 55

Online 15 minutes

Students will work online **independently** to complete activities on Vocabulary words. Help students locate the online activities, and provide support as needed.

Practice

Ordinal Words

Students will practice the ordinal words *first, second, third, fourth, fifth,* and *last.*

Offline Alternative

No computer access? At any time, you can print a list of the unit Vocabulary words and their definitions from the online lesson. Use this list to review the words with students offline. In addition, if students made their own flash cards, these can be used for offline review.

Objectives

- Increase oral vocabulary.
- Increase reading vocabulary.
- Increase concept vocabulary.

Ordinal Words (B)

Lesson Overview

Offline	15 minutes
Vocabulary	Introduce Ordinal Words
	OPTIONAL: Make Your Own Flash Cards
Online	**15 minutes**
Skills Update	Review Feeling Words
Learn	Introduce Ordinal Words

Materials

Supplied
- *K*[12] *Language Arts Activity Book*, p. LS 56

Also Needed
- household objects – buttons or other small, round objects (5)
- index cards (5) (optional)

Offline 15 minutes

Work **together** with students to complete an offline Vocabulary activity.

Vocabulary

Introduce Ordinal Words

Help students learn the following ordinal words:

tenth	**thirtieth**	**hundredth**
twentieth	**fortieth**	

1. Say each word to the students.
2. Gather five buttons or other small, round objects to use as markers and page LS 56 in *K*[12] *Language Arts Activity Book.*
3. Ask students to put a marker on the thirtieth star, and then write the word *thirtieth* above it.
4. Ask students to put a marker on the tenth star, and then write the word *tenth* above it.
5. Ask students to put a marker on the hundredth star, and then write the word *hundredth* above it.

Objectives
- Increase oral vocabulary.
- Increase reading vocabulary.
- Increase concept vocabulary.

6. Ask students to put a marker on the fortieth star, and then write the word *fortieth* above it.
7. Ask students to put a marker on the twentieth star, and then write the word *twentieth* above it.
8. Assist students as needed with spelling and writing the words.

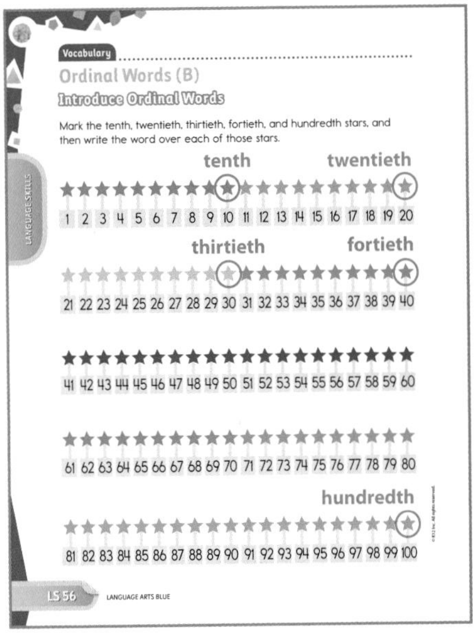
Vocabulary

Ordinal Words (B)

Introduce Ordinal Words

Mark the tenth, twentieth, thirtieth, fortieth, and hundredth stars, and then write the word over each of those stars.

tenth twentieth

1 2 3 4 5 6 7 8 9 10 11 12 13 14 15 16 17 18 19 20

thirtieth fortieth

21 22 23 24 25 26 27 28 29 30 31 32 33 34 35 36 37 38 39 40

41 42 43 44 45 46 47 48 49 50 51 52 53 54 55 56 57 58 59 60

61 62 63 64 65 66 67 68 69 70 71 72 73 74 75 76 77 78 79 80

hundredth

81 82 83 84 85 86 87 88 89 90 91 92 93 94 95 96 97 98 99 100

LS 56 LANGUAGE ARTS BLUE

⊕ OPTIONAL: Make Your Own Flash Cards

This activity is intended for students who have extra time and would benefit from practicing their vocabulary words with flash cards. Feel free to skip this activity.

Gather five index cards. Have students create flash cards by writing each vocabulary word on the front of an index card and their own definition or picture for each word on the back. Help students with spelling as necessary.

Online 15 minutes

Students will work online **independently** to complete activities on Vocabulary words. Help students locate the online activities, and provide support as needed.

Skills Update

Review Feeling Words

Students will answer a few questions to refresh their Vocabulary knowledge.

Objectives
- Increase oral vocabulary.
- Increase reading vocabulary.
- Increase concept vocabulary.

Learn

Introduce Ordinal Words

Students will be introduced to the ordinal words *tenth, twentieth, thirtieth, fortieth,* and *hundredth.*

Objectives
- Increase oral vocabulary.
- Increase reading vocabulary.
- Increase concept vocabulary.
- Use suffixes.

A Race with My Friends and Ordinal Words (B)

Lesson Overview

Offline	15 minutes
All About Me	A Race with My Friends
Online	**15 minutes**
Practice	Ordinal Words

Materials

Supplied
- K^{12} *All About Me*, p. 31

Also Needed
- crayons

Offline 15 minutes

Work **together** with students to complete an offline All About Me activity.

All About Me

A Race with My Friends

Students will complete page 31 in K^{12} *All About Me*.

1. Have students complete their drawing of the results of a race with two of their friends.
2. Have students label each runner *first*, *second*, or *third*. They may also use the label *last* for the third runner. Make sure students use only lowercase letters in their labels. Help students if necessary.
3. Have students explain their drawing, pointing to and reading aloud each label.

Objectives
- Draw a picture or write about an idea generated through discussion.
- Reread own writing.
- Add supporting details to written or drawn work.
- Discuss own drawing.
- Share finished written and drawn works.
- Draw and label pictures.

Online 15 minutes

Students will work online **independently** to complete activities on Vocabulary words. Help students locate the online activities, and provide support as needed.

Practice

Ordinal Words

Students will practice the ordinal words *tenth, twentieth, thirtieth, fortieth,* and *hundredth.*

Offline Alternative

No computer access? At any time, you can print a list of the unit Vocabulary words and their definitions from the online lesson. Use this list to review the words with students offline. In addition, if students made their own flash cards, these can be used for offline review.

Objectives

- Increase oral vocabulary.
- Increase reading vocabulary.
- Increase concept vocabulary.
- Use suffixes.

"from Teddy Bear" and Ordinal Words

Lesson Overview

Offline	15 minutes
Poetry	"from Teddy Bear"
	OPTIONAL: Get Moving!
Online	**15 minutes**
Practice	Ordinal Words

Materials

Supplied
- *Tomie dePaola's Rhyme Time*

Also Needed
- crayons
- paper, drawing

Advance Preparation

Before reading today's poem, you will need to find the poem in *Tomie dePaola's Rhyme Time.* If your book has page numbers, turn to page 4. Otherwise, you will need to use a pencil to number the pages in the book. Mark the title page as page 1.

Offline 15 minutes

Work **together** with students to complete an offline Poetry activity.

Poetry

"from Teddy Bear"

It's time to read "from Teddy Bear" from *Tomie dePaola's Rhyme Time.*

1. Ask students to tell you what they know about exercise. Answers to questions will vary.
   - What is exercise?
   - Do you exercise? If so, what do you do?
   - Why do people exercise?
2. As necessary, tell students that people exercise to stay healthy and to make themselves feel good. Point out that while people and animals can exercise, things that are not alive cannot exercise.

Objectives
- Listen to and discuss poetry.
- Make connections with text: text-to-text, text-to-self, text-to-world.
- Respond to text through art, writing, and/or drama.
- Describe character(s).

3. Have students sit next to you so they can see the picture and words while you **read aloud the entire poem**, and then ask:
   - What two words describe the teddy bear in this poem? *short; fat*
   - What "exercise" does the teddy bear do? He falls off the ottoman.
   - Why can't the teddy bear clamber—or climb—back onto the ottoman after he falls? Answers will vary, but students should understand that the teddy bear is not alive and cannot move on his own.
4. As necessary, tell students that an ottoman is a piece of furniture.
   - Is the teddy bear in this poem truly exercising? No
   - Why is this poem funny or silly? Answers will vary.
   - Do you have a teddy bear? If so, what sorts of things do you like to imagine your teddy bear doing? Answers will vary.
5. Gather crayons and paper. Have students draw a picture of the teddy bear in the poem as you reread the poem.

OPTIONAL: Get Moving!

This activity is intended for students who have extra time and would benefit from getting up and moving around a bit. Feel free to skip this activity.

Have students pretend to be the teddy bear in the poem. As you read, have them act out the descriptions of the teddy bear and what he does.

Online 15 minutes

Students will work online **independently** to complete activities on Vocabulary words. Help students locate the online activities, and provide support as needed.

Practice

Ordinal Words

Students will practice the ordinal words *tenth, twentieth, thirtieth, fortieth,* and *hundredth.*

Objectives

- Increase oral vocabulary.
- Increase reading vocabulary.
- Increase concept vocabulary.
- Use suffixes.

Offline Alternative

No computer access? At any time, you can print a list of the unit Vocabulary words and their definitions from the online lesson. Use this list to review the words with students offline. In addition, if students made their own flash cards, these can be used for offline review.

Sequence Words (A)

Lesson Overview

Offline	15 minutes
Vocabulary	Introduce Sequence Words
	OPTIONAL: Make Your Own Flash Cards
Online	**15 minutes**
Skills Update	Review Community Words
Learn	Introduce Sequence Words

Materials

Supplied

- There are no supplied materials to gather for this lesson.

Also Needed

- crayons
- index cards (4) (optional)

Offline 15 minutes

Work **together** with students to complete an offline Vocabulary activity.

Vocabulary

Introduce Sequence Words

Introduce students to the following sequence words:

after	**next**
before	**then**

1. Tell students that these words keep things in order when you want to tell about those things.
   - Can you think of any groups of things that you might want to keep in order? Possible answers: numbers; alphabet letters; things that someone does
2. Have students write the numbers 1 through 10 on a piece of paper.
   - What number comes *after* 5? 6
   - What number comes *before* 5? 4
   - If you count to 8, what number comes *next*? 9
   - *Then,* what number is next? 10

Objectives

- Increase oral vocabulary.
- Increase concept vocabulary.

3. **Say:** Wake up in the morning. Get out of bed. Get dressed. Go outside.
4. Ask students to repeat these steps, adding sequence words. (If they have trouble remembering the sequence, have them draw pictures of each step in the sequence on a piece of paper.) Possible answer: After I wake up in the morning, I get out of bed. Next, I get dressed, and then I can go outside. Before I can go outside, I have to get dressed.

OPTIONAL: Make Your Own Flash Cards

This activity is intended for students who have extra time and would benefit from practicing their vocabulary words with flash cards. Feel free to skip this activity.

Gather four index cards. Have students create flash cards by writing each vocabulary word on the front of an index card and their own definition for each word on the back. Help students with spelling as necessary.

Online 15 minutes

Students will work online **independently** to complete activities on Vocabulary words. Help students locate the online activities, and provide support as needed.

Skills Update

Review Community Words
Students will answer a few questions to refresh their Vocabulary knowledge.

Objectives
- Increase oral vocabulary.
- Increase concept vocabulary.

Learn

Introduce Sequence Words
Students will be introduced to the sequence words *after, before, next,* and *then.*

Objectives
- Increase oral vocabulary.
- Increase reading vocabulary.
- Increase concept vocabulary.

My Mornings and Sequence Words (A)

Lesson Overview

Offline	15 minutes
All About Me	My Mornings

Online	15 minutes
Practice	Sequence Words

Materials

Supplied

- *K*[12] *All About Me*, pp. 32–33

Also Needed

- crayons

Offline 15 minutes

Work **together** with students to complete an offline All About Me activity.

All About Me

My Mornings

Students will begin pages 32 and 33 in *K*[12] *All About Me*; they will complete these pages over two lessons.

1. Help students point to and read the words *first, next, then,* and *finally.*
2. Ask students to describe four things they do each morning. Encourage them to use the words *first, next, then,* and *finally* in their description.
3. Point to and read aloud the first incomplete sentence to students.
4. Have students repeat the first part of the sentence and tell you an answer to write in the blank space.
5. Read the complete sentence to students, pointing to each word.
6. Have students repeat the complete sentence and point to the word *first* in the sentence.
7. Repeat Steps 3–6 with the remaining sentences, asking students to point to the words *next, then,* and *finally.*

Objectives

- Dictate or write simple sentences describing experiences, stories, people, objects, or events.

Online 15 minutes

Students will work online **independently** to complete activities on Vocabulary words. Help students locate the online activities, and provide support as needed.

Practice

Sequence Words

Students will practice the sequence words *after, before, next,* and *then.*

Offline Alternative

No computer access? At any time, you can print a list of the unit Vocabulary words and their definitions from the online lesson. Use this list to review the words with students offline. In addition, if students made their own flash cards, these can be used for offline review.

Objectives

- Increase oral vocabulary.
- Increase reading vocabulary.
- Increase concept vocabulary.

"Patty-Cake, Patty-Cake" and Vocabulary Unit Review

Lesson Overview

Offline	15 minutes
Poetry	"Patty-Cake, Patty-Cake"
Online	**15 minutes**
Unit Review	Ordinal and Sequence Words

Materials

Supplied

- *The Rooster Crows*

Advance Preparation

Before reading today's poem, you will need to find the poem in *The Rooster Crows.* If your book has page numbers, turn to page 24. Otherwise, you will need to use a pencil to number the pages in the book. Mark the title page as page 1.

Offline 15 minutes

Work **together** with students to complete an offline Poetry activity.

Poetry

"Patty-Cake, Patty-Cake"

It's time to read "Patty-Cake, Patty-Cake" from *The Rooster Crows.*

Objectives

- Listen to and discuss poetry.
- Make connections with text: text-to-text, text-to-self, text-to-world.
- Identify rhyme and rhythm in poetry.

1. Tell students that sometimes when we say poems, we play games with our hands, or we clap or move our bodies.
   - Do you know any poems that have movements that go with them? If so what are they? Answers will vary.

   As necessary, recite "The Itsy Bitsy Spider" or "Where is Thumbkin?" with appropriate hand gestures.
2. Tell students that even if a poem does not have movements that go with it, we can always clap along to the rhythm. As necessary, remind students that **rhythm** is a pattern of beats or sounds in a poem.

3. Have students sit next to you so they can see the picture and words while you **read aloud the entire poem**, and then ask:
   - What does the person in the poem want the baker's man to do? bake him a cake as fast as he can
   - Where does the poem tell the baker's man to put the cake? in the pan
   - Name another word that rhymes with *man*, *can*, and *pan*. Answers will vary.
4. Tell students to clap along with the rhythm of the poem as you read it again. Each clap should be on a syllable shown in bold type:

   Pat**ty-cake, **pat**ty-cake, **Ba**ker's **man
   Bake** me a **cake** as **fast** as you **can
   ***Roll** it up and **roll** it up*
   *And **put** it **in** the **pan**.*
5. Tell students that "Patty-Cake, Patty-Cake" is a poem we can say while playing a game with our hands. Play "patty-cake" with students while reciting the poem and miming the motions for rolling up the cake and putting it in the pan.

Online 15 minutes

Students will work online **independently** to complete an activity on Vocabulary words. Help students locate the online activity, and provide support as needed.

Unit Review

Ordinal and Sequence Words

Students will review all words from the unit to prepare for the Unit Checkpoint.

Objectives
- Increase oral vocabulary.
- Increase reading vocabulary.
- Increase concept vocabulary.

Offline Alternative

No computer access? At any time, you can print a list of the unit Vocabulary words and their definitions from the online lesson. Use this list to review the words with students offline. In addition, if students made their own flash cards, these can be used for offline review.

Unit Checkpoint

Lesson Overview

Online	30 minutes
Unit Checkpoint	Ordinal and Sequence Words

Materials

There are no materials to gather for this lesson.

Online 30 minutes

Students will work online to complete the Unit Checkpoint. Help students locate the Unit Checkpoint, and provide support as needed.

Unit Checkpoint

Ordinal and Sequence Words

Explain that students are going to show what they have learned about ordinal and sequence vocabulary words.

Objectives

- Increase oral vocabulary.
- Increase reading vocabulary.
- Increase concept vocabulary.

Sequence Words (B)

Unit Overview

In this unit, students will

- Learn vocabulary words for sequences of events
- Complete the *All About Me* pages *My Mornings* and *When I Grow Up*
- Explore the poems "The Land of Counterpane," "Johnny on the Woodpile," and "Finger Games"

Materials

Supplied

- There are no supplied materials to gather for this lesson.

Also Needed

- index cards (5) (optional)

Lesson Overview

Offline	15 minutes
Vocabulary	Introduce Sequence Words
	OPTIONAL: Make Your Own Flash Cards
Online	15 minutes
Skills Update	Review Position Words
Learn	Introduce Sequence Words

Offline 15 minutes

Work **together** with students to complete an offline Vocabulary activity.

Vocabulary

Introduce Sequence Words

Introduce students to the following words about sequences:

during	**once**
finally	**soon**
following	

1. Explain to students that **sequence** is the order in which things happen. This lesson's words help identify when in a sequence things happen.
2. Read aloud the following example of a story that uses the sequence vocabulary words, emphasizing the vocabulary words.
   - *Once* I wanted to make cookies.
   - I mixed the batter and put the cookies in the oven.

Objectives

- Increase oral vocabulary.
- Increase reading vocabulary.
- Increase concept vocabulary.

- *Soon* a wonderful smell filled the kitchen.
- *During* the time the cookies were in the oven, I got hungrier and hungrier.
- *Finally* the cookies were ready. I ate the whole batch!
- *Following* my gobbling of the cookies, I got a stomach ache.

3. Ask students to make up a story using the sequence words. If they have trouble thinking of a topic for the story, ask them to use the story of their life, or of a typical day.

OPTIONAL: Make Your Own Flash Cards

This activity is intended for students who have extra time and would benefit from practicing their vocabulary words with flash cards. Feel free to skip this activity.

Gather five index cards. Have students create flash cards by writing each vocabulary word on the front of an index card and their own definition for each word on the back. Help students with spelling as necessary.

TIP If students are not ready to read and write on their own, skip this optional activity.

Online 15 minutes

Students will work online **independently** to complete activities on Vocabulary words. Help students locate the online activities, and provide support as needed.

Skills Update

Review Position Words

Students will answer a few questions to refresh their Vocabulary knowledge.

Objectives
- Increase oral vocabulary.
- Increase reading vocabulary.
- Increase concept vocabulary.

Learn

Introduce Sequence Words

Students will be introduced to the sequence words *once, soon, during, following,* and *finally*.

Objectives
- Increase oral vocabulary.
- Increase reading vocabulary.
- Increase concept vocabulary.

My Mornings and Sequence Words (B)

Lesson Overview

Offline	15 minutes
All About Me	My Mornings

Online	15 minutes
Practice	Sequence Words

Materials

Supplied
- *K¹² All About Me*, pp. 32–33

Also Needed
- crayons

Offline 15 minutes

Work **together** with students to complete an offline All About Me activity.

All About Me

My Mornings

Students will complete pages 32 and 33 in *K[12] All About Me*.

1. Discuss with students what a typical morning is like for them. As necessary, prompt students with questions such as the following:
   - What's the first thing you do in the morning when you get up?
   - What happens next?
   - Then what do you do?
2. Help students point to and read the words *first*, *next*, *then*, and *finally*.
3. Referring back to your discussion about a typical morning, help students complete the sentences about their morning.
4. Have students illustrate their sentences in the spaces provided.

Objectives
- Sequence pictures of events in proper order.
- Write and/or draw narrative text.
- Discuss own drawing.
- Share finished written and drawn works.
- Draw and label pictures.

Online 15 minutes

Students will work online **independently** to complete activities on Vocabulary words. Help students locate the online activities, and provide support as needed.

Practice

Sequence Words

Students will practice the sequence words *once, soon, during, following,* and *finally*.

Offline Alternative

No computer access? At any time, you can print a list of the unit Vocabulary words and their definitions from the online lesson. Use this list to review the words with students offline. In addition, if students made their own flash cards, these can be used for offline review.

Objectives

- Increase oral vocabulary.
- Increase reading vocabulary.
- Increase concept vocabulary.

"The Land of Counterpane" and Sequence Words

Lesson Overview

Offline	15 minutes
Poetry	"The Land of Counterpane"
Online	**15 minutes**
Practice	Sequence Words

Materials

Supplied

- *Tomie dePaola's Rhyme Time*
- *K[12] Language Arts Activity Book*, p. LS 57

Also Needed

- crayons

Advance Preparation

Before reading today's poem, you will need to find the poem in *Tomie dePaola's Rhyme Time*. If your book has page numbers, turn to page 29. Otherwise, you will need to use a pencil to number the pages in the book. Mark the title page as page 1.

Offline 15 minutes

Work **together** with students to complete an offline Poetry activity.

Poetry

Objectives

- Listen to and discuss poetry.
- Make predictions based on title, illustrations, and/or context clues.
- Make connections with text: text-to-text, text-to-self, text-to-world.
- Respond to text through art, writing, and/or drama.

"The Land of Counterpane"

It's time to read "The Land of Counterpane" from *Tomie dePaola's Rhyme Time*.

1. Tell students that a *counterpane* is a bedspread, and then state the title of the poem.
   - What do you think this poem will be about? Answers will vary.

   Remind students that a **stanza** is a group of lines in a poem.
2. Have students sit next to you so they can see the picture and words while you **read aloud the entire poem**, and then ask:
   - Where does this poem take place? in a bed
   - Are the ships, trees, and houses in the third stanza real or are they toys? They are toys.
   - Why does the person in the poem call himself a "giant"? He is much bigger than his toys.

3. Have students recall the prediction they made before hearing the poem. Answers to questions will vary.
   - Did you guess what this poem would be about?
   - Did what the poem described sound like fun to you? Why or why not?
4. Have students think about what they like to do when they are sick. Answers to questions will vary.
   - Do you ever play make-believe with your toys when you are sick?
   - If so, what do you pretend? If not, what would you pretend if you did play make-believe?
5. Turn to page LS 57 in *K*[12] *Language Arts Activity Book*. As students color the picture, reread the poem and discuss with them how they would play with each toy in the picture.

Online 15 minutes

Students will work online **independently** to complete activities on Vocabulary words. Help students locate the online activities, and provide support as needed.

Practice

Sequence Words

Students will practice the sequence words *once, soon, during, following,* and *finally*.

Objectives
- Increase oral vocabulary.
- Increase reading vocabulary.
- Increase concept vocabulary.

Offline Alternative

No computer access? At any time, you can print a list of the unit Vocabulary words and their definitions from the online lesson. Use this list to review the words with students offline. In addition, if students made their own flash cards, these can be used for offline review.

Growing Words (A)

Lesson Overview

Offline		15 minutes
Vocabulary	Introduce Growing Words	
	OPTIONAL: Make Your Own Flash Cards	
Online		15 minutes
Skills Update	Review Color Words	
Learn	Introduce Growing Words	

Materials

Supplied

- *K*[12] *Language Arts Activity Book*, p. LS 59

Also Needed

- index cards (6) (optional)
- scissors, round-end safety

Offline 15 minutes

Work **together** with students to complete an offline Vocabulary activity.

Vocabulary

Introduce Growing Words

Help students learn the following growing words:

adult	**fruit**
baby	**plant**
child	**seed**

1. Have students cut out the cards on page LS 59 in *K*[12] *Language Arts Activity Book*.
2. Read aloud each card.
   - What do the words *baby, child,* and *adult* have in common? They are all words for people.
   - What is the difference between the words? The baby is beginning to grow, the child is growing, and the adult is grown.
   - What do the words *seed, plant,* and *fruit* have in common? They are all words for plants.
   - What is the difference between the words? The seed is beginning to grow, the plant is growing, and the fruit is grown.

Objectives

- Increase oral vocabulary.
- Increase reading vocabulary.
- Increase concept vocabulary.
- Classify and sort common words into categories.

3. Shuffle the cards. Ask students to put them in two piles—those that show a person and those that show a plant. Have students arrange the cards in each pile from beginning to growing to grown.

OPTIONAL: Make Your Own Flash Cards

This activity is intended for students who have extra time and would benefit from practicing their vocabulary words with flash cards. Feel free to skip this activity.

Gather six index cards. Have students create flash cards by writing each vocabulary word on the front of an index card and their own definition for each word on the back. Help students with spelling as necessary.

Online 15 minutes

Students will work online **independently** to complete activities on Vocabulary words. Help students locate the online activities, and provide support as needed.

Skills Update

Review Color Words

Students will answer a few questions to refresh their Vocabulary knowledge.

Objectives

- Increase oral vocabulary.
- Increase concept vocabulary.

Learn

Introduce Growing Words

Students will be introduced to the growing words *baby, adult, child, seed, plant,* and *fruit.*

Objectives

- Increase oral vocabulary.
- Increase reading vocabulary.
- Increase concept vocabulary.
- Classify and sort common words into categories.

When I Grow Up and Growing Words (A)

Lesson Overview

Offline		15 minutes
All About Me	When I Grow Up	
Online		15 minutes
Practice	Growing Words	

Materials

Supplied
- *K[12] All About Me*, pp. 34–35

Also Needed
- crayons

Offline 15 minutes

Work **together** with students to complete an offline All About Me activity.

All About Me

When I Grow Up

Students will begin pages 34 and 35 in *K[12] All About Me*; they will complete these pages over two lessons.

1. Discuss with students what they would like to do when they grow up. Have them explain why they chose that particular career. Answers will vary.
   - What do you think you will do each day at work?
   - Do you know anyone who has that job?
   - Is this the same career you chose at the beginning of the year? Why or why not?
2. Read aloud the incomplete sentence on page 34. Have students repeat the first part of the sentence and tell you a word to write in the blank space.
3. Read the complete sentence to students, pointing to each word.
4. Repeat Steps 2 and 3 to complete page 35.
5. If time permits, have students begin illustrating their sentences.

Objectives
- Dictate or write simple sentences describing experiences, stories, people, objects, or events.
- Write and/or draw narrative text.

Online 15 minutes

Students will work online **independently** to complete activities on Vocabulary words. Help students locate the online activities, and provide support as needed.

Practice

Growing Words

Students will practice the growing words *baby, adult, child, seed, plant,* and *fruit.*

Offline Alternative

No computer access? At any time, you can print a list of the unit Vocabulary words and their definitions from the online lesson. Use this list to review the words with students offline. In addition, if students made their own flash cards, these can be used for offline review.

Objectives

- Increase oral vocabulary.
- Increase reading vocabulary.
- Increase concept vocabulary.
- Classify and sort common words into categories.

"Johnny on the Woodpile" and Growing Words

Lesson Overview

Offline	15 minutes
Poetry	"Johnny on the Woodpile"
Online	**15 minutes**
Practice	Growing Words

Materials

Supplied

- *The Rooster Crows*

Advance Preparation

Before reading today's poem, you will need to find the poem in *The Rooster Crows.* If your book has page numbers, turn to page 11. Otherwise, you will need to use a pencil to number the pages in the book. Mark the title page as page 1.

Offline 15 minutes

Work **together** with students to complete an offline Poetry activity.

Poetry

"Johnny on the Woodpile"

It's time to read "Johnny on the Woodpile" from *The Rooster Crows.*

1. Tell students that there is an old saying that a picture is worth a thousand words.
   - What do you think that saying means? Answers will vary.
2. As necessary, explain to students that the saying means that a picture can show us a lot. Tell them that when a poem has a picture with it, the picture can often help us understand the poem better.
3. **Note: For this lesson, do not have students sit next to you while you read the poem. You will show them the picture later in the lesson.**

Objectives

- Listen to and discuss poetry.
- Use visual text features to aid understanding of text.
- Identify rhyme and rhythm in poetry.
- Describe character(s).

4. **Read aloud the entire poem**, and then ask:
   - Which two things does the poem say Johnny is on? the woodpile; the fence
   - What word in this poem rhymes with *fence*? *cents*
   - How much does Johnny's haircut cost? 15 cents
5. Show students the picture above the poem in *The Rooster Crows.*
   - Which person is Johnny? the boy getting his hair cut
   - How do you know? Answers will vary.
6. Have students describe how Johnny looks.
   - Does Johnny seem happy to be getting a haircut? No
   - How do you know? Answers will vary.
7. Discuss with students whether or not the picture was "worth a thousand words." Guide them to talk about things they learned from the picture that they would not have learned from just hearing the poem read. As necessary, point out details like the following:
   - Where Johnny is getting his hair cut
   - What is on Johnny's head
   - Who is cutting Johnny's hair

Online 15 minutes

Students will work online **independently** to complete an activity on Vocabulary words. Help students locate the online activity, and provide support as needed.

Practice

Growing Words

Students will practice the growing words *baby, adult, child, seed, plant,* and *fruit.*

Offline Alternative

No computer access? At any time, you can print a list of the unit Vocabulary words and their definitions from the online lesson. Use this list to review the words with students offline. In addition, if students made their own flash cards, these can be used for offline review.

Objectives

- Increase oral vocabulary.
- Increase reading vocabulary.
- Increase concept vocabulary.
- Classify and sort common words into categories.

Growing Words (B)

Lesson Overview

Offline	15 minutes
Vocabulary	Introduce Growing Words OPTIONAL: Make Your Own Flash Cards
Online	**15 minutes**
Skills Update	Review Manners Words
Learn	Introduce Growing Words

Materials

Supplied

- *K[12] Language Arts Activity Book*, p. LS 61

Also Needed

- index cards (6) (optional)
- scissors, round-end safety

Offline 15 minutes

Work **together** with students to complete an offline Vocabulary activity.

Vocabulary

Introduce Growing Words

Introduce the following growing words:

bud	**garden**	**seedling**
flower	**grain**	**vegetable**

1. Have students cut out the cards on page LS 61 in *K[12] Language Arts Activity Book.*

Objectives

- Increase oral vocabulary.
- Increase reading vocabulary.
- Increase concept vocabulary.
- Classify and sort common words into categories.

2. Read each card to students. Ask them to pick the cards with words relating to
   - Food
   - Flowers
   - Plants

⊕ OPTIONAL: Make Your Own Flash Cards

This activity is intended for students who have extra time and would benefit from practicing their vocabulary words with flash cards. Feel free to skip this activity.

Gather six index cards. Have students create flash cards by writing each vocabulary word on the front of an index card and their own definition for each word on the back. Help students with spelling as necessary.

Online 15 minutes

Students will work online **independently** to complete activities on Vocabulary words. Help students locate the online activities, and provide support as needed.

Skills Update

Review Manners Words

Students will answer a few questions to refresh their Vocabulary knowledge.

Objectives
- Increase oral vocabulary.
- Increase reading vocabulary.
- Increase concept vocabulary.

Learn

Introduce Growing Words

Students will be introduced to the growing words *bud, flower, garden, grain, seedling,* and *vegetable.*

Objectives
- Increase oral vocabulary.
- Increase reading vocabulary.
- Increase concept vocabulary.
- Classify and sort common words into categories.

When I Grow Up and Growing Words (B)

Lesson Overview

Offline	15 minutes
All About Me	When I Grow Up

Online	15 minutes
Practice	Growing Words

Materials

Supplied

- K^{12} *All About Me*, pp. 34–35

Also Needed

- crayons

Offline 15 minutes

Work **together** with students to complete an offline All About Me activity.

All About Me

Objectives

- Write and/or draw narrative text.
- Add supporting details to written or drawn work.
- Discuss own drawing.
- Share finished written and drawn works.
- Draw and label pictures.

When I Grow Up

Students will complete pages 34 and 35 in K^{12} *All About Me.*

1. Have students finalize their drawing of themselves as adults working in their chosen profession and explain their illustration when they complete it.
2. Have students label their picture. Encourage them to use the sentence you completed if they need help with spelling.
3. Turn to page 6 in K^{12} *All About Me* to find the career choice students made at the beginning of the year.
4. Have students compare their two career choices. Encourage them to discuss similarities and differences in their choices and in their drawings.

Online 15 minutes

Students will work online **independently** to complete activities on Vocabulary words. Help students locate the online activities, and provide support as needed.

Practice

Growing Words

Students will practice the growing words *bud, flower, garden, grain, seedling,* and *vegetable.*

Offline Alternative

No computer access? At any time, you can print a list of the unit Vocabulary words and their definitions from the online lesson. Use this list to review the words with students offline. In addition, if students made their own flash cards, these can be used for offline review.

Objectives

- Increase oral vocabulary.
- Increase reading vocabulary.
- Increase concept vocabulary.
- Classify and sort common words into categories.

"Finger Games" and Vocabulary Unit Review

Lesson Overview

Offline	15 minutes
Poetry	"Finger Games"
	OPTIONAL: Another Finger Game
Online	**15 minutes**
Unit Review	Sequence and Growing Words

Materials

Supplied

- *The Rooster Crows*

Advance Preparation

Before reading today's poem, you will need to find the poem in *The Rooster Crows.* If your book has page numbers, turn to page 46. Otherwise, you will need to use a pencil to number the pages in the book. Mark the title page as page 1.

Offline 15 minutes

Work **together** with students to complete an offline Poetry activity.

Poetry

"Finger Games"

It's time to read some poems about finger games from *The Rooster Crows.*

1. Remind students that some poems are meant to be said while doing movements with our bodies or our hands. Help them to recall how they rolled their arms, for example, while saying "Patty-Cake, Patty-Cake." Tell them that some poems go with games we play with our fingers.

   As an example, sing "Where is Thumbkin?," "The Itsy, Bitsy Spider," or another finger game poem while doing the appropriate hand gestures. Tell students that the poems they will hear today are all meant to be said while doing things with our fingers.

Objectives

- Listen to and discuss poetry.
- Use visual text features to aid understanding of text.
- Respond to text through art, writing, and/or drama.
- Identify rhyme and rhythm in poetry.

2. Have students sit next to you so they can see the pictures and words while you **read aloud all five poems** in the "Finger Games" section, and then ask:
   - What word in "Here Is the Bee-Hive" rhymes with *bee-hive* and *alive*? five
   - Which rabbit in "Five Little Rabbits" says, "I will not run!"? the second one
   - Where are the two blackbirds sitting? on a hill
   - What is the minister doing in "Here Is the Church, Here Is the Steeple"? saying his prayers
3. Have students choose one of the following poems: "Here Is the Bee-hive," "These Are Mother's Knives and Forks," or "Here Is the Church, Here Is the Steeple." Show students the hand-gesture illustrations that go with the poem they chose. Tell students that they are going to learn to play the finger game that goes with this poem.
4. Help students make the appropriate hand gestures as you recite the poem aloud. As they get better at making the hand gestures, encourage them to repeat after you and recite the poem aloud themselves.

OPTIONAL: Another Finger Game

This activity is intended for students who have extra time and would benefit from learning another finger game. Feel free to skip this activity.

Have students choose one of the poems with hand-gesture illustrations that they have not yet learned. Practice the finger game that goes with it while reciting the poem aloud.

Online 15 minutes

Students will work online **independently** to complete an activity on Vocabulary words. Help students locate the online activity, and provide support as needed.

Unit Review

Sequence and Growing Words

Students will review all words from the unit to prepare for the Unit Checkpoint.

Objectives

- Increase oral vocabulary.
- Increase reading vocabulary.
- Increase concept vocabulary.
- Classify and sort common words into categories.

Offline Alternative

No computer access? At any time, you can print a list of the unit Vocabulary words and their definitions from the online lesson. Use this list to review the words with students offline. In addition, if students made their own flash cards, these can be used for offline review.

Unit Checkpoint

Lesson Overview

Online	30 minutes
Unit Checkpoint	Sequence and Growing Words

Materials

There are no materials to gather for this lesson.

Online 30 minutes

Students will work online to complete the Unit Checkpoint. Help students locate the Unit Checkpoint, and provide support as needed.

Unit Checkpoint

Sequence and Growing Words

Explain that students are going to show what they have learned about sequence and growing vocabulary words.

Objectives

- Increase oral vocabulary.
- Increase reading vocabulary.
- Increase concept vocabulary.
- Classify and sort words into common categories.

Adult and Baby Words (A)

Unit Overview

In this unit, students will

- Learn vocabulary words for adult, babies, and homographs.
- Complete the *All About Me* pages *My Hand, My Foot, My Body Language,* and *Things I Can Do.*
- Explore the poems "from The Three Foxes," "from A Good Play," and "Three Little Kittens."

Materials

Supplied

- *K[12] Language Arts Activity Book*, p. LS 63

Also Needed

- scissors, round-end safety
- index cards (8) (optional)

Lesson Overview

Offline	15 minutes
Vocabulary	Introduce Adult and Baby Words
	OPTIONAL: Make Your Own Flash Cards
Online	15 minutes
Skills Update	Review Food Words
Learn	Introduce Adult and Baby Words

Offline 15 minutes

Work **together** with students to complete an offline Vocabulary activity.

Vocabulary

Introduce Adult and Baby Words

Play a memory game to help students learn the following adult and baby words:

cow	**cat**	**dog**	**goose**
calf	**kitten**	**puppy**	**gosling**

1. Help students cut out the cards on page LS 63 in *K[12] Language Arts Activity Book.*
2. Shuffle the cards and place them face down on a flat surface.

Objectives

- Increase oral vocabulary.
- Increase reading vocabulary.
- Increase concept vocabulary.
- Classify and sort common words into categories.

3. Determine who will go first. Have that student select a card by flipping it over and then select another card by flipping it over. If the word and picture match, the student keeps the cards. If the word and picture do not match, the student returns the cards to the face-down position.
4. Continue playing until all of the matches have been found.
5. If time permits, have students play again, but this time have them match the adult animal with the baby animal.

Vocabulary
Adult and Baby Words (A)
Introduce Adult and Baby Words
Cut out each animal and word card.
dog
gosling
calf
kitten
goose
cat
puppy
cow
LANGUAGE SKILLS
LANGUAGE ARTS BLUE
LS 63

⊕ OPTIONAL: Make Your Own Flash Cards

This activity is intended for students who have extra time and would benefit from practicing vocabulary words with flash cards. Feel free to skip this activity.

Gather eight index cards. Have students create flash cards by writing each vocabulary word on the front of an index card and their own definition for each word on the back. Help students with spelling as necessary.

TIP If students are not ready to read and write on their own, skip this optional activity.

Online 15 minutes

Students will work online **independently** to complete activities on Vocabulary words. Help students locate the online activities, and provide support as needed.

Skills Update

Review Food Words

Students will answer a few questions to refresh their Vocabulary knowledge.

Objectives
- Increase oral vocabulary.
- Increase concept vocabulary.

Learn

Introduce Adult and Baby Words

Students will be introduced to the adult and baby words *dog, puppy, cat, kitten, cow, calf, goose,* and *gosling*.

Objectives
- Increase oral vocabulary.
- Increase reading vocabulary.
- Increase concept vocabulary.
- Classify and sort common words into categories.

My Hand & My Foot and Adult & Baby Words

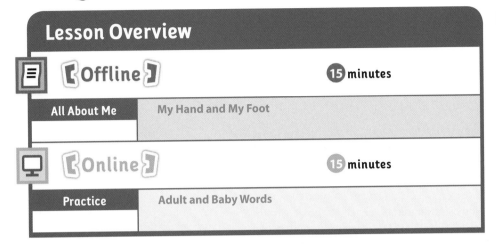

Lesson Overview

Offline	15 minutes
All About Me	My Hand and My Foot
Online	**15 minutes**
Practice	Adult and Baby Words

Materials

Supplied
- K^{12} *All About Me*, pp. 36–37

Also Needed
- crayons

Offline 15 minutes

Work **together** with students to complete an offline All About Me activity.

All About Me

My Hand and My Foot

Students will complete pages 36 and 37 in K^{12} *All About Me*.

1. Have students trace either foot, but make sure the hand they trace is **not** the hand with which they write. (Right-handed students should trace their left hand, and left-handed students should trace their right hand.) If time permits, have students color their tracings.
2. Have students write the labels *hand* and *foot* on the line under the appropriate picture. Make sure they use only lowercase letters.
3. Turn to pages 2 and 3 to find the hand and foot tracings students made at the beginning of the year.
4. Have students compare their tracings. Encourage them to discuss similarities and differences in the sizes of their hand and foot.

Objectives
- Draw and label pictures.
- Discuss own drawing.
- Share finished written and drawn works.

[Online] 15 minutes

Students will work online **independently** to complete activities on Vocabulary words. Help students locate the online activities, and provide support as needed.

Practice

Adult and Baby Words

Students will practice the adult and baby words *dog, puppy, cat, kitten, cow, calf, goose,* and *gosling.*

Offline Alternative

No computer access? At any time, you can print a list of the unit Vocabulary words and their definitions from the online lesson. Use this list to review the words with students offline. In addition, if students made their own flash cards, these can be used for offline review.

Objectives

- Increase oral vocabulary.
- Increase reading vocabulary.
- Increase concept vocabulary.
- Classify and sort common words into categories.

"from The Three Foxes" and Adult & Baby Words

Lesson Overview

Offline	15 minutes
Poetry	"from The Three Foxes"
Online	**15 minutes**
Practice	Adult and Baby Words

Materials

Supplied

- *Tomie dePaola's Rhyme Time*
- *K[12] Language Arts Activity Book*, p. LS 65

Also Needed

- crayons

Advance Preparation

Before reading today's poem, you will need to find the poem in *Tomie dePaola's Rhyme Time*. If your book has page numbers, turn to page 16. Otherwise, you will need to use a pencil to number the pages in the book. Mark the title page as page 1.

Offline 15 minutes

Work **together** with students to complete an offline Poetry activity.

Poetry

"from The Three Foxes"

It's time to read "from The Three Foxes" from *Tomie dePaola's Rhyme Time.*

1. Tell students that some poems use made-up words. Made-up words can make a poem silly or funny. Sometimes, a writer can make us understand what a made-up word means.
   - Do you know any poems that contain made-up words? If so, which ones? Answers will vary.
2. Prompt students to recall other poems or stories they have heard that contain made-up words. For example, many stories by Dr. Seuss contain made-up words. Some poems found in *The Rooster Crows* contain made-up words as well.
3. **Say:** I am going to read a poem. Listen carefully for any made-up words.

Objectives

- Listen to and discuss poetry.
- Identify unknown words in text.
- Respond to text through art, writing, and/or drama.
- Identify rhyme and rhythm in poetry.
- Describe character(s).

4. Have students sit next to you so they can see the picture and words while you **read aloud the entire poem**, and then ask:
   - What two things does the first stanza say the foxes do not wear? stockings and sockses
   - What three words rhyme in the first stanza? *foxes, sockses,* and *boxes*
   - Who do the foxes play "Touch last" with? a family of "mouses"
5. Reread the first stanza. Tell students that the word *sockses* is made up, but we can understand what it means.
   - What are *sockses*? socks
   - Why do you think the poet made up this word? Answers will vary.
6. As necessary, guide students to understand that the word is fun and it rhymes with two other words in this stanza.
   - What words in the second stanza are made up? *trousies* and *mouses*
   - What do these words mean? *trousers* and *mice*
7. Turn to page LS 65 in *K*[12] *Language Arts Activity Book*. Have students draw the place where the poem says the three foxes live. As necessary, guide them to draw three little houses in a forest. Reread the second stanza of the poem if students need help remembering what to draw.

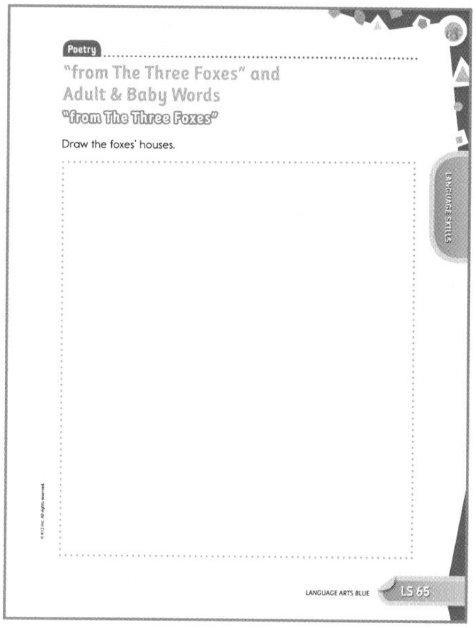
Poetry
"from The Three Foxes" and Adult & Baby Words
"from The Three Foxes"
Draw the foxes' houses.
LANGUAGE SKILLS
LANGUAGE ARTS BLUE LS 65

Online 15 minutes

Students will work online **independently** to complete activities on Vocabulary words. Help students locate the online activities, and provide support as needed.

Practice

Adult and Baby Words

Students will practice the adult and baby words *dog, puppy, cat, kitten, cow, calf, goose,* and *gosling.*

Offline Alternative

No computer access? At any time, you can print a list of the unit Vocabulary words and their definitions from the online lesson. Use this list to review the words with students offline. In addition, if students made their own flash cards, these can be used for offline review.

Objectives
- Increase oral vocabulary.
- Increase reading vocabulary.
- Increase concept vocabulary.
- Classify and sort common words into categories.

Adult and Baby Words (B)

Lesson Overview

Offline		15 minutes
Vocabulary	Introduce Adult and Baby Words OPTIONAL: Make Your Own Flash Cards	
Online		15 minutes
Skills Update	Review Traffic Words	
Learn	Introduce Adult and Baby Words	

Materials

Supplied
- *K[12] Language Arts Activity Book*, p. LS 67

Also Needed
- scissors, round-end safety
- index cards (8) (optional)

Offline 15 minutes

Work **together** with students to complete an offline Vocabulary activity.

Vocabulary

Introduce Adult and Baby Words

Play a game with students to help them sort the following adult and baby words:

chicken	**goat**	**sheep**	**pig**
chick	**kid**	**lamb**	**piglet**

1. Help students cut out the cards on page LS 67 in *K[12] Language Arts Activity Book*.
2. Point to the picture of each animal. Ask students to name each animal and the sound it makes. Tell them the name and sound of any animal they don't know.

Objectives
- Increase oral vocabulary.
- Increase reading vocabulary.
- Increase concept vocabulary.
- Classify and sort common words into categories.
- Identify and use new meanings for known words.

3. Spread the animal cards on the floor or table. Ask students to sort the cards into two groups: adult animals and baby animals. adult: *chicken, goat, pig, sheep*; baby: *chick, kid, piglet, lamb*

4. Shuffle the cards, and then ask students to sort the cards into adult and baby pairs. goat, kid; chicken, chick; sheep, lamb; pig, piglet

OPTIONAL: Make Your Own Flash Cards

This activity is intended for students who have extra time and would benefit from practicing their vocabulary words with flash cards. Feel free to skip this activity.

Gather eight index cards. Have students create flash cards by writing each vocabulary word on the front of an index card and their own definition for each word on the back. Help students with spelling as necessary.

Online 15 minutes

Students will work online **independently** to complete activities on Vocabulary words. Help students locate the online activities, and provide support as needed.

Skills Update

Review Traffic Words

Students will answer a few questions to refresh their Vocabulary knowledge.

Objectives

- Increase oral vocabulary.
- Increase reading vocabulary.
- Increase concept vocabulary.

Learn

Introduce Adult and Baby Words

Students will be introduced to the adult and baby words *goat, kid, sheep, lamb, chicken, chick, pig,* and *piglet.*

Objectives

- Increase oral vocabulary.
- Increase reading vocabulary.
- Increase concept vocabulary.
- Classify and sort common words into categories.
- Identify and use new meanings for known words.

My Body Language and Adult & Baby Words

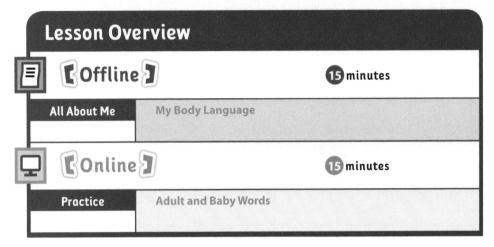

Lesson Overview

Offline 15 minutes

All About Me	My Body Language

Online 15 minutes

Practice	Adult and Baby Words

Materials

Supplied

- K^{12} *All About Me*, pp. 38–39

Also Needed

- crayons

Offline 15 minutes

Work **together** with students to complete an offline All About Me activity.

All About Me

My Body Language

Students will complete pages 38 and 39 in K^{12} *All About Me.*

1. Discuss with students the different ways people communicate (talking in person, talking on the phone, and sending letters, e-mails, text messages, and so on).
2. Explain to students that people also communicate without using words or voices. Ask them if they can think of times when they have communicated without words.
3. Read aloud the first incomplete sentence on page 38, pointing to each word as you read. Have students repeat the first part of the sentence and write the answer in the blank space. head
4. Read the complete sentence to students, pointing to each word.
5. Repeat Steps 3 and 4 with the remaining two sentences. Students should complete the second sentence with the word *shoulders* and the third sentence with the word *mouth.*
6. On page 39, have students illustrate one of their completed sentences and explain.

Objectives

- Dictate or write simple sentences describing experiences, stories, people, objects, or events.
- Write and/or draw narrative text.
- Discuss own drawing.
- Share finished written and drawn works.
- Draw and label pictures.

[Online] 15 minutes

Students will work online **independently** to complete activities on Vocabulary words. Help students locate the online activities, and provide support as needed.

Practice

Adult and Baby Words

Students will practice the adult and baby words *goat, kid, sheep, lamb, chicken, chick, pig,* and *piglet.*

Offline Alternative

No computer access? At any time, you can print a list of the unit Vocabulary words and their definitions from the online lesson. Use this list to review the words with students offline. In addition, if students made their own flash cards, these can be used for offline review.

Objectives

- Increase oral vocabulary.
- Increase reading vocabulary.
- Increase concept vocabulary.
- Classify and sort common words into categories.
- Identify and use new meanings for known words.

"from A Good Play" and Adult & Baby Words

Lesson Overview

Offline	15 minutes
Poetry	"from A Good Play"
	OPTIONAL: Build a Fort
Online	**15 minutes**
Practice	Adult and Baby Words

Materials

Supplied

- *Tomie dePaola's Rhyme Time*

Also Needed

- household items – pillows, blankets (optional)

Advance Preparation

Before reading today's poem, you will need to find the poem in *Tomie dePaola's Rhyme Time.* If your book has page numbers, turn to page 37. Otherwise, you will need to use a pencil to number the pages in the book. Mark the title page as page 1.

Offline 15 minutes

Work **together** with students to complete an offline Poetry activity.

Poetry

"from A Good Play"

It's time to read "from A Good Play" from *Tomie dePaola's Rhyme Time.*

1. Tell students to imagine that they are in a room with no toys but with many blankets, boxes, and bowls. Answers to questions will vary.
   - Would you be able to play with these things?
   - What might you do?
2. Tell students that even the most ordinary objects can be fun to play with if you use your imagination. Tell them that this is exactly what the children in today's poem do.

Objectives

- Listen to and discuss poetry.
- Make connections with text: text-to-text, text-to-self, text-to-world.
- Respond to text through art, writing, and/or drama.
- Identify rhyme and rhythm in poetry.

3. Have students sit next to you so they can see the picture and words while you **read aloud the entire poem**, and then ask:
   - What is the ship in the poem made of? back-bedroom chairs
   - What word in the second stanza rhymes with *nails*? *pails*
   - What two things does Tom say they should take with them? an apple and a slice of cake
4. Have students discuss whether they think the "ship" that the children in this poem build would be fun to play on. Answers to questions will vary.
   - Where would go if you built a ship like that?
   - If your ship needed sails, what would you use?
   - How would you steer your ship?
5. Have students pretend to be the captain of a ship and give orders about what to bring and what to do once at sea.

OPTIONAL: Build a Fort

This activity is optional. It is intended for students who have extra time and would benefit from imaginative play like that described in the poem. Feel free to skip this activity.

Have students gather pillows and blankets and build a fort among living room or kitchen furniture. As they work, have them tell you what they are doing and why.

Online 15 minutes

Students will work online **independently** to complete activities on Vocabulary words. Help students locate the online activities, and provide support as needed.

Practice

Adult and Baby Words

Students will practice the adult and baby words *goat, kid, sheep, lamb, chicken, chick, pig,* and *piglet.*

Offline Alternative

No computer access? At any time, you can print a list of the unit Vocabulary words and their definitions from the online lesson. Use this list to review the words with students offline. In addition, if students made their own flash cards, these can be used for offline review.

Objectives

- Increase oral vocabulary.
- Increase reading vocabulary.
- Increase concept vocabulary.
- Classify and sort common words into categories.
- Identify and use new meanings for known words.

Homographs

Lesson Overview

Offline		15 minutes
Vocabulary	Homographs	
	OPTIONAL: Make Your Own Flash Cards	
Online		15 minutes
Skills Update	Review Opposite Words	
Learn	Homographs	

Materials

Supplied

- There are no supplied materials to gather for this lesson.

Also Needed

- index cards (6) (optional)

Offline 15 minutes

Work **together** with students to complete an offline Vocabulary activity.

Vocabulary

Homographs

Help students learn the following homographs:

bow **dove** **lead**

1. **Say:** A homograph is a word that can be pronounced two different ways and have two different meanings.
2. Pronounce *bow* two different ways: /bow/ (rhymes with *cow*) and /bō/ (rhymes with *toe*). Explain what each one means.
   - Bow, pronounced /bow/, means "the front part of a ship."
   - Bow, pronounced /bō/, means "a curved piece of wood with a tight string between two ends, used for shooting arrows."

Objectives

- Increase oral vocabulary.
- Increase concept vocabulary.
- Increase reading vocabulary.
- Identify homographs.

3. Pronounce *dove* two different ways: /dŭv/ (rhymes with *love*) and /dōv/ (rhymes with *cove*). Explain what each one means.
    - Dove, pronounced /dŭv/, means "a small white bird."
    - Dove, pronounced /dōv/, means "moved from a high place with your head going first."
4. Pronounce *lead* two different ways: /lēd/ (rhymes with *speed*) and /lĕd/ (rhymes with *bed*). Explain what each one means.
    - Lead, pronounced /lēd/, means "to direct or guide something."
    - Lead, pronounced /lĕd/, means "a heavy gray metal."
5. Read the following sentences aloud. Have students determine which missing word best fits the sentence.
    - The ________ part of the ship was damaged from the hurricane. /bow/
    - The ________ flew from one branch to another. /dŭv/
    - ________ is used to make batteries. /lĕd/
    - My dad is really good at shooting a ________ and arrow. /bō/
    - The boy ________ headfirst under his covers to hide when he heard his mom coming. /dōv/
    - I saw the basketball coach ________ the team onto the court for warm-ups. /lēd/

⊕ OPTIONAL: Make Your Own Flash Cards

This activity is intended for students who have extra time and would benefit from practicing their vocabulary words with flash cards. Feel free to skip this activity.

Gather six index cards. Have students create flash cards by writing each vocabulary word on the front of an index card and their own definition for each word on the back. (For each word, students should make two cards—one for each pronunciation.) Help students with spelling as necessary.

Online 15 minutes

Students will work online **independently** to complete activities on Vocabulary words. Help students locate the online activities, and provide support as needed.

Skills Update

Review Opposite Words

Students will answer a few questions to refresh their Vocabulary knowledge.

Objectives

- Increase oral vocabulary.
- Increase reading vocabulary.
- Increase concept vocabulary.

Learn

Homographs

Students will be introduced to the homographs *bow, dove,* and *lead.*

Objectives

- Increase oral vocabulary.
- Increase reading vocabulary.
- Increase concept vocabulary.
- Identify homographs.

Things I Can Do and Homographs

Lesson Overview

Offline	15 minutes
All About Me	Things I Can Do
Online	**15 minutes**
Practice	Homographs

Materials

Supplied

- *K[12] All About Me*, p. 40

Also Needed

- crayons

Offline 15 minutes

Work **together** with students to complete an offline All About Me activity.

All About Me

Things I Can Do

Students will begin page 40 in *K[12] All About Me*; they will complete this page over two lessons.

1. Have students think of something they can do that makes them proud. Possible answers: I can tie my shoes; I can run fast; I can read.
2. Read aloud the first incomplete sentence to students, pointing to each word as you read.
3. Have students repeat the first part of the sentence and tell you an answer to write in the blank space. Have them explain why they are proud of that particular ability. Answers to questions will vary.
   - When did you learn how to do this?
   - Do any of your friends know how to do this?
4. Repeat Steps 2 and 3 with the remaining sentences.
5. Have students choose a sentence to illustrate and explain.

Objectives

- Dictate or write simple sentences describing experiences, stories, people, objects, or events.
- Write and/or draw narrative text.

Online 15 minutes

Students will work online **independently** to complete activities on Vocabulary words. Help students locate the online activities, and provide support as needed.

Practice

Homographs

Students will practice the homographs *bow, dove,* and *lead.*

Objectives

- Increase oral vocabulary.
- Increase reading vocabulary.
- Increase concept vocabulary.
- Identify homographs.

Offline Alternative

No computer access? At any time, you can print a list of the unit Vocabulary words and their definitions from the online lesson. Use this list to review the words with students offline. In addition, if students made their own flash cards, these can be used for offline review.

"Three Little Kittens" and Vocabulary Unit Review

Lesson Overview

Offline	15 minutes
Poetry	"Three Little Kittens"
Online	**15 minutes**
Unit Review	Adult & Baby Words and Homographs

Materials

Supplied

- *K*[12] *Read Aloud Treasury*, pp. 164–167

Offline 15 minutes

Work **together** with students to complete an offline Poetry activity.

Poetry

Objectives

- Listen to and discuss poetry.
- Identify author's use of sensory language.
- Describe character(s).
- Sequence events from a text.

"Three Little Kittens"

It's time to read "Three Little Kittens" from *K*[12] *Read Aloud Treasury.*

1. Remind students that some words are used to help readers imagine how things sound. The word *boom*, for example, helps readers imagine a loud noise. Tell students that sound words are often used to help readers imagine the noises made by animals.
   - What noise does a cow make? moo

   Write *m-o-o* on a piece of paper so that students can see the word that represents this sound.
2. Tell students that today's poem has sound words that help us imagine the noises made by kittens. Tell them to listen for these words in the poem.
3. Have students sit next to you so they can see the pictures and words while you **read aloud the entire poem**, and then ask:
   - What do the kittens lose in the first stanza? their mittens
   - What food do the kittens get when they find their mittens in stanza 2? pie
   - Who are the kittens afraid of in stanza 4? the rat

4. Tell students that "Three Little Kittens" has two words that help us imagine how the kittens sound.
   - What are these two words? *mee-ow* and *purr-r*
5. Tell students that the kittens say *mee-ow* when they feel one way and they say *purr-r* when they feel another way.
   - When do the kittens say *mee-ow*? when they are scared or unhappy
   - When do the kittens say *purr-r*? when they are happy
6. Have students pretend to be kittens and say *mee-ow* or *purr-r* in various situations that you suggest. For instance, if you say that they are being gently petted, they would say *purr-r*. If you say they are cold and wet from rain, they would say *mee-ow*.

Online 15 minutes

Students will work online **independently** to complete an activity on Vocabulary words. Help students locate the online activity, and provide support as needed.

Unit Review

Adult & Baby Words and Homographs

Students will review all words from the unit to prepare for the Unit Checkpoint.

Offline Alternative

No computer access? At any time, you can print a list of the unit Vocabulary words and their definitions from the online lesson. Use this list to review the words with students offline. In addition, if students made their own flash cards, these can be used for offline review.

Objectives

- Identify homographs.
- Classify and sort common words into categories.
- Identify and use new meanings for known words.
- Increase oral vocabulary.
- Increase reading vocabulary.
- Increase concept vocabulary.

Unit Checkpoint

Lesson Overview

Online — 30 minutes

Unit Checkpoint	Adult & Baby Words and Homographs

Materials

There are no materials to gather for this lesson.

Online — 30 minutes

Students will work online to complete the Unit Checkpoint. Help students locate the Unit Checkpoint, and provide support as needed.

Unit Checkpoint

Adult & Baby Words and Homographs

Explain that students are going to show what they have learned about vocabulary words for adults, babies, and homographs.

Objectives

- Increase oral vocabulary.
- Increase reading vocabulary.
- Increase concept vocabulary.
- Identify homographs.
- Classify and sort common words into categories.
- Identify and use new meanings for known words.

Review Words (A)

Unit Overview

In this unit, students will

- Review vocabulary words.
- Complete the *All About Me* pages *Things I Can Do, What I Have Learned,* and *Self-Portrait.*
- Explore counting-out rhymes and the poems "The Storm" and "We're Racing, Racing down the Walk."

Materials

Supplied

- *K[12] Language Arts Activity Book,* p. LS 69

Also Needed

- scissors, round-end safety

Lesson Overview

Offline	15 minutes
Vocabulary	Introduce Review Words
Online	15 minutes
Skills Update	Review Ordinal Words
Learn	Introduce Review Words

Offline 15 minutes

Work **together** with students to complete an offline Vocabulary activity.

Vocabulary

Introduce Review Words

Play a memory game to help students review the following vocabulary words:

baker	**cow**	**horse**	**mom**
cat	**farmer**	**kitten**	**mother**

1. Help students cut out the cards on page LS 69 in *K[12] Language Arts Activity Book.*
2. Shuffle the cards and place them face down on a flat surface.

Objectives

- Increase oral vocabulary.
- Increase reading vocabulary.
- Increase concept vocabulary.
- Classify and sort common words into categories.
- Use synonyms.

3. Determine who will go first. Have that student select a card and flip it over, then select another card and flip it over as well. If the word and picture match, the student keeps the cards. If the word and picture do not match, the student returns the cards to the face-down position.
4. Continue playing until all the matches have been found.
5. If time permits, have students sort the cards into two groups, people and animals.

Vocabulary
Review Words (A)
Introduce Review Words
Cut out each picture and word card.

baker	cow	horse	mother
cat	farmer	kitten	mom

LANGUAGE ARTS BLUE LS 69

Online 15 minutes

Students will work online **independently** to complete activities on Vocabulary words. Help students locate the online activities, and provide support as needed.

Skills Update

Review Ordinal Words

Students will answer a few questions to refresh their Vocabulary knowledge.

Objectives

- Increase oral vocabulary.
- Increase reading vocabulary.
- Increase concept vocabulary.

Learn

Introduce Review Words

Students will be introduced to the review words *mother, mom, baker, farmer, horse, cow, cat,* and *kitten.*

Objectives

- Increase oral vocabulary.
- Increase reading vocabulary.
- Increase concept vocabulary.
- Classify and sort common words into categories.
- Use synonyms.

Things I Can Do and Review Words

Lesson Overview

Offline		15 minutes
All About Me	Things I Can Do	
Online		15 minutes
Practice	Review Words	

Materials

Supplied
- *K*[12] *All About Me*, p. 40

Also Needed
- crayons

Offline 15 minutes

Work **together** with students to complete an offline All About Me activity.

All About Me

Things I Can Do

Students will complete page 40 in *K*[12] *All About Me.*

1. Have students finalize their illustration of an ability that makes them feel proud of themself.
2. Have students explain their illustration. Encourage them to describe their picture in as much detail as possible.

TIP If time permits, have students illustrate and explain multiple sentences.

Objectives
- Write and/or draw narrative text.
- Add supporting details to written or drawn work.
- Discuss own drawing.
- Share finished written and drawn works.

Online 15 minutes

Students will work online **independently** to complete activities on Vocabulary words. Help students locate the online activities, and provide support as needed.

Practice

Review Words

Students will practice the review words *mother, mom, baker, farmer, horse, cow, cat,* and *kitten.*

Objectives

- Increase oral vocabulary.
- Increase reading vocabulary.
- Increase concept vocabulary.
- Classify and sort common words into categories.
- Use synonyms.

Offline Alternative

No computer access? At any time, you can print a list of the unit Vocabulary words and their definitions from the online lesson. Use this list to review the words with students offline. In addition, if students made their own flash cards, these can be used for offline review.

Counting-Out Rhymes and Review Words

Lesson Overview

Offline	15 minutes
Poetry	Counting-Out Rhymes
	OPTIONAL: Play Potatoes
Online	**15 minutes**
Practice	Review Words

Materials

Supplied

- *The Rooster Crows*

Advance Preparation

Before reading today's poems, you will need to find the poems in *The Rooster Crows.* If your book has page numbers, turn to pages 51–54. Otherwise, you will need to use a pencil to number the pages in the book. Mark the title page as page 1.

Offline 15 minutes

Work **together** with students to complete an offline Poetry activity.

Poetry

Counting-Out Rhymes

Explore counting-out rhymes with students in the poems "Entry, Kentry, Cutry, Corn," "Onery, Uery, Ickory Ann," and "One Potato, Two Potatoes."

1. **Say:** Some poems are used to play games. Many of these are called counting-out rhymes. These rhymes can help us choose who will be "It" in a game or to narrow down a group of people or things to just one.
   - "Eeny, meeny, miney, moe" is a counting-out rhyme. Do you know the rest of this rhyme? If so, how does it go? Answers will vary.
2. As necessary, say the rest of the rhyme. Then explain how it might be used in a game of hide-and-seek to choose the seeker.

Objectives

- Listen to and discuss poetry.
- Make connections with text: text-to-text, text-to-self, text-to-world.
- Use visual text features to aid understanding of text.
- Identify rhyme and rhythm in poetry.
- Identify the purpose of a text.

3. Have students sit next to you so they can see the pictures and words while you **read the three poems aloud**, and then ask:
   - Which word in "Entry, Kentry, Cutry, Corn" rhymes with *west*—*east*, *flew*, or *nest*? *nest*
   - Are *onery* and *uery* real words? No
   - What is the last number in "One Potato, Two Potatoes"? seven
4. Read the first line of "Entry, Kentry, Cutry, Corn." Tell students that two of the words you just read are made-up.
   - Which words are not real words? *kentry* and *cutry*
   - Why do you think the poem has nonsense words in it? Answers will vary.
5. Explain that these poems are meant to be fun. Point to the picture above "One Potato, Two Potatoes." Answers to questions will vary.
   - What are the children doing?
   - Have you ever used a counting-out rhyme in a game?

OPTIONAL: Play Potatoes

This activity is optional. It is intended for students who have extra time and would benefit from seeing a counting-out rhyme in action. Feel free to skip this activity.

Have students hold out two fists, and hold out one of your own. Then alternate touching each fist while reciting "One Potato, Two Potatoes." Put down the fist you are touching when the poem ends. Repeat until only one fist remains.

Online 15 minutes

Students will work online **independently** to complete activities on Vocabulary words. Help students locate the online activities, and provide support as needed.

Practice

Review Words

Students will practice the review words *mother, mom, baker, farmer, horse, cow, cat,* and *kitten*.

Objectives
- Increase oral vocabulary.
- Increase reading vocabulary.
- Increase concept vocabulary.
- Classify and sort common words into categories.
- Use synonyms.

Offline Alternative

No computer access? At any time, you can print a list of the unit Vocabulary words and their definitions from the online lesson. Use this list to review the words with students offline. In addition, if students made their own flash cards, these can be used for offline review.

Review Words (B)

Lesson Overview

Offline		15 minutes
Vocabulary	Introduce Review Words	
Online		15 minutes
Skills Update	Review Writing Words	
Learn	Introduce Review Words	

Materials

Supplied

- *K*[12] *Language Arts Activity Book,* p. LS 71

Also Needed

- scissors, round-end safety

Offline 15 minutes

Work **together** with students to complete an offline Vocabulary activity.

Vocabulary

Introduce Review Words

Have students review the following vocabulary words:

back	**loud**	**purple**	**sky blue**
front	**navy blue**	**quiet**	**yellow**

1. Turn to page LS 71 in *K*[12] *Language Arts Activity Book.*
2. Point to each item. Ask students to name each item.
3. For the pairs of cards that are antonyms, have students demonstrate each word: *back, front, loud,* and *quiet.*

Objectives

- Increase oral vocabulary.
- Increase concept vocabulary.
- Increase reading vocabulary.
- Describe people, places, things, locations, actions, events, and/or feelings.
- Use antonyms.

4. For the color cards, have students describe how each color makes them feel. Possible answers: yellow = happy; purple = calm; navy blue = grumpy; sky blue = playful
5. Help students cut out the cards. Shuffle the cards, and ask students to sort the cards into two piles: antonyms and colors. antonyms: *back, front, loud, quiet*; colors: *yellow, purple, navy blue, sky blue*

Online 15 minutes

Students will work online **independently** to complete activities on Vocabulary words. Help students locate the online activities, and provide support as needed.

Skills Update

Review Writing Words

Students will answer a few questions to refresh their Vocabulary knowledge.

Objectives
- Increase oral vocabulary.
- Increase concept vocabulary.

Learn

Introduce Review Words

Students will be introduced to the review words *yellow, purple, sky blue, navy blue, back, front, loud,* and *quiet*.

Objectives
- Increase oral vocabulary.
- Increase reading vocabulary.
- Increase concept vocabulary.
- Describe people, places, things, locations, actions, events, and/or feelings.
- Use antonyms.

What I Have Learned and Review Words

Lesson Overview

Offline	15 minutes
All About Me	What I Have Learned
Online	**15 minutes**
Practice	Review Words

Materials

Supplied
- *K*[12] *All About Me,* p. 41

Also Needed
- crayons

Offline 15 minutes

Work **together** with students to complete an offline All About Me activity.

All About Me

What I Have Learned

Students will complete page 41 in *K*[12] *All About Me.*

1. Talk with students about the things they have learned this year. If necessary, prompt them by asking about their favorite subjects, activities, books, and so on.
2. Have students dictate a list of things they have learned this year. Write the list on the top half of the page.
3. Have students provide a few details about each thing they have learned.
   - Was it easy or difficult to learn?
   - How has it helped you?
   - Did you have fun learning it? Why or why not?
4. Have students choose one of the things on their list to illustrate and explain.

Objectives
- Dictate or write simple sentences describing experiences, stories, people, objects, or events.
- Discuss own drawing.
- Share finished written and drawn works.

Online 15 minutes

Students will work online **independently** to complete activities on Vocabulary words. Help students locate the online activities, and provide support as needed.

Practice

Review Words

In this activity, students will practice the review words *yellow, purple, sky blue, navy blue, back, front, loud,* and *quiet.*

Offline Alternative

No computer access? At any time, you can print a list of the unit Vocabulary words and their definitions from the online lesson. Use this list to review the words with students offline. In addition, if students made their own flash cards, these can be used for offline review.

Objectives

- Increase oral vocabulary.
- Increase reading vocabulary.
- Increase concept vocabulary.
- Describe people, places, things, locations, actions, events, and/or feelings.
- Use antonyms.

"The Storm" and Review Words

Lesson Overview

Offline	15 minutes
Poetry	"The Storm"
Online	**15 minutes**
Practice	Review Words

Materials

Supplied
- *Tomie dePaola's Rhyme Time*
- *K[12] Language Arts Activity Book*, p. LS 73

Also Needed
- crayons

Advance Preparation

Before reading today's poem, you will need to find the poem in *Tomie dePaola's Rhyme Time.* If your book has page numbers, turn to page 12. Otherwise, you will need to use a pencil to number the pages in the book. Mark the title page as page 1.

Offline 15 minutes

Work **together** with students to complete an offline Poetry activity.

Poetry

"The Storm"

It's time to read "The Storm" from *Tomie dePaola's Rhyme Time.*

1. Remind students that poems use words to help us imagine how things look and sound. Tell them that today's poem is about a rainstorm. Answers to questions will vary.
   - What do rainstorms look like?
   - What sounds do you hear when it rains?
2. Have students make the sound of thunder and the sound of rain as it hits the ground, a window, or a car.

Objectives
- Listen to and discuss poetry.
- Identify author's use of sensory language.
- Identify words that create mental imagery.
- Respond to text through art, writing, and/or drama.

3. Have students sit next to you so they can see the picture and words while you **read aloud the entire poem**, and then ask:
   - ▸ Where is the boy during the storm? in his bed
   - ▸ Which is louder—the thunder or the rain? the thunder
   - ▸ What does the poem say has fingers? lightning
4. Read aloud the first two lines of the poem. Stress the word *listen*.
   - ▸ What do we use when we listen? our ears
5. Point out that the next two lines describe things that we hear with our ears. Read them.
   - ▸ Which words describe how the thunder sounds? *rumbles*, *loud*, and *grand*
   - ▸ Which words describe how the rain sounds? *splash* and *whisper*
6. Read the last two lines of the poem. Tell students that these lines do not describe how something sounds, but rather how something looks.
   - ▸ What words describe how the lightning looks? *sharp* and *bright*
   - ▸ What does the last line of the poem compare the lightning to? a hand with fingers
7. Have students turn to page LS 73 in *K*[12] *Language Arts Activity Book*. Have them color the picture of the stormy night. As students work, have them tell you how things look and what the storm might sound like.

Online 15 minutes

Students will work online **independently** to complete activities on Vocabulary words. Help students locate the online activities, and provide support as needed.

Practice

Review Words

Students will practice the review words *yellow*, *purple*, *sky blue*, *navy blue*, *back*, *front*, *loud*, and *quiet*.

Offline Alternative

No computer access? At any time, you can print a list of the unit Vocabulary words and their definitions from the online lesson. Use this list to review the words with students offline. In addition, if students made their own flash cards, these can be used for offline review.

Objectives

- Increase oral vocabulary.
- Increase reading vocabulary.
- Increase concept vocabulary.
- Describe people, places, things, locations, actions, events, and/or feelings.
- Use antonyms.

Review Words (C)

Lesson Overview

Offline	15 minutes
Vocabulary	Review Words

Online	15 minutes
Skills Update	Review Subject Words
Learn	Introduce Review Words

Materials

Supplied

- There are no supplied materials to gather for this lesson.

Also Needed

- household objects – items of graduated sizes (4); pictures of stop sign and caution sign; pennies or other small tokens (10)

Advance Preparation

Gather four household objects of graduated sizes, such as a tennis ball, a book, a small waste basket, and a chair. Gather pictures of a stop sign and caution sign from a magazine, photo, or the Internet. Gather 10 pennies or other small tokens.

Offline 15 minutes

Work **together** with students to complete an offline Vocabulary activity.

Vocabulary

Review Words

Have students review the following vocabulary words:

caution	**larger**	**stop**
large	**largest**	**tenth**

1. Gather the four household objects. Place the objects next to each other, in order from smallest to largest (with the smallest item on the left end). Tell students that you are going to compare the sizes of the items.
   - Point to the second item from the left.
     Say: This [item] is large compared to this [smallest item].

Objectives

- Increase oral vocabulary.
- Increase concept vocabulary.
- Increase reading vocabulary.
- Classify and sort common words into categories.
- Identify purpose of environmental print.
- Use suffixes.

- Point to the third item from the left.
  Say: This [item] is larger than this [second item from the left].
- Point to the item at far right.
  Say: This [item] is the largest of all four items.

If time permits, have students gather four additional items of graduated sizes. Have them describe each item using the vocabulary words.

2. Show students a picture of a stop sign. Ask them what this sign means. Explain why it is important for drivers and pedestrians to understand what a stop sign means.
3. Show students a picture of a caution sign. Ask them what this sign means. Explain why it is important for drivers and pedestrians to understand what a caution sign means.
4. Place 10 pennies or other small tokens on the table. Ask students to line them up. Have them point to the tenth penny in the row to demonstrate their understanding of the word *tenth*.

Online 15 minutes

Students will work online **independently** to complete activities on Vocabulary words. Help students locate the online activities, and provide support as needed.

Skills Update

Review Subject Words
Students will answer a few questions to refresh their Vocabulary knowledge.

Objectives
- Increase oral vocabulary.
- Increase concept vocabulary.

Learn

Introduce Review Words
Students will be introduced to the review words *stop, caution, large, larger, largest,* and *tenth.*

Objectives
- Increase oral vocabulary.
- Increase reading vocabulary.
- Increase concept vocabulary.
- Classify and sort common words into categories.
- Identify purpose of environmental print.
- Use suffixes.

Self-Portrait and Review Words

Lesson Overview

Offline	15 minutes
All About Me	Self-Portrait
Online	**15 minutes**
Practice	Review Words

Materials

Supplied

- *K[12] All About Me,* p. 42

Also Needed

- crayons

Offline 15 minutes

Work **together** with students to to complete an offline All About Me activity.

All About Me

Objectives

- Capitalize proper names.
- Draw and label pictures.

Self-Portrait

Students will begin page 42 in *K[12] All About Me*; they will complete this page over two lessons.

1. Discuss with students the features of their heads (hair color, eye color, nose, mouth, ears, and so on).
2. Have students draw a self-portrait, focusing only on their head and face rather than drawing their entire body.
3. Have students write their first and last names on the line provided. Make sure they capitalize only the first letter of their first and last names.
4. If time permits, have students compare their self-portrait to the drawing on page 1 of *K[12] All About Me.*

Online 15 minutes

Students will work online **independently** to complete activities on Vocabulary words. Help students locate the online activities, and provide support as needed.

Practice

Review Words

Students will practice the review words *stop, caution, large, larger, largest,* and *tenth.*

Offline Alternative

No computer access? At any time, you can print a list of the unit Vocabulary words and their definitions from the online lesson. Use this list to review the words with students offline. In addition, if students made their own flash cards, these can be used for offline review.

Objectives

- Increase oral vocabulary.
- Increase reading vocabulary.
- Increase concept vocabulary.
- Classify and sort common words into categories.
- Identify purpose of environmental print.
- Use suffixes.

"We're Racing, Racing down the Walk" and Vocabulary Unit Review

Lesson Overview

Offline	15 minutes
Poetry	"We're Racing, Racing down the Walk"
Online	**15 minutes**
Unit Review	Review Words

Materials

Supplied

- *Tomie dePaola's Rhyme Time*

Advance Preparation

Before reading today's poem, you will need to find the poem in *Tomie dePaola's Rhyme Time*. If your book has page numbers, turn to page 24. Otherwise, you will need to use a pencil to number the pages in the book. Mark the title page as page 1.

Offline 15 minutes

Work **together** with students to complete an offline Poetry activity.

Poetry

"We're Racing, Racing down the Walk"

It's time to read "We're Racing, Racing down the Walk" from *Tomie dePaola's Rhyme Time.*

Objectives

- Listen to and discuss poetry.
- Identify author's use of sensory language.
- Identify words that create mental imagery.

1. Remind students that poems often use words that help us imagine how things sound and feel. Tell them that today's poem is about roller-skating. Answers to questions will vary.
   - Have you ever been on roller-skates? If not, have you ever seen people on roller-skates?
   - If you had to describe roller-skating, what noises and feelings would you talk about?

2. Have students sit next to you so they can see the picture and words while you **read aloud the entire poem**, and then ask:
   - Where do the girls in the poem roller-skate? around their block
   - Why does the girls' hair fly backward? because they are moving fast
   - Which words describe how the girls talk to each other? *roar* and *shout*
3. Read the first four lines of the poem. Stress the words *racing* and *rumble*.
   - Are the girls moving fast or slow? fast
4. Point out that the next two lines describe some of the sounds that the girls hear. Read them. Answers to questions will vary.
   - What might the words *whish* and *whirr* describe?
   - Why do the girls have to *roar* and *shout* to each other?
5. Read the last three lines of the poem. Tell students that these lines do not describe the sounds of roller-skating, but rather how roller-skating feels.
   - What words describe how roller-skating feels? *rattle* and *rock*
6. Have students tell you whether or not they think the girls enjoy roller-skating, and why. Encourage them to tell you whether they think this poem makes roller-skating seem like fun, and why.

Online 15 minutes

Students will work online **independently** to complete an activity on Vocabulary words. Help students locate the online activity, and provide support as needed.

Unit Review

Review Words

Students will review all words from the unit to prepare for the Unit Checkpoint.

Offline Alternative

No computer access? At any time, you can print a list of the unit Vocabulary words and their definitions from the online lesson. Use this list to review the words with students offline. In addition, if students made their own flash cards, these can be used for offline review.

Objectives

- Increase oral vocabulary.
- Increase reading vocabulary.
- Increase concept vocabulary.
- Classify and sort common words into categories.
- Identify purpose of environmental print.
- Use suffixes.
- Use synonyms.
- Use antonyms.

Unit Checkpoint

Lesson Overview

Online	30 minutes
Unit Checkpoint	Review Words

Materials

There are no materials to gather for this lesson.

Online 30 minutes

Students will work online to complete the Unit Checkpoint. Help students locate the Unit Checkpoint, and provide support as needed.

Objectives

- Increase oral vocabulary.
- Increase reading vocabulary.
- Increase concept vocabulary.
- Classify and sort common words into categories.
- Identify purpose of environmental print.
- Use suffixes.
- Use synonyms.
- Use antonyms.

Unit Checkpoint

Review Words

Explain that students are going to show what they have learned about vocabulary review words.

Literature & Comprehension

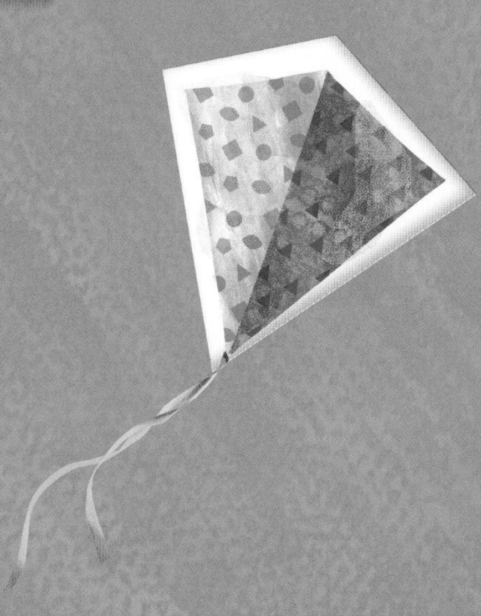

Introduce "Migrating Monarchs: A Butterfly Vacation"

Unit Overview

In this unit, students will explore the theme of *Amazing Tales* through the following reading selections:

- "Migrating Monarchs: A Butterfly Vacation"
- *A Story, A Story*
- "Spider and Turtle and Good Manners"

Lesson Overview

Offline	"Migrating Monarchs: A Butterfly Vacation"	30 minutes
Get Ready	The Main Idea and Reality	
	Words to Know	
Read Aloud	Book Walk	
	"Migrating Monarchs: A Butterfly Vacation"	
Check Your Reading	"Migrating Monarchs: A Butterfly Vacation"	

Advance Preparation

Read "Migrating Monarchs: A Butterfly Vacation" before beginning the Read Aloud activities, to locate Words to Know within the text. Note that students will identify their own Words to Know as they read.

Big Ideas

Early learners acquire vocabulary through active exposure (by talking and listening, being read to, and receiving explicit instruction).

Materials

Supplied

- "Migrating Monarchs: A Butterfly Vacation," *Animals Around the World*, pp. 18–23

Also Needed

- dictionary

Story Synopsis

Not everyone has a warm home to protect them from a cold winter. That's why millions of monarch butterflies take flight and migrate south to Mexico every fall. Their journey is one of nature's most spectacular events.

Keywords

main idea – the most important idea in a paragraph or text

Offline 30 minutes

"Migrating Monarchs: A Butterfly Vacation"

Work **together** with students to complete offline Get Ready, Read Aloud, and Check Your Reading activities.

Get Ready

The Main Idea and Reality

Introduce students to main idea and reality.

1. Tell students that they are going to read an article called "Migrating Monarchs: A Butterfly Vacation."
2. Point out that everything in this article is true, or real. **Everything in the article exists in real life**, and everything that happens in the article is true.
3. Explain that, even though there are several paragraphs in the article, **the overall article is mostly about one thing**, which is called the **main idea** of the article. Tell them to listen carefully so they can figure out the main idea, or what the article is mostly about.

Objectives

- Identify and define reality.
- State the main idea of a text.
- Make predictions based on title, illustrations, and/or context clues.

Words to Know

In this lesson, you'll introduce students to the Words to Know as you read the article.

adjust – to get used to something
instinct – knowing how to do something without having to learn it
migrate – to go from one place to another with the change of seasons
migration – the act of going from one place to another with the change of seasons
season – one of the four times of the year: spring, summer, fall, or winter

Read Aloud

Book Walk

Prepare students by taking them on a Book Walk of "Migrating Monarchs: A Butterfly Vacation." Scan the magazine article together and ask students to make predictions about the text. Answers to questions may vary.

1. Have students turn to the **table of contents**. Ask them what information is found on this page. Help students find today's selection, and turn to that page.
2. Point to and read aloud the **title of the article**.
3. Have students look at the **pictures** in the article.
   - What do you think the article is about?
   - Do you know of any animals that go south for the winter?
4. Point to and read aloud any **headers, captions, or other features** that stand out.
   - What do you think the article might tell us about monarch butterflies?

Objectives

- Read and listen to a variety of texts for information and pleasure independently or as part of a group.
- Identify unknown words in text.
- Increase concept and content vocabulary.

"Migrating Monarchs: A Butterfly Vacation"

Now it's time to read the article. Have students sit next to you so that they can see the pictures and words while you read the article aloud. Gather the dictionary.

1. **Read aloud the entire article.** Tell students to listen carefully so they can figure out what the article is mostly about. Tell them that good readers stop to find out what words mean to make sure they understand what they're reading.
2. Pause after each paragraph that includes a word in boldface. Ask students if there were any words in that portion of the text that they didn't understand.
   - Encourage students to mention *any* word that is unclear.
   - If students don't mention a boldfaced word, review it with them to guarantee they hear the correct meaning. Refer to the definitions in Words to Know.
3. Use the dictionary to define words that are not listed in Words to Know. If you're using a children's dictionary, the word might not be included, and you may have to use your own words for the definition.
4. Jot down **all** the words students identify as unknown.

Check Your Reading

"Migrating Monarchs: A Butterfly Vacation"

Have students retell the article in their own words to develop grammar, vocabulary, comprehension, and fluency skills.

1. Ask students the following questions to **check understanding of main idea and reality**.
   - What is this article mostly about? how monarch butterflies fly, or migrate, to Mexico every winter
   - Is everything in the article true? Yes
   - What does it mean if everything in the article is true? It means everything in the article is real; it means everything in the article exists, or happens, in the real world.
2. Gather the list of unknown words that students identified when you read the article. **Ask the following questions for each word on the list.**
   - What does [word] mean? If students cannot or do not define the word correctly, read the definition.
   - Can you use [word] in a sentence? If students cannot or do not use the word in a sentence correctly, help them construct a sentence.

Objectives

- State the main idea of a text.
- Identify and define reality.
- Identify unknown words in text.
- Increase concept and content vocabulary.
- Use new vocabulary in written and spoken sentences.

Explore "Migrating Monarchs: A Butterfly Vacation"

Lesson Overview

Offline	"Migrating Monarchs: A Butterfly Vacation"	30 minutes
Get Ready	Sequence Events to Check Understanding	
	Words to Know	
Read Aloud	Book Walk	
	"Migrating Monarchs: A Butterfly Vacation"	
Check Your Reading	"Migrating Monarchs: A Butterfly Vacation"	
Reading for Meaning	Sequence of a Monarch Migration	

Materials

Supplied

- "Migrating Monarchs: A Butterfly Vacation," *Animals Around the World*, pp. 18–23

Keywords

sequence – order

Advance Preparation

Before working with students, gather the list of Words to Know that students identified as they read "Migrating Monarchs: A Butterfly Vacation" and spend a few minutes reviewing the words. Then review the Check Your Reading and Reading for Meaning activities to familiarize yourself with the questions and answers.

Big Ideas

- Comprehension entails an understanding of the organizational patterns of text.
- Comprehension requires the reader to self-monitor understanding.

Offline 30 minutes

"Migrating Monarchs: A Butterfly Vacation"

Work **together** with students to complete offline Get Ready, Read Aloud, Check Your Reading, and Reading for Meaning activities.

Get Ready

Sequence Events to Check Understanding

Tell students that it's important to think about the sequence of events in a story or article. **Thinking about the sequence, or order, of events helps good readers check their understanding of what they're reading.**

1. **Read aloud** the following paragraph to explain a sequence of events: Listen carefully to the order in which things happen in this short story. Yesterday Pedro and his father went to the animal shelter to adopt a puppy. Pedro picked a puppy named Barney. Pedro and his father brought Barney home. Then Pedro and Barney played fetch all afternoon.
2. Tell students the sequence in which things happened.
   - Pedro and his father went to the animal shelter.
   - Pedro picked a puppy named Barney.
   - Pedro and his father brought Barney home.
   - Pedro and Barney played fetch.
3. Tell students that it's now their turn. Reread the paragraph, and ask students to tell you the sequence of events.

Objectives

- Sequence information in text.
- Increase concept and content vocabulary.
- Use new vocabulary in written and spoken sentences.

Words to Know

Before reading "Migrating Monarchs: A Butterfly Vacation,"

1. Gather the list of Words to Know that students identified. The definitions for the boldfaced words in the article are provided for you, but you may have additional words on your list.
2. Have students say each word aloud.
3. Ask students if they know what each word means.
   - If students know a word's meaning, have them define it and use it in a sentence.
   - If students don't know a word's meaning, read them the definition and discuss the word with them.

adjust – to get used to something
instinct – knowing how to do something without having to learn it
migrate – to go from one place to another with the change of seasons
migration – the act of going from one place to another with the change of seasons
season – one of the four times of the year: spring, summer, fall, or winter

Read Aloud

Book Walk

Prepare students by taking them on a Book Walk of "Migrating Monarchs: A Butterfly Vacation." Scan the magazine article together to revisit the text.

1. Turn to today's selection.
2. Point to and read aloud the **title of the article**.
3. Have students look at the **pictures** in the article. Answers to questions may vary.
   - What is something you learned about monarch butterflies that you didn't already know?
   - Have you ever seen a monarch butterfly? If so, what was it doing?

Objectives

- Activate prior knowledge by previewing text and/or discussing topic.
- Read and listen to a variety of texts for information and pleasure independently or as part of a group.

"Migrating Monarchs: A Butterfly Vacation"

Now it's time to read the article. Have students sit next to you so that they can see the pictures and words while you read the article aloud.

Read aloud the entire article. Tell students to listen carefully to see if they can hear the sequence of events in the article.

Check Your Reading

"Migrating Monarchs: A Butterfly Vacation"

Have students retell the article in their own words to develop grammar, vocabulary, comprehension, and fluency skills. When finished, **ask students the following questions** to check comprehension and encourage discussion. If students have trouble responding to a question, **help them locate the answer in the text or pictures**.

- Where do monarch butterflies that live in parts of Canada and the United States fly every year? Mexico; a mountain range in central Mexico; a special place in Mexico
- Why do monarch butterflies fly to Mexico? It's too cold during the winter where they live.
- What do the butterflies do when they get to Mexico? They rest on tree trunks.
- How many butterflies rest on one tree trunk? thousands
- How do the butterflies know it's time to fly home? Their instinct tells them it's time to go.
- When does a female monarch butterfly lay her eggs? when she gets back home from Mexico

Objectives

- Answer questions requiring literal recall of details.

Reading for Meaning

Sequence of a Monarch Migration

Ask students the following questions to check their understanding of sequence. When appropriate, **reread parts of the article and point to pictures** to help students remember the sequence of events.

- What is the first thing the butterflies do in the article? They start to fly to Mexico.
- How long do the butterflies fly? for days and days
- What do the butterflies do when they get to Mexico? They rest close to each other on tree trunks.
- How long do the butterflies stay on the tree trunks? all winter long
- What happens when winter is over? The butterflies fly home.
- What do the female butterflies do when they get home? They find a place to lay their eggs.
- What happens next? The eggs hatch.
- What happens after the eggs hatch? They grow to become new monarch butterflies.
- What happens when winter comes again? The migration begins again; the butterflies fly to Mexico again.

TIP If students are having difficulty understanding sequence, tell them a short story with several events and review the sequence of events with them. Tell them the sequence of events, and then have them tell you the events in their own words.

Objectives

- Sequence information in text.
- Answer questions requiring literal recall of details.

Review "Migrating Monarchs: A Butterfly Vacation"

Lesson Overview

Offline "Migrating Monarchs: A Butterfly Vacation" **30 minutes**

Get Ready	Words to Know
	Reread or Retell
Reading for Meaning	Visual Text Features in "Migrating Monarchs: A Butterfly Vacation"
Making Connections	Fly, Butterfly, Fly
Beyond the Lesson	**OPTIONAL:** Gotta Go to Mexico!

Materials

Supplied

- "Migrating Monarchs: A Butterfly Vacation," *Animals Around the World*, pp. 18–23
- *K[12] Language Arts Activity Book*, p. LC 39

Also Needed

- scissors, round-end safety

Keywords

retelling – using your own words to tell a story that you have listened to or read

sequence – order

text feature – part of a text that helps a reader locate information and determine what is most important; examples include the title, table of contents, headings, pictures, and glossary

Advance Preparation

Before working with students, gather the list of Words to Know that students identified as they read "Migrating Monarchs: A Butterfly Vacation."

Big Ideas

- Readers who visualize, or form mental pictures, while they read have better recall of text than those who do not.
- Comprehension is facilitated by an understanding of physical presentation (headings, subheads, graphics, and other features).
- Comprehension entails an understanding of the organizational patterns of text.

Offline 30 minutes

"Migrating Monarchs: A Butterfly Vacation"

Work **together** with students to complete offline Get Ready, Reading for Meaning, Making Connections, and Beyond the Lesson activities.

Get Ready

Words to Know

Ask students to define the Words to Know that they identified and use them in a sentence. The following words may be on their lists:

adjust	**migration**
instinct	**season**
migrate	

Correct any incorrect or vague definitions.

Objectives

- Increase concept and content vocabulary.
- Use new vocabulary in written and spoken sentences.

Reread or Retell

If you'd like to, reread the article to students. Otherwise, have students retell the article using the pictures as a guide, or move on to the next activity.

Reading for Meaning

Visual Text Features in "Migrating Monarchs: A Butterfly Vacation"

Tell students that sometimes the ideas in a magazine article can be hard to understand or imagine. That's why **features such as pictures, graphics (for example, maps and charts), and headings are an important part of magazine articles**. These features can give extra information that may not be found in the written words. They also help readers form their own mental pictures, which can make it easier to understand and remember the ideas in a text. **Ask students the following questions** to check understanding of visual text features.

Objectives

- Use visual text features to aid understanding of text.

1. Point to the monarch butterfly on page 18.
   - Why is this picture in the article? to show what a monarch butterfly looks like
2. Point to the map on page 19.
   - Why are there arrows on the map? to show where the butterflies begin flying and where they're flying to; to show how far the butterflies fly
3. Point to the picture of the tree covered with butterflies on page 21.
   - What does this picture show? how the butterflies rest close to each other to stay warm; how many butterflies rest on one tree

4. Point to the alarm clock, and read aloud the line of text next to it on pages 22–23.
   - What do the alarm clock and this sentence tell us? that the butterflies' instinct tells them when it's time to fly home
5. Point to the picture of the butterflies leaving the trees on pages 22–23.
   - Why is this picture in the article? to show how all the butterflies start flying home at the same time

Making Connections

Fly, Butterfly, Fly

Have students retell the order of events in the monarch butterfly migration.

Objectives

- Compare and contrast two texts on the same topic.
- Compare and contrast informational text and literary text.

1. Have students cut out the monarch butterfly and the arrow on page LC 39 in *K*[12] *Language Arts Activity Book.*
2. Have students retell the four main events in the butterfly migration sequence using the butterfly, arrow, and map: (1) fly south to Mexico; (2) rest on trees all winter; (3) fly back home to the north; (4) lay eggs. Have them lay the arrow on the map to show the direction in which the butterflies fly on each leg of their journey—pointing down to fly south, pointing up to fly north.

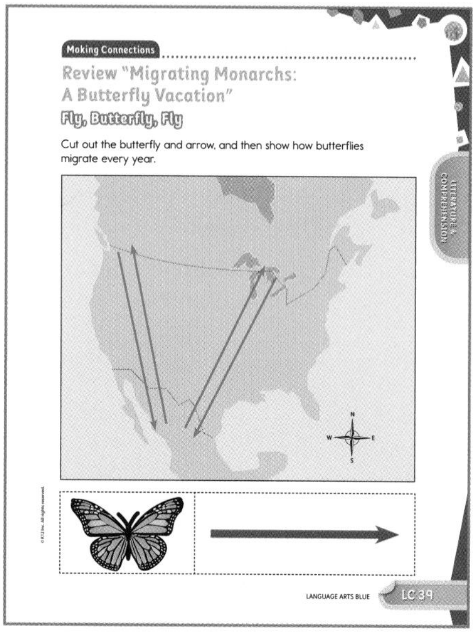
Making Connections
Review "Migrating Monarchs: A Butterfly Vacation"
Fly, Butterfly, Fly
Cut out the butterfly and arrow, and then show how butterflies migrate every year.
LITERATURE & COMPREHENSION
LANGUAGE ARTS BLUE LC 39

Beyond the Lesson

OPTIONAL: Gotta Go to Mexico!

This activity is intended for students who have extra time and would benefit from reading a story about a migrating butterfly. Feel free to skip this activity.

- Go to a library and look for a copy of *Gotta Go! Gotta Go!* by Sam Swope and Sue Riddle or *Hurry and the Monarch* by Antoine O. Flatharta.
- Lead a Book Walk, and then read aloud the story.
- Have students tell how the book and the article are alike and different. Be sure students recognize that the library book is fiction, while the article is nonfiction.
- Have them tell which account they like better, and why.

Objectives

- Compare and contrast two texts on the same topic.
- Compare and contrast informational text and literary text.

Introduce *A Story, A Story*

Lesson Overview

Offline *A Story, A Story* **30 minutes**

Get Ready	The Purpose of a Text
	Words to Know
	Pronunciation Guide
Read Aloud	Book Walk
	A Story, A Story
Check Your Reading	*A Story, A Story*

Advance Preparation

Read *A Story, A Story* before beginning the Read Aloud activities, to locate Words to Know within the story.

Materials

Supplied

- *A Story, A Story*, retold by Gail E. Haley

Story Synopsis

This myth explains that long ago, there were no stories on earth because they all belonged to the Sky God, Nyame. Ananse, the Spider Man, is told he can buy the stories and give them to the people of earth if he can bring three elusive creatures to Nyame. Can he do it using his trickery?

Keywords

author's purpose – the reason the author wrote a text: to entertain, to inform, to express an opinion, or to persuade

Offline 30 minutes

A Story, A Story

Work **together** with students to complete offline Get Ready, Read Aloud, and Check Your Reading activities.

Get Ready

The Purpose of a Text

Explore the author's purpose.

1. Tell students that an author writes an article or story for a particular reason, or **purpose**. Authors write for the following reasons: to teach or tell us something, to entertain us, to convince us of something, or to tell us their opinion.
2. Tell students that newspaper articles are written to tell us something. Magazine articles are often written to teach us something. Authors who write children's books usually want to entertain us, but sometimes they do it to teach us something at the same time.

Objectives

- Identify the purpose of a text.
- Build vocabulary through listening, reading, and discussion.
- Use new vocabulary in written and spoken sentences.

Words to Know

Before reading *A Story, A Story,*

1. Have students say each word aloud.
2. Ask students if they know what each word means.
   - If students know a word's meaning, have them define it and use it in a sentence.
   - If students don't know a word's meaning, read them the definition and discuss the word with them.

bind – to tie up something
calabash – a container made from a dried, hollowed-out gourd
captive – a person or animal that has been taken prisoner
demand – to ask for something firmly
hornet – an insect that stings; a large wasp
reply – to answer
scatter – to go in different directions
stir – to move slightly
stop – to plug up

Pronunciation Guide

A Story, A Story has words that may be difficult to pronounce correctly. Review these words and their pronunciations:

Ananse (ah-NAHN-see)
Mmboro (moh-BOR-oh)
Mmoatia (m-MOH-AH-tee-ah)
Nyame (nye-AH-mee)
Osebo (oh-SAY-boh)
twe (chweh)
yiridi (yee-ree-dee)

Read Aloud

Book Walk

Prepare students by taking them on a Book Walk of *A Story, A Story*. Scan the book together, and ask students to make predictions about the story.

1. Ask students to point to the front cover of the book, and then have them point to the back cover.
2. Have students look at the pictures on the cover.
3. Have students point to the **title**, and then read aloud the title.
   - What do you think the book is about? Answers will vary.
4. Have students point to the name of the **author**. Read aloud the name of the author.
5. Have students locate the **title page**.
   - What information is found on the title page? title and name of the author and illustrator.
6. Look through the book. Have students describe what they see in the **pictures**. Answers to questions may vary.
   - Where do you think the story takes place?
   - What do you think might happen in the story?
   - Has anyone ever tricked you into doing something?

Objectives

- Make predictions based on title, illustrations, and/or context clues.
- Listen and respond to texts representing a variety of cultures, time periods, and traditions.

A Story, A Story

Now it's time to read the story. Have students sit next to you so that they can see the pictures and words while you read the story aloud.

Read aloud the entire story. Emphasize Words to Know as you come to them. If appropriate, use the pictures to help show what each word means.

Check Your Reading

A Story, A Story

Have students retell the story in their own words to develop grammar, vocabulary, comprehension, and fluency skills. When finished, **ask students the following questions** to check understanding of author's purpose and the story's details and events.

- Why did the author write this story? to tell how stories came to be on earth; to entertain
- Who has all the stories at the beginning of the tale? the Sky God (Nyame) Where does he keep them? in a golden box
- What does the Sky God say is his price for the stories? the leopard (Osebo), the hornet (Mmboro), and the fairy (Mmoatia)
- How does Ananse capture the leopard? He tricks the leopard into playing a game, and then ties him up.
- What does Ananse use to capture the fairy? a sticky doll; the Gum baby
- What does the Sky God do when Ananse brings him the leopard, the hornet, and the fairy? He gives Ananse his stories.

Objectives

- Identify the purpose of a text.
- State the details of a text.

Explore *A Story, A Story*

Lesson Overview

Offline *A Story, A Story* 30 minutes

Get Ready	Use Words with More Than One Meaning
	Words to Know
Read Aloud	Book Walk
	A Story, A Story
Check Your Reading	*A Story, A Story*
Reading for Meaning	Sensory Language: Sounds and Repeated Words

Materials

Supplied

- *A Story, A Story*, retold by Gail E. Haley

Keywords

context clue – a word or phrase in a text that helps you figure out the meaning of an unknown word

sensory language – language that appeals to the five senses

Advance Preparation

Before working with students, spend a few minutes reviewing Words to Know. Then review the Check Your Reading and Reading for Meaning activities to familiarize yourself with the questions and answers.

Read the third paragraph in the introduction to *A Story, A Story* (next to the dedication page) to familiarize yourself with the use of sensory and repeated words in the story.

Big Ideas

- Early learners acquire vocabulary through active exposure (by talking and listening, being read to, and receiving explicit instruction).
- Comprehension entails actively thinking about what is being read.

Offline 30 minutes

A Story, A Story

Work **together** with students to complete offline Get Ready, Read Aloud, Check Your Reading, and Reading for Meaning activities.

Get Ready

Use Words with More Than One Meaning

Tell students that **some words can mean more than one thing**. We use multiple-meaning words all the time; for instance, the word *watch* can mean the action of looking at something or it can mean the thing that's worn on a wrist for telling time. Good readers look for clues in the surrounding text to figure out which meaning an author is using for a word in a sentence.

1. Model how to locate and determine the meaning of a word with more than one meaning.
2. Ask students if they know what the word *light* means. The word *light* can mean "a lamp" or it can be used to describe something that's not heavy.
   Say: Listen to this sentence: Mason turned on the light when he came into the room.
   - Which meaning of the word *light* makes sense in this sentence? a lamp
   - What clues helped you figure out the correct meaning? turned on
3. Ask students if they know what the word *stopped* means. The word *stopped* can mean either "ended" or "plugged up."
4. **Read aloud:**
   ". . . the hornets . . . flew into the calabash—fom! Ananse quickly stopped the mouth of the gourd."
   - Which meaning of *stopped* makes sense in the sentence? plugged up

Objectives

- Identify multiple-meaning words.
- Identify and use context clues to define words.
- Build vocabulary through listening, reading, and discussion.
- Use new vocabulary in written and spoken sentences.

Words to Know

Before reading *A Story, A Story*,

1. Have students say each word aloud.
2. Ask students if they know what each word means.
   - If students know a word's meaning, have them define it and use it in a sentence.
   - If students don't know a word's meaning, read them the definition and discuss the word with them.

bind – to tie up something
calabash – a container made from a dried, hollowed-out gourd
captive – a person or animal that has been taken prisoner
demand – to ask for something firmly
hornet – an insect that stings; a large wasp
reply – to answer
scatter – to go in different directions
stir – to move slightly
stop – to plug up

Read Aloud

Book Walk

Prepare students by taking them on a Book Walk of *A Story, A Story*. Scan the book together to revisit the characters and events.

1. Read aloud the **book title**.
2. Have students locate the name of the **author**. Read the name of the author.
3. Have students locate the name of the **illustrator**. Read the name of the illustrator.
4. Look through the book. Have students describe what they see in the **pictures.**
   - Name a creature that Ananse captures. Possible answers: leopard, hornet, fairy
   - What sound do you think the hornets might make when they realize that Ananse has trapped them? Answers will vary.

Objectives

- Activate prior knowledge by previewing text and/or discussing topic.
- Listen and respond to texts representing a variety of cultures, time periods, and traditions.

A Story, A Story

Now it's time to read the story. Have students sit next to you so that they can see the pictures and words while you read the story aloud.

Read aloud the entire story. Tell students to listen for words that have more than one meaning and words that help them imagine sounds. Be sure to emphasize words that represent sounds.

Check Your Reading

A Story, A Story

Have students retell the story in their own words to develop grammar, vocabulary, comprehension, and fluency skills. When finished, **ask students the following questions** to check understanding of multiple-meaning words.

Objectives

- Identify multiple-meaning words.
- Identify and use context clues to define words.

1. **Read aloud:**
   "... the Sky God called together all the nobles of his court ..."
   - Which word has more than one meaning? *court*
   - What does the word *court* mean in the sentence? the people who work for the king What is another meaning for that word? the area where you play a game like basketball or tennis; the place where a judge works
2. **Read aloud:**
   "'Don't you reply when I thank you?' cried the angered fairy. The doll did not stir."
   - Which word has more than one meaning? *stir*
   - What does the word *stir* mean in the sentence? to move a little bit What is another meaning for that word? to mix with a spoon
3. **Read aloud:**
   "[The fairy] pushed against the doll with her feet, and they also stuck fast."
   - What does the word *fast* mean in the sentence? firm; unable to move What is another meaning for *fast*? quick; speedy
   - Was there a clue that helped you figure out the meaning of *fast* in the sentence? the word *stuck*; if something is stuck, it can't move

Reading for Meaning

Sensory Language: Sounds and Repeated Words

Tell students that **authors sometimes use words to help readers imagine the sounds of a story**: balloons pop, whips crack, and the wind howls. In some African stories, the author also repeats words to make them stronger. For example, "So small, so small, so small" means very, very small.

Objectives

- Identify author's use of sensory language.
- Identify repetitive text.

1. **Read aloud:**
   "When the Sky God heard what Ananse wanted, he laughed: 'Twe, twe, twe.'"
   - Which words help you to imagine, or hear, the Sky God laughing? *twe, twe, twe*
   - What words would you use to stand for a character laughing? Possible answers: ha, ha, ha; hee, hee, hee
2. **Read aloud:**
   "He crept through the tall grasses, sora, sora, sora, till he came to the nest of Mmboro ..."
   - Which words did you hear repeated? *sora, sora, sora* What do these words stand for? the sound Ananse makes when he moves through the grass

3. **Read aloud:**
"The rest [of the water] he emptied over the hornet's nest and cried: 'It is raining, raining, raining.'"
    - Why does the author repeat the word *raining* three times? to make it stronger; to say it's raining very hard

4. **Read aloud:**
"'Thank you, thank you,' hummed the hornets, and they flew into the calabash—fom! Ananse quickly stopped the mouth of the gourd."
    - Which word helps you imagine the sound of Ananse quickly plugging the mouth of the gourd? *fom*

5. **Read aloud:**
"'Let go of my hand, or I'll slap you again.' Pa!"
    - Which word helps you hear the sound of the fairy slapping the doll, or Gum baby? *Pa*

6. **Read aloud:**
"'From this day and going on forever,' proclaimed the Sky God, 'my stories belong to Ananse and shall be called Spider Stories.' 'Eeeee, Eeeee, Eeeee,' shouted all the assembled nobles."
    - Which words do you hear repeated? *Eeeee, Eeeee, Eeeee* What do these words stand for? the sound of the nobles cheering

Review *A Story, A Story*

Lesson Overview

Offline *A Story, A Story* — 30 minutes

Get Ready	Words to Know
	Reread or Retell
Reading for Meaning	Characters and Their Actions in *A Story, A Story*
Making Connections	An A-Maze-ing Tale

Materials

Supplied

- *A Story, A Story*, retold by Gail E. Haley
- *K[12] Language Arts Activity Book*, p. LC 41

Keywords

character – a person or animal in a story

retelling – using your own words to tell a story that you have listened to or read

sequence – order

Big Ideas

Comprehension requires an understanding of story structure.

Offline 30 minutes

A Story, A Story

Work **together** with students to complete offline Get Ready, Reading for Meaning, and Making Connections activities.

Get Ready

Words to Know

Ask students to define the following words and use them in a sentence:

bind	**demand**	**reply**	**stir**
calabash	**hornet**	**scatter**	**stop**
captive			

Correct any incorrect or vague definitions.

Objectives

- Build vocabulary through listening, reading, and discussion.
- Use new vocabulary in written and spoken sentences.

Reread or Retell

If you'd like to, reread the story to students. Otherwise, have students retell the story using the pictures as a guide, or move on to the next activity.

Reading for Meaning

Characters and Their Actions in *A Story, A Story*

Tell students that you will discuss the characters in the story and how they act.

1. **Say:** To better understand characters' actions, it's helpful to think about our own actions in different situations. Answers to questions will vary.
   - Did you ever have to do a chore to get something you wanted? How did that make you feel? Do you think Ananse might have felt the same?
   - Did you ever give something of yours to another person? Why?
   - Why do you think Ananse gives the Sky God's stories to the world?
2. Remind students that the most important character in a story is called the main character, and the things characters do help us understand what they are like.

Objectives

- Activate prior knowledge by previewing text and/or discussing topic.
- Identify the main character(s).
- Describe character(s).
- Identify details that explain characters' actions.

3. **Ask students the following questions** to check understanding of characters and their actions.
   - Who is the main, or most important, character in the story? Ananse; the Spider Man
   - What words would you use to describe Ananse? Possible answers: brave; clever; tricky; generous Why did you pick these words? Give examples from the story. Answers may vary.
   - Why does Ananse ask the leopard to play a game with him? to trick the leopard so Ananse can tie him up
   - How does Ananse capture the hornets? He gets them to fly into a calabash.
   - Why does Ananse cover the doll he makes with sticky latex gum? to capture the fairy; to get the fairy stuck to it
   - How would you describe the Sky God? Possible answers: cheerful; asks for a lot; fair; like a king Why did you describe him this way? Give examples from the story. Answers may vary.

Making Connections

An A-Maze-ing Tale

Have students use their knowledge of the sequence of events in *A Story, A Story* to help them complete the maze on page LC 41 in *K[12] Language Arts Activity Book.*

1. Tell students that Ananse needs their help to find the path to the Sky God.
2. Explain to students that to complete the maze, they must draw a line to each creature in the same order in which Ananse captures them in the book.
3. Have students retell the story and explain how Ananse captures each creature.

Objectives

- Sequence events from a text.
- Retell read-aloud stories.

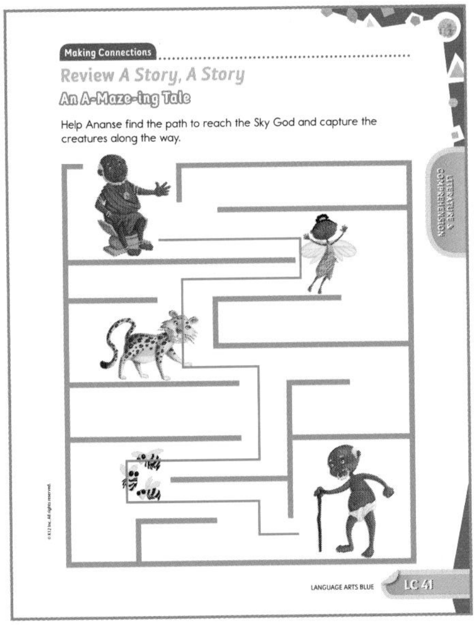

Introduce "Spider and Turtle and Good Manners"

Lesson Overview

Offline	"Spider and Turtle and Good Manners"	30 minutes
Get Ready	Stories with Morals	
	Words to Know	
Read Aloud	Book Walk	
	"Spider and Turtle and Good Manners"	
Check Your Reading	"Spider and Turtle and Good Manners"	

Advance Preparation

Read "Spider and Turtle and Good Manners" before beginning the Read Aloud activities, to locate Words to Know within the text.

Materials

Supplied

- "Spider and Turtle and Good Manners," *K[12] Read Aloud Treasury*, pp. 94–98

Story Synopsis

Spider pretends he's willing to share his dinner with the very hungry Turtle, but he really wants all the potatoes for himself. Turtle is tricked out of a good meal, but he still invites his ill-mannered host to dinner at his house. Little does Spider know that Turtle has every intention of getting even and teaching him a lesson about good manners.

Keywords

moral – the lesson of a story, particularly a fable

Offline 30 minutes

"Spider and Turtle and Good Manners"

Work **together** with students to complete offline Get Ready, Read Aloud, and Check Your Reading activities.

Get Ready

> **Objectives**
> - Identify the moral or lesson of a text.
> - Build vocabulary through listening, reading, and discussion.
> - Use new vocabulary in written and spoken sentences.

Stories with Morals

Introduce the idea of a story that has a moral.

1. Explain that a story can be written to teach a lesson. The characters in this kind of story are often animals that act like people.
2. Tell students that the lesson a story teaches is called a **moral**. One well-known moral is "honesty is the best policy," which means that it's always best to tell the truth.
3. Have students practice figuring out the moral of a story.
   Say: It was a hot day, and Frog was very thirsty because the marsh had dried up. He hopped around, looking for water, until he came upon a deep well. "I smell water!" he exclaimed. Without thinking, he jumped into the deep well to quench his thirst. And there he remained, trapped forever.
   - Does this story teach a lesson? Yes
   - What do we call the lesson that a story teaches? a moral
   - What do you think is the lesson, or moral, of this story? Answers will vary; guide students to recognize that the moral is "look before you leap" or "think before you act."

Words to Know

Before reading "Spider and Turtle and Good Manners,"

1. Have students say each word aloud.
2. Ask students if they know what each word means.
   - If students know a word's meaning, have them define it and use it in a sentence.
   - If students don't know a word's meaning, read them the definition and discuss the word with them.

blush – to become red in the face due to shame, embarrassment, or shyness
creek – a very small river
dainty – fine; delicate
manners – polite behavior
spell – a period of time
surface – the outside or flat top part of something

Read Aloud

Book Walk

Prepare students by taking them on a Book Walk of "Spider and Turtle and Good Manners." Scan the story together.

1. Turn to the **table of contents**. Help students find today's selection, and turn to that page.
2. Point to and read aloud the **title of the story**.
3. Have students look at the **pictures** of the story. Answers to questions may vary.
   - What do you think the story is about?
   - Where do you think the story takes place?
   - Did anyone ever ask you to share something, but you didn't want to? What did you do?
   - What is an example of good manners? What is an example of bad manners?

Objectives

- Make predictions based on title, illustrations, and/or context clues.
- Activate prior knowledge by previewing text and/or discussing topic.
- Listen and respond to texts representing a variety of cultures, time periods, and traditions.

"Spider and Turtle and Good Manners"

Now it's time to read the story. Have students sit next to you so that they can see the pictures and words while you read the story aloud.

Read aloud the entire story. Emphasize Words to Know as you come to them. If appropriate, use the pictures to help show what each word means. Tell students to listen carefully to hear the moral of the story.

Check Your Reading

"Spider and Turtle and Good Manners"

Have students retell the story in their own words to develop grammar, vocabulary, comprehension, and fluency skills. When finished, **ask students the following questions** to check comprehension and encourage discussion.

- What is the moral of the story? Good manners should help you be good, not bad.
- What does the moral mean? Answers may vary; guide students to understand that it's good manners to share your food with your guests, and it's bad manners to trick someone.
- What is Spider cooking for dinner when Turtle comes by? potatoes
- Where does Spider tell Turtle to wash his toenails? in the creek
- Where does Turtle live? at the bottom of the river
- What is Spider wearing when he visits Turtle? a coat

Objectives

- Identify the moral or lesson of a text.
- Answer questions requiring literal recall of details.

Explore "Spider and Turtle and Good Manners"

Lesson Overview

Offline	"Spider and Turtle and Good Manners"	30 minutes
Get Ready	Draw and Support a Conclusion	
	Words to Know	
Read Aloud	Book Walk	
	"Spider and Turtle and Good Manners"	
Check Your Reading	"Spider and Turtle and Good Manners"	
Reading for Meaning	Draw Conclusions in "Spider and Turtle and Good Manners"	

Materials

Supplied

- **"Spider and Turtle and Good Manners," *K[12] Read Aloud Treasury*, pp. 94–98**

Keywords

draw a conclusion – to make a decision about something not stated directly in a text by considering information provided and what you know from past experience

Advance Preparation

Before working with students, spend a few minutes reviewing Words to Know. Then review the Check Your Reading and Reading for Meaning activities to familiarize yourself with the questions and answers.

Big Ideas

Comprehension entails actively thinking about what is being read.

Offline 30 minutes

"Spider and Turtle and Good Manners"

Work **together** with students to complete offline Get Ready, Read Aloud, Check Your Reading, and Reading for Meaning activities.

Get Ready

Draw and Support a Conclusion

Introduce the idea of drawing and supporting a conclusion.

1. Tell students that sometimes an author doesn't tell us everything in the words of a story. Good readers look for clues in the words and pictures to help them figure out things such as what a character is thinking or why a character is doing something. Along with these clues, good readers think about what they know from personal experience. When readers do this, they **draw a conclusion.** A conclusion is based on what you read and see, together with your knowledge learned from personal experience.
2. Model how to draw and support a conclusion. **Read aloud:** Jerry opened his umbrella when he went outside for a walk.

   Say: Even though the sentence doesn't say that it's raining, I can draw the conclusion that it is. I can figure this out because Jerry opened his umbrella, and I know we use umbrellas to keep dry when it's raining.
3. Help students to draw and support a conclusion. **Read aloud:** Ramona put a bag of rabbit food in her shopping cart.
   - Why do you think Ramona put rabbit food in her shopping cart? She owns a rabbit.
   - How do you know this? People don't eat rabbit food, so it must be for her rabbit.

Objectives

- Draw conclusions using text, illustrations, and/or prior knowledge.
- Support conclusions using text, illustrations, and/or prior knowledge.
- Build vocabulary through listening, reading, and discussion.
- Use new vocabulary in written and spoken sentences.

Words to Know

Before reading "Spider and Turtle and Good Manners,"

1. Have students say each word aloud.
2. Ask students if they know what each word means.
   - If students know a word's meaning, have them define it and use it in a sentence.
   - If students don't know a word's meaning, read them the definition and discuss the word with them.

blush – to become red in the face due to shame, embarrassment, or shyness
creek – a very small river
dainty – fine; delicate
manners – polite behavior
spell – a period of time
surface – the outside or flat top part of something

Read Aloud

Book Walk

Prepare students by taking them on a Book Walk of "Spider and Turtle and Good Manners." Scan the story together to revisit the characters and events.

1. Turn to today's selection. Point to and read aloud the **title of the story**.
2. Have students look at the **pictures** of the story. Answers to questions may vary.
   - Why might Turtle have chosen to live at the bottom of a river?
   - Why might Spider have been wearing a coat when he goes to Turtle's house for dinner?

Objectives

- Draw conclusions using text, illustrations and/or prior knowledge.
- Listen and respond to texts representing a variety of cultures, time periods, and traditions.

"Spider and Turtle and Good Manners"

Now it's time to read the story. Have students sit next to you so that they can see the pictures and words while you read the story aloud.

Read aloud the entire story. Remind students that both the words and pictures give clues to help them understand parts of the story that aren't directly stated by the author.

Check Your Reading

"Spider and Turtle and Good Manners"

Have students retell the story in their own words to develop grammar, vocabulary, comprehension, and fluency skills. When finished, **ask students the following questions** to check comprehension and encourage discussion.

- Why is Turtle hungry at the beginning of the story? because he's been crawling all day long
- Why does Turtle crawl to Spider's camp? to ask Spider if he'll share his potatoes
- What does Spider tell Turtle to do to show that he has good manners? wash his dirty toenails
- Why is Spider hungry in the middle of the story? There's been a dry spell, and he can't catch any food.
- What does Turtle tell Spider to do to show that he has good manners? take off his coat before he has dinner
- What happens when Spider takes off his coat? He pops up to the surface of the river like a bubble.

Objectives

- Answer questions requiring literal recall of details.

Reading for Meaning

Draw Conclusions in "Spider and Turtle and Good Manners"

Remind students that sometimes they can figure out something the author doesn't state directly by using clues in the words and the pictures, along with thinking about their own experiences. **Ask the following questions** to check students' understanding of drawing and supporting a conclusion.

Objectives

- Draw conclusions using text, illustrations, and/or prior knowledge.
- Support conclusions using text, illustrations, and/or prior knowledge.

1. **Read aloud:**
   "Turtle said, 'I am so hungry. Can you share your potatoes with me?' 'Of course!' said Anansi. But he really wanted to keep all his potatoes for himself. On the outside, he smiled. Inside, he kept thinking and thinking."
   - Is Spider telling the truth when he says he'll share the potatoes? No
   - Why is Spider smiling on the outside? He wants Turtle to believe that he will share the potatoes.
   - What is Spider "thinking and thinking" about? how to trick Turtle so he can keep all the potatoes for himself
   - How do you know all this? The story says that Spider wants the potatoes for himself, and then he tricks Turtle into going to the creek so he can eat the potatoes while Turtle is gone.
2. **Read aloud:**
   "Turtle's toenails had gotten dirt in them again when he crawled back from the creek. Turtle blushed, and went back to wash again in the creek."
   - Why does Turtle blush? He's embarrassed that his toenails are dirty again.
   - How do you know? Answer may vary; guide students to think about a time when somebody pointed out a mistake they had made, and how it probably made them feel embarrassed.
3. **Read aloud:**
   "Well, Anansi. It's been a long time since I've seen you. Every time my stomach has growled, I have thought of you."
   - Why does Turtle think of Spider every time his stomach growls? because it makes him think of the time Spider tricked him out of a meal when he was hungry
4. Point to the picture of Spider putting pebbles in his pocket, and **read aloud:**
   "To sink, I'll fill the eight pockets on my coat with pebbles."
   - Why would putting pebbles in his pockets make Spider sink? the pebbles are heavy and will pull Spider down
5. Point to the picture of Spider holding on to the reed, and **read aloud:**
   "Spider popped up to the surface like a bubble. He grabbed a reed with two of his legs. He looked back down into the water. Turtle was laughing and enjoying his big meal all by himself."
   - Why is Turtle laughing? because he tricked Spider out of a meal, just like Spider had tricked him before

TIP Remember that *Anansi* and *Spider* are two names for the same character.

Review "Spider and Turtle and Good Manners"

Lesson Overview

Offline	"Spider and Turtle and Good Manners"	30 minutes
Get Ready	Words to Know	
	Reread or Retell	
Reading for Meaning	Spider and Turtle and Their Actions	
Making Connections	A Literary Progress Report	

Materials

Supplied

- "Spider and Turtle and Good Manners," *K[12] Read Aloud Treasury*, pp. 94–98
- *K[12] Language Arts Activity Book*, p. LC 42

Keywords

character – a person or animal in a story

Big Ideas

- Comprehension entails actively thinking about what is being read.
- Comprehension is facilitated when readers connect new information to information previously learned.

Offline 30 minutes

Spider and Turtle and Good Manners

Work **together** with students to complete offline Get Ready, Reading for Meaning, and Making Connections activities.

Get Ready

Words to Know

Ask students to define the following words and use them in a sentence:

blush	**dainty**	**spell**
creek	**manners**	**surface**

Correct any incorrect or vague definitions.

Objectives

- Build vocabulary through listening, reading, and discussion.
- Use new vocabulary in written and spoken sentences.

Reread or Retell

If you'd like to, reread the story to students. Otherwise, have students retell the story using the pictures as a guide, or move on to the next activity.

Reading for Meaning

Spider and Turtle and Their Actions

Tell students that you will be discussing the characters Spider and Turtle and how they act.

1. Tell students that to better understand characters' actions, it's helpful to think about our own actions in different situations. Answers to questions may vary.
   - Did you ever play a trick on someone? Why? How did it make you feel?
   - Do you think Spider felt the same way when he tricked Turtle?
2. **Ask students the following questions** to check ability to describe characters and their actions.
   - What words would you use to describe Spider? Possible answers: greedy; tricky; has bad manners Why did you pick these words? Give examples from the story. Answers will vary.
   - Why does Spider tell Turtle to wash his toenails in the creek? to trick Turtle out of eating his potatoes
   - Why does Spider laugh when Turtle leaves his camp without dinner? Answers will vary; guide students to understand that Spider is laughing because he tricked Turtle.
   - How would you describe Turtle? Possible answers: slow; patient; has good manners; clever Why did you describe him this way? Give examples from the story. Answers will vary.
   - Why does Turtle tell Spider to take off his coat? to trick him out of his dinner; because it will make him pop back up to the surface of the river

Objectives

- Make connections with text: text-to-text, text-to-self, text-to-world.
- Describe character(s).
- Identify details that explain characters' actions.

Making Connections

A Literary Progress Report

Have students use their knowledge of Spider in "Spider and Turtle and Good Manners" to help them complete the citizenship progress report on page LC 42 in K^{12} *Language Arts Activity Book.*

1. Tell students that they are going to help fill out a progress report that evaluates how Spider acts.
2. Read aloud what each "grade" represents.
3. Read aloud the first skill, the grade Spider received, and the comment that justifies the grade. Discuss why Spider received an "N" for the "Is honest" skill.
4. Read aloud the next skill, and write the grade that students conclude Spider should receive.
5. Have students explain why they assigned Spider that grade. Write students' explanation in the Comment column. Answers will vary; possible answers are shown.
6. Repeat Steps 4 and 5 for the next two skills on the progress report. Answers will vary; possible answers are shown.

Objectives

- Draw conclusions using text, illustrations and/or prior knowledge.
- Support conclusions using text, illustrations and/or prior knowledge.
- Describe character(s).

Making Connections

Review "Spider and Turtle and Good Manners"

A Literary Progress Report

Help grade Spider on his citizenship.

Aesop's Academy
Citizenship Progress Report

Student: Spider

G = Good   S = Satisfactory   N = Needs to improve

Skill	Grade	Comment
Is honest.	N	Spider didn't tell Turtle the truth when he said he was willing to share his potatoes.
Shows respect for others.	N	Spider tricked Turtle. Spider laughed at Turtle.
Is smart or clever.	G	Spider's trick was clever.
Has good manners.	N	Spider was selfish with his food.

LC 42 LANGUAGE ARTS BLUE

Introduce "The Wombat and the Kangaroo"

Unit Overview

In this unit, students will explore the theme of *A Visit to Australia* through the following reading selections:

- "The Wombat and the Kangaroo"
- "Go, Kangaroos, Go!"

Lesson Overview

Offline "The Wombat and the Kangaroo" **30 minutes**

Get Ready	The Purpose of Text
	Words to Know
Read Aloud	Book Walk
	"The Wombat and the Kangaroo"
Check Your Reading	"The Wombat and the Kangaroo"

Advance Preparation

Read "The Wombat and the Kangaroo" before beginning the Read Aloud activity, to locate Words to Know within the text.

Big Ideas

Comprehension entails actively thinking about what is being read.

Materials

Supplied

- **"The Wombat and the Kangaroo," K[12] *Read Aloud Treasury*, pp. 100–103**

Story Synopsis

"The Wombat and the Kangaroo" is a "how things came to be" story. In this case, we learn that kangaroos didn't always have a pouch and we discover what one particularly selfless mother kangaroo does to deserve one.

Keywords

author's purpose – the reason the author wrote a text: to entertain, to inform, to express an opinion, or to persuade

Offline 30 minutes

"The Wombat and the Kangaroo"

Work **together** with students to complete offline Get Ready, Read Aloud, and Check Your Reading activities.

Get Ready

The Purpose of Text

Introduce students to the reasons why an author writes a text.

1. Explain to students that an author writes a text for a certain reason, or **purpose**. Good readers can figure out the purpose of a text by asking questions.
   - Does the author give facts or explain something? If so, the author wrote the text to teach us something.
   - Does the author tell a made-up story with characters? If so, the author wrote the story to entertain us.
   - Does the author want us to believe something? If so, the author wrote the text to convince us, or to tell us his or her opinion.

   Sometimes an author writes for more than one reason. For example, an author can write a story to entertain but also to teach something.
2. Have students practice naming the purpose of a text.
   Say: Listen carefully as I read the title of a text and what it's about. "Roar Went the Dinosaur" is a story about Denny the Dinosaur, who likes to scare other animals with his loud roar.
   - This is a made-up story with characters. Why do you think the author wrote this story? to entertain us
   - At the end of the story, Denny the Dinosaur learns a lesson about manners. What might be another reason the author wrote the story? to teach us something

Objectives

- Identify the purpose of a text.
- Build vocabulary through listening, reading, and discussion.
- Use new vocabulary in written and spoken sentences.

Words to Know

Before reading "The Wombat and the Kangaroo,"

1. Have students say each word aloud.
2. Ask students if they know what each word means.
   - If students know a word's meaning, have them define it and use it in a sentence.
   - If students don't know a word's meaning, read them the definition and discuss the word with them.

burrow – a tunnel or hole in the ground dug by an animal
common sense – making good choices based on what you've learned from everyday life; for example, it's common sense to wear a jacket if it's cold outside
dilly bag – a small bag, often made of dried grass and used for carrying small things, such as food
marsupial – any kind of animal that has a pouch on the belly of the mother to carry her baby
selfless – to care about others more than yourself; unselfish
stubby – short and thick
tracks – the marks animals or people leave on the ground when they walk

Read Aloud

Book Walk

Prepare students by taking them on a Book Walk of "The Wombat and the Kangaroo." Scan the story together.

1. Turn to the **table of contents**. Help students find today's selection, and turn to that page.
2. Point to and read aloud the **title of the story**.
3. Have students look at the **pictures** of the story. Answers to questions may vary.
   - What do you think the story is about?
   - Where do you think the story takes place?
   - Do you think the wombat and the kangaroo are friends in the story?

Objectives

- Make predictions based on title, illustrations, and/or context clues.
- Listen and respond to texts representing a variety of cultures, time periods, and traditions.

"The Wombat and the Kangaroo"

Now it's time to read the story. Have students sit next to you so that they can see the pictures and words while you read the story aloud.

Read aloud the entire story. Emphasize Words to Know as you come to them. If appropriate, use the pictures to help show what each word means. Remind students to think about why the author wrote the story as they listen.

Check Your Reading

"The Wombat and the Kangaroo"

Have students retell the story in their own words to develop grammar, vocabulary, comprehension, and fluency skills. When finished, **ask students the following questions** to check comprehension and encourage discussion.

- Is this a made-up story with characters? Yes Why do you think the author wrote it? to entertain us
- Does the story also explain something? Yes Because it explains something, what might be another reason that the author wrote the story? to teach us something
- What does the story (attempt to) teach us? how animals like the kangaroo and the koala got a pouch
- What makes the mother kangaroo and her joey wake up at the beginning of the story? someone moaning; a lonely wombat
- How does the mother kangaroo help the wombat get to the spear grass? She has him hold on to her tail while she hops.
- Why does the mother kangaroo tell the wombat to run? because she sees a hunter sneaking up on him
- Why does the god Byamee give the mother kangaroo a pouch? because she had the kindest heart; because she takes care of others

Objectives

- Identify the purpose of a text.
- Answer questions requiring literal recall of details.

Explore "The Wombat and the Kangaroo"

Lesson Overview

Offline	"The Wombat and the Kangaroo"	30 minutes
Get Ready	Use Context Clues to Understand Unknown Words	
	Words to Know	
Read Aloud	Book Walk	
	"The Wombat and the Kangaroo"	
Check Your Reading	"The Wombat and the Kangaroo"	
Reading for Meaning	Use Context Clues in "The Wombat and the Kangaroo"	

Materials

Supplied

- "The Wombat and the Kangaroo," K[12] *Read Aloud Treasury*, pp. 100–103

Keywords

context – the parts of a sentence or passage surrounding a word

context clue – a word or phrase in a text that helps you figure out the meaning of an unknown word

Advance Preparation

Before working with students, spend a few minutes reviewing Words to Know. Then review the Check Your Reading and Reading for Meaning activities to familiarize yourself with the questions and answers.

Big Ideas

Early learners acquire vocabulary through active exposure (by talking and listening, being read to, and receiving explicit instruction).

Offline 30 minutes

"The Wombat and the Kangaroo"

Work **together** with students to complete offline Get Ready, Read Aloud, Check Your Reading, and Reading for Meaning activities.

Get Ready

Use Context Clues to Understand Unknown Words

Explore the idea that the surrounding **words and pictures provide context clues to help define unknown words in a story**.

1. Turn to page 101 of "The Wombat and the Kangaroo." Show students the picture of the wombat holding on to the kangaroo's tail.
   Say: The story is about a wombat. But, I don't know what the word *wombat* means.
2. Model how to use clues to figure out what a word means.
   Say: The text tells us that the wombat grabbed the mother kangaroo's tail. So I know that when I look at the picture I can try to figure out what a wombat is by looking at the animal that is holding on to the kangaroo's tail. Now I need to look carefully at the animal in the picture.
   - What clue in this picture can help us figure out what the word *wombat* means? There's a small, furry animal with short legs holding on to the kangaroo's tail, so a *wombat* must be some kind of little, furry animal with short legs.

Objectives

- Identify and use context clues to define words.
- Identify and use picture clues to define words.
- Build vocabulary through listening, reading, and discussion.
- Use new vocabulary in written and spoken sentences.

Words to Know

Before reading "The Wombat and the Kangaroo,"

1. Have students say each word aloud.
2. Ask students if they know what each word means.
   - If students know a word's meaning, have them define it and use it in a sentence.
   - If students don't know a word's meaning, read them the definition and discuss the word with them.

burrow – a tunnel or hole in the ground dug by an animal
common sense – making good choices based on what you've learned from everyday life; for example, it's common sense to wear a jacket if it's cold outside
dilly bag – a small bag, often made of dried grass and used for carrying small things, such as food
marsupial – any kind of animal that has a pouch on the belly of the mother to carry her baby
selfless – to care about others more than yourself; unselfish
stubby – short and thick
tracks – the marks animals or people leave on the ground when they walk

Read Aloud

Book Walk

Prepare students by taking them on a Book Walk of "The Wombat and the Kangaroo." Scan the story together to revisit the characters and events.

1. Turn to today's selection. Point to and read aloud the **title of the story**.
2. Have students look at the **pictures** of the story. Answers to questions may vary.
   - What are some things you know about the mother kangaroo?
   - What are some things you know about the wombat?

Objectives

- Activate prior knowledge by previewing text and/or discussing topic.
- Listen and respond to texts representing a variety of cultures, time periods, and traditions.

"The Wombat and the Kangaroo"

Now it's time to read the story. Have students sit next to you so that they can see the pictures and words while you read the story aloud.

Read aloud the entire story. Tell students to listen carefully to the words before and after an unknown word or phrase to help figure out what it means. Remind them to follow along and look for clues in the pictures, as well.

Check Your Reading

"The Wombat and the Kangaroo"

Have students retell the story in their own words. When finished, **ask the following questions** to check students' ability to use words and pictures at the same time as context clues.

1. Point to the picture on page 102, and **read aloud**: "The joey was still asleep under the gum tree."
   - What is a *joey*? a baby kangaroo
   - What clues are in the sentence? Guide students to recognize that the words "asleep under the gum tree" tell us where to look in the picture for a clue.
   - What do you see in the picture that gives you a clue? the little kangaroo sleeping under the tree
2. Point to the picture of the mother kangaroo with the joey in her pouch on page 103, and **read aloud**: "The kangaroo mother was very happy with her new pouch. She was so happy that she put her joey in it!"
   - What is a *pouch*? a pocket on the belly of a kangaroo
   - What word clues are in the sentences? Guide students to recognize that the words "she put her joey in it" tell the reader what to look for in the picture.
   - What do you see in the picture that gives you a clue? the joey sitting in it

Objectives

- Identify and use context clues to define words.
- Identify and use picture clues to define words.

Reading for Meaning

Use Context Clues in "The Wombat and the Kangaroo"

Remind students that sometimes they can discover the meaning of an unknown word by reading the words that surround it in the story.

Objectives

- Identify and use context clues to define words.
- Identify and use picture clues to define words.

1. **Read aloud** from page 100: "The joey fell asleep. The mother fell asleep, too. Suddenly they were both startled by a sad moan . . . The mother kangaroo looked around."
   - What does *suddenly* mean? all at once; quickly
   - What clues are in the sentences? Guide students to recognize that first the kangaroos are asleep, and then the mother wakes up and looks around because she hears a sad moan. This tells us something made her wake up all at once or quickly.
2. **Read aloud** from page 100: "[The hunter] had spotted the wombat and was sneaking up on him."
   - What does *spotted* mean? saw
   - What word clues are in the sentences? Guide students to recognize that the words "sneaking up on him" tell us that the hunter had to see the wombat first.
3. **Read aloud** from page 100: "'Run, friend wombat, run!' she hollered."
   Say: In this part of the story, the hunter is sneaking up on the wombat.
   - Why is the mother kangaroo telling the wombat to run? She's warning him. Do you think she would say this in a normal voice or in a loud voice? loud
   - Knowing that she probably said it in a loud voice, what do you think the word *hollered* means? shouted; yelled
4. **Read aloud** from page 102: "The kangaroo hopped out of the burrow and hopped as fast as she could back to her joey . . . She caught her breath while he finished his nap."
   - What does *caught her breath* mean? rested for a moment until she could breathe regularly again
   - What word clues are in the sentences? Guide students to recognize that the words "hopped as fast as she could" tell us that the kangaroo was breathing hard. They know this from personal experience.
5. **Read aloud** from page 102: "She hid there and saw the hunter run by. Then she saw the hunter turn around and run the other way. And then she saw the hunter run the first way again. 'He's going in two directions, like me!' she thought."
   - What does *going in two directions* mean? going back and forth
   - What word clues are in the sentences? Guide students to recognize that the words "she . . . saw the hunter run by" followed by "run the other way" and "then she saw the hunter run the first way again" tell us that the hunter is running back and forth.

Review "The Wombat and the Kangaroo"

Lesson Overview

Offline	"The Wombat and the Kangaroo"	30 minutes
Get Ready	Words to Know	
	Reread or Retell	
Reading for Meaning	Recognize Fiction Stories	
Making Connections	A Picture's Worth a Thousand Words	

Materials

Supplied

- "The Wombat and the Kangaroo," *K*[12] *Read Aloud Treasury*, pp. 100–103
- *K*[12] *Language Arts Activity Book*, p. LC 43

Keywords

fiction – make-believe stories

nonfiction – writings about true things

Big Ideas

- Comprehension requires an understanding of story structure.
- Early learners acquire vocabulary through active exposure (by talking and listening, being read to, and receiving explicit instruction).

Offline 30 minutes

"The Wombat and the Kangaroo"

Work **together** with students to complete offline Get Ready, Reading for Meaning, and Making Connections activities.

Get Ready

Words to Know

Ask students to define the following words and use them in a sentence:

burrow
common sense
dilly bag
marsupial
selfless
stubby
tracks

Correct any incorrect or vague definitions.

Objectives

- Build vocabulary through listening, reading, and discussion.
- Use new vocabulary in written and spoken sentences.

Reread or Retell

If you'd like to, reread the story to students. Otherwise, have students retell the story using the pictures as a guide, or move on to the next activity.

Reading for Meaning

Recognize Fiction Stories

Explore characteristics of fiction texts.

1. Tell students that a make-believe story is called **fiction**. This is different from nonfiction writing, which is about true things. Good readers can tell that a story is fiction, or make-believe, if things in the story (such as talking animals) couldn't happen in real life.
2. **Ask students the following questions** to check their ability to distinguish fiction text from nonfiction text and their general comprehension of the story.
   - Is "The Wombat and the Kangaroo" a real story or a made-up story? made-up How can you tell? Possible answers: the animals talk; the wombat is a god What do we call a made-up story? fiction
   - Point to the picture of the kangaroo and wombat on page 101. What clue in the picture helps you know this story is make-believe? The animals are wearing clothes; the wombat is wearing glasses.
   - Why does the wombat want to give the kangaroo mother a gift? Possible answers: She's kind to him; she's a good mother who helps everybody around her.
   - What does the wombat give the kangaroo mother? a pouch
   - What does the kangaroo mother ask the wombat to do after she gets a pouch? to give one to all of her other animal friends that make good choices

Objectives

- Identify different types of text.
- Distinguish fiction text from nonfiction text.
- Answer questions requiring literal recall of details.

Making Connections

A Picture's Worth a Thousand Words

Help students use their knowledge of word meanings in "The Wombat and the Kangaroo" to match the words with real-life situations on page LC 43 in *K¹² Language Arts Activity Book.*

1. Have students look at the pictures on the Actvity Book page.
2. In row 1, have students circle the picture that shows someone who is using common sense. If students have trouble remembering the meaning of *common sense,* review the definition with them.
3. In row 2, have students circle the picture that shows someone who could use a pouch.
4. In row 3, have students circle the picture that shows someone leaving tracks.
5. Have students explain their choices by describing what they see in the pictures they circled.

Objectives

- Increase concept and content vocabulary.
- Build vocabulary through listening, reading, and discussion.
- Demonstrate understanding through drawing, discussion, and/or writing.

Making Connections

Review "The Wombat and the Kangaroo"

A Picture's Worth a Thousand Words

Circle the picture that answers the question.

1. Which person is using common sense?
2. Which person could use a pouch?
3. Which person is leaving tracks?

LITERATURE & COMPREHENSION

LANGUAGE ARTS BLUE LC 43

Introduce "Go, Kangaroos, Go!"

Lesson Overview

Offline "Go, Kangaroos, Go!" 30 minutes

Get Ready	Learn to Read for Meaning
	Words to Know
Read Aloud	Book Walk
	"Go, Kangaroos, Go!"
Check Your Reading	"Go, Kangaroos, Go!"

Advance Preparation

Read "Go, Kangaroos, Go!" before beginning the Read Aloud activity, to locate Words to Know within the text.

Review the KWL chart on page LC 44 in *K[12] Language Arts Activity Book*. Keep the chart handy for use during Get Ready and Read Aloud activities.

Big Ideas

- Comprehension entails having and knowing a purpose for reading.
- Comprehension entails asking and answering questions about the text.
- Self-questioning improves comprehension and ensures that reading is an interactive process.
- Comprehension is facilitated when readers connect new information to information previously learned.
- Comprehension strategies can be taught through explicit instruction.

Materials

Supplied

- "Go, Kangaroos, Go!," *Animals Around the World*, pp. 24–29
- *K[12] Language Arts Activity Book*, p. LC 44

Story Synopsis

Long considered a symbol of the land "down under," kangaroos are arguably one of the most unusual-looking animals on the planet. These giant marsupials—best known for carrying their young in pouches—can jump over a car, out-hop a dingo, and go for a week without a sip of water!

Keywords

graphic organizer – a visual tool used to show relationships between key concepts; formats include webs, diagrams, and charts

prior knowledge – things you already know from past experience

Offline 30 minutes

"Go, Kangaroos, Go!"

Work **together** with students to complete offline Get Ready, Read Aloud, and Check Your Reading activities.

Get Ready

Learn to Read for Meaning

Introduce students to prereading activities and reading for a specific purpose. Turn to page LC 44 in *K*[12] *Language Arts Activity Book*.

1. **Say:** This is called a KWL chart. It will help us get ready to read. It will also help us organize our thoughts on what we want to know.
2. Point to the K column.
   Say: The *K* stands for "know." Good readers ask, "What do I already **know** about this subject?" before they read an article.
   - Thinking about what we already know helps us get our brain ready to learn more about the subject.
3. Point to the W column.
   Say: The *W* stands for "want." Good readers ask, "What do I **want** to know, or wonder, about this subject?" before they read an article.
   - Good readers ask questions and then look for the answers while they read. Looking for the answers is our **purpose** for reading this article.
   - Asking questions arouses our curiosity and motivates us to read.
4. Point to the L column.
   Say: The *L* stands for "learn." Good readers write down what they **learn** after they read an article.
5. Tell students that before they read "Go, Kangaroos, Go!" they will work on the K and W columns of the chart. They will complete the L column after they read.

Objectives

- Demonstrate understanding through graphic organizers.
- Identify purpose for reading text.
- Generate literal level questions.
- Increase concept and content vocabulary.
- Use new vocabulary in written and spoken sentences.

Words to Know

Before reading "Go, Kangaroos, Go!,"

1. Have students say each word aloud.
2. Ask students if they know what each word means.
   - If students know a word's meaning, have them define it and use it in a sentence.
   - If students don't know a word's meaning, read them the definition and discuss the word with them.

dingo – a wild dog that lives in Australia
joey – a baby or young kangaroo
mob – a group of kangaroos
pouch – a pocket on the belly of a female kangaroo

Read Aloud

Book Walk

Gather the KWL chart on page LC 44 in *K[12] Language Arts Activity Book*. Prepare students by taking them on a Book Walk of "Go, Kangaroos, Go!" Scan the magazine article together, and ask students to make predictions about the text. Answers to questions may vary.

1. Turn to the **table of contents.** Help students find today's selection, and turn to that page.
2. Point to and read aloud the **title of the article**.
3. Have students look at the **pictures** in the article.
   - What do you already know about kangaroos? [Write each fact in the K column of the KWL chart.]
   - Name at least three things that you wonder about or want to learn about kangaroos. [Write what students dictate in the W column of the chart.]

   If students have difficulty thinking of things they'd like to learn, suggest one or more of the following questions: What do kangaroos eat? How far can they jump in one hop? How high they can jump?
4. Point to and read aloud any **headers, captions, or other features** that stand out.
   - What do you think the article might tell us about kangaroos?
5. Keep the Activity Book page handy so students can complete it later.

Objectives

- Activate prior knowledge by previewing text and/or discussing topic.
- Make predictions based on title, illustrations, and/or context clues.
- Read and listen to a variety of texts for information and pleasure independently or as part of a group.
- Demonstrate understanding through graphic organizers.
- Identify purpose for reading text.
- Generate literal level questions.

"Go, Kangaroos, Go!"

Now it's time to read the article. Have students sit next to you so that they can see the pictures and words while you read the article aloud.

Read aloud the entire article. Emphasize Words to Know as you come to them. If appropriate, use the pictures to help show what each word means.

Check Your Reading

"Go, Kangaroos, Go!"

Have students retell the article in their own words to develop grammar, vocabulary, comprehension, and fluency skills. When finished, **ask students the following questions** to check comprehension and encourage discussion.

- How far can a kangaroo jump? about 30 feet
- Why can a kangaroo jump so far? It has strong back legs.
- Where does a mother kangaroo keep her baby? in her pouch
- What kind of animal likes to hunt kangaroos? dingo

Objectives

- Answer questions requiring literal recall of details.

Explore "Go, Kangaroos, Go!"

Lesson Overview

Offline	"Go, Kangaroos, Go!"	30 minutes
Get Ready	Read to Find Answers	
	Words to Know	
Read Aloud	Book Walk	
	"Go, Kangaroos, Go!"	
Check Your Reading	"Go, Kangaroos, Go!"	
Reading for Meaning	What Did I Learn?	

Materials

Supplied

- "Go, Kangaroos, Go!," *Animals Around the World*, pp. 24–29
- *K*[12] *Language Arts Activity Book*, p. LC 44

Keywords

graphic organizer – a visual tool used to show relationships between key concepts; formats include webs, diagrams, and charts

Advance Preparation

Before working with students, spend a few minutes reviewing Words to Know. Then review the Check Your Reading activity to familiarize yourself with the questions and answers. Review the Reading for Meaning activity to familiarize yourself with the process for completing the KWL chart on page LC 44 in *K*[12] *Language Arts Activity Book*.

Big Ideas

- Comprehension entails having and knowing a purpose for reading.
- Comprehension entails asking and answering questions about the text.
- Self-questioning improves comprehension and ensures that reading is an interactive process.
- Comprehension is facilitated when readers connect new information to information previously learned.
- Comprehension strategies can be taught through explicit instruction.

Offline 30 minutes

"Go, Kangaroos, Go!"

Work **together** with students to complete offline Get Ready, Read Aloud, and Check Your Reading, and Reading for Meaning activities.

Get Ready

Read to Find Answers

Prepare students to read a text for a specific purpose. Turn to the KWL chart on page LC 44 in *K[12] Language Arts Activity Book.*

1. Refresh students' memories of what they already knew about kangaroos by reading what's written in the K column.
2. Remind students that they are reading the article to answer their questions about kangaroos. This is their reason, or **purpose**, for reading.
3. Read aloud the questions written in the W column.
4. Explain that the answers to some of these questions might not be in the article. However, thinking about the questions will help students listen carefully to the article and better remember the information they hear.
5. Tell students that they will fill in the last column of the chart after listening to the article again.

Objectives

- Demonstrate understanding through graphic organizers.
- Identify purpose for reading text.
- Increase concept and content vocabulary.
- Use new vocabulary in written and spoken sentences.

Words to Know

Before reading "Go, Kangaroos, Go!,"

1. Have students say each word aloud.
2. Ask students if they know what each word means.
   - If students know a word's meaning, have them define it and use it in a sentence.
   - If students don't know a word's meaning, read them the definition and discuss the word with them.

dingo – a wild dog that lives in Australia
joey – a baby or young kangaroo
mob – a group of kangaroos
pouch – a pocket on the belly of a female kangaroo

Read Aloud

Book Walk

Prepare students by taking them on a Book Walk of "Go, Kangaroos, Go!" Scan the magazine article together to revisit the text.

1. Turn to today's selection.
2. Point to and read aloud the **title of the article**.
3. Have students look at the **pictures** in the article. Answers to questions may vary.
   - Which picture do you like most?
   - What does the picture show?

Objectives

- Activate prior knowledge by previewing text and/or discussing topic.
- Read and listen to a variety of texts for information and pleasure independently or as part of a group.

"Go, Kangaroos, Go!"

Now it's time to read the article. Have students sit next to you so that they can see the pictures and words while you read the article aloud.

Read aloud the entire article. Remind students to listen for answers to the questions in the W column of the KWL chart.

TIP If students interrupt your reading because they hear an answer to one of their questions, be sure to praise them for their careful listening. You can either write the answer in the KWL chart immediately or wait until you have finished reading the article. Choose the method that you feel will best maintain students' interest.

Check Your Reading

"Go, Kangaroos, Go!"

Have students retell the article in their own words to develop grammar, vocabulary, comprehension, and fluency skills. When finished, **ask students the following questions** to check understanding of the purpose of reading the article, as well as basic comprehension.

- Why did we read this article? to learn about kangaroos; to find answers to our questions about kangaroos
- How do kangaroos get from one place to another? They hop.
- How does a kangaroo use its tail? to keep from tipping over
- What does a mother kangaroo keep in her pouch? her joey; her baby kangaroo
- What do you call a bunch of kangaroos that hop around together? a mob

Objectives

- Identify purpose for reading text.
- Answer questions requiring literal recall of details.

Reading for Meaning

What Did I Learn?

Have students use the KWL chart to record answers to the questions they previously generated. Turn to page LC 44 in *K[12] Language Arts Activity Book*.

1. Read aloud the first question written in the W column.
   - Ask students if they heard the answer in the article. If students know the answer, write it in the L column of the chart across from the question.
   - If the answer is in the article but students cannot remember it, return to the article and help students locate the answer. Then write it in the L column across from the question.
   - If the answer to the question is not in the article, remind students that we don't always find the answers to our questions in the articles we read. But asking the questions still helps us become better readers because it helps us to read or listen carefully to a text. Leave the area across from the unanswered question blank.
2. Repeat Step 1 for each of the remaining questions in the W column.
3. After the last question is answered, have students tell any additional facts that they learned about kangaroos from reading the article, and write them at the end of the L column.
4. Keep the KWL chart handy so students can use it to do more research later.

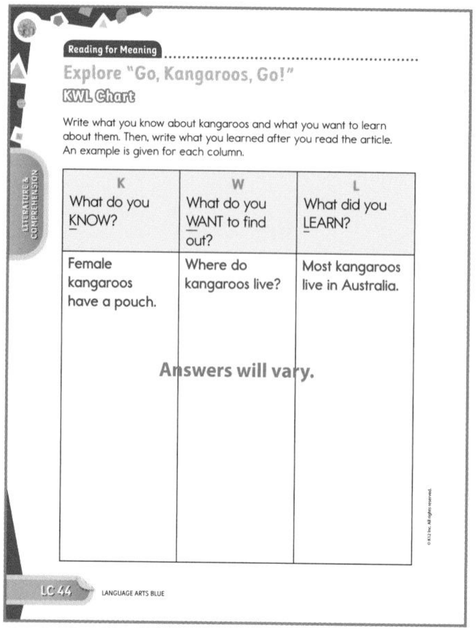

Reading for Meaning

Explore "Go, Kangaroos, Go!"

KWL Chart

Write what you know about kangaroos and what you want to learn about them. Then, write what you learned after you read the article. An example is given for each column.

K What do you KNOW?	W What do you WANT to find out?	L What did you LEARN?
Female kangaroos have a pouch.	Where do kangaroos live?	Most kangaroos live in Australia.

Answers will vary.

LC 44 LANGUAGE ARTS BLUE

Objectives

- Demonstrate understanding through graphic organizers.
- Seek information in provided sources to answer questions.

Review "Go, Kangaroos, Go!"

Lesson Overview

Offline	"Go, Kangaroos, Go!"	30 minutes
Get Ready	Words to Know	
	Reread or Retell	
Reading for Meaning	Distinguish Fiction from Nonfiction	
Making Connections	Jump for It!	
Beyond the Lesson	OPTIONAL: Seek and Find	

Materials

Supplied

- "Go, Kangaroos, Go!," *Animals Around the World*, pp. 24–29
- *K[12] Language Arts Activity Book*, p. LC 44

Also Needed

- tape, masking
- yardstick
- crayons
- paper, drawing

Keywords

fact – something that can be proven true

fiction – make-believe stories

nonfiction – writings about true things

Advance Preparation

Gather the KWL chart from page LC 44 in *K[12] Language Arts Activity Book.*

Big Ideas

Comprehension entails asking and answering questions about text.

Offline 30 minutes

"The Go, Kangaroos, Go!"

Work **together** with students to complete offline Get Ready, Reading for Meaning, Making Connections, and Beyond the Lesson activities.

Get Ready

Words to Know

Ask students to define the following words and use them in a sentence:

dingo **mob**
joey **pouch**

Correct any incorrect or vague definitions.

Objectives

- Use new vocabulary in written and spoken sentences.
- Increase concept and content vocabulary.

Reread or Retell

If you'd like to, reread the story to students. Otherwise, have students retell the story using the pictures as a guide, or move on to the next activity.

Reading for Meaning

Distinguish Fiction from Nonfiction

Explore characteristics of nonfiction texts.

Objectives

- Identify different types of text.
- Distinguish fiction text from nonfiction text.
- Compare and contrast informational text and literary text.

1. Tell students that a text about real things is called **nonfiction**. This is different from fiction writing, which is about made-up characters and events. Good readers can tell that a text is nonfiction, or about real things, if it tells facts about real-life things, such as the fact that kangaroos live in Australia.
2. **Ask students the following questions** to check their ability to distinguish nonfiction text from fiction stories, and their general comprehension of the article.
   - Is "Go, Kangaroos, Go!" about real or made-up things? real things How can you tell? It tells facts, or real things, about kangaroos. What do we call a text like this article about kangaroos? nonfiction
   - Think about the story "The Wombat and the Kangaroo." How are that story and the article "Go, Kangaroos, Go!" the same? Possible answers: They both have kangaroos in them; they both have joeys; they both have kangaroos that hop around.
   - How are they different? Possible answers: The kangaroos in the story are make-believe and can talk, but the kangaroos in the article are real and can't talk; the kangaroo in the story gets a pouch as a gift, but the kangaroos in the article already have pouches; the kangaroos in the story wear clothes, but the kangaroos in the article just have fur.

Making Connections

Jump for It!

Have students see how far they can jump compared to a kangaroo.

1. Tape a 12-inch strip of masking tape to the ground.
2. Lay the yardstick vertically against the edge of the tape strip.
3. Ask students to predict how far they think they can jump in one hop.
4. Have students line up their toes against the edge of the strip and jump from a standing position, using both feet.
5. Measure and record the distance that each student jumps.
6. Discuss how much farther a kangaroo can jump.
   - If students don't recall the distance a kangaroo can jump in one hop, help them look it up in the article, "Go, Kangaroos, Go!" or the KWL chart that they completed on page LC 44 in the *K[12] Language Arts Activity Book*.
7. Demonstrate how far 30 feet is by going outside, and laying the yardstick on the ground and flipping it over end-to-end 10 times.
8. Remind students that a kangaroo can also jump high enough to leap over a car.
9. Have students draw a picture of what they would like to jump over if they were a kangaroo.

Objectives

- Make connections with text: text-to-text, text-to-self, text-to-world.
- Respond to text through art, writing, and/or drama.
- Create illustrations that represent personal connections to text.

Beyond the Lesson

OPTIONAL: Seek and Find

This activity is intended for students who have extra time and would benefit from further research on kangaroos. Feel free to skip this activity.

1. Gather the KWL chart from page LC 44 in the *K[12] Language Arts Activity Book*.
2. Help students look for answers to their unanswered questions about kangaroos on their KWL charts. Use one or more of the following sources:
   - Encyclopedias
   - Science magazines, such as *National Geographic Kids*
   - Nonfiction library books about kangaroos
   - The Internet, using the search words "kangaroo facts"
3. If students find an answer, write it in the L column across from the question in the W column of the KWL chart.
4. If students find additional information about kangaroos that they find interesting, write these facts at the end of the L column in the chart.

Objectives

- Seek information in provided sources to answer questions.
- Demonstrate understanding through graphic organizers.

Introduce "Insects of the Rain Forest"

Unit Overview

In this unit, students will explore the theme of *Creature Features* through the following reading selections:

- "Insects of the Rain Forest"
- *Tikki Tikki Tembo*
- "The Story of Chicken Little"

Lesson Overview

Offline	"Insects of the Rain Forest"	30 minutes
Get Ready	Identify the Main Idea	
	Words to Know	
Read Aloud	Book Walk	
	"Insects of the Rain Forest"	
Check Your Reading	"Insects of the Rain Forest"	

Advance Preparation

Read "Insects of the Rain Forest" before beginning the Read Aloud activity, to locate Words to Know within the text.

Big Ideas

Comprehension entails an understanding of the organizational patterns of text.

Materials

Supplied

- "Insects of the Rain Forest," *Animals Around the World*, pp. 30–35

Story Synopsis

The Amazon rain forest is teeming with life, including thousands of types of rare and unusual insects. Some have horns, some blend in with the background, and some eat leaf fungus. One thing is certain—they're all unique!

Keywords

main idea – the most important idea in a paragraph or text

supporting detail – a detail that gives more information about a main idea

Offline 30 minutes

"Insects of the Rain Forest"

Work **together** with students to complete offline Get Ready, Read Aloud, and Check Your Reading activities.

Get Ready

Identify the Main Idea

Explore identifying the main idea with students.

1. Tell students that they are going to read an article called "Insects of the Rain Forest." There are several paragraphs in the article. **Each paragraph has a main idea, or is mostly about one thing.** Good readers listen carefully so they can figure out what a paragraph is mostly about.
2. **Read aloud** the following paragraph, and then model how to determine the main idea:
   The Amazon River is the longest river in South America. Over 3,000 different kinds of fish live in it. There is more water in the Amazon River than any other river in the world.
   Say: The paragraph mentions things like fish, water, and South America, but all of these things are information about the Amazon River. **The paragraph is mostly about the Amazon River.**
3. **Read aloud** the following paragraph, and then ask the question for student practice:
   The piranha is a fish that lives in the Amazon River. It has many sharp, pointed teeth. People who live near the Amazon River like to catch and eat this fish.
   - Which of the following tells what the paragraph is mostly about, the main idea? (a) Piranhas have teeth; (b) People like to eat piranhas; (c) The piranha is a type of fish. (c) The piranha is a type of fish.
   - Why do you think answer C is correct? Guide students to recognize that each sentence gives information about piranhas, so the paragraph is mostly about piranhas.

TIP *Piranha* is pronounced "puh-RAH-nuh."

Objectives

- Identify the main idea.
- Increase concept and content vocabulary.
- Use new vocabulary in written and spoken sentences.

Words to Know

Before reading "Insects of the Rain Forest,"

1. Have students say each word aloud.
2. Ask students if they know what each word means.
   - If students know a word's meaning, have them define it and use it in a sentence.
   - If students don't know a word's meaning, read them the definition and discuss the word with them.

Amazon rain forest – the world's largest tropical rain forest
sap – the liquid inside a plant
twig – a small, thin branch
unusual – different; something you don't see very often

Read Aloud

Book Walk

Prepare students by taking them on a Book Walk of "Insects of the Rain Forest." Scan the magazine article together, and ask students to make predictions about the text. Answers to questions may vary.

1. Turn to the **table of contents**. Help students find today's selection, and turn to that page.
2. Point to and read aloud the **title of the article**.
3. Have students look at the **pictures** in the article.
   - What do you think the article is about?
   - What kinds of insects do you think live in the Amazon rain forest?
4. Point to and read aloud any **headers, captions, or other features** that stand out.
   - What do you think the article might tell us about insects that live in the Amazon rain forest?

Objectives

- Make predictions based on title, illustrations, and/or context clues.
- Read and listen to a variety of texts for information and pleasure independently or as part of a group.

"Insects of the Rain Forest"

Now it's time to read the article. Have students sit next to you so that they can see the pictures and words while you read the article aloud. Tell students to listen carefully so they can discover what each paragraph is mostly about.

Read aloud the entire article. Emphasize Words to Know as you come to them. If appropriate, use the pictures to help show what each word means.

Check Your Reading

"Insects of the Rain Forest"

Have students retell the article in their own words to develop grammar, vocabulary, comprehension, and fluency skills. When finished, **ask students the following questions** to check ability to identify or state the main idea of a paragraph.

1. **Read aloud** the last paragraph on page 30.
   - Which of the following sentences tells what the paragraph is mostly about? (a) Insects are pesky; (b) There are thousands of insects in the Amazon rain forest; (c) Insects crawl, hop, and fly. (b) There are thousands of insects in the Amazon rain forest.
2. **Read aloud** the first paragraph on page 33.
   - What is the paragraph mostly about? the rhinoceros beetle's horn
3. **Read aloud** the second paragraph on page 34.
   - Which of the following sentences tells what the paragraph is mostly about? (a) Leaf-cutter ants spend all day cutting up and carrying leaves; (b) Leaf-cutter ants have sharp mouths. (a) Leaf-cutter ants spend all day cutting up and carrying leaves.

Objectives

- Identify the main idea.
- State the main idea of a text.

Explore "Insects of the Rain Forest"

Lesson Overview

Offline "Insects of the Rain Forest" 30 minutes

Get Ready	Details Support the Main Idea
	Words to Know
Read Aloud	Book Walk
	"Insects of the Rain Forest"
Check Your Reading	"Insects of the Rain Forest"
Reading for Meaning	Support the Main Idea with Details

Materials

Supplied

- "Insects of the Rain Forest," *Animals Around the World*, pp. 30–35

Keywords

main idea – the most important idea in a paragraph or text

self-monitor – to notice if you do or do not understand what you are reading

supporting detail – a detail that gives more information about a main idea

Advance Preparation

Before working with students, spend a few minutes reviewing Words to Know. Then review the Check Your Reading activity to familiarize yourself with the questions and answers.

Big Ideas

- Comprehension entails an understanding of the organizational patterns of text.
- Comprehension requires the reader to self-monitor understanding.

Offline 30 minutes

"Insects of the Rain Forest"

Work **together** with students to complete offline Get Ready, Read Aloud, Check Your Reading, and Reading for Meaning activities.

Get Ready

Details Support the Main Idea

Remind students that **every paragraph in an article has a main idea**. The main idea is what a paragraph is mostly about. The other information in a paragraph tells other things, or **details,** about the main idea. The details in a paragraph help readers better understand the main idea.

1. **Read aloud** the following paragraph:
   The macaw is a bird that lives in the Amazon rain forest. It has a big, curved beak and makes loud, squawking noises. A macaw has bright blue, green, yellow, or red feathers. This bird likes to eat things such as fruit, nuts, and insects.
2. Tell students that this paragraph is about a bird called a macaw. That is the main idea of the paragraph. The other things in the paragraph are details about the macaw.
   - What is the paragraph mostly about? a bird called a macaw
   - Name a bit of information, or a detail, about a macaw. Possible answers: big, curved beak; makes loud, squawking noises; has bright feathers; eats things like fruit, nuts, and insects
3. If students have trouble naming a detail about a macaw, read aloud the paragraph again, pausing to point out each detail.

TIP Identifying the main idea of an article is one way readers can check their understanding of what they read. This is called **self-monitoring** comprehension.

Objectives

- State the main idea of a text.
- Identify supporting details.
- Increase concept and content vocabulary.
- Use new vocabulary in written and spoken sentences.

Words to Know

Before reading "Insects of the Rain Forest,"

1. Have students say each word aloud.
2. Ask students if they know what each word means.
   - If students know a word's meaning, have them define it and use it in a sentence.
   - If students don't know a word's meaning, read them the definition and discuss the word with them.

Amazon rain forest – the world's largest tropical rain forest
sap – the liquid inside a plant
twig – a small, thin branch
unusual – different; something you don't see very often.

Read Aloud

Book Walk

Prepare students by taking them on a Book Walk of "Insects of the Rain Forest." Scan the magazine article together to revisit the text.

1. Turn to today's selection.
2. Point to and read aloud the **title of the article**.
3. Have students look at the **pictures** in the article. Answers to questions may vary.
   - Which insect do you like most?
   - What is something you learned about this insect?

Objectives

- Activate prior knowledge by previewing text and/or discussing topic.
- Read and listen to a variety of texts for information and pleasure independently or as part of a group.

"Insects of the Rain Forest"

Now it's time to read the article. Have students sit next to you so that they can see the pictures and words while you read the article aloud.

Read aloud the entire article. Tell students to listen carefully so they can discover what each paragraph is mostly about.

Check Your Reading

"Insects of the Rain Forest"

Check students' comprehension of the article.

1. **Have students retell the article in their own words** to develop grammar, vocabulary, comprehension, and fluency skills.
2. **Read aloud** the following paragraph: "The rhinoceros beetle doesn't need to worry about blending in with the background. It has a big, pointed horn on its head, just like the animal it's named after. The big horn scares away other insects."
3. **Ask students questions** to focus on the main idea and supporting details.
   - The main idea is what the paragraph talks about the most. What is the main idea of this paragraph? the rhinoceros beetle's horn
   - What is one detail about the beetle's horn? Possible answers: it's big; it's pointed; it scares away other insects.
   - What animal is the beetle named after? rhinoceros

Objectives

- State the main idea of a text.
- Identify supporting details.

Reading for Meaning

Support the Main Idea with Details

Ask students the following questions to further **check understanding of the main idea and supporting details**. Read aloud paragraphs from the article as directed.

1. **Read aloud:** "The walking stick likes to eat leaves at night. So, this insect spends most of its day hiding under plants, pretending to be a twig. Sometimes, it won't move for hours."
   - What is the main idea of this paragraph? the walking stick
   - Which of the following is a detail in this paragraph that tells more about the walking stick? (a) A walking stick eats leaves; (b) Many insects live in the Amazon rain forest. (a) A walking stick eats leaves.
   - Where does a walking stick like to hide? under plants
   - What does a walking stick pretend to be? a twig
2. **Read aloud:** "Another insect that can blend into the background is the blue morpho butterfly. You can see this butterfly's beautiful blue wings when it's flying. But, sometimes the blue morpho needs to rest on a tree or on the ground. When it does, it folds up its blue wings. Then, all that shows is the brown underside of its wings."
   - What is the main idea of this paragraph? The blue morpho butterfly can blend into the background.
   - When can you see this butterfly's blue wings? when it's flying
   - When does the blue morpho butterfly need to blend into the background? when it wants to rest
   - What color is the underside of a blue morpho butterfly's wings? brown
3. **Read aloud:** "The brown color of the folded-up wings makes this butterfly look like tree bark or a dead leaf. By folding up its wings, the blue morpho can hide from bigger, hungry insects or animals that might want to eat it."
   - What is the main idea of this paragraph? how the blue morpho butterfly can hide
   - What does the brown color of the wings make the butterfly look like? tree bark or a dead leaf
   - What does the blue morpho butterfly hide from? hungry insects and animals

Objectives

- State the main idea of a text.
- Identify supporting details.
- Retell the main idea and supporting details.

Review "Insects of the Rain Forest"

Lesson Overview

Offline "Insects of the Rain Forest" **30 minutes**

Get Ready	Words to Know
	Reread or Retell
Reading for Meaning	Compare and Contrast Insects of the Rain Forest
Making Connections	Plus or Minus

Materials

Supplied

- "Insects of the Rain Forest," *Animals Around the World,* pp. 30–35
- *K[12] Language Arts Activity Book*, p. LC 45

Also Needed

- crayons

Keywords

compare – to explain how two or more things are alike

contrast – to explain how two or more things are different

Offline 30 minutes

"Insects of the Rain Forest"

Work **together** with students to complete offline Get Ready, Reading for Meaning, and Making Connections activities.

Get Ready

Words to Know

Ask students to define the following words and use them in a sentence:

Amazon rain forest	**twig**
sap	**unusual**

Correct any incorrect or vague definitions.

Objectives

- Use new vocabulary in written and spoken sentences.
- Increase concept and content vocabulary.

Reread or Retell

If you'd like to, reread the story to students. Otherwise, have students retell the story using the pictures as a guide, or move on to the next activity.

Reading for Meaning

Compare and Contrast Insects of the Rain Forest

Compare and contrast insects of the Amazon rain forest.

Objectives

- Compare and contrast elements within a text.

1. Tell students that the insects in the article are alike in some ways and different in other ways. Good readers look for these things so they can better understand what they read.
2. **Ask students the following questions** to check their ability to recognize how insects in the article are the same and how they are different.
   - How many insects in the article have a horn? one Which insect is it? the rhinoceros beetle
   - How are the blue morpho butterfly and the walking stick alike? Both can blend into the background; both have six legs.
   - The rhinoceros beetle has wings, even though you can't see them in the picture. Which other insect in the article has wings? the blue morpho butterfly Which ones don't have wings? the walking stick and the leaf-cutter ant
   - How are the walking stick and the leaf-cutter ant alike? Possible answers: the walking stick eats leaves, and the leaf-cutter ant chews up leaves to make food (or fungus); they both have six legs.

Making Connections

Plus or Minus

Have students complete a chart on page LC 45 in K^{12} *Language Arts Activity Book* to help them recognize how Amazon rain forest insects are alike and different.

1. Point to and read aloud the column headings, one by one. Explain that each heading is something that may or may not describe each of the insects pictured in the first column of the chart.
2. Help students determine if the characteristic at the top of each column describes each insect.
   - Tell students to put a plus sign in the box if the column heading describes that insect.
   - Tell students to put a minus sign in the box if it doesn't.
   - If students have trouble recalling details about an insect, refer back to the pictures and text of the article.
3. Help students determine which insects are most alike because they share the most characteristics.
   - Look for the insects that have the most plus signs in common. For example, there should be a plus sign in the "Lives in Amazon rain forest" and "Blends in with background" boxes for both the walking stick and the blue morpho butterfly. So they share those characteristics.
4. Have students draw an insect of their choice in the first box of the empty row at the bottom of the chart. Some suggestions are bee, ladybug, grasshopper, dragonfly, or firefly.
   - Be sure students choose an insect that has one or more things in common with the insects in the chart.
   - Be sure students choose an insect, not another type of animal. For example, spiders, caterpillars, and worms are not insects.

Objectives

- Demonstrate understanding through graphic organizers.
- Seek information in provided sources to answer questions.
- Compare and contrast elements within a text.
- Make connections with text: text-to-text, text-to-self, text-to-world.

5. Read aloud each column heading again, and have students put plus or minus signs in the boxes for the insect they chose.
6. Have students determine which Amazon rain forest insect is most like theirs by looking at how many plus signs they have in common.

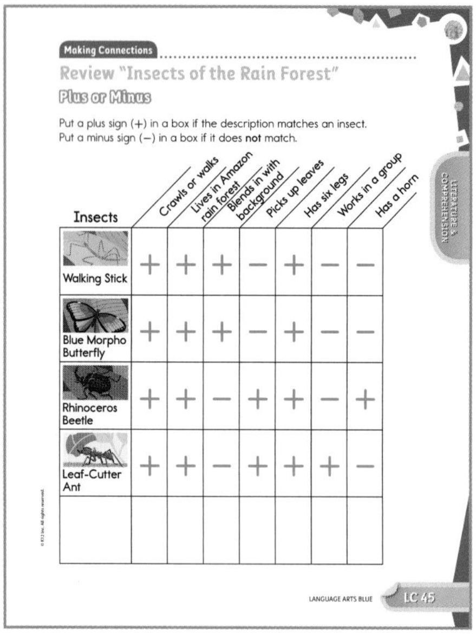
Making Connections

Review "Insects of the Rain Forest"

Plus or Minus

Put a plus sign (+) in a box if the description matches an insect.
Put a minus sign (–) in a box if it does **not** match.

Insects	Crawls or walks	Lives in Amazon rain forest	Blends in with background	Picks up leaves	Has six legs	Works in a group	Has a horn
Walking Stick	+	+	+	–	+	–	–
Blue Morpho Butterfly	+	+	+	–	+	–	–
Rhinoceros Beetle	+	+	–	+	+	–	+
Leaf-Cutter Ant	+	+	–	+	+	+	–

© K12 Inc. All rights reserved.

LANGUAGE ARTS BLUE LC 45

Introduce *Tikki Tikki Tembo*

Lesson Overview

Offline	*Tikki Tikki Tembo*	30 minutes
Get Ready	Why Good Readers Make Predictions	
	Words to Know	
Read Aloud	Book Walk	
	Tikki Tikki Tembo	
Check Your Reading	*Tikki Tikki Tembo*	

Materials

Supplied

- *Tikki Tikki Tembo*, retold by Arlene Mosel

Story Synopsis

Long ago in China, the first-born son of a family was given a long and honorable name. But, as poor Tikki tikki tembo-no sa rembo-chari bari ruchi-pip peri pembo soon finds out, longer isn't necessarily better.

Keywords

prediction – a guess about what might happen that is based on information in a story and what you already know

Advance Preparation

Read *Tikki Tikki Tembo* before beginning the Read Aloud activities, to locate Words to Know within the text.

Review the second Read Aloud activity so you will be prepared to pause at certain points in the story to allow students to make predictions. Locate and bookmark these pages in the story to serve as a reminder to pause while reading.

Big Ideas

- Comprehension entails actively thinking about what is being read.
- Comprehension is facilitated when new information is connected to information previously learned.

Offline 30 minutes

Tikki Tikki Tembo

Work **together** with students to complete offline Get Ready, Read Aloud, and Check Your Reading activities.

Get Ready

Why Good Readers Make Predictions

Explore the strategy of making predictions.

1. Tell students that **good readers make predictions**, or guesses, about what will happen in a story. Making predictions helps us to be active readers. It makes us want to keep reading a story to see if what we predict happens or not. We use clues in the story and what we know from our own experiences to guess, or predict, what will happen next.
2. Have students practice making a prediction.
   Say: It was a very hot day. Jana was so thirsty! She went to the kitchen, got a clean glass, and put it on the table. Then she opened the refrigerator door and looked inside.
   - What do you think, or predict, will happen next? Answers may vary but should involve Jana getting something cold to drink.
   - What clues from the story did you use to make your guess? Possible answers: it was hot; Jana was thirsty; she got a glass.
   - What do you know from your own experiences that helped you make your prediction? I like something cold to drink when it's hot outside; cold drinks are kept in the refrigerator.

TIP Do not describe a prediction as "wrong," which may discourage students from attempting to make predictions. Predictions are neither right nor wrong. Readers make the best prediction possible, based on the available information.

Objectives

- Make predictions before and during reading.
- Build vocabulary through listening, reading, and discussion.
- Use new vocabulary in written and spoken sentences.

Words to Know

Before reading *Tikki Tikki Tembo,*

1. Have students say each word aloud.
2. Ask students if they know what each word means.
   - If students know a word's meaning, have them define it and use it in a sentence.
   - If students don't know a word's meaning, read them the definition and discuss the word with them.

custom – something you do regularly; a tradition
heir – someone who has been or will be left money, property, or a title by another person, usually a parent
honored – treated with special attention and great respect
possess – to own
pump – an up-and-down action that empties water out of something
reverence – great respect
unfortunate – unlucky
well – a deep hole in the ground from which you can get water
youth – the time when a person is young

Read Aloud

Book Walk

Prepare students by taking them on a Book Walk of *Tikki Tikki Tembo*. Scan the book together, and ask students to make predictions about the story.

1. Have students look at the pictures on the cover. Point to and read aloud the **book title**.
2. Read aloud the names of the **author** and the **illustrator**.
3. Ask students the following questions. Answers to questions may vary.
   - Where do you think the story takes place?
   - What do you think might happen in the story?
   - Did anyone ever tell you **not** to do something, but you did it anyway? What happened?

Objectives

- Make predictions based on title, illustrations, and/or context clues.
- Listen and respond to texts representing a variety of cultures, time periods, and traditions.
- Make predictions before and during reading.

Tikki Tikki Tembo

Now it's time to read the story. Have students sit next to you so that they can see the pictures and words while you read the story aloud.

Read aloud the entire story. Pause at the following points in the story to ask students what they predict will happen next. Jot down their predictions for later reference.

- After the mother first warns her sons not to go near the well
- After the boys run to the well to eat their rice cakes
- After Chang wakes up the Old Man With The Ladder
- After the Old Man With The Ladder pumps water out of Tikki tikki tembo and pushes air into him

TIP Reading aloud the long name might be easier if you break it into parts: Tikki tikki tembo / no sa rembo / chari bari / ruchi pip / peri pembo.

Check Your Reading

Tikki Tikki Tembo

Have students retell the story in their own words to develop grammar, vocabulary, comprehension, and fluency skills. When finished, **ask students the following questions** to check their predictions. **Refer to the predictions you jotted down, as necessary.** Answers to questions may vary.

- What did you predict would happen after the mother tells her two sons not to go near the well?
- Were you surprised that the boys run to play on the well again after Chang fell inside? Why or why not?
- Did you think the Old Man With The Ladder would get up from his nap to help Chang get his brother out of the well? Why or why not?
- What did you predict would happen after Tikki tikki tembo gets the water pumped out of him and the air pushed in? What really happened?

Objectives

- Evaluate predictions.

Explore *Tikki Tikki Tembo*

Lesson Overview

Offline	*Tikki Tikki Tembo*	30 minutes
Get Ready	Characters' Actions and Experiences	
	Words to Know	
Read Aloud	Book Walk	
	Tikki Tikki Tembo	
Check Your Reading	*Tikki Tikki Tembo*	
Reading for Meaning	Compare and Contrast Characters' Actions and Experiences	

Materials

Supplied

- *Tikki Tikki Tembo*, retold by Arlene Mosel

Keywords

author's purpose – the reason the author wrote a text: to entertain, to inform, to express an opinion, or to persuade

character – a person or animal in a story

Advance Preparation

Before working with students, spend a few minutes reviewing Words to Know. Then review the Check Your Reading and Reading for Meaning activities to familiarize yourself with the questions and answers.

Offline 30 minutes

Tikki Tikki Tembo

Work **together** with students to complete offline Get Ready, Read Aloud, Check Your Reading, and Reading for Meaning activities.

Get Ready

Characters' Actions and Experiences

Explore characters' actions and their experiences.

1. Tell students that it's important to notice the things that characters do and the experiences that they have so we can better understand the characters and the story. Sometimes the same thing can happen to two people, but they will react in different ways.
2. Have students practice comparing shared experiences and characters' reactions.
   Say: Carla and Maria were walking to the park after it rained. When Carla stepped into a puddle on the sidewalk, she laughed at how her shoes started to make a squishy sound. At the park, Maria stepped into a puddle near the swings. Maria got mad. "Now my feet are all wet," she complained.
   - What happens to Carla and Maria that is the same? They both step into a puddle.
   - What does Carla do when she steps into a puddle? She laughs.
   - What does Maria do when she steps into a puddle? She gets mad.
   - What do Carla's and Maria's reactions tell us about them? Possible answers: Carla is happy, Maria is unhappy; Carla doesn't mind getting wet, but Maria doesn't like to get wet.

Objectives

- Identify details that explain characters' actions.
- Compare and contrast experiences of characters in a text.
- Build vocabulary through listening, reading, and discussion.
- Use new vocabulary in written and spoken sentences.

Words to Know

Before reading *Tikki Tikki Tembo*,

1. Have students say each word aloud.
2. Ask students if they know what each word means.
   - If students know a word's meaning, have them define it and use it in a sentence.
   - If students don't know a word's meaning, read them the definition and discuss the word with them.

custom – something you do regularly; a tradition
heir – someone who has been or will be left money, property, or a title by another person, especially a parent
honored – treated with special attention and great respect
possess – to own

pump – an up-and-down action that empties water out of something
reverence – great respect
unfortunate – unlucky
well – a deep hole in the ground from which you can get water
youth – the time when a person is young

Read Aloud

Book Walk

Prepare students by taking them on a Book Walk of *Tikki Tikki Tembo*. Scan the book together to revisit the text.

1. Read aloud the **book title**.
2. Have students locate the name of the **author**. Read the name of the author.
3. Have students locate the name of the **illustrator**. Read the name of the illustrator.
4. Look through the book. Have students describe what they see in the **pictures**.
   - Why did Chang and Tikki tikki tembo need help? They fell in the well.
   - Were you ever in trouble and needed help? Who helped you? What did that person do to help? Answers will vary.

Objectives

- Activate prior knowledge by previewing text and/or discussing topic.
- Listen and respond to texts representing a variety of cultures, time periods, and traditions.

Tikki Tikki Tembo

Now it's time to read the story. Have students sit next to you so that they can see the pictures and words while you read the story aloud.

Read aloud the entire story. Remind students to pay attention to the things that happen to the characters and the things that they do.

Check Your Reading

Tikki Tikki Tembo

Tell students that you will be discussing the characters in the story and how they act.

1. To better understand characters' actions, it's helpful to think about our own actions in different situations. Answers to questions may vary.
   - Did you ever help someone in trouble? What did you do to help?
   - Think about what Chang did to help his brother. How is what you did the same? How is it different?
2. **Ask students the following questions** to check their ability to describe characters and their actions.
   - Why does the mother tell her two sons not to play near the well? because she thinks they could fall in
   - Why do the brothers play on the well anyway? because they don't always mind their mother

Objectives

- Identify details that explain characters' actions.

- Why don't the boys play near the well for several months? because Change fell inside and they know it's dangerous
- Why does the Old Man With The Ladder tell Chang that he is a "miserable child"? because Chang woke him up while he was dreaming

Reading for Meaning

Compare and Contrast Characters' Actions and Experiences

Complete the following activity to help students develop a deeper understanding of the story.

1. Remind students that **why** characters do something is just as important as **what** they do. How characters think and act tells us what kind of people they are.
   - What does Tikki tikki tembo do when his brother falls into the well? He runs to tell their mother.
   - What does Chang do when his brother falls into the well? He runs to tell their mother.
   - What does the mother do when Tikki tikki tembo tells her that Chang has fallen into the well? Possible answers: she calls Chang a "troublesome boy"; she tells Tikki tikki tembo to get the Old Man With The Ladder.
   - The final time that Chang tells his mother that Tikki tikki tembo has fallen into the well, he bows his head clear to the sand and takes a deep breath. Why does he do this? He's out of breath because his brother's name is so long, and he's already said it three times after running all the way from the well.
   - Why is the mother more upset when she hears that Tikki tikki tembo has fallen into the well than when Chang fell in? Tikki tikki tembo is her first and honored son.
   - What happens after Tikki tikki tembo gets the water pumped out of him and the air pushed in? The moon rose many times before he was the same. How is this different from what happens to Chang? Chang is as good as ever very soon.
   - Why does it take Tikki tikki tembo longer to get better? because he was in the well longer than Chang
   - Why was Tikki tikki tembo in the well longer than Chang? because it took so long for Chang to say Tikki tikki tembo's whole name to his mother and to the Old Man With The Ladder
2. Remind students that the author writes a story for a particular reason: to teach or tell us something; to entertain us; to convince us of something; or to tell us his or her opinion.
   - Did the author write this story to entertain us? Yes
   - Did the author also write this story to tell us something? Yes What does the author tell us? Possible answers: why parents in China no longer give their children long names; why it's not safe to play on a well; why you should always listen to your mother

Objectives

- Identify details that explain characters' actions.
- Compare and contrast experiences of characters in a text.
- Identify the purpose of a text.

Review *Tikki Tikki Tembo*

Lesson Overview

Offline	*Tikki Tikki Tembo*	30 minutes
Get Ready	Words to Know	
	Reread or Retell	
Reading for Meaning	Words Can Help You See and Imagine	
Making Connections	What's in a Name?	

Materials

Supplied

- *Tikki Tikki Tembo*, retold by Arlene Mosel
- *K[12] Language Arts Activity Book*, p. LC 46

Also Needed

- crayons

Keywords

imagery – language that helps readers imagine how something looks, sounds, smells, feels, or tastes

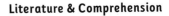

Big Ideas

Readers who visualize, or form mental pictures, when they read have better recall of text than those who do not.

Offline 30 minutes

Tikki Tikki Tembo

Work **together** with students to complete offline Get Ready, Reading for Meaning, and Making Connections activities.

Get Ready

Words to Know

Ask students to define the following words and use them in a sentence:

custom	**possess**	**unfortunate**
heir	**pump**	**well**
honored	**reverence**	**youth**

Correct any incorrect or vague definitions.

Objective

- Use new vocabulary in written and spoken sentences.

Reread or Retell

If you'd like to, reread the story to students. Otherwise, have students retell the story using the pictures as a guide, or move on to the next activity.

Reading for Meaning

Words Can Help You See and Imagine

Tell students that authors often use words that help readers imagine how things would sound, look, smell, feel, or taste in a story. **Ask the following questions to check ability to identify words that create mental imagery.** Have students close their eyes as you read the text excerpts to help them form mental images as they listen.

Objective

- Identify words that create mental imagery.

1. Have students compare the imagery in two sentences.
   - Which of the following sentences makes it easier for you to imagine what's happening in the story? (a) The boy ran to his mother; (b) The boy ran as fast as his little legs could carry him to his mother. The boy ran as fast as his little legs could carry him to his mother.
2. **Read aloud**: "The water roars . . . I cannot hear you."
   - Which word in the sentence helps you imagine the sound of the water? *roars*

3. **Read aloud**: "Step over step, step over step [the Old Man With The Ladder] went into the well."
   - How do the words *step over step, step over step* help you imagine what is happening? Answers will vary; guide students to recognize that these words help you imagine the Old Man With The Ladder slowly climbing down the ladder.
4. **Read aloud**: "I had floated into a purple mist . . . ."
   - Which words in the sentence help paint a picture in your head? *a purple mist*
   - How does the word *floated* make you feel? light; weightless
5. **Read aloud**: "There were glittering gateways and jeweled blossoms."
   - Which words in the sentence help paint a picture in your head? *glittering gateways; jeweled blossoms*
   - What do you see in your head when you think of a glittering gateway and a jeweled blossom? Answers will vary.

Making Connections

What's in a Name?

Help students invent a new, long name for themselves.

1. Tell students there are fifty letters in the name Tikki tikki tembo-no sa rembo-chari bari ruchi-pip peri pembo.
2. Help students come up with their own long name to write on page LC 46 in *K[12] Language Arts Activity Book*. Here are some suggestions for expanding a name, using the name Megan Tamara Jeeters as an example:
   - Repeat the first name. (Megan megan)
   - Break the middle name up. (tama-ra)
   - Add a nonsense syllable and a word that rhymes with the first part of the middle name. (fa lama-)
   - Rhyme two words about something the student likes to play or do. (dancer prancer)
   - Break up the last name and add a nonsense syllable that starts with the same letter as the last part of the last name. (jee-ters ti)
   - Add a nonsense syllable or word that rhymes with first part of the middle name. (sama)
   - String all the names together. (Megan megan tama-ra fa lama-dancer prancer jee-ters ti sama)

Objective

- Make connections with text: text-to-text, text-to-self, text-to-world.

3. Help students write the long name in the space provided below the dragon.
4. Have students tell how having such a long name could cause problems. If students can't think of any problems, suggest any of the following: it's too long to write on an envelope or a name tag; it's hard to remember; it takes too long to say.
5. Have students color the dragon, if time allows.

Making Connections

Review *Tikki Tikki Tembo*

What's in a Name?

Make up a long name for yourself, and write it in the box. Then, color the dragon.

Write student's long name in this box.

LC 46 LANGUAGE ARTS BLUE

Introduce "The Story of Chicken Little"

Lesson Overview

Offline	"The Story of Chicken Little"	30 minutes
Get Ready	Predictions Cause Active Reading	
	Words to Know	
Read Aloud	Book Walk	
	"The Story of Chicken Little"	
Check Your Reading	"The Story of Chicken Little"	

Materials

Supplied

- "The Story of Chicken Little," *K¹² Read Aloud Treasury,* pp. 106–109

Story Synopsis

The sky is falling, and Chicken Little rushes to tell the King the bad news. Each friend she encounters along the way wants to join her, but one sly character has an ulterior motive for offering to lead the way.

Keywords

prediction – a guess about what might happen that is based on information in a story and what you already know

Advance Preparation

Read "The Story of Chicken Little" before beginning the Read Aloud activity, to locate Words to Know within the text.

Big Ideas

- Comprehension entails actively thinking about what is being read.
- Comprehension is facilitated when readers connect new information to information previously learned.

Offline 30 minutes

"The Story of Chicken Little"

Work **together** with students to complete offline Get Ready, Read Aloud, and Check Your Reading activities.

Get Ready

Predictions Cause Active Reading

Explore the strategy of making predictions.

1. Tell students that **good readers make predictions**, or guesses, about what will happen in a story. Making predictions makes us want to keep reading a story to see if what we predict happens or not. We use clues in the story and what we know from our own experiences to guess, or predict, what will happen next.
2. Remind students that good readers learn to change their predictions as they read more of a story and get more information.
3. Have students practice making and changing a prediction. **Read aloud** this passage, which is the beginning of a short story: Jason was sitting in the living room when he heard a whistling noise. He got up and looked out the window. The wind was so strong that it was blowing leaves down the street.
   - What do you think will happen next? Answers will vary.
4. Have students revise their prediction after you **read aloud** the rest of the short story: "Hooray!" Jason shouted. He ran into his room and grabbed his jacket and his new kite.
   - Now what do you think, or predict, will happen? Answers will vary but should involve Jason going outside to fly his kite.
   - Did you change your prediction? If you did, what new clue from the story did you use to change your guess? Jason grabs his kite.
   - What do you know from your own experiences that helped you make your prediction? You need wind to fly a kite.

TIP Do not describe a prediction as "wrong," which may discourage students from attempting to make predictions. Readers make the best prediction possible, based on the available information. Encourage students to revise their predictions as they get more information from the story.

Objectives

- Make predictions before and during reading.
- Build vocabulary through listening, reading, and discussion.
- Use new vocabulary in written and spoken sentences.

Words to Know

Before reading "The Story of Chicken Little,"

1. Have students say each word aloud.
2. Ask students if they know what each word means.
   - If students know a word's meaning, have them define it and use it in a sentence.
   - If students don't know a word's meaning, read them the definition and discuss the word with them.

acorn – the large seed of an oak tree
den – the home of a wild animal, often a cave

Read Aloud

Book Walk

Prepare students by taking them on a Book Walk of "The Story of Chicken Little." Scan the story together.

1. Turn to the **table of contents**. Help students find today's selection, and turn to that page.
2. Point to and read aloud the **title of the story**.
3. Have students look at the picture on the first page of the story.
   Answers to questions may vary.
   - Where do you think the story takes place?
   - What do you think might happen in the story?
   - Did you ever have to run to tell someone something important?

Objectives

- Make predictions based on title, illustrations, and/or context clues.
- Listen and respond to texts representing a variety of cultures, time periods, and traditions.
- Make predictions before and during reading.

"The Story of Chicken Little"

Now it's time to read the story. Have students sit next to you so that they can see the pictures and words while you read the story aloud.

Read aloud the entire story. Pause at the following points in the story to ask students what they predict will happen next. Jot down their predictions for later reference.

- Page 106: After Chicken Little tells Henny Penny that the sky is falling and she is going to tell the King
- Page 106: After the animals tell Ducky Lucky that the sky is falling and they are going to tell the King
- Page 108: After the animals tell Turkey Lurkey that the sky is falling and they are going to tell the King
- Page 109: After the animals tell Foxy Loxy that the sky is falling and they are going to tell the King

Check Your Reading

"The Story of Chicken Little"

Have students retell the story in their own words to develop grammar, vocabulary, comprehension, and fluency skills. When finished, **ask students the following questions** to check their predictions. **Refer to the predictions you jotted down, as necessary.**

- What did you predict would happen after Chicken Little tells Henny Penny that the sky is falling and she is going to tell the King? Answers may vary.
- Were you surprised that every animal wants to go with Chicken Little to tell the King that the sky is falling? Why or why not? Answers may vary.
- The story tells us that the animals never see the King after Foxy Loxy leads them into his den. What do you think might have happened to the animals? Foxy Loxy probably ate them.
- Think about the fox in "The Gingerbread Man" or another story. What do you already know about foxes that gave you a clue about what might have happened to the animals? Possible answers: foxes are tricky; foxes are hungry; foxes eat other animals.

Objectives

- Evaluate predictions.
- Make inferences based on text and/or prior knowledge.

Explore "The Story of Chicken Little"

Lesson Overview

Offline "The Story of Chicken Little" 30 minutes

Get Ready	Parts of a Story
	Words to Know
Read Aloud	Book Walk
	"The Story of Chicken Little"
Check Your Reading	"The Story of Chicken Little"
Reading for Meaning	Identify the Story Elements of "The Story of Chicken Little"

Materials

Supplied

- "The Story of Chicken Little," K^{12} *Read Aloud Treasury*, pp. 106–109

Keywords

character – a person or animal in a story

plot – what happens in a story

setting – when and where a story takes place

story events – the things that happen in a story; the plot

story structure elements – components of a story; they include character, setting, plot, problem, and solution

Advance Preparation

Before working with students, spend a few minutes reviewing Words to Know. Then review the Check Your Reading and Reading for Meaning activities to familiarize yourself with the questions and answers.

Big Ideas

Comprehension requires an understanding of story structure.

Offline 30 minutes

"The Story of Chicken Little"

Work **together** with students to complete offline Get Ready, Read Aloud, Check Your Reading, and Reading for Meaning activities.

Get Ready

Parts of a Story

Tell students that every story has certain parts, or elements. These parts include the characters, the setting, and the plot.

1. Remind students that the characters are the people or animals in a story. The setting is where and when a story takes place.
2. Tell students that this part of the lesson focuses mainly on the plot. **The plot is the most important things that happen in a story**, or the most important events.
3. **Say:** Think of the story of "Little Red Riding Hood." This is the plot for "Little Red Riding Hood": A girl goes to see her grandmother. On the way, she meets a wolf who tricks her into picking flowers. The wolf arrives at grandmother's house first, swallows her, and gets in her bed. When the girl arrives, the wolf swallows her. A woodman comes and rescues the girl and her grandmother.
4. Have students practice identifying the plot of "Cinderella."
   - What happens in the story? Example of the plot: A girl named Cinderella has two mean stepsisters who make her do all the chores. One day, a fairy appears and helps Cinderella go to a ball. At the ball, she dances with the Prince, loses her glass slipper, and then runs away. The Prince searches until he finds the girl whose foot fits the glass slipper.

TIP If students do not know the story of "Little Red Riding Hood" or "Cinderella," substitute a favorite story that they do know.

Objectives

- Identify story structure elements: plot, setting, character(s).
- Build vocabulary through listening, reading, and discussion.
- Use new vocabulary in written and spoken sentences.

Words to Know

Before reading "The Story of Chicken Little,"

1. Have students say each word aloud.
2. Ask students if they know what each word means.
   - If students know a word's meaning, have them define it and use it in a sentence.
   - If students don't know a word's meaning, read them the definition and discuss the word with them.

acorn – the large seed of an oak tree
den – the home of a wild animal, often a cave

Read Aloud

Book Walk

Prepare students by taking them on a Book Walk of "The Story of Chicken Little." Scan the story together to revisit the characters and events.

1. Turn to today's selection. Point to and read aloud the **title of the story.**
2. Have students look at the **pictures** of the story.
   - Where do you think the story takes place? the woods
   - Who are some of the story's characters? Possible answers: Chicken Little; Henny Penny; Cocky Locky; Ducky Lucky; Goosey Loosey; Turkey Lurkey; Foxy Loxy

Objectives

- Identify story structure elements: plot, setting, character(s).
- Listen and respond to texts representing a variety of cultures, time periods, and traditions.

"The Story of Chicken Little"

Now it's time to read the story. Have students sit next to you so that they can see the pictures and words while you read the story aloud.

Read aloud the entire story. Encourage students to join in saying the following repeated phrases as you come to them:

- "Where are you going?"
- "The sky is falling, and we are going to tell the King."
- "I will go with you, if I may."

Check Your Reading

"The Story of Chicken Little"

Have students retell the story in their own words to develop grammar, vocabulary, comprehension, and fluency skills. When done, **ask the following questions** to check their ability to identify repetitive text in the story.

Read aloud: "When they came to the pond, they saw Ducky Lucky. 'Where are you going, Cocky Locky?' asked Ducky Lucky."

- Which words are repeated over and over in the story? "Where are you going?"
- What is the answer when a character asks where the animals are going? "The sky is falling, and we are going to tell the King."
- What does each character say when he or she hears that the animals are going to see the King? "I will go with you, if I may."

Objectives

- Identify repetitive text.

Reading for Meaning

Identify the Story Elements of "The Story of Chicken Little"

Complete the following activity to check students' comprehension.

1. **Ask students the following questions to check general comprehension** of the story.
   - Why does Chicken Little think the sky is falling? an acorn falls on her head
   - Who is the first character that Chicken Little meets on the way to see the King? Henny Penny
   - Where do all the characters that Chicken Little meets on the road want to go? They all want to go with her to see the King.
   - Who is the last animal Chicken Little meets on the road to see the King? Foxy Loxy
   - What does Foxy Loxy offer to do? show the way
   - Where does Foxy Loxy really take the animals? to his den; to his home
2. **Ask students the following questions to check their ability to identify the story elements** of character, setting, and plot.
   - Who is the most important character in the story? Chicken Little
   - Where does the story take place? Possible answers: in the woods; where Chicken Little lives; Foxy Loxy's den
   - What happens in the story? Name only the most important things that happen. Example of the plot: An acorn falls on Chicken Little's head, so she thinks the sky is falling. Chicken Little runs to tell the King, and she meets many animals on the way who want to go with her. The animals meet Foxy Loxy and follow him into his den; they're never seen again.

Objectives

- Answer questions requiring literal recall of details.
- Identify story structure elements: plot, setting, character(s).

Review "The Story of Chicken Little"

Lesson Overview

Offline	"The Story of Chicken Little"	30 minutes
Get Ready	Words to Know	
	Reread or Retell	
Reading for Meaning	Summarize "The Story of Chicken Little"	
Making Connections	Chicken Little & Co.	
Beyond the Lesson	OPTIONAL: Henny Penny	

Materials

Supplied

- "The Story of Chicken Little," *K[12] Read Aloud Treasury*, pp. 106–109
- *K[12] Language Arts Activity Book*, p. LC 47

Also Needed

- glue stick
- paper, drawing
- scissors, round-end safety

Big Ideas

- Comprehension requires an understanding of story structure.
- Comprehension requires the reader to self-monitor understanding.

Keywords

self-monitor – to notice if you do or do not understand what you are reading

summarize – to tell the most important ideas or events of a text

summary – a short retelling that includes only the most important ideas or events of a text

Offline 30 minutes

"The Story of Chicken Little"

Work **together** with students to complete offline Get Ready, Reading for Meaning, Making Connections, and Beyond the Lesson activities.

Get Ready

Words to Know

Ask students to define the following words and use them in a sentence:

acorn **den**

Correct any incorrect or vague definitions.

Objectives

- Build vocabulary through listening, reading, and discussion.
- Use new vocabulary in written and spoken sentences.

Reread or Retell

If you'd like to, reread the story to students. Otherwise, have students retell the story using the pictures as a guide, or move on to the next activity.

Reading for Meaning

Summarize "The Story of Chicken Little"

Tell students that one way readers can check their own understanding of a story is by giving a summary.

Objectives

- Summarize read-aloud stories.

1. Tell students that a **summary** is a very short retelling that **includes only the most important things that happen in a story in the order in which they happen.**
2. Point out that a summary is not the same as retelling a story because it does not include very many details.
3. Ask students to complete the following steps to summarize the story:
   - Tell what happens at the beginning of the story in one or two sentences. Example: An acorn falls on Chicken Little's head; she runs to tell the King that the sky is falling.
   - Tell what happens in the middle of the story in one or two sentences. Example: Chicken Little meets many animals on the way to see the King; every animal want to go with Chicken Little to see the King.
   - Tell what happens at the end of the story in one or two sentences. Example: Foxy Loxy offers to show the animals the way, but he really takes them to his den; the animals never see the King.
   - Tell what happens in the story in just a few sentences. Answers should be a combination of the preceding summaries for the beginning, middle, and end of the story. The summary of the full story should tell the events in the order in which they happen.

Making Connections

Chicken Little & Co.

Have students practice their sequencing skills by putting the characters in the order in which they appear in the story. Turn to page LC 47 in *K[12] Language Arts Activity Book*.

1. Have students cut out the pictures of the animals.
2. Have students glue the animals to a piece of drawing paper in the order in which they appear in the story. Have them refer to the story and pictures to help recall the correct order.
3. Have students dictate the name of each character, and then write the name below each animal's picture.

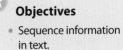

Objectives

- Sequence information in text.

Beyond the Lesson

OPTIONAL: Henny Penny

This activity is intended for students who have extra time and would benefit from reading another version of the story. Feel free to skip this activity.

1. Go to a library and look for a copy of *Henny Penny* by Paul Galdone.
2. Lead a Book Walk, and read aloud the different version of the story.
3. Have students compare the two stories and tell how they are alike and different.
4. Ask them to tell which version of the story is their favorite, and why.

Objectives

- Compare and contrast two texts on the same topic.

Introduce "The Foolish Rabbit"

Unit Overview

In this unit, students will explore the theme of *Listen to Learn* through the following reading selections:

- "The Foolish Rabbit"
- "Being Nosy About Smells"
- "The Honest Woodsman"

Lesson Overview

Offline	"The Foolish Rabbit"	30 minutes
Get Ready	How Illustrations Relate to Story Events	
	Words to Know	
Read Aloud	Book Walk	
	"The Foolish Rabbit"	
Check Your Reading	"The Foolish Rabbit"	

Advance Preparation

Read "The Foolish Rabbit" before beginning the Read Aloud activity, to locate Words to Know within the text.

Materials

Supplied

- "The Foolish Rabbit," *K[12] Read Aloud Treasury*, pp. 112–115

Story Synopsis

A rabbit hears a falling coconut hit the ground, and he immediately and erroneously thinks the world is breaking into pieces. Widespread panic occurs when he tells his animal friends the bad news. Will the voice of reason be heard?

Keywords

illustration – a drawing

story events – the things that happen in a story; the plot

Offline 30 minutes

"The Foolish Rabbit"

Work **together** with students to complete offline Get Ready, Read Aloud, and Check Your Reading activities.

Get Ready

How Illustrations Relate to Story Events

Explore the idea of how illustrations help readers better understand story events.

1. Tell students that the pictures in a story aren't just fun to look at—they usually help readers better understand what happens in the story.
2. Explain that looking at and describing what is in pictures is a way to retell the story. It is also a step toward learning how to give a summary of a story. A summary is like retelling, but it is shorter and does not have as many details as a retelling.
3. Turn to page 2 in K[12] *Read Aloud Treasury* and point to the first picture from "Little Red Riding Hood."
   - What is happening in this picture? Little Red Riding Hood is setting off on the path through the woods so she can take food to her sick grandmother.
4. **Say:** Telling what's happening in this picture is a good way to begin retelling the story.

Objectives

- Describe illustrations and their relationship to story events.
- Build vocabulary through listening, reading, and discussion.
- Use new vocabulary in written and spoken sentences.

Words to Know

Before reading "The Foolish Rabbit,"

1. Have students say each word aloud.
2. Ask students if they know what each word means.
   - If students know a word's meaning, have them define it and use it in a sentence.
   - If students don't know a word's meaning, read them the definition and discuss the word with them.

foot – the bottom or lower end of something, like the foot of a cliff or the foot of your bed
join – to come together with someone or something
stop in one's tracks – to stop suddenly because one is startled, scared, or surprised
wise – being able to use what you've learned from experience to make good choices; smart

Read Aloud

Book Walk

Prepare students by taking them on a Book Walk of "The Foolish Rabbit." Scan the story together, and ask students to make predictions.

1. Turn to the **table of contents**. Help students find today's selection, and turn to that page.
2. Point to and read aloud the **title of the story**. Answers to questions may vary.
   - Where do you think the story takes place?
   - What do you think might happen in the story?
   - Why might the rabbit in the story be called foolish?

Objectives

- Make predictions based on title, illustrations, and/or context clues.
- Listen and respond to texts representing a variety of cultures, time periods, and traditions.

"The Foolish Rabbit"

Now it's time to read the story. Have students sit next to you so that they can see the pictures and words while you read the story aloud.

Read aloud the entire story. Emphasize Words to Know as you come to them. If appropriate, use the pictures to help show what each word means.

Check Your Reading

"The Foolish Rabbit"

Have students retell the story in their own words to develop grammar, vocabulary, comprehension, and fluency skills. When finished, **ask students the following questions** to check their ability to use illustrations to describe story events.

1. Turn to page 113 and point to the monkeys in the tree.
   - What are the monkeys doing? throwing coconuts
2. Point to the rabbit on pages 112 and 113.
   - What does the look on the rabbit's face tell you? He's scared.
   - What scared the rabbit? the sound of a coconut falling on the ground
   - What does the rabbit think the sound means? He thinks the world is breaking into pieces.
3. Turn to page 114 and point to the animals running together.
   - What part of the story does this picture show? how each animal the rabbit meets while he's running starts to run with him
4. Turn to page 115 and point to the lion.
   - What part of the story does this picture show? how the lion roars to get the animals to stop running and listen to him

Objectives

- Describe illustrations and their relationship to story events.

Explore "The Foolish Rabbit"

Lesson Overview

Offline	"The Foolish Rabbit"	30 minutes
Get Ready	Parts of a Story	
	Words to Know	
Read Aloud	Book Walk	
	"The Foolish Rabbit"	
Check Your Reading	"The Foolish Rabbit"	
Reading for Meaning	Story Structure Elements in "The Foolish Rabbit"	

Materials

Supplied

- "The Foolish Rabbit," *K[12] Read Aloud Treasury*, pp. 112–115

Keywords

character – a person or animal in a story

plot – what happens in a story

setting – when and where a story takes place

story events – the things that happen in a story; the plot

story structure elements – components of a story; they include character, setting, plot, problem, and solution

Advance Preparation

Before working with students, spend a few minutes reviewing Words to Know. Then review the Check Your Reading and Reading for Meaning activities to familiarize yourself with the questions and answers.

Big Ideas

Comprehension requires an understanding of story structure.

Offline 30 minutes

"The Foolish Rabbit"

Work **together** with students to complete offline Get Ready, Read Aloud, Check Your Reading, and Reading for Meaning activities.

Get Ready

Parts of a Story

Explore the idea that stories have distinct parts, or elements.

1. Tell students that every story has certain parts, or elements. These parts include the characters, the setting, and the plot.
2. Explain that the characters are the people or animals in a story. The setting is where and when a story takes place. **The plot is the most important things that happen in a story.**
3. Model telling the plot of a familiar story.
   Say: This is the plot of "The Gingerbread Man." A woman who is baking a Gingerbread Man tells her son to watch the oven. The Gingerbread Man jumps out of the oven and runs down the road. He runs away from many people and animals on the road, and then he meets a fox. The fox tricks the Gingerbread Man into stopping, and then the fox eats him in one big bite.
4. Have students practice telling the plot of "The Elves and the Shoemaker."
   - What happens in the story? Example of the plot: It's too late for a shoemaker to finish a pair of shoes he's making, so he goes to bed. When he gets up the next morning, he finds the shoes are done. This happens several times. The shoemaker and his wife hide one night and find out that elves are doing the work. They make the elves new clothes to thank them. The elves do a dance and are never seen again. The shoemaker has good luck from that day on.

TIP If students do not know the story of "The Gingerbread Man" or "The Elves and the Shoemaker," use a favorite story that they do know for the example or the practice.

Objectives

- Identify story structure elements: plot, setting, character(s).
- Build vocabulary through listening, reading, and discussion.
- Use new vocabulary in written and spoken sentences.

Words to Know

Before reading "The Foolish Rabbit,"

1. Have students say each word aloud.
2. Ask students if they know what each word means.
   - If students know a word's meaning, have them define it and use it in a sentence.
   - If students don't know a word's meaning, read them the definition and discuss the word with them.

foot – the bottom or lower end of something, like the foot of a cliff or the foot of your bed
join – to come together with someone or something
stop in one's tracks – to stop suddenly because one is startled, scared, or surprised
wise – being able to use what you've learned from experience to make good choices; smart

Read Aloud

Book Walk

Prepare students by taking them on a Book Walk of "The Foolish Rabbit." Scan the story together to revisit the characters and events.

1. Turn to the **table of contents**. Help students find today's selection, and turn to that page.
2. Point to and read aloud the **title of the story**.
   - Who are some of the characters in the story? Possible answers: the monkeys; the rabbits; the deer; the elephant; the lion
   - Have you ever heard a loud noise that scared you? What did you do when you heard it? What made the noise? Answers will vary.

Objectives

- Listen and respond to texts representing a variety of cultures, time periods, and traditions.
- Identify character(s).

"The Foolish Rabbit"

Now it's time to read the story. Have students sit next to you so that they can see the pictures and words while you read the story aloud.

Read aloud the entire story. Tell students to listen for the most important things that happen in the story.

Check Your Reading

"The Foolish Rabbit"

Have students retell the story in their own words to develop grammar, vocabulary, comprehension, and fluency skills. When finished, **ask students the following questions** to check their ability to recognize how story illustrations relate to story events.

- Why does the rabbit think the world is breaking into pieces? He hears a falling coconut hit the ground.
- What does the rabbit do when he thinks the world is breaking apart? He gets scared and starts to run.
- Name two of the animals the rabbit meets while he is running. Possible answers: rabbits; a deer; a fox; an elephant
- What does the lion do to get the animals to stop running? He roars three times.
- What does the lion do when he hears that the world is breaking up? He asks if anyone saw it happen.
- Why is the title of the story "The Foolish Rabbit"? The rabbit is foolish because he doesn't stop to look to see what made the noise; instead, he just figures the world is breaking up, which isn't true.

Objectives

- Answer questions requiring literal recall of details.
- Make inferences based on text and/or prior knowledge.

Reading for Meaning

Story Structure Elements in "The Foolish Rabbit"

Ask students the following questions to check their ability to identify the story structure elements.

- Who is the most important character in the story? the rabbit who thinks the world is breaking into pieces; the foolish rabbit
- Where does the story take place? Possible answers: in a jungle or rain forest; where the rabbit lives
- What happens in the beginning of the story? Name only the most important things that happen. Example: A sleeping rabbit wakes up and hears a coconut hit the ground. He thinks the noise means the world is breaking into pieces, and he starts to run.
- What happens in the middle of the story? Name only the most important things that happen. Example: The rabbit tells other animals, and they run with him. The lion sees them all running and roars to make them stop.
- What happens in the end of the story? Name only the most important things that happen. Example: The lion and the rabbit go back to the place where the rabbit was sleeping. The lion figures out that the rabbit heard the falling coconut and the world is not breaking apart.
- Tell the plot of "The Foolish Rabbit." Tell only the most important parts of the story. Students should repeat the answers for what happens in the beginning, middle, and end of the story, in the correct order.

TIP It is often impossible to identify *when* a story takes place, such as in "The Foolish Rabbit." Therefore, that aspect of the setting is not addressed in this activity.

Objectives

- Identify story structure elements: plot, setting, character(s).
- Retell the beginning, middle, and end of a story.

Review "The Foolish Rabbit"

Lesson Overview

Offline	"The Foolish Rabbit"	30 minutes
Get Ready	Words to Know	
	Reread	
Reading for Meaning	A Summary of "The Foolish Rabbit"	
Making Connections	The Foolish Rabbit and His Foolish Friends	
Beyond the Lesson	OPTIONAL: The Sky Is Falling vs. The World Is Breaking Up	

Materials

Supplied

- "The Foolish Rabbit," *K*[12] *Read Aloud Treasury*, pp. 112–115
- *K*[12] *Language Arts Activity Book*, p. LC 49

Also Needed

- craft sticks
- glue stick
- scissors, round-end safety

Big Ideas

- Comprehension requires an understanding of story structure.
- Comprehension requires the reader to self-monitor understanding.

Keywords

compare – to explain how two or more things are alike

contrast – to explain how two or more things are different

self-monitor – to notice if you do or do not understand what you are reading

summarize – to tell the most important ideas or events of a text

summary – a short retelling that includes only the most important ideas or events of a text

Offline 30 minutes

"The Foolish Rabbit"

Work **together** with students to complete offline Get Ready, Reading for Meaning, Making Connections, and Beyond the Lesson activities.

Get Ready

Words to Know

Ask students to define the following words and use them in a sentence:

foot **stop in one's tracks**
join **wise**

Correct any incorrect or vague definitions.

Objectives

- Build vocabulary through listening, reading, and discussion.
- Use new vocabulary in written and spoken sentences.

Reread

If you'd like to, reread the story to students. Otherwise, move on to the next activity.

Reading for Meaning

A Summary of "The Foolish Rabbit"

Tell students that one way readers can check their own understanding of a story is by giving a summary.

Objectives

- Summarize read-aloud stories.

1. Tell students that a **summary** is a very short retelling that **includes only the most important things that happen in a story in the order in which they happen.**
2. Explain that a summary is not the same as retelling a story because it does not include very many details.
3. Ask students to complete the following steps to summarize the story:
   - Tell what happens at the beginning of the story in one or two sentences. Example summary of the beginning of the story: A rabbit hears a noise and thinks the world is breaking apart; he starts to run.
   - Tell what happens in the middle of the story in one or two sentences. Example summary of the middle of the story: The rabbit runs by many animals; he tells each one the world is breaking apart, and each animal starts to run with him.
   - Tell what happens at the end of the story in one or two sentences. Example summary of the end of the story: The lion finds out that no one saw the world start to break up; he takes the rabbit back to where he heard the noise and they find out that it was just a falling coconut.
   - Tell what happens in the story in just a few sentences. Answers should be a combination of the preceding summaries for the beginning, middle, and end of the story. The summary should tell the events of the story in the order in which they happen.

Making Connections

The Foolish Rabbit and His Foolish Friends

Help students practice their sequencing skills by using stick puppets to reenact the story. Turn to page LC 49 in K^{12} *Language Arts Activity Book*.

1. Have students cut out the pictures of the animals.
2. Have students glue the animals to craft sticks to use as handles for puppets.
3. Have students reenact the story using the animal puppets.
   - Be sure students tell the story in the correct sequence.
   - Refer back to the story pictures and text if students need help recalling the order in which the other animals join the rabbit.

Objectives

- Sequence information in text.
- Reenact a story in the correct sequence.
- Respond to text through art, writing, and/or drama.

Making Connections

Review "The Foolish Rabbit"

The Foolish Rabbit and His Foolish Friends

Cut out the pictures of the characters. Glue them to sticks to make puppets. Then, use the puppets to tell the story.

LITERATURE & COMPREHENSION

LANGUAGE ARTS BLUE LC 49

Beyond the Lesson

OPTIONAL: The Sky Is Falling vs. The World Is Breaking Up

This activity is intended for students who have extra time and would benefit from hearing a similar story. Feel free to skip this activity.

1. Tell students that they are going to hear a story that is like "The Foolish Rabbit."
2. On page 106 in K^{12} *Read Aloud Treasury,* read aloud "The Story of Chicken Little."
3. Have students compare and contrast the pictures, main characters, and story events of the two stories.
4. Have students tell which story they like best, and why.

Objectives

- Compare and contrast two texts on the same topic.

Introduce "Being Nosy About Smells"

Lesson Overview

Offline	"Being Nosy About Smells"	30 minutes
Get Ready	Organize Information in a KWL Chart	
	Words to Know	
Read Aloud	Book Walk	
	"Being Nosy About Smells"	
Check Your Reading	"Being Nosy About Smells"	

Advance Preparation

Read "Being Nosy About Smells" before beginning the Read Aloud activity, to locate Words to Know within the text.

Review the KWL chart on page LC 51 in K^{12} *Language Arts Activity Book*. Keep the chart handy for use during Get Ready and Read Aloud activities.

Big Ideas

- Comprehension entails having and knowing a purpose for reading.
- Comprehension entails asking and answering questions about the text.
- Self-questioning improves comprehension and ensures that reading is an interactive process.
- Comprehension is facilitated when readers connect new information to information previously learned.
- Comprehension strategies can be taught through explicit instruction.

Materials

Supplied

- "Being Nosy About Smells," *Our Busy Bodies*, pp. 2–11
- K^{12} *Language Arts Activity Book*, p. LC 51

Story Synopsis

Have you ever noticed that you can't taste food when you have a stuffed-up nose? Why would that be? What does your sense of taste have to do with your sense of smell? Read on to solve the mystery.

Keywords

graphic organizer – a visual tool used to show relationships between key concepts; formats include webs, diagrams, and charts

prior knowledge – things you already know from past experience

Offline 30 minutes

"Being Nosy About Smells"

Work **together** with students to complete offline Get Ready, Read Aloud, and Check Your Reading activities.

Get Ready

Organize Information in a KWL Chart

Introduce students to prereading strategies and reading for a specific purpose. Turn to page LC 51 in *K*[12] *Language Arts Activity Book.*

1. **Say:** This is called a KWL chart. It is a tool that helps you organize your thoughts and get ready to read a text.
2. Point to the K column.
   Say: The *K* stands for "know." Good readers ask, "What do I already **know** about this subject?" before reading. This gets your brain ready to learn more about the subject.
3. Point to the W column.
   Say: The *W* stands for "want." Good readers ask, "What do I **want to know** or wonder about this subject?" before they read a text. Looking for answers to "What do I want to know?" questions is your reason, or **purpose**, for reading a text.
4. Point to the L column.
   Say: The *L* stands for "learn." Good readers ask, "What did I **learn**?" after reading an article.
5. Tell students that before they read "Being Nosy About Smells," they will work on the K and W columns of the chart. They will complete the L column after they read the article.

Objectives

- Demonstrate understanding through graphic organizers.
- Identify purpose for reading text.
- Generate literal level questions.
- Increase concept and content vocabulary.
- Use new vocabulary in written and spoken sentences.

Words to Know

Before reading "Being Nosy About Smells,"

1. Have students say each word aloud.
2. Ask students if they know what each word means.
   - If students know a word's meaning, have them define it and use it in a sentence.
   - If students don't know a word's meaning, read them the definition and discuss the word with them.

molecules – very small bits; tiny particles
nasal cavity – the air-filled space above and behind the nose; air passes through the nose and into this space when a person breathes
nerves – long, thin fibers that send messages to and from the brain and other parts of the body; nerves give us the sense of touch and let us feel things such as heat and cold

nostrils – the two openings at the end of the nose that we breathe through
odors – smells
sense of smell – one of the five senses; the sense used to detect odors by sniffing air into the nose
spices – parts of plants that are dried or made into powder and put in food to give it flavor
spoiled – gone bad; rotten

Read Aloud

Book Walk

Turn to the KWL chart on page LC 51 *K[12] Language Arts Activity Book*. Prepare students by taking them on a Book Walk of "Being Nosy About Smells." Scan the magazine article together, and ask students to make predictions about the text. Answers to questions may vary.

1. Turn to the **table of contents.** Help students find today's selection, and turn to that page.
2. Point to and read aloud the **title of the article**.
3. Have students look at the **pictures** in the article.
   - What do you already know about your sense of smell or how you use your nose to smell things? [Write each fact in the K column of the KWL chart.]
   - Name at least three things that you wonder about or would like to know about your sense of smell. [Write what students dictate in the W column of the chart.]

   If students have difficulty thinking of things they'd like to know, suggest one or more of the following questions: Why do some things smell bad? How does my sense of smell work? Why can't I taste food if I can't smell it, like when I have a cold?
4. Point to and read aloud any **headers, captions, or other features** that stand out.
   - What do you think the article might tell us about our sense of smell?

Objectives

- Activate prior knowledge by previewing text and/or discussing topic.
- Make predictions based on title, illustrations, and/or context clues.
- Read and listen to a variety of texts for information and pleasure independently or as part of a group.
- Demonstrate understanding through graphic organizers.
- Identify purpose for reading text.
- Generate literal level questions.

"Being Nosy About Smells"

Now it's time to read the article. Have students sit next to you so that they can see the pictures and words while you read the article aloud.

Read aloud the entire article. Emphasize Words to Know as you come to them. If appropriate, use the pictures to help show what each word means.

Check Your Reading

"Being Nosy About Smells"

Have students retell the article in their own words to develop grammar, vocabulary, comprehension, and fluency skills. When finished, **ask students the following questions** to check comprehension and encourage discussion.

- What part of your body do you use to smell things? your nose
- Can you taste a cookie without your sense of smell? No
- How does your nose help you taste a cookie? It tells your brain the flavor of the cookie.
- What do we call the tiny things that float way up into our nose and help us smell things? molecules

Objectives

- Answer questions requiring literal recall of details.

Explore "Being Nosy About Smells"

Lesson Overview

Offline	"Being Nosy About Smells"	30 minutes
Get Ready	Read to Find Answers	
	Words to Know	
Read Aloud	Book Walk	
	"Being Nosy About Smells"	
Check Your Reading	"Being Nosy About Smells"	
Reading for Meaning	Record and Check What You Learned	

Materials

Supplied

- "Being Nosy About Smells," *Our Busy Bodies*, pp. 2–11
- *K[12] Language Arts Activity Book*, p. LC 51

Keywords

graphic organizer – a visual tool used to show relationships between key concepts; formats include webs, diagrams, and charts

Advance Preparation

Before working with students, spend a few minutes reviewing Words to Know. Then review the Check Your Reading activity to familiarize yourself with the questions and answers.

Review the Reading for Meaning activity to familiarize yourself with the process for completing the KWL chart on page LC 51 in *K[12] Language Arts Activity Book.*

Big Ideas

- Comprehension entails having and knowing a purpose for reading.
- Comprehension entails asking and answering questions about the text.
- Self-questioning improves comprehension and ensures that reading is an interactive process.
- Comprehension is facilitated when readers connect new information to information previously learned.
- Comprehension strategies can be taught through explicit instruction.

Offline 30 minutes

"Being Nosy About Smells"

Work **together** with students to complete offline Get Ready, Read Aloud, Check Your Reading, and Reading for Meaning activities.

Get Ready

Read to Find Answers

Prepare students to read a text for a specific purpose. Turn to the KWL chart on page LC 51 in *K[12] Language Arts Activity Book.*

1. Refresh students' memory of what they already know about the sense of smell by reading what's written in the K column.
2. Remind students that they are reading the article to answer their questions about the sense of smell. This is their reason, or **purpose**, for reading.
3. Read aloud students' questions written in the W column.
4. Explain that the answers to some of these questions might not be in the article. However, thinking about the questions will help students listen carefully to the article and better remember the information they hear.
5. Tell students that they will fill in the last column of the chart after listening to the article again.

Objectives

- Demonstrate understanding through graphic organizers.
- Activate prior knowledge by previewing text and/or discussing topic.
- Identify purpose for reading text.
- Increase concept and content vocabulary.
- Use new vocabulary in written and spoken sentences.

Words to Know

Before reading "Being Nosy About Smells,"

1. Have students say each word aloud.
2. Ask students if they know what each word means.
   - If students know a word's meaning, have them define it and use it in a sentence.
   - If students don't know a word's meaning, read them the definition and discuss the word with them.

molecules – very small bits; tiny particles
nasal cavity – the air-filled space above and behind the nose; air passes through the nose and into this space when a person breathes
nerves – long, thin fibers that send messages to and from the brain and other parts of the body; nerves give us the sense of touch and let us feel things such as heat and cold
nostrils – the two openings at the end of the nose that we breathe through
odors – smells
sense of smell – one of the five senses; the sense used to detect odors by sniffing air into the nose
spices – parts of plants that are dried or made into powder and put in food to give it flavor
spoiled – gone bad; rotten

Read Aloud

Book Walk

Prepare students by taking them on a Book Walk of "Being Nosy About Smells." Scan the magazine article together to revisit the text.

1. Turn to today's selection.
2. Point to and read aloud the **title of the article**.
3. Have students look at the **pictures** in the article. Answers to questions may vary.
   - What is one of your favorite smells?
   - What **don't** you like to smell?
   - Did you ever sneeze after smelling pepper or breathing in dust? Why do you think that happened?

Objectives

- Activate prior knowledge by previewing text and/or discussing topic.
- Read and listen to a variety of texts for information and pleasure independently or as part of a group.

"Being Nosy About Smells"

Now it's time to read the article. Have students sit next to you so that they can see the pictures and words while you read the article aloud.

Read aloud the entire article. Remind students to listen for answers to the questions in the W column of the KWL chart. Take time to pause during reading to ask students if they heard an answer to any of their questions.

TIP If students interrupt your reading because they hear an answer to one of their questions, be sure to praise them for their careful listening. You can either write the answer in the KWL chart immediately or wait until you have finished reading the article. Choose the method that you feel will best maintain students' interest.

Check Your Reading

"Being Nosy About Smells"

Have students retell the article in their own words to develop grammar, vocabulary, comprehension, and fluency skills. When finished, **ask students the following questions** to check understanding of the purpose of reading the article, as well as basic comprehension.

- Why did we read this article? to learn about the sense of smell; to find answers to our questions about the sense of smell
- How do molecules from a flower get into a person's nose? They float up through your nostrils.
- What do the nerves at the top of your nasal cavity do? They send a message to your brain, and then your brain figures out what the smell is.
- How can our sense of smell warn us of danger? We can smell smoke if there's a fire; we can smell if food is spoiled so we don't eat it.
- Why are some dogs specially trained to find things? Their sense of smell is very strong.

Objectives

- Identify purpose for reading text.
- Answer questions requiring literal recall of details.

Reading for Meaning

Record and Check What You Learned

Have students use the KWL chart to record answers to the questions they previously generated. Return to the KWL chart on page LC 51 in *K*[12] *Language Arts Activity Book*.

1. Read aloud the first question written in the W column.
   - Ask students if they heard the answer in the article. If students know the answer, write it in the L column of the chart across from the question.
   - If the answer is in the article but students cannot remember it, return to the article and help students locate the answer. Then write it in the L column across from the question.
   - If the answer to the question is not in the article, remind students that we don't always find the answers to our questions in the articles we read. But asking the questions still helps us become better readers because it helps us read or listen carefully to a text. Leave the area across from the unanswered question blank.
2. Repeat Step 1 for each of the remaining questions in the W column.
3. Have students tell any additional facts they learned about the sense of smell from reading the article, and write them at the end of the L column.

Objectives

- Demonstrate understanding through graphic organizers.
- Seek information in provided sources to answer questions.

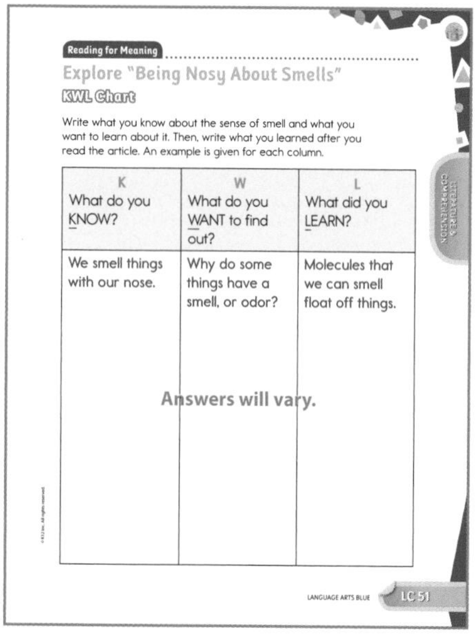

Reading for Meaning

Explore "Being Nosy About Smells"

KWL Chart

Write what you know about the sense of smell and what you want to learn about it. Then, write what you learned after you read the article. An example is given for each column.

K What do you KNOW?	W What do you WANT to find out?	L What did you LEARN?
We smell things with our nose.	Why do some things have a smell, or odor?	Molecules that we can smell float off things.

Answers will vary.

LANGUAGE ARTS BLUE LC 51

Review "Being Nosy About Smells"

Lesson Overview

Offline	"Being Nosy About Smells"	30 minutes
Get Ready	Words to Know	
	Reread or Retell	
Reading for Meaning	Seeing Is Understanding	
Making Connections	Smells Like . . .	
Beyond the Lesson	OPTIONAL: Sniff It Out	

Materials

Supplied

- "Being Nosy About Smells," *Our Busy Bodies*, pp. 2–11
- *K[12] Language Arts Activity Book*, p. LC 52

Also Needed

- crayons

Keywords

sequence – order

topic – the subject of a text

visual text support – a graphic feature that helps a reader better understand text, such as a picture, chart, or map

Big Ideas

- Comprehension entails an understanding of the organizational patterns of text.
- Comprehension is facilitated by an understanding of physical presentation (headings, subheads, graphics, and other features).
- Comprehension is enhanced when information is presented through more than one learning modality; learning modalities are visual (seeing), auditory (hearing), and kinesthetic (touching).

Offline 30 minutes

"Being Nosy About Smells"

Work **together** with students to complete offline Get Ready, Reading for Meaning, Making Connections, and Beyond the Lesson activities.

Get Ready

Words to Know

Ask students to define the following words and use them in a sentence:

molecule	**odors**
nasal cavity	**sense of smell**
nerves	**spices**
nostrils	**spoiled**

Correct any incorrect or vague definitions.

Objectives

- Use new vocabulary in written and spoken sentences.
- Increase concept and content vocabulary.

Reread or Retell

If you'd like to, reread the story to students. Otherwise, have students retell the article using the pictures as a guide, or move on to the next activity.

Reading for Meaning

Seeing Is Understanding

Check students' ability to identify the topic of a text and use visual text features to better understand text information.

1. Remind students that the **topic is the main focus of a text**, or what it's mostly about.
   - What is the article "Being Nosy About Smells" mostly about? the sense of smell; how we use our noses to smell
2. Tell students that **visual text supports such as pictures and diagrams** provide information that we can see. We learn and remember information more easily if we see it as well as hear it. So looking at things like pictures and diagrams while we listen to or read an article can help us to better understand the article.
3. Point to the diagram on page 4.
   - What does this picture show? how we smell molecules
4. Point to the picture of the children and the trash can on page 3.
   - Why are the children holding their nose? to show that the trash smells bad

Objectives

- Identify the topic.
- Identify purpose of information provided by illustrations, titles, charts, and graphs.
- Use visual text features to aid understanding of text.

5. Point to the diagram on page 6.
   - What does this picture show? how the sense of smell helps us taste things
6. Point to the smoking oven on page 8.
   - What does this picture show? how something that's burning or on fire makes smoke
   - Why is it important to be able to smell smoke? to keep us out of danger; to know when there's a fire

Making Connections

Smells Like . . .

Have students show understanding of how the sense of smell works by drawing a personal picture. Turn to page LC 52 in *K[12] Language Arts Activity Book.*

1. Have students draw something they like to smell below the nose, such as a particular food or flower. Be sure students include lines coming from the item to represent odor molecules.
2. Have students tell how they are able to smell the item, step by step. Allow them to use the diagram from the article as a guide.
3. If time allows, students may color the nasal cavity and the brain inside the head.

Objectives

- Respond to text through art, writing, and/or drama.
- Create illustrations that represent personal connections to text.
- Sequence information from a text.

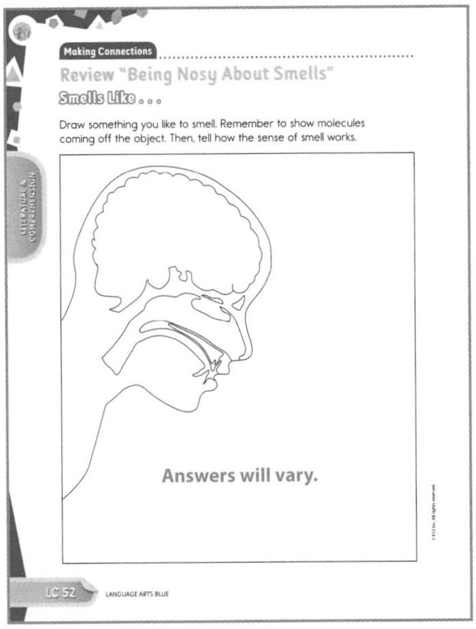

Beyond the Lesson

OPTIONAL: Sniff It Out

This activity is intended for students who have extra time and would benefit from further research on the sense of smell. Feel free to skip this activity.

1. Turn to the KWL chart on page LC 51 *K12 Language Arts Activity Book*.
2. Help students look for answers to their unanswered questions on their KWL charts. Use one or more of the following sources:
   - Library books, such as *The Sense of Smell* by Ellen Weiss or *You Can't Smell a Flower with Your Ear!* by Joanna Cole
   - An Internet search engine (use the words "sense of smell") or the site http://kidshealth.org/kid/ (enter "smell" in the search box)
3. If students find an answer, write it in the L column in the chart, across from the corresponding question.
4. If students find additional information about the sense of smell that they find interesting, write these facts at the end of the L column.

Objectives

- Seek information in provided sources to answer questions.
- Demonstrate understanding through graphic organizers.

Introduce "The Honest Woodsman"

Lesson Overview

Offline	"The Honest Woodsman"	30 minutes
Get Ready	Morals	
	Words to Know	
Read Aloud	Book Walk	
	"The Honest Woodsman"	
Check Your Reading	"The Honest Woodsman"	

Materials

Supplied

- "The Honest Woodsman," K^{12} *Read Aloud Treasury*, pp. 116–121

Also Needed

- dictionary

Advance Preparation

Read "The Honest Woodsman" before beginning the Read Aloud activities, to locate Words to Know within the text.

Read the directions for the second Read Aloud activity to become familiar with how to model asking and answering questions about unknown words.

Big Ideas

- Early learners acquire vocabulary through active exposure (by talking and listening, being read to, and receiving explicit instruction).
- Comprehension entails asking and answering questions about the text.
- Self-questioning improves comprehension and ensures that reading is an interactive process.

Story Synopsis

What would you do if you lost an important item only to have a more valuable version mistakenly returned to you? Would you be happy to keep it, or would you be honest and say it wasn't yours? Such is the dilemma facing a poor woodsman who loses his prized ax.

Keywords

context clue – a word or phrase in a text that helps you figure out the meaning of an unknown word

moral – the lesson of a story, particularly a fable

Offline 30 minutes

"The Honest Woodsman"

Work **together** with students to complete offline Get Ready, Read Aloud, and Check Your Reading activities.

Get Ready

Morals

Explore the idea that a story can teach a lesson that can be applied to everyday living.

1. Explain that a story can be written to teach a lesson. The lesson that a story teaches is called a **moral**. Some well-known morals are "One man's trash is another man's treasure," "Choose your friends wisely," and "Look before you leap."
2. Have students recall the moral of the fable "The Lion and the Mouse" in *K¹² Read Aloud Treasury,* pages 82–86.
   Say: Think about the fable of the lion and the mouse. The lion captured the mouse and then let him go. The mouse was grateful and said that maybe someday he'd be able to help the lion. The lion laughed at this because the mouse was so small. Later the lion was trapped by hunters and the mouse helped the lion to escape.
   - What was the lesson, or moral, of that fable? No matter how small you are, you can always help others.

Objectives

- Identify the moral or lesson of a text.
- Build vocabulary through listening, reading, and discussion.
- Use new vocabulary in written and spoken sentences.

Words to Know

Before reading "The Honest Woodsman,"

1. Have students say each word aloud.
2. Ask students if they know what each word means.
   - If students know a word's meaning, have them define it and use it in a sentence.
   - If students don't know a word's meaning, read them the definition and discuss the word with them.

bank – the raised area at the edge of a river, pond, or canal
cease – to stop
remain – to stay
seek – to look for
sorrow – great sadness
stroke – the hitting of one thing against another, as in the stroke of an ax

Read Aloud

Book Walk

Prepare students by taking them on a Book Walk of "The Honest Woodsman." Scan the story together and ask students to make predictions.

1. Turn to the **table of contents**. Help students find today's selection, and turn to that page.
2. Point to and read aloud the **title of the story**.
3. Have students look at the **pictures** of the story. Answers to questions may vary.
   - What do you think the story is about?
   - Where do you think the story takes place?
   - Did you ever lose something that was important to you?

Objectives

- Make predictions based on title, illustrations, and/or context clues.
- Listen and respond to texts representing a variety of cultures, time periods, and traditions.
- Identify unknown words in text.
- Ask and answer questions about unknown words in text.

"The Honest Woodsman"

Now it's time to read the story. Have students sit next to you so that they can see the pictures and words while you read the story aloud. Students will learn how to identify and ask questions about unknown words. Gather the dictionary.

1. **Begin to read aloud.** Near the end of page 116, pause after reading the sentence with the word *gazed* in it.
   Say: I wonder what *gazed* means. In the picture the woodsman is looking at the stream where his ax fell. I can say, "The woodsman looked into the stream." That makes sense, so I think that *gazed* means *looked*. I'm going to check the dictionary to make sure.
2. Look up *gaze* in the dictionary and read aloud the definition.
3. Have students raise their hand if they hear a word they don't know as you read the rest of the story.
4. While reading, pause at the end of pages 118 and 120 to ask students if they heard any words they don't know. Help students use clues in the story and the dictionary to figure out the meaning of any unknown words.

Check Your Reading

"The Honest Woodsman"

Have students retell the story in their own words to develop grammar, vocabulary, comprehension, and fluency skills. When finished, **ask students the following questions** to check comprehension and encourage discussion.

- How does the woodsman lose his ax? He trips on the ax and it slides into the river.
- Who helps the woodsman find his ax? the water fairy
- What does the woodsman do when the fairy asks if the silver ax is his? He says it's not his ax.
- What does the woodsman do when the fairy asks if the gold ax is his? He says it's not his ax.
- How does the fairy reward the woodsman for being honest? She gives him the gold and silver axes.
- What is the moral of the story? Answers will vary; guide students to understand that the moral is "Honesty is the best policy" or "Always tell the truth."

Objectives

- Answer questions requiring literal recall of details.
- Identify the moral or lesson of a text.

Explore "The Honest Woodsman"

Lesson Overview

Offline	"The Honest Woodsman"	30 minutes
Get Ready	Identify and Use Multiple-Meaning Words	
	Words to Know	
Read Aloud	Book Walk	
	"The Honest Woodsman"	
Check Your Reading	"The Honest Woodsman"	
Reading for Meaning	Multiple-Meaning Words in "The Honest Woodsman"	

Materials

Supplied

- "The Honest Woodsman," *K[12] Read Aloud Treasury,* pp. 116–121

Keywords

multiple-meaning word – a word that has more than one meaning

problem – an issue a character must solve in a story

solution – how a character solves a problem in a story

story structure elements – components of a story; they include character, setting, plot, problem, and solution

Advance Preparation

Before working with students, spend a few minutes reviewing Words to Know. Then review the Check Your Reading and Reading for Meaning activities to familiarize yourself with the questions and answers.

Big Ideas

- Comprehension requires an understanding of story structure.
- Early learners acquire vocabulary through active exposure (by talking and listening, being read to, and receiving explicit instruction).

Offline 30 minutes

"The Honest Woodsman"

Work **together** with students to complete offline Get Ready, Read Aloud, Check Your Reading, and Reading for Meaning activities.

Get Ready

Identify and Use Multiple-Meaning Words

Tell students that **a word can mean more than one thing**. We use multiple-meaning words all the time; for instance, the word *bat* can mean the wooden club you use to hit a ball or it can mean the small, winged animal that flies at night. Good readers look for clues in the surrounding text to figure out which meaning is being used in a sentence.

1. Model how to figure out the meaning of a word in a sentence that has more than one meaning.
2. Tell students that the word *ring* can be a piece of jewelry you wear on your finger or it can be used to describe the sound that a bell makes.
   Say: Listen to this sentence: The prince wore a large gold ring on his right hand.
   - In this sentence, I know the word *ring* is a piece of jewelry that you wear on your finger.
   - I know this because the words *wore*, *gold*, and *hand* are clues that help me figure it out.
3. Ask students if they know more than one meaning for the word *trip*. It can mean either "to travel from one place to another, like a vacation" or "to fall over something."
4. **Read aloud** from the story: "But he tripped against his ax . . . ."
   - Which meaning of *trip* makes sense in the sentence? to fall over something

Objectives

- Identify multiple-meaning words.
- Identify and use context clues to define words.
- Build vocabulary through listening, reading, and discussion.
- Use new vocabulary in written and spoken sentences.

Words to Know

Before reading "The Honest Woodsman,"

1. Have students say each word aloud.
2. Ask students if they know what each word means.
   - If students know a word's meaning, have them define it and use it in a sentence.
   - If students don't know a word's meaning, read them the definition and discuss the word with them.

bank – the raised area at the edge of a river, pond, or canal
cease – to stop
remain – to stay
seek – to look for
sorrow – great sadness
stroke – the hitting of one thing against another, as in the stroke of an ax

Read Aloud

Book Walk

Prepare students by taking them on a Book Walk of "The Honest Woodsman." Scan the story together to revisit the characters and events.

1. Turn to today's selection. Point to and read aloud the **title of the story**.
2. Have students look at the **pictures** of the story.
   - Why does a lady live in the river? She's a water fairy.
   - Why does the woodsman have three axes in the last picture? The fairy found his ax and gave it back to him. She also gave him the silver and gold axes because he was so honest.

Objectives

- Listen and respond to texts representing a variety of cultures, time periods, and traditions.
- Activate prior knowledge by previewing text and/or discussing topic.

"The Honest Woodsman"

Now it's time to read the story. Have students sit next to you so that they can see the pictures and words while you read the story aloud. Tell students to listen carefully for the woodsman's problem and how the problem is solved.

Check Your Reading

"The Honest Woodsman"

Remind students that the main character is the person or animal that the story is mostly about, and **the main character usually has a problem that needs to be solved**.

- Where does the story take place? in the woods
- Who is the story mostly about? the woodsman
- What is the woodsman's problem? His ax fell into the river and he needs to get it back.
- How is the woodsman's problem solved? The water fairy finds his ax in the river and gives it back to him.
- Why doesn't the woodsman take the silver ax or the gold ax when the fairy asks if they are his? because neither one is his ax, and he feels it would be wrong to take what doesn't belong to him
- What does the fairy do when the woodsman says that the ax made of wood and steel is his? She gives him the silver ax and the gold ax, too.
- Describe the woodsman with one word. Answers will vary; if students have trouble answering, remind them that the title of the story is "The Honest Woodsman."
- Describe the fairy with one word. Possible answers: helpful; generous; kind; beautiful

Objectives

- Identify story structure elements: plot, setting, character(s).
- Identify story structure elements: problem and solution.
- Identify the main character(s).
- Describe character(s).

Reading for Meaning

Multiple-Meaning Words in "The Honest Woodsman"

Have students retell the story in their own words to develop grammar, vocabulary, comprehension, and fluency skills. When finished, **ask students the following questions** to check understanding of multiple-meaning words. Tell students that you will read aloud sentences from the story. They should listen carefully for words with more than one meaning.

Objectives

- Identify multiple-meaning words.
- Identify and use context clues to define words.

1. **Read aloud**: "He selected a large oak tree near the riverside. He swung his ax steadily as he chopped away at the trunk."
   - Which word has more than one meaning? *trunk* What does the word *trunk* mean in the sentence? the thick, woody part of a tree What is another meaning for that word? Possible answers: an elephant's nose; the space in the back of a car that's used to carry things
2. **Read aloud**: "The chips flew fast at every stroke."
   Say: There are two words in this sentence with more than one meaning. The first one is *chips*.
   - What does the word *chips* mean in the sentence? small, cut-off pieces What is another meaning for that word? a snack food, like potato chips or tortilla chips
3. **Read the sentence aloud** again: "The chips flew fast at every stroke."
   Say: The other word in the sentence that has more than one meaning is *stroke*. It can mean "to rub gently" like you would stroke a cat's fur, or it can be used to describe hitting one thing against another.
   - What does the word *stroke* mean in the sentence? hitting one thing against another
4. **Read aloud**: "But he tripped against his ax, and before he could catch it, it slid down the bank into the river. . . ."
   - Which word has more than one meaning? *bank* What are two meanings for *bank*? the place where you keep your money; the edge of a river
   - What does *bank* mean in the sentence? the edge of a river What clue helped you figure out the meaning of *bank* in the sentence? the word *river,* because a river has an edge
5. **Read aloud**: "She sank, and then, quick as a wink, she rose again."
   - The word *rose* can mean "a kind of flower" or it can describe how something came back up. What does *rose* mean in the sentence? came back up
   - What clue in the sentence helped you figure out that *rose* means "came back up"? the word *sank,* because it tells us the fairy went down into the river, and then she *rose* or "came back up"

Review "The Honest Woodsman"

Lesson Overview

Offline	"The Honest Woodsman"	30 minutes
Get Ready	Words to Know	
	Reread or Retell	
Reading for Meaning	Hear and See "The Honest Woodsman"	
Making Connections	Draw What You Hear	

Materials

Supplied

- "The Honest Woodsman," K[12] *Read Aloud Treasury*, pp. 116–121
- *K[12] Language Arts Activity Book*, p. LC 53

Also Needed

- crayons

Big Ideas

Readers who visualize, or form mental pictures, when they read have better recall of text than those who do not.

Keywords

sensory language – language that appeals to the five senses

Offline 30 minutes

"The Honest Woodsman"

Work **together** with students to complete offline Get Ready, Reading for Meaning, and Making Connections activities.

Get Ready

Words to Know

Ask students to define the following words and use them in a sentence:

bank	**seek**
cease	**sorrow**
remain	**stroke**

Correct any incorrect or vague definitions.

Objectives

- Build vocabulary through listening, reading, and discussion.
- Use new vocabulary in written and spoken sentences.

Reread or Retell

If you'd like to, reread the story to students. Otherwise, have students retell the story using the pictures as a guide, or move on to the next activity.

Reading for Meaning

Hear and See "The Honest Woodsman"

Remind students that authors sometimes use words to help readers imagine the sounds of a story. Authors also use words to help paint pictures in readers' heads. **Ask students the following questions** to check understanding of sensory language.

Objectives

- Identify author's use of sensory language.

1. **Read aloud**: ". . . a rushing river that foamed and sparkled. . . ."
   - What words help you hear and see how the river moves? *rushing; foamed; sparkled*
2. **Read aloud**: "The sound of the ax ringing against the wood echoed so clearly. . . ."
   - What words help you imagine, or hear, the ax hitting the tree? *ringing; echoed*
3. **Read aloud**: ". . . she spoke to him in a voice that was like the sweet, tuneful tinkle of flowing water."
   - Which words help you hear the fairy's voice? *sweet, tuneful tinkle* Describe how you imagine her voice might sound. Answers will vary.

4. **Read aloud**: "She sank beneath the water, and then popped back up again."
   - How do the words *sank* and *popped* help you imagine how the fairy moved in the water? Answers will vary.
5. **Read aloud**: "The woodsman looked at the gold ax and the silver ax, glittering in the grass."
   - What word helps you imagine how the gold and silver axes look? *glittering* Describe what you see in your head. Answers will vary.

Making Connections

Draw What You Hear

Students will explore how descriptive and sensory words can help them see pictures in their minds as they listen to a story. Turn to page LC 53 in K[12] *Language Arts Activity Book.*

Objectives

- Identify author's use of sensory language.
- Demonstrate understanding through drawing, discussion and/or writing.
- Create illustrations that represent personal connections to text.

1. Have students close their eyes and listen as you read the following excerpt from the story:
   Once upon a time, out in the green, silent woods, near a rushing river that foamed and sparkled as it hurried along, there lived a good man whose work was chopping wood. One fine autumn day, he started out on his walk to the forest, with his strong, sharp ax over his shoulder. He selected a large oak tree near the riverside. He swung his ax steadily as he chopped away at the trunk.
2. Have students draw a picture of what they imagined as they listened with their eyes closed.
3. Ask students to describe their picture. Encourage them to use words that appeal to the senses.

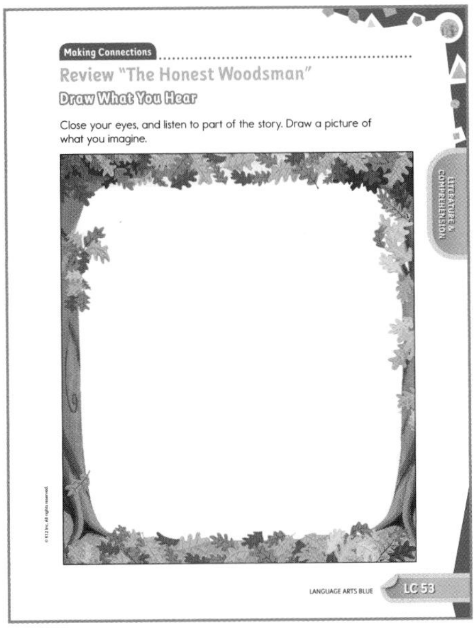

Introduce "Diamonds and Toads"

Unit Overview

In this unit, students will explore the theme of *Out of the Mouths* through the following reading selections:

- "Diamonds and Toads"
- "Talk"
- "That's Tasty!"

Lesson Overview

Offline "Diamonds and Toads" **30 minutes**

Get Ready	Identify Fantasy
	Words to Know
Read Aloud	Book Walk
	"Diamonds and Toads"
Check Your Reading	"Diamonds and Toads"

Advance Preparation

Read "Diamonds and Toads" before beginning the Read Aloud activity, to locate Words to Know within the text.

Materials

Supplied

- "Diamonds and Toads," *K^{12} Read Aloud Treasury*, pp. 122–127

Story Synopsis

A young girl with a kind heart is rewarded for her generosity in a most unexpected way. Her bad-mannered sister, on the other hand, learns a hard lesson when she treats a stranger rudely.

There is a brief reference to snakes near the end of the story.

Keywords

fantasy – a story with characters, settings, or other elements that could not really exist

moral – the lesson of a story, particularly a fable

Offline 30 minutes

"Diamonds and Toads"

Work **together** with students to complete offline Get Ready, Read Aloud, and Check Your Reading activities.

Get Ready

Identify Fantasy

Explore elements of fantasy in a story.

1. Explain to students that a **fantasy is a story that has make-believe things in it**. Parts of a story that are fantasy could never happen in the real world. For example, in the real world, a woman cannot live in a river. Good readers look for hints in the pictures and the words of a story to find out if it is a fantasy.
2. Ask students the following questions.
   - Is a hen that lays eggs real or fantasy? real How do you know? Hens lay eggs in the real world.
   - Is a hen that lays *golden* eggs real or fantasy? fantasy How do you know? A hen can't lay a golden egg in the real world.

Objectives

- Identify and define fantasy.
- Build vocabulary through listening, reading, and discussion.
- Use new vocabulary in written and spoken sentences.

Words to Know

Before reading "Diamonds and Toads,"

1. Have students say each word aloud.
2. Ask students if they know what each word means.
   - If students know a word's meaning, have them define it and use it in a sentence.
   - If students don't know a word's meaning, read them the definition and discuss the word with them.

astonished – surprised
pitcher – a container for liquids like water, which usually has a handle for carrying and a spout for pouring
rude – not polite; having bad manners
spring – a place where water rises up from under the ground
sweet-tempered – being kind and gentle
viper – a poisonous snake

Read Aloud

Book Walk

Prepare students by taking them on a Book Walk of "Diamonds and Toads." Scan the story together.

1. Turn to the **table of contents**. Help students find the selection, and turn to that page.
2. Point to and read aloud the **title of the story**.
3. Have students look at the **pictures** of the story. Answers to questions may vary.
   - What do you think the story is about?
   - Where do you think the story takes place?
   - Has anyone ever spoken to you in a rude way? How did it make you feel?

Objectives

- Make predictions based on title, illustrations, and/or context clues.
- Listen and respond to texts representing a variety of cultures, time periods, and traditions.

"Diamonds and Toads"

Now it's time to read the story. Have students sit next to you so that they can see the pictures and words while you read the story aloud.

Read aloud the entire story. Tell students to listen carefully because there is a moral, or lesson, to the story.

Check Your Reading

"Diamonds and Toads"

Have students retell the story in their own words to develop grammar, vocabulary, comprehension, and fluency skills. When finished, **ask students the following questions** to check comprehension and encourage discussion.

- What happens when the younger daughter gives a drink of water to the old woman? The old woman gives her the gift of flowers and jewels coming from her mouth for being so kind.
- The mother scolds the younger daughter for staying so long at the spring. What happens when the younger daughter apologizes to her mother? Diamonds, pearls, and roses come out of her mouth. Can this happen in real life? No
- What kind of story has things that can't happen in real life? fantasy
- Why does the mother send the elder daughter to get water? She wants the elder daughter to find the old woman so she can have jewels and flowers come out of her mouth, too.
- What happens when the elder daughter talks at the end of the story? Snakes and toads come out of her mouth.
- What is the moral of the story? Possible answers: Use kind words when talking to others; be careful about what you say and how you say it.

Objectives

- Identify the moral or lesson of a story.
- Identify and define fantasy.
- Answer questions requiring literal recall of details.

Explore "Diamonds and Toads"

Lesson Overview

Offline "Diamonds and Toads" 30 minutes

Get Ready	Characters and Their Actions
	Words to Know
Read Aloud	Book Walk
	"Diamonds and Toads"
Check Your Reading	"Diamonds and Toads"
Reading for Meaning	Characters' Actions in "Diamonds and Toads"

Materials

Supplied

- "Diamonds and Toads," *K[12] Read Aloud Treasury*, pp. 122–127

Keywords

character – a person or animal in a story
compare – to explain how two or more things are alike
contrast – to explain how two or more things are different
illustration – a drawing

Advance Preparation

Before working with students, spend a few minutes reviewing Words to Know. Then review the Check Your Reading and Reading for Meaning activities to familiarize yourself with the questions and answers.

Offline 30 minutes

"Diamonds and Toads"

Work **together** with students to complete offline Get Ready, Read Aloud, Check Your Reading, and Reading for Meaning activities.

Get Ready

Characters and Their Actions

Discuss how characters act and respond to the things that happen in a story.

1. Explain that sometimes the same thing can happen to two people, but they will react in different ways.
2. Have students practice comparing shared experiences and characters' reactions.
   Say: Martin and Pedro watched a movie together. Part of the movie was scary. Martin thought the scary part was fun and exciting. Pedro didn't like the scary part and covered his eyes.
   - What happens to Martin and Pedro that is the same? They both see a movie.
   - What does Martin think about the scary part of the movie? He thinks it's fun and exciting.
   - What does Pedro think about the scary part of the movie? He doesn't like it.
   - What do Martin's and Pedro's reactions tell us about them? Possible answer: Martin likes to be scared, but Pedro doesn't.

Objectives

- Compare and contrast actions of characters in a text.
- Identify details that explain characters' actions.
- Build vocabulary through listening, reading, and discussion.
- Use new vocabulary in written and spoken sentences.

Words to Know

Before reading "Diamonds and Toads,"

1. Have students say each word aloud.
2. Ask students if they know what each word means.
   - If students know a word's meaning, have them define it and use it in a sentence.
   - If students don't know a word's meaning, read them the definition and discuss the word with them.

astonished – surprised
pitcher – a container for liquids like water, which usually has a handle for carrying and a spout for pouring
rude – not polite; having bad manners
spring – a place where water rises up from under the ground
sweet-tempered – being kind and gentle
viper – a poisonous snake

Read Aloud

Book Walk

Prepare students by taking them on a Book Walk of "Diamonds and Toads." Scan the story together to revisit the characters and events.

1. Turn to the **table of contents**. Help students find the selection, and turn to that page.
2. Point to and read aloud the **title of the story**.
3. Have students look at the **pictures** of the story.
   - Have you ever been rude or mean to another person? What did you say or do? Answers will vary.
   - Has anyone ever been rude or mean to you? How did it make you feel? Answers will vary.
   - The poor woman and the princess are the same person. How can this be? She's a fairy and can change what she looks like.

Objectives

- Activate prior knowledge by previewing text and/or discussing topic.
- Listen and respond to texts representing a variety of cultures, time periods, and traditions.

"Diamonds and Toads"

Now it's time to read the story. Have students sit next to you so that they can see the pictures and words while you read the story aloud.

Read aloud the entire story. Tell students to listen carefully to hear how the characters act and why they do the things they do.

Check Your Reading

"Diamonds and Toads"

Have students retell the story in their own words to develop grammar, vocabulary, comprehension, and fluency skills. When finished, **ask students the following questions** to check comprehension and encourage discussion.

1. Point to the picture on page 122.
   - Which daughter is more like the mother? the elder daughter
2. Point to the picture on page 123.
   - What part of the story does this picture show? the younger daughter giving the poor woman some water
   - What is the younger daughter holding? a pitcher Why does she have a pitcher? Getting water is one of her chores.
3. Point to the pictures on page 125.
   - Why does the younger daughter looked surprised? Jewels and flowers are coming out of her mouth.
4. Point to the picture on page 126.
   - Why are snakes and toads coming out of the elder daughter's mouth? She was rude to the princess (fairy), so the princess gave her a gift that fit her actions.

Objectives

- Describe illustrations and their relationship to story events.

Reading for Meaning

Characters' Actions in "Diamonds and Toads"

Remind students that characters sometimes share experiences, but they don't always react to them in the same way. **Ask students the following questions** to check understanding of characters and their actions.

- The mother has two daughters. Which daughter does she treat better? the elder daughter Why? because she looks and acts like the mother
- How does the mother treat the younger daughter? She makes the younger daughter do all the housework. Why? She doesn't like her; she likes the elder daughter better.
- What does the younger daughter do when the poor woman asks her for a drink? She gets her some water from the clearest part of the spring.
- Why is the younger daughter happy to get the poor woman a drink? Possible answers: because she's a sweet-tempered girl; because she's kind.
- What does the elder daughter do when the princess asks her for a drink? She tells the princess that she can get it herself; she throws the pitcher at her feet.
- Why does the elder daughter treat the princess this way? Possible answers: because she's a disagreeable girl; because she's rude, mean, nasty, or spoiled
- The fairy disguises herself as a poor woman and a princess. She makes jewels and flowers come out of the younger daughter's mouth, but she makes snakes and toads come out of the elder daughter's mouth. Why does the fairy treat the daughters differently? because the younger daughter is nice to her, but the elder daughter is mean
- Do you think what the fairy does to the two daughters is fair? Why or why not? Answers will vary.

Objectives

- Compare and contrast actions of characters in a text.
- Identify details that explain characters' actions.
- Demonstrate understanding through drawing, discussion, and/or writing.

Review "Diamonds and Toads"

Lesson Overview

Offline "Diamonds and Toads" **30 minutes**

Get Ready	Words to Know
	Reread
Reading for Meaning	Summarize "Diamonds and Toads"
Making Connections	You Are What You Speak
Beyond the Lesson	**OPTIONAL:** Diamonds and Toads and Eggs, Oh My!

Materials

Supplied

- "Diamonds and Toads," *K12 Read Aloud Treasury*, pp. 122–127
- *K12 Language Arts Activity Book*, p. LC 55

Also Needed

- crayons

Keywords

summarize – to tell the most important ideas or events of a text

summary – a short retelling that includes only the most important ideas or events of a text

Big Ideas

- Comprehension requires an understanding of story structure.
- Comprehension requires the reader to self-monitor understanding.

Offline 30 minutes

"Diamonds and Toads"

Work **together** with students to complete offline Get Ready, Reading for Meaning, Making Connections, and Beyond the Lesson activities.

Get Ready

Words to Know

Ask students to define the following words and use them in a sentence:

astonished	**rude**	**sweet-tempered**
pitcher	**spring**	**viper**

Correct any incorrect or vague definitions.

Objectives

- Build vocabulary through listening, reading, and discussion.
- Use new vocabulary in written and spoken sentences.

Reread

If you'd like to, reread the story to students. Otherwise, move on to the next activity.

Reading for Meaning

Summarize "Diamonds and Toads"

Have students check their understanding of a story by giving a summary.

Objectives

- Summarize read-aloud stories.

1. Tell students that a **summary** is a very short retelling that **includes only the most important things that happen in a story, in the order in which they happen**.
2. Point out that a summary is not the same as retelling a story because it does not include very many details.
3. Ask students to complete the following steps to summarize the story.
   - Tell what happens at the beginning of the story in one or two sentences. Example: There is a mother with two daughters. The mother likes the elder daughter and is mean to the younger daughter.
   - Tell what happens in the middle of the story in one or two sentences. Example: The younger daughter gives an old woman some water, and then flowers and jewels come out of her mouth when she talks. The mother sends the elder daughter to find the old woman.
   - Tell what happens at the end of the story in one or two sentences. Example: The elder daughter finds a princess but is rude to her; after that, whenever she speaks, snakes and toads fall out of her mouth.
   - Tell what happens in the story in just a few sentences. Answers should be a combination of the preceding summaries for the beginning, middle, and end of the story. The summary of the full story should tell the events in the order in which they happen.

Making Connections

You Are What You Speak

Encourage students to evaluate their own behavior and create a personal drawing.

1. Ask students to think about how they speak to other people.
2. On page LC 55 in *K[12] Language Arts Activity Book*, have them draw what would come out of their mouth based on past behavior. Have students use one of the following situations for their picture:
   - Think of a time when you said something nice to someone.
   - Think of a time when you said something to someone when you were feeling angry.
3. Have students explain their drawing.

Objectives

- Create illustrations that represent personal connections to text.

Making Connections
Review "Diamonds and Toads"
You Are What You Speak
Think about how you speak to other people. Draw a picture of what would come out of your mouth.
Answers will vary.
LANGUAGE ARTS BLUE LC 55

Beyond the Lesson

OPTIONAL: Diamonds and Toads and Eggs, Oh My!

This activity is intended for students who have extra time and would benefit from reading another version of "Diamonds and Toads." Feel free to skip this activity.

1. Go to a library and look for a copy of *The Talking Eggs* by Robert D. San Souci.
2. Lead a Book Walk, and then read aloud the story.
3. Have students tell how "Diamonds and Toads" and *The Talking Eggs* are alike and different.
4. Ask them to tell which story is their favorite and why.

Objectives

- Compare and contrast two texts on the same topic.

Introduce "Talk"

Lesson Overview

Offline	"Talk"	30 minutes
Get Ready	Identify Fantasy	
	Words to Know	
Read Aloud	Book Walk	
	"Talk"	
Check Your Reading	"Talk"	

Materials

Supplied

- "Talk," *K[12] Read Aloud Treasury*, pp. 128–132

Story Synopsis

Have you ever heard the expression, "If these walls could talk. . . ."? In this West African folktale, the walls might not be talking—but everything else is!

There is a brief reference to wanting to whip a dog, but it never happens.

Keywords

fantasy – a story with characters, settings, or other elements that could not really exist

Advance Preparation

Read "Talk" before beginning the Read Aloud activity, to locate Words to Know within the text.

Offline 30 minutes

"Talk"

Work **together** with students to complete offline Get Ready, Read Aloud, and Check Your Reading activities.

Get Ready

Identify Fantasy

Explore the concept of fantasy.

1. Explain that a **fantasy** is a story that has make-believe things in it. The parts of a story that are fantasy could never happen in the real world. For example, a toy rabbit is real, but a toy rabbit cannot think or move in the real world.
2. Ask students the following questions.
   - Imagine that you read a story about a fairy who turns pebbles into gold coins. Is this real or fantasy? fantasy How do you know? Fairies don't exist in the real world.
   - Imagine that you read a story about a family going on a trip in a car. Is this real or fantasy? real How do you know? A family can take a trip in a car in the real world.
   - Imagine that you read a story about a family that lives in a castle on a cloud. Is this real or fantasy? fantasy How do you know? A family can't live on a cloud in the real world.

Objectives

- Distinguish fantasy from realistic text.
- Build vocabulary through listening, reading, and discussion.
- Use new vocabulary in written and spoken sentences.

Words to Know

Before reading "Talk,"

1. Have students say each word aloud.
2. Ask students if they know what each word means.
   - If students know a word's meaning, have them define it and use it in a sentence.
   - If students don't know a word's meaning, read them the definition and discuss the word with them.

bundle – something wrapped or tied up for carrying
chief – the leader of a group of people
ford – a shallow part of a river where a person can cross by walking
position – the place where someone or something is
recite – to tell about in detail
refrain – to hold yourself back from doing something
scowl – to frown in an angry way
tone – the sound of somebody's voice that shows how they are feeling

Read Aloud

Book Walk

Prepare students by taking them on a Book Walk of "Talk." Scan the story together.

1. Turn to the **table of contents**. Help students find the selection, and turn to that page.
2. Point to and read aloud the **title of the story**.
3. Have students look at the **pictures** of the story. Answers to questions may vary.
   - What do you think the story is about?
   - Where do you think the story takes place?
   - What do you think your shoe would say if it could talk?
   - What object would you like to talk to you? Why?

Objectives

- Make predictions based on title, illustrations, and/or context clues.
- Listen and respond to texts representing a variety of cultures, time periods, and traditions.

"Talk"

Now it's time to read the story. Have students sit next to you so that they can see the pictures and words while you read the story aloud.

Read aloud the entire story. Emphasize Words to Know as you come to them. If appropriate, use the pictures to help show what each word means. Tell students to listen carefully for things that couldn't happen in the real world.

TIP *Guinea* is pronounced "GIH-nee."

Check Your Reading

"Talk"

Have students retell the story in their own words to develop grammar, vocabulary, comprehension, and fluency skills. When finished, **ask students the following questions** to check their understanding of the story, with a focus on fantasy.

- Can a man really use a stick to dig up a yam? Yes
- Can a yam really talk? No
- The dog tells the farmer that it was the yam that spoke. Is this fantasy or something that could really happen? fantasy
- Name something else in the story that is fantasy. Answers will vary; be sure students mention something that couldn't happen in real life.
- Who is the first person that the farmer tells about the talking things? the fisherman
- What does the fisherman do when the fish trap says something to him? He throws the trap on the ground and starts to run.

Objectives

- Distinguish fantasy from realistic text.
- Answer questions requiring literal recall of details.

Explore "Talk"

Lesson Overview

Offline "Talk" — 30 minutes

Get Ready	Recognize Cause and Effect
	Words to Know
Read Aloud	Book Walk
	"Talk"
Check Your Reading	"Talk"
Reading for Meaning	Cause and Effect in "Talk"

Materials

Supplied

- "Talk," *K[12] Read Aloud Treasury*, pp. 128–132

Also Needed

- household objects – globe or world map

Keywords

cause – the reason why something happens

character – a person or animal in a story

effect – the result of a cause

setting – when and where a story takes place

Advance Preparation

Before working with students, spend a few minutes reviewing Words to Know. Then review the Check Your Reading and Reading for Meaning activities to familiarize yourself with the questions and answers.

Gather a globe or world map for use in the Read Aloud activity.

Big Ideas

Comprehension requires an understanding of story structure.

Offline 30 minutes

"Talk"

Work **together** with students to complete offline Get Ready, Read Aloud, Check Your Reading, and Reading for Meaning activities.

Get Ready

Recognize Cause and Effect

Explore cause-and-effect relationships with students.

1. Tell students that doing one thing can make another thing happen. The thing that you do is called the **cause**, and the thing that happens is called the **effect**.
2. Explain that sometimes the cause and effect are things we can see and touch. Other times, they are things we say or do. Examples of cause and effect are all around us.
   - **Cause:** You drop a bowl of popcorn.
     Effect: Popcorn falls all over the floor.
   - **Cause:** You feel cold.
     Effect: You put on a sweater.
3. Have students practice figuring out cause-and-effect relationships.
   - The box of cookies is empty. What might have caused this? Possible answer: Someone ate them.
   - You forget to water the flowers in the garden. What might happen next? Possible answers: The flowers might wilt, die, or turn brown.
4. Tell students that they will hear more examples of cause and effect in the story "Talk."

Objectives

- Describe cause-and-effect relationships in text.
- Build vocabulary through listening, reading, and discussion.
- Use new vocabulary in written and spoken sentences.

Words to Know

Before reading "Talk,"

1. Have students say each word aloud.
2. Ask students if they know what each word means.
   - If students know a word's meaning, have them define it and use it in a sentence.
   - If students don't know a word's meaning, read them the definition and discuss the word with them.

bundle – something wrapped or tied up for carrying
chief – the leader of a group of people
ford – a shallow part of a river where a person can cross by walking
position – the place where someone or something is
recite – to tell about in detail
refrain – to hold yourself back from doing something
scowl – to frown in an angry way
tone – the sound of somebody's voice that shows how they are feeling

Read Aloud

Book Walk

Prepare students by taking them on a Book Walk of "Talk." Scan the story together to revisit the characters and events.

1. Turn to the **table of contents**. Point to and read aloud the **title of the story**.
2. Have students look at the **pictures** of the story.
3. Point to the picture on pages 130 and 131.
   - Why are the characters running to the village chief? They want to tell him about all the items talking.
   - Why do you think the story is call "Talk?" Answers will vary.
4. Gather the world map or globe.
   - Point to Ghana in West Africa.
   - Tell students the story takes place in Accra, Ghana. Ghana is a country in Africa.

Objectives

- Activate prior knowledge by previewing text and/or discussing topic.
- Listen and respond to texts representing a variety of cultures, time periods, and traditions.

"Talk"

Now it's time to read the story. Have students sit next to you so that they can see the pictures and words while you read the story aloud.

Read aloud the entire story. Tell students to listen carefully to hear how one thing causes another throughout the story.

Check Your Reading

"Talk"

Have students retell the story in their own words to develop grammar, vocabulary, comprehension, and fluency skills. When finished, **ask students the following questions** to check ability to identify characters and setting.

- Name a character from the story. Possible answers: the farmer; the fisherman; the weaver; the man in the river (the bather); the chief
- Do any of the characters in the story have a name? No
- Where does the story take place? Possible answers: Africa; Gulf of Guinea; Ghana; Accra; a village
- Who does the farmer think is talking to him at first? his cow
- Who is really talking? his dog
- Where does the end of the story take place? at the house of the chief

Objectives

- Identify setting.
- Identify character(s).
- Answer questions requiring literal recall of details.

Reading for Meaning

Cause and Effect in "Talk"

Remind students that doing one thing can make another thing happen. **Ask students the following questions** to check ability to identify cause-and-effect relationships.

- Why does the man want to dig up some yams? He wants to take them to the market.
- Why is the yam angry with the man? because the man never weeded it
- Why does the man become angry? He doesn't like how the dog speaks to him.
- What happens when the man cuts a branch from the palm tree? The tree tells him to put it down.
- What happens when the man puts the branch on the stone? The stone tells him to take it off.
- What does the man do when the stone talks to him? He starts to run.
- What happens after the man tells the fisherman about all the talking things? The fisherman says that it's not so frightening, and then the fish trap asks a question and scares the fisherman.

Objectives

- Describe cause-and-effect relationships in text.
- Identify details that explain characters' actions.

Review "Talk"

Lesson Overview

Offline	"Talk"	30 minutes
Get Ready	Words to Know	
	Reread or Retell	
Reading for Meaning	Use Pictures to Recognize Cause and Effect	
Making Connections	And Then . . .	

Materials

Supplied

- "Talk," *K[12] Read Aloud Treasury*, pp. 128–132
- *K[12] Language Arts Activity Book*, p. LC 56

Also Needed

- crayons

Keywords

cause – the reason why something happens

effect – the result of a cause

illustration – a drawing

Big Ideas

- Comprehension requires an understanding of story structure.
- Comprehension is enhanced when information is presented through more than one learning modality; learning modalities are visual (seeing), auditory (hearing), and kinesthetic (touching).

Offline 30 minutes

"Talk"

Work **together** with students to complete offline Get Ready, Reading for Meaning, and Making Connections activities.

Get Ready

Words to Know

Ask students to define the following words and use them in a sentence:

bundle	**position**	**scowling**
chief	**recite**	**tone**
ford	**refrain**	

Correct any incorrect or vague definitions.

Objectives

- Build vocabulary through listening, reading, and discussion.
- Use new vocabulary in written and spoken sentences.

Reread or Retell

If you'd like to, reread the story to students. Otherwise, have students retell the story using the pictures as a guide, or move on to the next activity.

Reading for Meaning

Use Pictures to Recognize Cause and Effect

Remind students that pictures can help readers understand story events. In this story, pictures can help readers see how one action leads to, or causes, another action.

Objectives

- Describe illustrations and their relationship to story events.
- Describe cause-and-effect relationships in text.

1. Point to the picture on page 128.
   - Why does the man look surprised? The yam is talking to him.
   - What does the yam say? to go away and leave him alone
2. Point to the picture on page 129.
   - Why does the man look surprised? because the stone is talking to him
   - What does the stone say? to take the branch off of him
3. Point to the picture on page 131.
   - Why are all the men talking to the village chief? They are telling him about all the talking things.
   - Does the chief believe them? No
4. Point to the picture on page 132.
   - Why does the chief looked surprised? because his stool is talking to him

Making Connections

And Then . . .

Have students demonstrate understanding of cause-and-effect relationships by imagining what would happen next in the story "Talk."

1. Have students study the picture on page LC 56 in *K[12] Language Arts Activity Book*.
2. Remind them that the last thing that happens in the story "Talk" is that the stool talks to the chief of the village.
3. Have students draw a picture of what they think the chief would do because of the talking stool.
4. Ask students to explain their drawing.

Objectives

- Describe cause-and-effect relationships in text.
- Respond to text through art, writing, and/or drama.

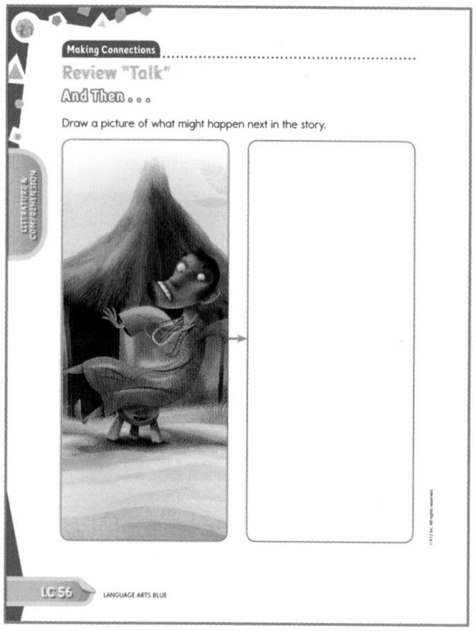
Making Connections
Review "Talk"
And Then . . .
Draw a picture of what might happen next in the story.
LITERATURE & COMPREHENSION
LC 56 LANGUAGE ARTS BLUE

Introduce "That's Tasty!"

Lesson Overview

Offline	"That's Tasty!"	30 minutes
Get Ready	Topic and Purpose of a Text	
	Words to Know	
Read Aloud	Book Walk	
	"That's Tasty!"	
Check Your Reading	"That's Tasty!"	

Advance Preparation

Read "That's Tasty!" before beginning the Read Aloud activity, to locate Words to Know within the text.

Big Ideas

Comprehension entails actively thinking about what is being read.

Materials

Supplied

- **"That's Tasty!," *Our Busy Bodies*, pp. 12–19**

Story Synopsis

Bite into a cupcake? *Sweet!* Bite into a lemon? *Sour!* A handful of chips? *Salty*! A sprig of parsley? *Bitter!*

Without the help of thousands of taste buds on our tongue, food would be pretty bland, and we'd never have a reason to say, "That's tasty!"

Keywords

nonfiction – writings about true things

topic – the subject of a text

[Offline] 30 minutes

"That's Tasty!"

Work **together** with students to complete offline Get Ready, Read Aloud, and Check Your Reading activities.

Get Ready

Topic and Purpose of a Text

Explore characteristics of nonfiction text.

1. Tell students that every magazine article has a **topic**. Good readers can figure out the topic by asking themselves, "What is this article mostly about?"
2. Explain that an author writes an article for a certain reason, or **purpose**. Good readers can figure out the purpose of an article by asking themselves, "Why did the author write this?
3. Tell students that authors write articles for one of the following reasons: to teach us something; to entertain us; to convince us of something; or to tell us their opinion.
4. Have students practice naming the topic and purpose of an article.
   Say: Listen carefully as I read the title of an article and what it's about. In the article "Roar!" the author tells interesting facts about lions.
   - What do you think is the topic of the article "Roar!"? lions
   - Why do you think the author wrote the article? to teach us things about lions

Objectives

- Identify the topic.
- Identify the purpose of a text.
- Increase concept and content vocabulary.
- Use new vocabulary in written and spoken sentences.

Words to Know

Before reading "That's Tasty!,"

1. Have students say each word aloud.
2. Ask students if they know what each word means.
   - If students know a word's meaning, have them define it and use it in a sentence.
   - If students don't know a word's meaning, read them the definition and discuss the word with them.

sense – to become aware of something; to recognize something
sense of taste – one of the five senses; the sense that makes it possible to recognize flavors when a person eats and drinks
signal – a message
taste buds – little bumps on the tongue that sense whether food is sweet, sour, salty, or bitter

Read Aloud

Book Walk

Prepare students by taking them on a Book Walk of "That's Tasty!" Scan the magazine article together, and ask students to make predictions about the text. Answers to questions may vary.

1. Turn to the **table of contents.** Help students find today's selection, and turn to that page.
2. Point to and read aloud the **title of the article**.
3. Have students look at the **pictures** in the article.
   - What do you think the article is about?
   - What do you already know about the sense of taste?
   - What is one of your favorite foods to eat? What do you like about the way it tastes?
4. Point to and read aloud any **headers, captions,** or **other features** that stand out.
   - What do you think the article might tell us about the sense of taste?

Objectives

- Activate prior knowledge by previewing text and/or discussing topic.
- Make predictions based on title, illustrations, and/or context clues.
- Read and listen to a variety of texts for information and pleasure independently or as part of a group.

"That's Tasty!"

Now it's time to read the article. Have students sit next to you so that they can see the pictures and words while you read the article aloud.

Read aloud the entire article. Emphasize Words to Know as you come to them. If appropriate, use the pictures to help show what each word means. Tell students to listen carefully to figure out the topic of the article and why the author most likely wrote it.

Check Your Reading

"That's Tasty!"

Have students retell the article in their own words to develop grammar, vocabulary, comprehension, and fluency skills. When finished, **ask students the following questions** to check comprehension and encourage discussion.

- What is the topic of this article? the sense of taste
- What question did you ask yourself to figure out the topic? What is this article mostly about?
- Why do you think the author wrote this article? to teach us about the sense of taste
- What are the four different tastes? sweet, sour, salty, bitter
- Name a food that tastes sour. Answers will vary.
- Name a food that tastes sweet. Answers will vary.

Objectives

- Identify the topic.
- Identify the purpose of a text.
- Answer questions requiring literal recall of details.

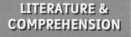

Explore "That's Tasty!"

Lesson Overview

Offline	"That's Tasty!"	30 minutes
Get Ready	It's in the Details	
	Words to Know	
Read Aloud	Book Walk	
	"That's Tasty!"	
Check Your Reading	"That's Tasty!"	
Reading for Meaning	Evaluate the Importance of a Detail	

Materials

Supplied

- "That's Tasty!," *Our Busy Bodies*, pp. 12–19

Keywords

detail – a piece of information in a text

informational text – text written to explain and give information about a topic

Advance Preparation

Before working with students, spend a few minutes reviewing Words to Know. Then review the Check Your Reading and Reading for Meaning activities to familiarize yourself with the questions and answers.

Big Ideas

Comprehension entails an understanding of the organizational patterns of text.

Offline 30 minutes

"That's Tasty!"

Work **together** with students to complete offline Get Ready, Read Aloud, Check Your Reading, and Reading for Meaning activities.

Get Ready

It's in the Details

Help students recognize the most important details in informational text.

1. Tell students that informational texts—such as magazine articles—are filled with details about the topic. However, one detail isn't automatically as important as another. **Details that help readers better understand the topic of an article are important.**
2. **Say:** Other details might be interesting, but they aren't essential to remember. For example, it's important to know that earth has one moon; although it's interesting to know that some people see a man's face when they look at the moon, it doesn't help us know more about the moon.
3. Tell students that learning to recognize the most important details helps good readers sort through information and make decisions about what they should remember.
4. Have students practice picking out an important detail.
   Say: The first person to walk on the moon was Neil Armstrong. His boot left a footprint in the moon dust that was 13 inches long and 6 inches wide.
   - Which detail is more important: that Neil Armstrong was the first person to walk on the moon, or that he left a footprint in the moon dust? that Neil Armstrong was the first person to walk on the moon

Objectives

- Identify important details in informational text.
- Distinguish the most important details from less important details in text.
- Increase concept and content vocabulary.
- Use new vocabulary in written and spoken sentences.

Words to Know

Before reading "That's Tasty!,"

1. Have students say each word aloud.
2. Ask students if they know what each word means.
   - If students know a word's meaning, have them define it and use it in a sentence.
   - If students don't know a word's meaning, read them the definition and discuss the word with them.

sense – to become aware of something; to recognize something
sense of taste – one of the five senses; the sense that makes it possible to recognize flavors when a person eats and drinks
signal – a message
taste buds – little bumps on the tongue that sense whether food is sweet, sour, salty, or bitter

Read Aloud

Book Walk

Prepare students by taking them on a Book Walk of "That's Tasty!" Scan the magazine article together to revisit the text.

1. Turn to the article.
2. Point to and read aloud the **title of the article**.
3. Have students look at the **pictures** in the article.
4. Point to the picture of the tongue on page 12.
   - ▸ What does this picture of a tongue show? the bumps that are taste buds
   - ▸ What is one of the tastes that your taste buds can sense? Possible answers: sweet; sour; salty; bitter

Objectives

- Activate prior knowledge by previewing text and/or discussing topic.
- Read and listen to a variety of texts for information and pleasure independently or as part of a group.

"That's Tasty!"

Now it's time to read the article. Have students sit next to you so that they can see the pictures and words while you read the article aloud.

Read aloud the entire article. Tell students to listen carefully for important details in the article.

Check Your Reading

"That's Tasty!"

Have students retell the article in their own words to develop grammar, vocabulary, comprehension, and fluency skills. When finished, **ask students the following questions** to check ability to state and identify details in an informational text.

- ▸ What do we call the bumps on our tongue? taste buds
- ▸ When you put food in your mouth, what do your taste buds do? sense what the food tastes like; send signals to the brain
- ▸ What are the four tastes? sweet; sour; salty; bitter
- ▸ Name a food from the article that tastes salty. pretzels; potato chips; crackers
- ▸ How does a dill pickle taste? sour
- ▸ How does our sense of taste help keep us safe? It can tell us when foods are moldy, rotten, or poisonous so we don't eat them.

Objectives

- State the details of a text.
- Identify important details in informational text.

Reading for Meaning

Evaluate the Importance of a Detail

Remind students that **some details in an article are more important to remember than others. Ask the following questions** to check ability to distinguish the most important details from less important details in an article.

- What's on your tongue that helps you taste food? taste buds Is this an important detail about the sense of taste? Yes
- How does honey taste? sweet
- What can happen if you eat too much sugar? It can make you feel sick.
- Which detail is more important: that a lemon is a food that tastes sour, or that eating a lemon might make your lips pucker? that a lemon is a food that tastes sour
- Which detail is more important: that "bitter" is one of the four tastes, or that some medicines taste bitter? that "bitter" is one of the four tastes
- Which detail is more important: that your sense of taste can keep you safe, or that you probably would spit out spoiled milk? that your sense of taste can keep you safe
- Which detail is more important: that many children don't like the taste of broccoli, or that the way things taste to you can change over time? that the way things taste to you can change over time

Objectives

- Identify important details in informational text.
- Distinguish the most important details from less important details in text.

Review "That's Tasty!"

Lesson Overview

Offline	"That's Tasty!"	30 minutes
Get Ready	Words to Know	
	Reread or Retell	
Reading for Meaning	How the Sense of Taste Works	
Making Connections	Four Tastes	

Materials

Supplied

- "That's Tasty!," *Our Busy Bodies*, pp. 12–19
- *K[12] Language Arts Activity Book*, p. LC 57

Also Needed

- crayons

Big Ideas

Comprehension entails an understanding of the organizational patterns of text.

Keywords

cause – the reason why something happens

effect – the result of a cause

graphic organizer – a visual tool used to show relationships between key concepts; formats include webs, diagrams, and charts

Offline 30 minutes

"That's Tasty!"

Work **together** with students to complete offline Get Ready, Reading for Meaning, and Making Connections activities.

Get Ready

Words to Know

Ask students to define the following words and use them in a sentence:

sense	**signals**
sense of taste	**taste buds**

Correct any incorrect or vague definitions.

Objectives

- Use new vocabulary in written and spoken sentences.
- Increase concept and content vocabulary.

Reread or Retell

If you'd like to, reread the article to students. Otherwise, have students retell the article using the pictures as a guide, or move on to the next activity.

Reading for Meaning

How the Sense of Taste Works

Remind students that one thing can lead to another. The thing that you do is called the **cause**, and the thing that happens is called the **effect**. **Ask students the following questions** to check understanding of cause-and-effect relationships and general comprehension.

- What happens when you put food in your mouth? Your taste buds send signals to your brain.
- What do the signals help your brain to do? figure out what the food tastes like
- Imagine that your lips are puckering and your mouth is watering. What might have caused that? You just put something that tastes sour in your mouth; you're eating something like a lemon or a dill pickle.
- What is the effect, or what happens, when people put salt on their food? It can make their food taste better.
- Why don't most people like to eat bitter foods? Those foods have a sharp taste; they don't taste good.

Objectives

- Describe cause-and-effect relationships in text.
- Answer questions requiring literal recall of details.

Making Connections

Four Tastes

Have students identify foods with the four basic tastes.

1. Turn to page LC 57 in *K^{12} Language Arts Activity Book*.
2. Point to the "sweet" circle and say the word aloud.
3. Point to and read aloud the name of the item already in the circle.
4. In the blank sections of the circle, have students draw foods that also have that taste.
   - If students have trouble thinking of foods for taste, help them find examples in the article.
5. Ask students to identify what they've drawn, and write what they dictate next to the drawings.
6. Repeat Steps 2–5 for the remaining circles.
7. Have students identify their favorite taste and foods with that taste.

Objectives

- Demonstrate understanding through graphic organizers.
- Increase concept and content vocabulary.

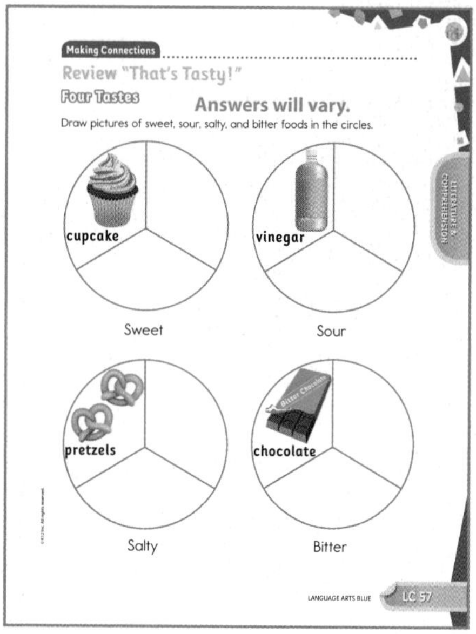

Introduce "The Story of Tom Thumb"

Unit Overview

In this unit, students will explore the theme of *Tiny People* through the following reading selections:

- "The Story of Tom Thumb"
- "Thumbelina"

Lesson Overview

Offline "The Story of Tom Thumb" 30 minutes

Get Ready	Predictions
	Words to Know
Read Aloud	Book Walk
	"The Story of Tom Thumb"
Check Your Reading	"The Story of Tom Thumb"

Advance Preparation

Read "The Story of Tom Thumb" before beginning the Read Aloud activity, to locate Words to Know within the text.

Read the Read Aloud directions to be aware of stopping points in the story at which students will make predictions.

Big Ideas

- Comprehension entails actively thinking about what is being read.
- Comprehension is facilitated when readers connect new information to information previously learned.

Materials

Supplied

- **"The Story of Tom Thumb," *K[12] Read Aloud Treasury*, pp. 134–141**

Story Synopsis

Imagine that you were no bigger than your father's thumb. What would you wear? Where would you sleep? How would you stay out of the way of animals and "big" people? Such are the concerns of one small lad known as Tom Thumb.

There is a reference to a wizard at the beginning of the story.

Keywords

prediction – a guess about what might happen that is based on information in a story and what you already know

prior knowledge – things you already know from past experience

Offline 30 minutes

"The Story of Tom Thumb"

Work **together** with students to complete offline Get Ready, Read Aloud, and Check Your Reading activities.

Get Ready

Predictions

Explore making predictions.

1. Tell students that **good readers make predictions**, or guesses, about what will happen in a story. **We use clues in the story and what we know from our own experiences to predict** what will happen next.
2. Explain that good readers learn to change their predictions as they read more of a story and get more information.
3. Have students practice making and revising a prediction.
   Say: Jana opened the refrigerator and took out a carton of milk.
   - What do you think will happen next? Answers will vary.
4. Have students revise their prediction.
   Say: Jana bent down and poured some milk into the saucer on the floor.
   - Now what do you think, or predict, will happen? Answers will vary but should involve Jana's cat drinking the milk.
   - Did you change your prediction? If you did, what new clue made you change your guess? Jana poured milk into a saucer on the floor.

Objectives

- Make predictions before and during reading.
- Evaluate predictions.
- Build vocabulary through listening, reading, and discussion.
- Use new vocabulary in written and spoken sentences.

Words to Know

Before reading "The Story of Tom Thumb,"

1. Have students say each word aloud.
2. Ask students if they know what each word means.
   - If students know a word's meaning, have them define it and use it in a sentence.
   - If students don't know a word's meaning, read them the definition and discuss the word with them.

beggar – someone who asks for food or money because he or she is very poor
might – strength; force
parasol – a kind of umbrella that helps block the sun
raven – a large black bird that looks like a crow
strut – to walk in a proud way as if you are very important
tailor – someone who makes clothes
thistle – a plant with prickly leaves and purple flowers
trousers – pants

Read Aloud

Book Walk

Prepare students by taking them on a Book Walk of "The Story of Tom Thumb." Scan the story together.

1. Turn to the **table of contents**. Help students find the selection, and turn to that page.
2. Point to and read aloud the **title of the story**.
3. Have students look at the picture on the first page of the story. Answers to questions may vary.
   - Where do you think the story takes place?
   - What do you think might happen in the story?
   - What do you think it would be like to be so small that you could fit in someone's hand?

Objectives

- Make predictions based on title, illustrations, and/or context clues.
- Listen and respond to texts representing a variety of cultures, time periods, and traditions.
- Make predictions before and during reading.

"The Story of Tom Thumb"

Now it's time to read the story. Have students sit next to you so that they can see the pictures and words while you read the story aloud.

Read aloud the entire story. Pause at the following points in the story to ask students what they predict will happen next. Jot down their predictions for later reference.

- Page 136: After Tom slips into the bowl of cake batter
- Page 137: After the cow picks up Tom with her mouth
- Page 138: After the raven drops Tom into the sea
- Page 139: After Tom says he wants to visit his parents

Check Your Reading

"The Story of Tom Thumb"

Have students retell the story in their own words to develop grammar, vocabulary, comprehension, and fluency skills. When finished, **ask students the following questions** to check their predictions. **Refer to the predictions you jotted down, as necessary.**

- What did you predict would happen after Tom slips into the bowl of cake batter? Answers will vary.
- Were you surprised that Tom got out of the cow's mouth? Why or why not? Answers will vary.
- What did you predict would happen after the raven drops Tom into the sea? Answers will vary. What really happens? A fish swallows him.
- What did you predict would happen after Tom tells the king he misses his parents? Answers will vary. What clues from the story did you use to make your prediction? Answers will vary.

Objectives

- Evaluate predictions.

Explore "The Story of Tom Thumb"

Lesson Overview

Offline — "The Story of Tom Thumb" — 30 minutes

Get Ready	Inferences
	Words to Know
Read Aloud	Book Walk
	"The Story of Tom Thumb"
Check Your Reading	"The Story of Tom Thumb"
Reading for Meaning	Inferences in "The Story of Tom Thumb"

Materials

Supplied

- "The Story of Tom Thumb," *K12 Read Aloud Treasury*, pp. 134–141

Keywords

detail – a piece of information in a text

infer – to use clues and what you already know to make a guess

inference – a guess you make using the clues in a text and what you already know

prior knowledge – things you already know from past experience

Advance Preparation

Before working with students, spend a few minutes reviewing Words to Know. Then review the Check Your Reading and Reading for Meaning activities to familiarize yourself with the questions and answers.

Big Ideas

- Comprehension entails actively thinking about what is being read.
- Comprehension is facilitated when readers connect new information to information previously learned.

Offline 30 minutes

"The Story of Tom Thumb"

Work **together** with students to complete offline Get Ready, Read Aloud, Check Your Reading, and Reading for Meaning activities.

Get Ready

Inferences

Explain what inferences are.

1. Tell students that good readers are able to **infer**, or figure out, things in a story that the author does not say directly. Good readers think about **clues in the story** and their own **prior knowledge from past experience** to make inferences.
2. Have students practice making inferences. **Read aloud:** Chris put on a pair of swim trunks and ran out to the garage. Dad was putting things in the van. "Sand pail, shovel, sun block, towels. Yep, it's all here. Let's go!" Chris jumped up and down with a big smile on his face. Mom came into the garage and handed Chris a pair of sunglasses. Then everyone piled into the van, and off they went.
   - Where is the family going? the beach What clues from the story helped you figure this out? swim trunks; the things Dad puts in the van; sunglasses
   - Is Chris a girl or a boy? boy What clue helped you figure this out? Boys wear swim trunks, not girls.
   - How does Chris feel? excited; happy What do you know from your own experiences that helped you figure this out? Possible answers: people smile when they're happy; people might jump up and down when they're excited; I feel happy and I get excited when I'm going to the beach.

Objectives

- Make inferences based on text and/or prior knowledge.
- Support inferences with evidence from text and/or prior knowledge.
- Build vocabulary through listening, reading, and discussion.
- Use new vocabulary in written and spoken sentences.

Words to Know

Before reading "The Story of Tom Thumb,"

1. Have students say each word aloud.
2. Ask students if they know what each word means.
   - If students know a word's meaning, have them define it and use it in a sentence.
   - If students don't know a word's meaning, read them the definition and discuss the word with them.

beggar – someone who asks for food or money because he or she is very poor
might – strength or force
parasol – a kind of umbrella that blocks the sun
raven – a large black bird that looks like a crow
strut – to walk in a proud way as if you are very important
tailor – someone who makes clothes
thistle – a plant with prickly leaves and purple flowers
trousers – pants

Read Aloud

Book Walk

Prepare students by taking them on a Book Walk of "The Story of Tom Thumb." Scan the story together to revisit the characters and events.

1. Turn to the selection. Point to and read aloud the **title of the story.**
2. Have students look at the **pictures** of the story. Answers to questions may vary.
   - What is your favorite picture in the story?
   - What part of the story does the picture show?

Objectives

- Listen and respond to texts representing a variety of cultures, time periods, and traditions.
- Describe illustrations and their relationship to story events.

"The Story of Tom Thumb"

Now it's time to read the story. Have students sit next to you so that they can see the pictures and words while you read the story aloud.

Read aloud the entire story. Remind students to listen for clues that might help them understand things in the story that the author doesn't say directly.

Check Your Reading

"The Story of Tom Thumb"

Have students retell the story in their own words to develop grammar, vocabulary, comprehension, and fluency skills. When finished, **ask students the following questions** to check comprehension and encourage discussion. Tell them that when they name the order of things that happen in a story, they are describing the **sequence**.

- Who gives Tom Thumb his name? the fairy queen
- What happens when Tom's mother hears something shaking and rattling in the oven? She gets frightened and throws the cake pan out the window. What happens next? A man picks up the cake with Tom in it and puts it in a basket on his back.
- Why does Tom's mother give him a bath? He's all sticky from being in the cake batter.
- What happens to Tom after the raven drops him in the sea? A fish swallows him.
- How does the king happen to meet Tom? The servants who find Tom in the fish bring him to meet the king.
- What happens when Tom returns to the king's palace after visiting his parents? The king has a tiny chair and a tiny palace made for Tom. He gives Tom a cart pulled by mice. Tom lives at King Arthur's court.

Objectives

- State the details of a text.
- Sequence events from a text.

Reading for Meaning

Inferences in "The Story of Tom Thumb"

Help students make inferences based on events in "Tom Thumb."

Objectives

- Make inferences based on text and/or prior knowledge.
- Support inferences with evidence from text and/or prior knowledge.
- Describe character(s).

1. Remind students that sometimes the author doesn't say things directly in a story. But good readers can figure out, or **infer**, things, such as why events happen, why a character does something, or how a character feels. **Ask students the following questions** to check their ability to make inferences.
2. Remind students that a raven drops Tom in the sea, and then **read aloud**: "Ah, what would have become of poor Tom if it had not been for his friends the fairies? He had hardly touched the water when a big fish swallowed him and swam away."
   - What do you think the fairies did to help Tom? They made a fish come by and swallow him to keep him from drowning.
3. **Read aloud:** "From that day forth, whenever the king rode out on horseback, he took Tom along with him. And if the rain came on, or if the wind blew chill, Tom would creep through a buttonhole and snuggle close to the great king's heart."
   - How do you think the king feels about Tom? Answers will vary; guide students to recognize that the king likes Tom. What do you know from your own experiences that helped you figure this out? If I want to spend time with someone, it's because I like them.
4. **Read aloud:** "When the time came for Tom to go back to King Arthur, it had rained so much that he could not travel."
   - Do you think the roads that Tom had to travel on were paved like roads are now, or were they dirt roads? dirt
   - Why do you think rain would keep Tom from traveling with his little cart? Possible answers: The roads were too muddy or slippery; the roads might have holes filled with water that Tom could fall into; trees might have fallen down and blocked the roads.
5. Have students make inferences about Tom.
   - What words would you use to describe Tom? Possible answers: brave; curious; adventurous; friendly; kind Give examples from the story that explain why you think those words describe Tom. Answers will vary.

Review "The Story of Tom Thumb"

Lesson Overview

Offline "The Story of Tom Thumb" 30 minutes

Get Ready	Words to Know
	Reread or Retell
Reading for Meaning	Story Structure Elements in "The Story of Tom Thumb"
Making Connections	First, Then, Next

Materials

Supplied

- "The Story of Tom Thumb," *K¹² Read Aloud Treasury,* pp. 134–141
- *K¹² Language Arts Activity Book,* p. LC 59

Keywords

plot – what happens in a story

story events – the things that happen in a story; the plot

story structure elements – components of a story; they include character, setting, plot, problem, and solution

Big Ideas

Comprehension requires an understanding of story structure.

[Offline] 30 minutes

"The Story of Tom Thumb"

Work **together** with students to complete offline Get Ready, Reading for Meaning, and Making Connections activities.

Get Ready

Words to Know

Ask students to define the following words and use them in a sentence:

beggar	**raven**	**thistle**
might	**strut**	**trousers**
parasol	**tailor**	

Correct any incorrect or vague definitions.

Objectives

- Build vocabulary through listening, reading, and discussion.
- Use new vocabulary in written and spoken sentences.

Reread or Retell

If you'd like to, reread "The Story of Tom Thumb" to students. Otherwise, have students retell the story using the pictures as a guide, or move on to the next activity.

Reading for Meaning

Story Structure Elements in "The Story of Tom Thumb"

Review plot, setting, and characters in "The Story of Tom Thumb."

1. Remind students that **a story has main parts—plot, setting, and characters.**
2. **Ask students the following questions** to verify understanding of the parts of a story.
   - Where does the story take place? England; in the country; at a farmer's house
   - Name three characters in the story. Possible answers: Tom Thumb; Merlin; Tom's mother and father; the fairies; the servants; King Arthur
   - Who is the main character? Tom Thumb How do you know this? Most of the story is about him.
   - Tell what happens in "The Story of Tom Thumb" in a few sentences. Example: A boy no bigger than his father's thumb is born to a poor farmer and his wife; Tom has many adventures, including falling into cake batter, almost getting eaten by a cow, being carried away by a raven, and being swallowed by a fish. Finally he ends up living with King Arthur.

Objectives

- Identify story structure elements—plot, setting, character(s).

Making Connections

First, Then, Next

Have students demonstrate understanding of sequence by numbering scenes from "The Story of Tom Thumb" in the order in which they happen.

1. On page LC 59 in *K*[12] *Language Arts Activity Book,* have students look at each picture and describe what it shows from the story.
2. Have students number the pictures from the story in the order in which they happen. The first picture has been numbered for them.
   - Refer back to the story if students need help remembering the sequence of events.
3. Have students retell "The Story of Tom Thumb" using the pictures as a guide.

Objectives

- Sequence events from a text.
- Describe illustrations and their relationship to story events.
- Retell a story using illustrations from the text as a guide.

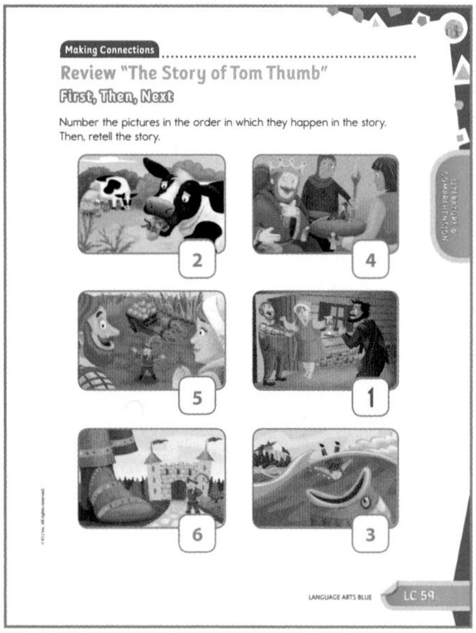
Making Connections

Review "The Story of Tom Thumb"

First, Then, Next

Number the pictures in the order in which they happen in the story. Then, retell the story.

2 4 5 1 6 3

Introduce "Thumbelina"

Lesson Overview

Offline	"Thumbelina"	30 minutes
Get Ready	Compare Characters	
	Words to Know	
Read Aloud	Book Walk	
	"Thumbelina"	
Check Your Reading	"Thumbelina"	

Materials

Supplied

- "Thumbelina," *K[12] Read Aloud Treasury*, pp. 142–147

Also Needed

- household objects – dictionary

Story Synopsis

Thumbelina—who is no bigger than her mother's thumb—has many adventures, including riding on the back of a grasshopper, sailing down a stream on a lily pad, and visiting Mrs. Mouse and her babies . . . all in one day!

Keywords

compare – to explain how two or more things are alike

context clue – a word or phrase in a text that helps you figure out the meaning of an unknown word

contrast – to explain how two or more things are different

Advance Preparation

Read "Thumbelina" before beginning the Read Aloud activities, to locate Words to Know within the text.

Read the Read Aloud directions to become familiar with how to model asking and answering questions about unknown words.

If students have not yet heard "The Story of Tom Thumb" on pages 134–141 in *K[12] Read Aloud Treasury*, read it to them **before** beginning this lesson.

Big Ideas

- Early learners acquire vocabulary through active exposure (by talking and listening, being read to, and receiving explicit instruction).
- Self-questioning improves comprehension and ensures that reading is an interactive process.

Offline 30 minutes

"Thumbelina"

Work **together** with students to complete offline Get Ready, Read Aloud, and Check Your Reading activities.

Get Ready

Compare Characters

Help students recognize similar characters in different literary works.

1. Tell students that **being familiar with characters from one story can help us understand the characters in another story**. The characters might be alike and do the same kinds of things. The characters in two different stories might have similar experiences, too. We know what to expect of certain characters because we've met similar characters in other stories.
2. Remind students of characters that they have met in previous stories.
   - A fox is often tricky and clever, and likes to eat other animals. We see this character in "The Gingerbread Man" and "The Story of Chicken Little."
   - A wolf in a story often acts like a fox. It is often mean or tricky. The wolf in "Little Red Riding Hood" is an example of a tricky wolf.

Objectives

- Build vocabulary through listening, reading, and discussion.
- Use new vocabulary in written and spoken sentences.
- Identify recurring characters in folk and fairy tales.

Words to Know

Before reading "Thumbelina,"

1. Have students say each word aloud.
2. Ask students if they know what each word means.
   - If students know a word's meaning, have them define it and use it in a sentence.
   - If students don't know a word's meaning, read them the definition and discuss the word with them.

bank – the raised area at the edge of a river, pond, or canal
dart – to move quickly
passageway – a narrow hallway or tunnel
thorn – a sharp point on the stem of a plant, such as a rose

Read Aloud

Book Walk

Prepare students by taking them on a Book Walk of "Thumbelina." Scan the story together.

1. Turn to the **table of contents**. Help students find the selection, and turn to that page.
2. Point to and read aloud the **title of the story**.
3. Have students look at the **pictures** of the story.
   - What do you think the story is about? Answers will vary.
   - Where do you think the story takes place? Answers will vary.
   - Does the little girl remind you of anyone from another story? Guide students to think about Tom Thumb.

Objectives

- Make predictions based on title, illustrations, and/or context clues.
- Listen and respond to texts representing a variety of cultures, time periods, and traditions.
- Identify unknown words in text.
- Ask and answer questions about unknown words in text.
- Identify and use picture clues to define words.

"Thumbelina"

Have students **identify unknown words and try to determine their meanings.**

1. Gather the dictionary, and have students sit next to you so that they can see the pictures and words while you read the story aloud.
2. Begin to read aloud. At the end of page 143, pause after reading the sentence with the word *stem* in it.
   Say: I wonder what *stem* means. It says the fish has the stem in his mouth, and I can see that he has something in his mouth in the picture on the next page. I think a stem is the part of a plant where the leaf is attached. I'm going to check the dictionary to make sure.
3. Look up *stem* in the dictionary and read aloud the definition.
4. As you read the rest of the story, have students raise their hand if they hear a word they don't know. Then help students use story clues and the dictionary to figure out what the word means.
5. If students don't identify unknown words on their own, pause at the end of pages 145 and 147, and ask them if they heard any words they don't know. Then help students to figure out the meaning of those words. Possible words to discuss are *crept*, *fetched*, and *skimmed*.

Check Your Reading

"Thumbelina"

Have students retell "Thumbelina" in their own words to develop grammar, vocabulary, comprehension, and fluency skills. When finished, **ask students the following questions** to check comprehension and encourage discussion.

- How are Thumbelina and Tom Thumb alike? They're both no bigger than a thumb.
- How is Thumbelina's experience with a fish different than Tom Thumb's? Thumbelina goes for a sail down the river with a fish; Tom is swallowed by one.
- Think about Tom Thumb's experience with a bird. How is Thumbelina's experience different? Tom is picked up by a bird and then dropped in the sea; Thumbelina goes for a ride on a bird's back.

Objectives

- Compare and contrast the experiences of Tom Thumb and Thumbelina.

Explore "Thumbelina"

Lesson Overview

Offline	"Thumbelina"	30 minutes
Get Ready	Sequence Events	
	Words to Know	
Read Aloud	Book Walk	
	"Thumbelina"	
Check Your Reading	"Thumbelina"	
Reading for Meaning	Use Pictures to Sequence Story Events	

Materials

Supplied

- "Thumbelina," *K[12] Read Aloud Treasury*, pp. 142–147

Keywords

sequence – order

Advance Preparation

Before working with students, spend a few minutes reviewing Words to Know. Then review the Check Your Reading and Reading for Meaning activities to familiarize yourself with the questions and answers.

Big Ideas

Comprehension requires an understanding of story structure.

Offline 30 minutes

"Thumbelina"

Work **together** with students to complete offline Get Ready, Read Aloud, Check Your Reading, and Reading for Meaning activities.

Get Ready

Sequence Events

Explore the order of events in a story.

1. Tell students that the order in which things happen in a story or article is called the **sequence**. Words like *first, next, before, after, then,* and *finally* help tell the sequence, or the order in which things happen.
2. Have students listen for words that tell the sequence, or order.
   Say: First, Maria watered the flowers in the garden. Then, she cut some roses. Next, she put water in a vase. Finally, she put the roses in the vase.
   - What happened first? Maria watered the flowers.
   - What happened next? She cut some roses.
   - What happened last? She put the roses in the vase.

Objectives

- Sequence events from a text.
- Build vocabulary through listening, reading, and discussion.
- Use new vocabulary in written and spoken sentences.

Words to Know

Before reading "Thumbelina,"

1. Have students say each word aloud.
2. Ask students if they know what each word means.
   - If students know a word's meaning, have them define it and use it in a sentence.
   - If students don't know a word's meaning, read them the definition and discuss the word with them.

bank – the raised area at the edge of a river, pond, or canal
dart – to move quickly
passageway – a narrow hallway or tunnel
thorn – a sharp point on the stem of a plant, such as a rose

Read Aloud

Book Walk

Prepare students by taking them on a Book Walk of "Thumbelina." Scan the story together to revisit the characters and events.

1. Point to the **table of contents**.
2. Turn to the selection. Point to and read aloud the **title of the story**.
3. Have students look at the **pictures** of the story. Answers to questions may vary.
   - Which picture is your favorite? Why?
   - What would you like to do if you were Thumbelina's size?

Objectives

- Activate prior knowledge by previewing text and/or discussing topic.
- Listen and respond to texts representing a variety of cultures, time periods, and traditions.

"Thumbelina"

Now it's time to read "Thumbelina." Have students sit next to you so that they can see the pictures and words while you read the story aloud.

Read aloud the entire story. Tell students to listen carefully to hear the order in which things happen in the story.

Check Your Reading

"Thumbelina"

Have students retell the story in their own words to develop grammar, vocabulary, comprehension, and fluency skills. When finished, **ask students the following questions** to check comprehension and encourage discussion.

- Who is first to ask Thumbelina if she would like to go for a ride? the grasshopper
- Who does Thumbelina meet after her ride on the grasshopper? the fish
- What do Thumbelina and the fish do? They sail down the river.
- Where does Mrs. Mouse live? underground
- What happens after Thumbelina leaves Mrs. Mouse's home? She hears a sick bird peeping.
- How does Thumbelina help the bird? She takes a thorn out of its foot.
- How does the story end? The bird takes Thumbelina home, and she tells her mother about all the things that happened to her.

Objectives

- Sequence events from a text.
- Answer questions requiring literal recall of details.

Reading for Meaning

Use Pictures to Sequence Story Events

Direct students to use the pictures in "Thumbelina" to recall the events in the story and the order in which they happen.

1. Explain to students that looking at **a story's pictures can help us remember the order** of the story's events.
2. Point to the picture on page 142.
   - Who is in this picture? Thumbelina and her mother
   - Where does Thumbelina sleep? in a walnut shell
   - Does this picture show something from the beginning, middle, or end of the story? beginning
3. Point to the picture at the top of page 143.
   - What is happening in this picture? Thumbelina is going for a ride on the grasshopper.
4. Point to the picture at the bottom of page 143.
   - Who is Thumbelina talking to? the fish
   - What does the fish ask Thumbelina? if she would like to go for a sail down the river
5. Point to the picture on page 144.
   - What is happening in this picture? Thumbelina is sitting on a lily pad, and the fish is pulling it by the stem.
   - When does this happen in the story? in the middle
6. Point to the picture on page 145.
   - Who is Thumbelina visiting in this picture? Mrs. Mouse and her children
7. Point to the picture on pages 146–147.
   - Why is Thumbelina riding on a bird? The bird is giving her a ride home.
   - When does this happen in the story? at the end

TIP Describing what is happening in a picture helps students develop their summarizing skills. If you accurately describe a picture in one or two sentences, you've given a good summary.

Objectives

- Describe illustrations and their relationship to story events.

Review "Thumbelina"

Lesson Overview

Offline	"Thumbelina"	30 minutes
Get Ready	Words to Know	
	Reread	
Reading for Meaning	Summarize "Thumbelina"	
Making Connections	Tom Thumb Meets Thumbelina	

Materials

Supplied

- "Thumbelina," *K¹² Read Aloud Treasury*, pp. 142–147
- *K¹² Language Arts Activity Book*, p. LC 60

Keywords

graphic organizer – a visual tool used to show relationships between key concepts; formats include webs, diagrams, and charts

self-monitor – to notice if you do or do not understand what you are reading

summarize – to tell the most important ideas or events of a text

summary – a short retelling that includes only the most important ideas or events of a text

Big Ideas

- Comprehension requires an understanding of story structure.
- Comprehension requires the reader to self-monitor understanding.

Offline 30 minutes

"Thumbelina"

Work **together** with students to complete offline Get Ready, Reading for Meaning, and Making Connections activities.

Get Ready

Words to Know

Ask students to define the following words and use them in a sentence:

bank	**passageway**
dart	**thorn**

Correct any incorrect or vague definitions.

Objectives

- Build vocabulary through listening, reading, and discussion.
- Use new vocabulary in written and spoken sentences.

Reread

If you'd like to, reread "Thumbelina" to students. Otherwise, move on to the next activity.

Reading for Meaning

Summarize "Thumbelina"

Help students check their understanding of "Thumbelina" by giving a summary.

Objectives

- Summarize read-aloud stories.

1. Tell students that a **summary** is a very short retelling that **includes only the most important things that happen in a story in the order in which they happen**.
2. Ask them to complete the following steps to summarize "Thumbelina."
   - Tell what happens at the beginning of the story in one or two sentences. Example: Thumbelina is a very tiny girl; she goes for a ride on the back of a grasshopper and sails down a river with a fish.
   - Tell what happens in the middle of the story in one or two sentences. Example: Thumbelina visits Mrs. Mouse and her children; on her way home, she finds a hurt bird.
   - Tell what happens at the end of the story in one or two sentences. Example: Thumbelina takes a thorn out of the bird's foot. The bird is so grateful that it flies Thumbelina home.
   - Tell what happens in the story in just a few sentences. Answers should be a combination of the preceding summaries for the beginning, middle, and end of the story. The summary of the full story should tell the events in the order in which they happen.

Making Connections

Tom Thumb Meets Thumbelina

Have students use a Venn diagram to compare and contrast "Thumbelina" and "The Story of Tom Thumb."

1. Turn to page LC 60 in K^{12} *Language Arts Activity Book*. Point to the illustration. **Say:** This is called a Venn diagram. We use it to show how things are alike and different. Let's use it to show how the characters in "Thumbelina" and "The Story of Tom Thumb" are alike in some ways and different in other ways.
2. Ask students to name things that describe only Thumbelina and her experiences, and write these attributes in the left circle of the Venn diagram. Possible answers: is polite; talks to animals; sails with a fish; helps a bird
3. Ask students to name things that describe only Tom Thumb and his adventures, and write these attributes in the right circle of the Venn diagram. Possible answers: is brave; gets baked into a cake; gets swallowed by a fish; meets a king
4. Ask students to name things that describe **both** Thumbelina and Tom Thumb, and write these attributes in the center of the Venn diagram, where the circles overlap. Possible answers: small size; the word "thumb" in their names

Objectives

- Make connections with text: text-to-text, text-to-self, text-to-world.
- Compare and contrast the experiences of Tom Thumb and Thumbelina.

Making Connections

Review "Thumbelina"

Tom Thumb Meets Thumbelina

Describe Thumbelina and Tom Thumb to complete the Venn diagram.

LC 60 LANGUAGE ARTS BLUE

Introduce "Germs—Our Unwanted Guests"

Unit Overview

In this unit, students will explore the theme of *Help Yourself and Others* through the following reading selections:

- "Germs—Our Unwanted Guests"
- "The Little Red Hen"

Lesson Overview

Offline	"Germs—Our Unwanted Guests"	30 minutes
Get Ready	The Purpose of an Article	
	Words to Know	
Read Aloud	Book Walk	
	"Germs—Our Unwanted Guests"	
Check Your Reading	"Germs—Our Unwanted Guests"	

Advance Preparation

Read "Germs—Our Unwanted Guests" before beginning the Read Aloud activity, to locate Words to Know within the text.

Materials

Supplied

- "Germs—Our Unwanted Guests," *Our Busy Bodies*, pp. 20–27

Story Synopsis

Germs are virtually everywhere, and some can't wait to get inside our bodies and make us sick. We can't stop germs completely, but we can learn how to take precautions to avoid inviting these unwanted guests inside.

Keywords

author's purpose – the reason the author wrote a text: to entertain, to inform, to express an opinion, or to persuade

Offline 30 minutes

"Germs—Our Unwanted Guests"

Work **together** with students to complete offline Get Ready, Read Aloud, and Check Your Reading activities.

Get Ready

The Purpose of an Article

Explore some of the characteristics of nonfiction text.

1. Tell students that an author writes an article for a certain reason, or **purpose**. Good readers can figure out the purpose of an article by asking themselves, "Why did the author write this?" Authors write articles for one of the following reasons: to teach us something; to entertain us; to convince us of something; or to tell us what they think about something.
2. Have students practice naming the purpose of articles.
   Say: Listen as I describe an article. In the article "Dogs Are Amazing Animals," the author tells interesting facts about dogs.
   - Why do you think the author wrote the article? to teach us something

   Say: Listen as I describe another article. In the article "My Dog Thinks She's My Sister," the author tells readers how her dog wants to eat, play, and study with her—just like her younger sister.
   - Why do you think the author wrote the article? to entertain us

Objectives

- Identify the purpose of a text.
- Increase concept and content vocabulary.
- Use new vocabulary in written and spoken sentences.

Words to Know

Before reading "Germs—Our Unwanted Guests,"

1. Have students say each word aloud.
2. Ask students if they know what each word means.
   - If students know a word's meaning, have them define it and use it in a sentence.
   - If students don't know a word's meaning, read them the definition and discuss the word with them.

cells – the tiny units that are the basic building blocks of all living things
germs – very small living things that cause illness
microscope – a scientific instrument that makes very small things look bigger
white blood cells – cells in the blood that fight infection

Read Aloud

Book Walk

Prepare students by taking them on a Book Walk of "Germs—Our Unwanted Guests." Scan the magazine article together, and ask students to make predictions about the text. Answers to questions may vary.

1. Turn to the **table of contents**. Help students find the selection, and turn to that page.
2. Point to and read aloud the **title of the article**.
3. Have students look at the **pictures** in the article.
   - ▸ What do you think the article is about?
   - ▸ When was the last time you were sick? How did you feel?
4. Point to and read aloud any **headers, captions,** or **other features** that stand out.
   - ▸ What do you think the article might tell us about germs?

Objectives

- Make predictions based on title, illustrations, and/or context clues.
- Read and listen to a variety of texts for information and pleasure independently or as part of a group.

"Germs—Our Unwanted Guests"

Now it's time to read the article. Have students sit next to you so that they can see the pictures and words while you read the article aloud.

Read aloud the entire article. Emphasize Words to Know as you come to them. If appropriate, use the pictures to help show what each word means. Tell students to listen carefully so that they can discover what the article is mostly about.

Check Your Reading

"Germs—Our Unwanted Guests"

Have students retell the article in their own words to develop grammar, vocabulary, comprehension, and fluency skills. When finished, **ask students the following questions** to check ability to identify the reason the author wrote the article and check general comprehension.

- ▸ Where can you find germs? almost everywhere; plants; animals; kitchens; bathrooms; water; dry land; air
- ▸ How do germs get into our bodies? They're so small that we can't stop them; we might breathe them in if they're in the air.
- ▸ Do all germs make us sick? No
- ▸ What kind of special cells fight germs? white blood cells
- ▸ Why is it a good idea to cover your mouth and nose when you sneeze? so you won't spread germs in the air
- ▸ Why do you think the author wrote this article? to teach us about germs

Objectives

- Identify the purpose of a text.
- Answer questions requiring literal recall of details.

Explore "Germs—Our Unwanted Guests"

Lesson Overview

Offline	"Germs—Our Unwanted Guests"	30 minutes
Get Ready	Cause and Effect	
	Words to Know	
Read Aloud	Book Walk	
	"Germs—Our Unwanted Guests"	
Check Your Reading	"Germs—Our Unwanted Guests"	
Reading for Meaning	Cause-and-Effect Relationships	

Materials

Supplied

- "Germs—Our Unwanted Guests," *Our Busy Bodies*, pp. 20–27

Keywords

cause – the reason why something happens

detail – a piece of information in a text

effect – the result of a cause

Advance Preparation

Before working with students, spend a few minutes reviewing Words to Know. Then review the Check Your Reading and Reading for Meaning activities to familiarize yourself with the questions and answers.

Big Ideas

Comprehension entails an understanding of the organizational patterns of text.

Offline 30 minutes

"Germs—Our Unwanted Guests"

Work **together** with students to complete offline Get Ready, Read Aloud, Check Your Reading, and Reading for Meaning activities.

Get Ready

Cause and Effect

Explore the idea that one thing can cause another to happen.

1. Tell students that doing one thing can make another thing happen. The thing that you do is called the **cause**, and the thing that happens is called the **effect**. Examples of cause and effect are all around us.
   - **Cause:** You push a button.
     Effect: A doorbell rings.
   - **Cause:** You kick a ball.
     Effect: The ball flies into the air.
   - **Cause:** You practice reading.
     Effect: You become a good reader.
2. Have students practice identifying cause and effect.
   - What happens, or what is the effect, if you stick a pin in a balloon? The balloon pops.
   - What is the cause of a broken glass on the floor? Possible answers: Someone dropped it; it got knocked over.

Objectives

- Describe cause-and-effect relationships in text.
- Increase concept and content vocabulary.
- Use new vocabulary in written and spoken sentences.

Words to Know

Before reading "Germs—Our Unwanted Guests,"

1. Have students say each word aloud.
2. Ask students if they know what each word means.
   - If students know a word's meaning, have them define it and use it in a sentence.
   - If students don't know a word's meaning, read them the definition and discuss the word with them.

cells – the tiny units that are the basic building blocks of all living things
germs – very small living things that cause illness
microscope – a scientific instrument that makes very small things look bigger
white blood cells – cells in the blood that fight infection

Read Aloud

Book Walk

Prepare students by taking them on a Book Walk of "Germs—Our Unwanted Guests." Scan the magazine article together to revisit the text.

1. Turn to the selection.
2. Point to and read aloud the **title of the article**.
3. Have students look at the **pictures** in the article.
   - Did you ever take medicine when you were sick? How did the medicine make you feel? Answers will vary.

Objectives

- Read and listen to a variety of texts for information and pleasure independently or as part of a group.
- Activate prior knowledge by previewing text and/or discussing topic.

"Germs—Our Unwanted Guests"

Now it's time to read the article. Have students sit next to you so that they can see the pictures and words while you read the article aloud.

Read aloud the entire article. Tell students to listen carefully to hear details about germs and what they can do. Remind students that they should listen for examples of cause and effect.

Check Your Reading

"Germs—Our Unwanted Guests"

Have students retell the article in their own words to develop grammar, vocabulary, comprehension, and fluency skills. When finished, **ask students the following questions** to check general comprehension.

- Can you see a germ with just your eyes? No
- What are all your body parts made out of? cells
- What do cells need to do their job well? food and energy
- What can germs do to the cells in our bodies? steal their food and energy
- Why should you cover your mouth and nose when you sneeze? It helps keep germs from getting in the air.

Objectives

- Identify important details in informational text.
- Answer questions requiring literal recall of details.

Reading for Meaning

Cause-and-Effect Relationships

After reading "Germs—Our Unwanted Guests," **ask students the following questions** to check understanding of cause-and-effect relationships and general comprehension.

- If you have a cold, what caused it? germs
- What happens when you look at germs through a microscope? The germs look bigger.
- Why do we feel weak and tired when some germs get into our bodies? The germs steal food and energy from our cells.
- What happens when white blood cells do their job? They keep you from getting sick; they fight germs.
- What happens, or what is the effect, if you take medicine when you're sick? It kills germs; it can make you feel better.
- What can happen if you don't cover your mouth when you cough? Germs get in the air; people breathe in your germs.
- Imagine that your friend is sick and drinks from a cup. What will your friend leave on the cup? germs What could happen if you take a drink from your sick friend's cup? The germs might get inside you; you might get sick, too.
- How can you keep germs off your hands? by washing your hands with soap and warm water

Objectives

- Describe cause-and-effect relationships in text.

Review "Germs—Our Unwanted Guests"

Lesson Overview

Offline	"Germs—Our Unwanted Guests"	30 minutes
Get Ready	Words to Know	
	Reread or Retell	
Reading for Meaning	Visual Text Features in "Germs—Our Unwanted Guests"	
Making Connections	Think! Use the Sink!	

Materials

Supplied

- "Germs—Our Unwanted Guests," *Our Busy Bodies*, pp. 20–27
- *K¹² Language Arts Activity Book*, p. LC 61

Also Needed

- crayons
- tape, clear
- scissors, round-end safety

Big Ideas

Comprehension is facilitated by an understanding of physical presentation (headings, subheads, graphics, and other features).

Keywords

text feature – part of a text that helps a reader locate information and determine what is most important; some examples include the title, table of contents, headings, pictures, and glossary

Offline 30 minutes

"Germs—Our Unwanted Guests"

Work **together** with students to complete offline Get Ready, Reading for Meaning, and Making Connections activities.

Get Ready

Words to Know

Ask students to define the following words and use them in a sentence:

cells **microscope**
germs **white blood cells**

Correct any incorrect or vague definitions.

Objectives

- Use new vocabulary in written and spoken sentences.
- Increase concept and content vocabulary.

Reread or Retell

If you'd like to, reread the article to students. Otherwise, have students retell the article using the pictures as a guide, or move on to the next activity.

Reading for Meaning

Visual Text Features in "Germs—Our Unwanted Guests"

Have students demonstrate the ability to identify and use visual text features such as pictures and headings.

1. Point to the microscopic view of cells on page 22.
   - What does this picture show? germs; how germs look through a microscope
2. Point to and read aloud the heading on page 24.
   - What is this part of the article about? things that help fight germs
3. Point to the picture of the germ holding up the bank on page 24.
   - What does this picture show? how germs rob your body of food and energy
4. Point to the picture of the germ that's been caught on page 25.
   - What caught the germ? the white blood cell What does this picture tell us? that white blood cells fight germs
5. Point to and read aloud the heading on page 26.
   - What is this part of the article about? ways to keep germs from making us sick; ways to keep germs away from us

Objectives

- Use visual text features to aid understanding of text.
- Identify the purpose of and information provided by illustrations, titles, charts, and graphs.

6. Point to the picture of the girl on page 26.
   - What is the girl doing? sneezing or coughing into her elbow Why is she doing this? to keep germs from getting into the air
7. Point to the picture of the hands being washed on page 27.
   - Why is there a picture of someone washing his or her hands? to show how to keep from spreading germs; to show how to get germs off your body

Making Connections

Think! Use the Sink!

Have students color a poster to help them to remember how to fight germs.

1. On page LC 61 in *K[12] Language Arts Activity Book*, point to and read aloud the words on the poster.
2. Ask students to explain why it's a good idea to wash their hands with soap and warm water.
3. Have students color the poster, and then cut it out.
4. Discuss with students the best place to display the poster. Help them hang up the poster in the place they decided upon.

Objectives

- Identify and comprehend environmental print.
- Make connections with text: text-to-text, text-to-self, text-to-world.

Introduce "The Little Red Hen"

Lesson Overview

Offline	"The Little Red Hen"	30 minutes
Get Ready	Morals	
	Words to Know	
Read Aloud	Book Walk	
	"The Little Red Hen"	
Check Your Reading	"The Little Red Hen"	

Advance Preparation

Read "The Little Red Hen"" before beginning the Read Aloud activity, to locate Words to Know within the text.

Materials

Supplied

- **"The Little Red Hen," *K*[12] *Read Aloud Treasury*, pp. 148–149**

Story Synopsis

No one wants to help the Little Red Hen do any work, but everyone wants to help her eat her fresh bread. Will she share the hard-earned fruit of her labors, or will she teach her barnyard friends a lesson?

Keywords

moral – the lesson of a story, particularly a fable

Offline 30 minutes

"The Little Red Hen"

Work **together** with students to complete offline Get Ready, Read Aloud, and Check Your Reading activities.

Get Ready

Morals

Explore the idea that a story can teach a lesson that can be applied to everyday living.

1. Explain that a story can be written to teach a lesson. The lesson that a story teaches is called a **moral**. Some well-known morals are "Two wrongs don't make a right," "Curiosity killed the cat," and "Waste not, want not."
2. Have students recall the moral of the story "The Honest Woodsman" in *K[12] Read Aloud Treasury,* pages 116–121.
   Say: Think about the story "The Honest Woodsman." A woodsman's old ax slides into the river. A river fairy dives into the river and brings back a silver ax and then a gold ax. Both times the woodsman says it's not his ax, even though the silver and gold axes are worth much more than his. At the end of the story, the river fairy rewards the woodsman for his honesty by giving him the silver and gold axes, as well as his old one.
   - What is the lesson, or moral, of the story? "Always tell the truth"; "Honesty is the best policy."

Objectives

- Identify the moral or lesson of a story.
- Build vocabulary through listening, reading, and discussion.
- Use new vocabulary in written and spoken sentences.

Words to Know

Before reading "The Little Red Hen,"

1. Have students say each word aloud.
2. Ask students if they know what each word means.
   - If students know a word's meaning, have them define it and use it in a sentence.
   - If students don't know a word's meaning, read them the definition and discuss the word with them.

grain – the seed of a cereal plant, such as wheat or rice
ground – crushed
mill – the place where wheat is turned into flour
ripe – ready to be picked or cut down

Read Aloud

Book Walk

Prepare students by taking them on a Book Walk of "The Little Red Hen." Scan the story together, and ask students to make predictions about the story.

1. Turn to the **table of contents**. Help students find the selection, and turn to that page.
2. Point to and read aloud the **title of the story**.
3. Have students look at the **pictures** of the story. Answers to questions may vary.
   - What do you think the story is about?
   - Where do you think the story takes place?
   - Did anyone ever ask you to help with a chore? Did you help?

Objectives

- Make predictions based on title, illustrations, and/or context clues.
- Listen and respond to texts representing a variety of cultures, time periods, and traditions.

"The Little Red Hen"

Now it's time to read the story. Have students sit next to you so that they can see the pictures and words while you read the story aloud.

Read aloud the entire story. Emphasize Words to Know as you come to them. If appropriate, use the pictures to help show what each word means.

Check Your Reading

"The Little Red Hen"

Have students retell the story in their own words to develop grammar, vocabulary, comprehension, and fluency skills. When finished, **ask students the following questions** to check ability to identify repetitive text and the moral of a story.

- What does each of the animals say when the little red hen asks who will help her plant the wheat? "I won't."
- What does each of the animals say when the little red hen asks who will help her cut the wheat? "I won't."
- What does each of the animals say when the little red hen asks who will help her take the wheat to the mill? "I won't."
- What does the little red hen say to the animals after they all say, "I won't"? "I will, then."
- What does each of the animals say when the little red hen asks who will help her eat the bread that she makes from the wheat? "I will!"
- What does the little red hen say to the animals after they say they will help eat the bread? "No, you won't."
- What is the moral of the story? Answers will vary; guide students to understand that the moral is "If you don't help, you don't get to share" or "Friends should help friends."

Objectives

- Identify repetitive text.
- Identify the moral or lesson of a text.

Explore "The Little Red Hen"

Lesson Overview

Offline "The Little Red Hen" 30 minutes

Get Ready	Characters in a Story
	Words to Know
Read Aloud	Book Walk
	"The Little Red Hen"
Check Your Reading	"The Little Red Hen"
Reading for Meaning	Compare and Contrast Characters

Materials

Supplied

- "The Little Red Hen," *K[12] Read Aloud Treasury*, pp. 148–149

Keywords

character – a person or animal in a story

compare – to explain how two or more things are alike

contrast – to explain how two or more things are different

Advance Preparation

Before working with students, spend a few minutes reviewing Words to Know. Then review the Check Your Reading and Reading for Meaning activities to familiarize yourself with the questions and answers.

Offline 30 minutes

"The Little Red Hen"

Work **together** with students to complete offline Get Ready, Read Aloud, Check Your Reading, and Reading for Meaning activities.

Get Ready

Characters in a Story

Review characters and main characters with students.

1. Tell students that a story has at least one character. **Characters** are the people or animals in a story. The most important character in a story is called the **main character**. For example, the characters in "Jack and the Beanstalk" are Jack, his mother, the giant, and the giant's wife.
2. Help students identify main characters by asking the following questions.
   - Who is the main character in the story "Jack and the Beanstalk"? Jack
   - How do you know? Most of the story is about Jack and what he does.
   - Think of the story "Little Red Riding Hood." Who are some of the characters in the story? Possible answers: Little Red Riding Hood; her mother; the wolf; her grandmother; the woodsman
   - Who is the main character in the story? Little Red Riding Hood
   - How do you know? Most of the story is about Little Red Riding Hood and what she does.

TIP If students have not yet read "Jack and the Beanstalk" or "Little Red Riding Hood," use stories with which they are familiar to ask the character questions.

Objectives

- Identify character(s).
- Identify the main character(s).
- Build vocabulary through listening, reading, and discussion.
- Use new vocabulary in written and spoken sentences.

Words to Know

Before reading "The Little Red Hen,"

1. Have students say each word aloud.
2. Ask students if they know what each word means.
   - If students know a word's meaning, have them define it and use it in a sentence.
   - If students don't know a word's meaning, read them the definition and discuss the word with them.

grain – the seed of a cereal plant, such as wheat or rice
ground – crushed
mill – the place where wheat is turned into flour
ripe – ready to be picked or cut down

Read Aloud

Book Walk

Prepare students by taking them on a Book Walk of "The Little Red Hen." Scan the story together to revisit the characters and events.

1. Turn to the selection. Point to and read aloud the **title of the story**.
2. Have students look at the **pictures** of the story.
3. Point to the pictures of the animals on page 148.
   - Name the animals in the picture. the little red hen; the dog; the cat; the pig; the turkey
   - What are some of the things the little red hen asks the animals to help her with? planting the wheat; cutting the wheat; taking the wheat to the mill; baking the bread; eating the bread

Objectives

- Listen and respond to texts representing a variety of cultures, time periods, and traditions.
- Activate prior knowledge by previewing text and/or discussing topic.

"The Little Red Hen"

Now it's time to read the story. Have students sit next to you so that they can see the pictures and words while you read the story aloud.

Read aloud the entire story. Remind students to listen to the story carefully so that they will be able to describe the characters. Encourage them to say aloud repetitive text, such as "I won't" and "I will, then."

Check Your Reading

"The Little Red Hen"

Have students retell the story in their own words to develop grammar, vocabulary, comprehension, and fluency skills. When finished, **ask students the following questions** to check ability to identify and describe characters in the story.

- Who are the characters in the story? the little red hen; the dog; the cat; the pig; the turkey; the little red hen's four little chicks
- Who is the main character in the story? the little red hen
- What makes the little red hen the main character? Most of the story is about her; she does all the work.

Objectives

- Identify character(s).
- Identify the main character(s).

Reading for Meaning

Compare and Contrast Characters

Remind students that sometimes characters act the same as each other, and sometimes they do the exact opposite of each other. Good readers look for these things so that they can better understand a story's characters. **Ask the following questions** to check ability to compare and contrast the animals in the story.

- How is the little red hen different from the other animals? She is willing to do all the work to make the bread.
- How are the dog, cat, pig, and turkey alike? None of them wants to help with the work.
- How are the dog, cat, pig, and turkey the same as the little red hen? They want to eat the bread.
- What words would you use to describe the little red hen? Give examples from the story that explain why you think those words describe her. Possible answers: hard worker; busy
- What words would you use to describe the dog, cat, pig, and turkey? Give examples from the story that explain why you chose those words. Possible answers: lazy; not helpful; don't like to do hard work
- How do you think the little red hen feels doing all the work by herself? Answers will vary.
- How do you think the other animals feel when the little red hen doesn't share the bread with them? Answers will vary.
- Do you think it was fair for the little red hen not to share the bread? Why or why not? Answers will vary.
- If you were the little red hen, what would you have done? Answers will vary.

Objectives

- Compare and contrast elements within a text.
- Describe character(s).
- Make inferences based on text and/or prior knowledge.
- Support inferences with evidence from text and/or prior knowledge.
- Make connections with text: text-to-text, text-to-self, text-to-world.

Review "The Little Red Hen"

Lesson Overview

Offline	"The Little Red Hen"	30 minutes
Get Ready	Words to Know	
	Reread	
Reading for Meaning	A Summary of "The Little Red Hen"	
Making Connections	Plant, Cut, Grind, Bake, . . . Eat!	
Beyond the Lesson	OPTIONAL: The Little Red Hen Revisited	

Materials

Supplied

- "The Little Red Hen," *K¹² Read Aloud Treasury*, pp. 148–149
- *K¹² Language Arts Activity Book*, p. LC 63

Also Needed

- glue stick
- scissors, round-end safety

Big Ideas

- Comprehension requires an understanding of story structure.
- Comprehension requires the reader to self-monitor understanding.

Keywords

self-monitor – to notice if you do or do not understand what you are reading

sequence – order

summarize – to tell the most important ideas or events of a text

summary – a short retelling that includes only the most important ideas or events of a text

Offline 30 minutes

"The Little Red Hen"

Work **together** with students to complete offline Get Ready, Reading for Meaning, Making Connections, and Beyond the Lesson activities.

Get Ready

Words to Know

Ask students to define the following words and use them in a sentence:

grain	**mill**
ground	**ripe**

Correct any incorrect or vague definitions.

Objectives

- Build vocabulary through listening, reading, and discussion.
- Use new vocabulary in written and spoken sentences.

Reread

If you'd like to, reread the story to students. Otherwise, move on to the next activity.

Reading for Meaning

A Summary of "The Little Red Hen"

Have students practice giving a summary of a story.

Objectives

- Summarize read-aloud stories.

1. Tell students that one way readers can check their own understanding of a story is by giving a summary.
   Say: A **summary** is a very short retelling that **includes only the most important things that happen in a story in the order in which they happen.**
2. Explain that a summary is not the same as retelling a story because it does not include very many details.
3. Ask students to complete the following steps to summarize the story.
   - Tell what happens at the beginning of the story in one or two sentences. Example: The little red hen finds a grain of wheat and asks the animals if they will help her plant it; they all say "I won't."
   - Tell what happens in the middle of the story in one or two sentences. Example: The little red hen asks the animals to help her cut the wheat and take it to the mill; they all say "I won't."
   - Tell what happens at the end of the story in one or two sentences. Example: The little red hen bakes bread and then asks the animals who will help her eat it; they all say "I will," but she only shares the bread with her four little chicks.
   - Tell what happens in the story in just a few sentences. Answers should be a combination of the preceding summaries for the beginning, middle, and end of the story. The summary should tell the events of the story in the order in which they happen.

Making Connections

Plant, Cut, Grind, Bake, . . . Eat!

Have students practice their sequencing skills by ordering pictures that represent the steps that lead up to baking bread.

1. On page LC 63 in K^{12} *Language Arts Activity Book,* have students cut out the pictures of what the little red hen had to do so she could bake bread and feed the bread to her chicks.
2. Have students glue the pictures to a large sheet of paper to show the correct sequence of events.
   - Have students refer back to the story if they need help remembering the order of the steps.
3. Have students retell the story of "The Little Red Hen" using the sequenced pictures as a guide.

Making Connections

Review "The Little Red Hen"

Plant, Cut, Grind, Bake, . . . Eat!

Cut out the pictures. Glue them to a sheet of paper in the correct order.

LANGUAGE ARTS BLUE LC 63

Objectives

- Sequence pictures illustrating story events.
- Retell a story using illustrations from the text as a guide.

Beyond the Lesson

OPTIONAL: The Little Red Hen Revisited

This activity is intended for students who have extra time and would benefit from hearing another version of the story. Feel free to skip this activity.

1. Go to a library and look for a copy of "The Little Red Hen."
2. Lead a Book Walk, and then read aloud the different version of the story.
3. Have students compare the two versions of the story and tell how they are alike and different.
4. If the book has a different ending, have students discuss it and tell which ending they like better.
5. Ask them to tell which book is their favorite and why.

Objectives

- Compare and contrast two texts on the same topic.

Introduce "The Three Bears"

Unit Overview

In this unit, students will explore the theme of *Three* through the following reading selections:

- "The Three Bears"
- "Three Billy Goats Gruff"
- "The Three Little Pigs"

Lesson Overview

Offline	"The Three Bears"	30 minutes
Get Ready	A Sequence of Events	
	Words to Know	
Read Aloud	Book Walk	
	"The Three Bears"	
Check Your Reading	"The Three Bears"	

Materials

Supplied

- **"The Three Bears," *K*[12] *Read Aloud Treasury*, pp. 150–153**

Story Synopsis

In this classic tale, a family of bears comes home to find that an uninvited guest has entered their house and has been using—and breaking—their things. Who is this intruder?

Keywords

sequence – order

Advance Preparation

Read "The Three Bears" before beginning the Read Aloud activity, to locate Words to Know within the text.

Big Ideas

Comprehension requires an understanding of story structure.

Offline 30 minutes

"The Three Bears"

Work **together** with students to complete offline Get Ready, Read Aloud, and Check Your Reading activities.

Get Ready

A Sequence of Events

Explore a story's sequence of events with students.

1. Tell students that the order in which things happen in a story or article is called the **sequence**. Words like *first, next, before, after, then,* and *finally* help tell the sequence, or the order in which things happen.
2. Have students practice listening for the sequence of events.
   Say: Listen for words that tell the sequence, or order, in this short story: It was a rainy day. First, Pedro put on his boots. Then, he put on his coat and gloves. Next, he grabbed his umbrella. Finally, he went outside. It was cold!
   - What happened first? Pedro put on his boots.
   - What happened last? Pedro went outside.

Objectives

- Sequence events from a text.
- Build vocabulary through listening, reading, and discussion.
- Use new vocabulary in written and spoken sentences.

Words to Know

Before reading "The Three Bears,"

1. Have students say each word aloud.
2. Ask students if they know what each word means.
   - If students know a word's meaning, have them define it and use it in a sentence.
   - If students don't know a word's meaning, read them the definition and discuss the word with them.

peep – to look at quickly; to glance
porridge – a hot breakfast food similar to oatmeal

Read Aloud

Book Walk

Prepare students by taking them on a Book Walk of "The Three Bears." Scan the story together, and ask students to make predictions.

1. Turn to the **table of contents**. Help students find the selection, and turn to that page.
2. Point to and read aloud the **title of the story**.

Objectives

- Make predictions based on title, illustrations, and/or context clues.
- Listen and respond to texts representing a variety of cultures, time periods, and traditions.

3. Have students look at the picture on the first page of the story. Answers to questions may vary.
    - Where do you think the story takes place?
    - What do you think might happen in the story?
    - Did you ever get caught using something that didn't belong to you?

"The Three Bears"

Now it's time to read "The Three Bears." Have students sit next to you so that they can see the pictures and words while you read the story aloud.

Read aloud the entire story. Emphasize Words to Know as you come to them. If appropriate, use the pictures to help show what each word means. Tell students to listen carefully to the order in which things happen.

Check Your Reading

"The Three Bears"

Have students retell "The Three Bears" in their own words to develop grammar, vocabulary, comprehension, and fluency skills. When finished, **ask students the following questions** to check ability to sequence story events.

- What happens right before Goldilocks arrives at the three bears' house? The bears go out to let their porridge cool off.
- When Goldilocks is in the house, what does she do first? She tastes the bowls of porridge until she finds the one that is just right.
- What does Goldilocks do next? She sits on the chairs until she finds the one that is just right. What happens to Baby Bear's chair? She breaks it.
- What does Goldilocks do after she breaks the chair? She goes upstairs; she tries the beds; she falls asleep.
- What do the bears do when they return home? They see that someone has eaten their porridge; they see that someone has sat in their chairs; they go upstairs and check their beds.
- When does Goldilocks wake up? after she hears Baby Bear's voice
- What is the last thing that happens in the story? Goldilocks runs out the door and into the woods.

Objectives

- Sequence events from a text.

Explore "The Three Bears"

Lesson Overview

Offline	"The Three Bears"	30 minutes
Get Ready	Parts of a Story	
	Words to Know	
Read Aloud	Book Walk	
	"The Three Bears"	
Check Your Reading	"The Three Bears"	
Reading for Meaning	Story Structure Elements in "The Three Bears"	

Materials

Supplied

- "The Three Bears," *K[12] Read Aloud Treasury*, pp. 150–153

Keywords

character – a person or animal in a story

plot – what happens in a story

setting – when and where a story takes place

story structure elements – components of a story; they include character, setting, plot, problem, and solution

Advance Preparation

Before working with students, spend a few minutes reviewing Words to Know. Then review the Check Your Reading and Reading for Meaning activities to familiarize yourself with the questions and answers.

Big Ideas

Comprehension requires an understanding of story structure.

Offline 30 minutes

"The Three Bears"

Work **together** with students to complete offline Get Ready, Read Aloud, Check Your Reading, and Reading for Meaning activities.

Get Ready

Parts of a Story

Review characters, setting, and plot with students.

1. Tell students that **every story has certain parts, or elements**. These parts include the **characters, setting,** and **plot**.
   - The characters are the people or animals in a story.
   - The setting is where and when a story takes place.
   - The **plot is the most important things that happen in a story**, or the most important events.
2. Help students practice naming the characters, setting, and plot of a familiar story.
   Say: Think of "The Story of Chicken Little." Here are the story's most important events, or the plot. An acorn falls on Chicken Little's head while she's in the forest; she runs to tell the king that the sky is falling. Chicken Little meets many animals on the way to see the king; every animal wants to go with Chicken Little to see the king.
   - Who are the characters? Chicken Little, the other animals
   - What is the setting, or where the story takes place? Possible answers: in the forest; on the road to the king's castle
   - How does the plot end? Example: Foxy Loxy offers to show the animals the way to the king's castle, but he really takes them to his den; the animals never see the king.

TIP If students have not yet read "The Story of Chicken Little," tell most of the plot of a familiar story, and then have students complete it.

Objectives

- Identify story structure elements—plot, setting, character(s).
- Build vocabulary through listening, reading, and discussion.
- Use new vocabulary in written and spoken sentences.

Words to Know

Before reading "The Three Bears,"

1. Have students say each word aloud.
2. Ask students if they know what each word means.
   - If students know a word's meaning, have them define it and use it in a sentence.
   - If students don't know a word's meaning, read them the definition and discuss the word with them.

peep – to look at quickly; to glance
porridge – a hot breakfast food similar to oatmeal

Read Aloud

Book Walk

Prepare students by taking them on a Book Walk of "The Three Bears." Scan the story together to revisit the characters and events.

1. Turn to the selection. Point to and read aloud the **title of the story**.
2. Have students look at the **pictures** of the story.
3. Point to the bear at the stove in the first picture of the story.
   - Who is this character? Mama Bear; the mother bear
   - What is Mama Bear doing? making porridge
   - Have you ever eaten anything like porridge? Answers will vary.

Objectives

- Listen and respond to texts representing a variety of cultures, time periods, and traditions.
- Activate prior knowledge by previewing text and/or discussing topic.

"The Three Bears"

Now it's time to read "The Three Bears." Have students sit next to you so that they can see the pictures and words while you read the story aloud.

Read aloud the entire story. Tell students to listen carefully to hear the names of characters and the most important things that happen in the story. Encourage them to say aloud repetitive text, such as "That was just right" and "Someone has been sitting in my chair!"

Check Your Reading

"The Three Bears"

Have students retell "The Three Bears" in their own words to develop grammar, vocabulary, comprehension, and fluency skills. When finished, **ask students the following questions** to check ability to identify repetitive text and general comprehension.

- What does each bear say when the bears first come home? "Someone has been eating my porridge!"
- What does each bear say when the bears see their chairs? "Someone has been sitting in my chair!"
- What does each bear say after the bears run upstairs? "Someone has been sleeping in my bed!"
- Why doesn't Goldilocks eat Papa Bear's porridge? It's too hot.
- Why doesn't Goldilocks sit in Mama Bear's chair? It's too soft.
- Why does Goldilocks sleep in Baby Bear's bed? It's just right.

Objectives

- Identify repetitive text.
- Answer questions requiring literal recall of details.

Reading for Meaning

Story Structure Elements in "The Three Bears"

Remind students that a story has certain parts, or elements. These parts include the characters, the setting, and the plot. **Ask students the following questions** to check their understanding of story structure elements.

- Who are the characters in "The Three Bears"? Papa Bear; Mama Bear; Baby Bear; Goldilocks
- Where does the story take place? in the woods; in a house in the woods; in the three bears' house
- Why do the three bears go for a walk? to let the porridge cool off
- Why does Goldilocks go upstairs? She feels sleepy.
- What is the first thing the bears notice when they come home? that someone's been sitting in their chairs
- Where do the bears find Goldilocks? sleeping in Baby Bear's bed; upstairs in bed
- What is the plot of "The Three Bears"? Example: A family of bears goes out for a walk. Goldilocks goes inside their house while they're gone. She eats their porridge, sits on their chairs, and then takes a nap in a bed. The bears come home and find her. She gets scared and runs away.

Objectives

- Identify story structure elements—plot, setting, character(s).

Review "The Three Bears"

Lesson Overview

Offline	"The Three Bears"	30 minutes
Get Ready	Words to Know	
	Reread	
Reading for Meaning	Retell "The Three Bears"	
Making Connections	Who, Where, What	

Materials

Supplied

- "The Three Bears," *K[12] Read Aloud Treasury*, pp. 150–153
- *K[12] Language Arts Activity Book*, p. LC 65

Keywords

graphic organizer – a visual tool used to show relationships between key concepts; formats include webs, diagrams, and charts

plot – what happens in a story

retelling – using your own words to tell a story that you have listened to or read

self-monitor – to notice if you do or do not understand what you are reading

story structure elements – components of a story; they include character, setting, plot, problem, and solution

Big Ideas

- Comprehension requires an understanding of story structure.
- Comprehension requires the reader to self-monitor understanding.

Offline 30 minutes

"The Three Bears"

Work **together** with students to complete offline Get Ready, Reading for Meaning, and Making Connections activities.

Get Ready

Words to Know

Ask students to define the following words and use them in a sentence:

peep
porridge

Correct any incorrect or vague definitions.

Objectives

- Build vocabulary through listening, reading, and discussion.
- Use new vocabulary in written and spoken sentences.

Reread

If you'd like to, reread the story to students. Otherwise, move on to the next activity.

Reading for Meaning

Retell "The Three Bears"

Guide students to demonstrate understanding by retelling "The Three Bears."

Objectives

- Retell familiar stories.

1. Tell students that one way readers can check their understanding of a story is by retelling it.
2. Remind students that **retelling means using your own words to tell a story** that you have listened to or read. **When good readers retell a story, they tell the most important things that happen in the beginning, middle, and end of the story.** They mention the characters and the things that the characters do.
3. **Ask the following questions** to check students' ability to retell a story.
   - In what part of the story does Mama Bear make the porridge? the beginning Retell that part of the story. Example: Mama Bear makes porridge; the three bears go for a walk while they wait for it to cool off.
   - In what part of the story does Goldilocks try things out at the bears' house? the middle Retell that part of the story. Example: Goldilocks comes into the bears' house and eats a bowl of porridge, sits in chairs, and then goes upstairs to take a nap.
   - In what part of the story do the bears come home? the end Retell that part of the story. Example: The bears come home and can tell that someone has been in their house; they go upstairs and find Goldilocks in bed; she gets scared and runs away.

Making Connections

Who, Where, What

Have students show an understanding of story structure elements by completing a graphic organizer called a story map.

1. On page LC 65 in *K[12] Language Arts Activity Book*, point to and read aloud the story title in the center of the story map.
2. Point to the Characters box and read aloud the label.
   - Have students say the names of the characters.
   - Write the names in the box.
   - If students forget a character, help them look back at the story for the name.
3. Repeat Step 2 for each box in the story map.

TIP If students enjoy drawing, an alternative is to read aloud the box labels and have students draw what goes inside each box.

Objectives

- Demonstrate understanding through graphic organizers.
- Identify story structure elements—plot, setting, character(s).

Making Connections
Review "The Three Bears"
Who, Where, What
Complete the story map.
Characters
Mama Bear, Papa Bear, Baby Bear, Goldilocks
Setting
the woods; the house where the three bears live
Title
"The Three Bears"
Plot
Beginning of story
Mama Bear makes porridge; it's too hot, so the bears go for a walk.
Middle of story
Goldilocks goes inside the bears' house, eats porridge, sits on chairs, and falls asleep in bed.
End of story
The bears come home, see that someone's been in their house, find a girl upstairs in bed, and scare her away.
LITERATURE & COMPREHENSION
LANGUAGE ARTS BLUE
LC 65

Introduce "Three Billy Goats Gruff"

Lesson Overview

Offline "Three Billy Goats Gruff" 30 minutes

Get Ready	A Play
	Words to Know
Read Aloud	Book Walk
	"Three Billy Goats Gruff"
Check Your Reading	"Three Billy Goats Gruff"

Advance Preparation

Read "Three Billy Goats Gruff" before beginning the Read Aloud activity, to locate Words to Know within the text.

Listen to the online audio recording of "Three Billy Goats Gruff" before beginning the Read Aloud activity. Decide whether to use this recording or read the play aloud, alone or with students.

Materials

Supplied

- "Three Billy Goats Gruff," *K12 Read Aloud Treasury*, pp. 154–159
- online audio recording of "Three Billy Goats Gruff" (optional)

Story Synopsis

This well-known story of three billy goats who outsmart a troll to get to a patch of grass is presented as a play.

Keywords

character – a person or animal in a story

genre – a category for classifying literary works

Offline 30 minutes

"Three Billy Goats Gruff"

Work **together** with students to complete offline Get Ready, Read Aloud, and Check Your Reading activities.

Get Ready

A Play

Introduce students to the written work known as a **play**.

1. Tell students that some stories are told as plays. Explain that a play is like a TV show. Both a play and a TV show have actors that act out a story. However, a play is different from a TV show because the actors perform live on a stage in front of people. A TV show is recorded, and people watch it at home.
2. Tell students they will see drawings of what a stage, actors, and an audience look like.

Objectives

- Identify genre.
- Build vocabulary through listening, reading, and discussion.
- Use new vocabulary in written and spoken sentences.

Words to Know

Before reading "Three Billy Goats Gruff,"

1. Have students say each word aloud.
2. Ask students if they know what each word means.
   - If students know a word's meaning, have them define it and use it in a sentence.
   - If students don't know a word's meaning, read them the definition and discuss the word with them.

brook – a small stream
troll – a fairy-tale character who is usually ugly and mean, and often lives in a cave or under a bridge

Read Aloud

Book Walk

Prepare students by taking them on a Book Walk of "Three Billy Goats Gruff." Scan the play together, and ask students to make predictions.

1. Turn to the **table of contents**. Help students find the selection, and turn to that page.
2. Point to and read aloud the **title of the play**.

Objectives

- Make predictions based on title, illustrations, and/or context clues.
- Listen and respond to texts representing a variety of cultures, time periods, and traditions.

3. Have students study the picture of the stage on page 155.
   - Point to the stage.
     Say: This is the stage. It's where the actors stand.
   - Point to the girl who is the narrator.
     Say: This person is the narrator. The narrator helps explain what's happening in the play.
   - Point to the two boys who are on the stage.
     Say: These two boys are actors in the play.
   - Point to the audience.
     Say: These people are the audience.
4. Ask students the following questions. Answers to questions may vary.
   - What do you think might happen in the play?
   - Have you ever been to a play?

"Three Billy Goats Gruff"

Now it's time to read the play. Have students sit next to you so that they can see the pictures and words while you read the play aloud.

Read aloud the entire play, or play the audio recording.

TIP The play has five characters. You may portray all the characters yourself, enlist several students to help, or play the online audio version instead of reading the story aloud.

Check Your Reading

"Three Billy Goats Gruff"

Have students retell the play in their own words to develop grammar, vocabulary, comprehension, and fluency skills. When finished, **ask students the following questions** to check understanding of the play.

- What do we call a story that is acted out on a stage? a play
- What does the narrator of the play do? helps tell what is happening in the play
- Who are the characters in the play "Three Billy Goats Gruff?" the troll; the three goats; the narrator
- Who lives under the bridge? a troll
- What does the troll want to do? eat one of the goats
- What do the goats want to do? cross the bridge to eat the grass on the hill

Objectives

- Identify genre.
- State the details of a text.
- Identify character(s).

Explore "Three Billy Goats Gruff"

Lesson Overview

Offline "Three Billy Goats Gruff" **30 minutes**

Get Ready	Problems and Solutions
	Words to Know
Read Aloud	Book Walk
	"Three Billy Goats Gruff"
Check Your Reading	"Three Billy Goats Gruff"
Reading for Meaning	How Characters Solve Their Problems

Materials

Supplied

- "Three Billy Goats Gruff," *K*[12] *Read Aloud Treasury*, pp. 154–159
- online audio recording of "Three Billy Goats Gruff" (optional)

Keywords

problem – an issue a character must solve in a story

solution – how a character solves a problem in a story

Advance Preparation

Before working with students, spend a few minutes reviewing Words to Know. Then review the Check Your Reading and Reading for Meaning activities to familiarize yourself with the questions and answers.

Listen to the online audio recording of "Three Billy Goats Gruff" before beginning the Read Aloud activity. Decide whether to use this recording or read the play aloud, alone or with students.

Big Ideas

- Comprehension requires an understanding of story structure.
- Comprehension is facilitated by an understanding of physical presentation (headings, subheads, graphics, and other features).

Offline 30 minutes

"Three Billy Goats Gruff"

Work **together** with students to complete offline Get Ready, Read Aloud, Check Your Reading, and Reading for Meaning activities.

Get Ready

Problems and Solutions

Explore the story structure elements of character, problem, and solution.

1. Tell students that the people and animals in a story are called **characters**.
2. Explain that **a character usually needs to solve a problem**. There can be more than one character that needs to solve a problem in a story.
3. Remind students of the story "The Little Red Hen."
   Say: A little red hen finds a grain of wheat. She wants to plant it so she can have flour to bake bread. She asks a dog, a cat, a pig, and a turkey for help, but they all say, "I won't." So the little red hen does all the work herself. In the end, she bakes the bread, and she shares it only with her four chicks.
   - Who are the characters in this story? the little red hen; the dog; the cat; the pig; the turkey; the four chicks
   - What is the little red hen's problem? The other animals won't help her do the work.
   - How does the little red hen solve her problem? She does the work herself.

Objectives

- Identify character(s).
- Identify story structure elements—problem and solution.
- Build vocabulary through listening, reading, and discussion.
- Use new vocabulary in written and spoken sentences.

Words to Know

Before reading "Three Billy Goats Gruff,"

1. Have students say each word aloud.
2. Ask students if they know what each word means.
   - If students know a word's meaning, have them define it and use it in a sentence.
   - If students don't know a word's meaning, read them the definition and discuss the word with them.

brook – a small stream
troll – a fairy-tale character who is usually ugly and mean, and often lives in a cave or under a bridge

Read Aloud

Book Walk

Prepare students by taking them on a Book Walk of "Three Billy Goats Gruff." Scan the play together to revisit the characters and events.

1. Turn to the selection. Point to and read aloud the **title of the play**.
2. Have students look at the **pictures** of the play.
   - What do the pictures show? children in a play; children on a stage
   - Why is there a character under the bridge? The troll lives there.
3. Point to the list of names under the title. Tell students that when we read a play, the characters' names are always listed at the beginning.
4. Point to an example of bold type at the beginning of a line. Explain that **the bold type tells us which character is speaking**. The words that follow are what the character says.
5. Point to the first occurrence of **TROLL**.
   - Who speaks the words that are written after **TROLL**? the troll

Objectives

- Identify genre.
- Listen and respond to texts representing a variety of cultures, time periods, and traditions.

"Three Billy Goats Gruff"

Now it's time to read "Three Billy Goats Gruff." Have students sit next to you so that they can see the pictures and words while you read the play aloud.

Read aloud the entire play, or play the audio recording. Tell students to listen carefully for the characters' problems and how they solve those problems.

Check Your Reading

"Three Billy Goats Gruff"

Have students retell the play in their own words to develop grammar, vocabulary, comprehension, and fluency skills. When finished, **ask students the following questions** to check their ability to identify characters and recognize features of a play.

1. Point to the list of names at the beginning of the play.
   - What is this list of names? the characters in the play
2. Point to the girl holding the papers in one of the pictures.
   - Who is this person? the narrator

Objectives

- Identify character(s).
- Identify genre.
- Identify author's use of sensory language.

3. Ask the following question using the text on pages 154 and 157.

   - When Little Billy Goat Gruff crosses the bridge, the text says "Trip-trap! Trip-trap!" in small letters. But when Big Billy Goat Gruff crosses the bridge, it says "TRIP-TRAP! TRIP-TRAP!" in all capital letters. Why is that? Big Billy Goat Gruff is the biggest goat, so he makes more noise than Little Billy Goat Gruff when he crosses the bridge.

4. Point to the audience in one of the pictures.

   - Who are these people and what are they doing? They're the audience, and they're watching the play.

TIP The play has five characters. You may portray all the characters yourself, enlist several students to help, or play the online audio version instead of reading the story aloud.

Reading for Meaning

How Characters Solve Their Problems

Remind students that characters often have a problem to solve. **Ask students the following questions** to check their understanding of problem and solution.

- What is Little Billy Goat Gruff's problem? how to get across the bridge without being eaten by the troll
- How does Little Billy Goat Gruff solve his problem? He tells the troll that his brother, Second Billy Goat Gruff, is coming, and that he is bigger.
- What problem does Second Billy Goat Gruff need to solve? how to get across the bridge without being eaten by the troll
- How does Second Billy Goat Gruff solve his problem? He tells the troll that his brother, Big Billy Goat Gruff, is coming, and that he is bigger.
- What is Big Billy Goat Gruff's problem? how to get across the bridge without being eaten by the troll
- How does Big Billy Goat Gruff solve his problem? He throws the troll off the bridge.
- What happens after Big Billy Goat Gruff solves his problem? Answer will vary; guide students to recognize that the goats can cross the bridge and eat as much grass as they want once the troll is gone.

Objectives

- Identify story structure elements—problem and solution.

Review "Three Billy Goats Gruff"

Lesson Overview

Offline	"Three Billy Goats Gruff"	30 minutes
Get Ready	Words to Know	
	Reread	
Reading for Meaning	Retell "Three Billy Goats Gruff"	
Making Connections	Play the Characters	
Beyond the Lesson	OPTIONAL: Narrative vs. Narrated	

Materials

Supplied

- "Three Billy Goats Gruff," *K[12] Read Aloud Treasury*, pp. 154–159
- *K[12] Language Arts Activity Book*, p. LC 67

Also Needed

- scissors, round-end safety
- craft sticks (4) (optional)
- glue (optional)

Big Ideas

- Comprehension requires an understanding of story structure.
- Comprehension requires the reader to self-monitor understanding.

Keywords

retelling – using your own words to tell a story that you have listened to or read

self-monitor – to notice if you do or do not understand what you are reading

sequence – order

Offline 30 minutes

"Three Billy Goats Gruff"

Work **together** with students to complete offline Get Ready, Reading for Meaning, Making Connections, and Beyond the Lesson activities.

Get Ready

Words to Know

Ask students to define the following words and use them in a sentence:

brook
troll

Correct any incorrect or vague definitions.

Objectives

- Build vocabulary through listening, reading, and discussion.
- Use new vocabulary in written and spoken sentences.

Reread

If you'd like to, reread the play to students. Otherwise, move on to the next activity.

Reading for Meaning

Retell "Three Billy Goats Gruff"

Help students check their understanding of "Three Billy Goats Gruff" by retelling it.

Objectives

- Retell a story using illustrations from the text as a guide.
- Sequence events from a text.

1. Remind students that **retelling means using your own words to tell what happens in a story or a play** that you have listened to or read.
2. Tell students that **when good readers retell a play, they tell the most important things that happen in the beginning, middle, and end of the play.** They mention the characters and the things that the characters do.
3. **Ask the following questions** to check students' ability to retell a play.
   - Point to the picture on page 155. Have students retell that part of the play.
     Example: Little Billy Goat Gruff tries to cross the bridge but is stopped by the hungry troll; he tells the troll to wait for his brother, who is bigger.
   - Point to the picture on page 156. Have students retell that part of the play.
     Example: Second Billy Goat Gruff tries to cross the bridge but is stopped by the hungry troll; he tells the troll to wait for his brother, who is bigger.
   - Point to the picture on page 157. Have students retell that part of the play.
     Example: Big Billy Goat Gruff tries to cross the bridge but is stopped by the hungry troll; he tells the troll he's not afraid of him.
   - Point to the picture on page 158. Have students retell that part of the play.
     Example: Big Billy Goat Gruff catches the troll in his horns and throws him into the brook; the troll is frightened and runs away.

Making Connections

Play the Characters

Have students show an understanding of a play and its sequence by reenacting "Three Billy Goats Gruff."

1. Help students cut out the finger puppets on page LC 67 in *K¹² Language Arts Activity Book*.
2. Cut out the finger holes on each puppet.
   - Demonstrate for students how to put your index and middle fingers through the holes on each puppet so your fingers act as the goats' front legs and the troll's arms.
3. Have students act out the play with the finger puppets.
   - Refer back to the play if students need help recalling events.
   - Act as narrator or play characters if students have trouble manipulating more than one puppet at a time.

TIP Glue the puppets to craft sticks if tearing is a concern.

Objectives

- Reenact a story in correct sequence.
- Respond to text through art, writing, and/or drama.

Beyond the Lesson

OPTIONAL: Narrative vs. Narrated

This activity is intended for students who have extra time and would benefit from hearing a narrative version of the play. Feel free to skip this activity.

1. Go to a library and look for a storybook version of "Three Billy Goats Gruff." **Note:** In some books, the troll suffers a violent ending.
2. Lead a Book Walk, and then read aloud the story.
3. Have students compare the narrative story and the play, and explain how they are alike and different.
4. If the book has a different ending, have students discuss it and tell which ending they like better.
5. Ask them to tell which version is their favorite and why.

Objectives

- Compare and contrast two texts on the same topic.

Introduce "The Three Little Pigs"

Lesson Overview

Offline	"The Three Little Pigs"	30 minutes
Get Ready	Recurring Characters	
	Words to Know	
Read Aloud	Book Walk	
	"The Three Little Pigs"	
Check Your Reading	"The Three Little Pigs"	

Advance Preparation

Read "The Three Little Pigs" before beginning the Read Aloud activity, to locate Words to Know within the text.

Materials

Supplied

- "The Three Little Pigs," *K[12] Read Aloud Treasury*, pp. 160–163

Story Synopsis

Three pigs, three houses, and one big, bad wolf. Is it a recipe for disaster, or will the pigs outsmart the wolf?

Keywords

character – a person or animal in a story

Offline 30 minutes

"The Three Little Pigs"

Work **together** with students to complete offline Get Ready, Read Aloud, and Check Your Reading activities.

Get Ready

Recurring Characters

Explore the idea that the same type of character can appear in different stories.

1. Explain to students that some characters appear over and over in fairy tales and other types of stories. Fairies are an example of a character that you will find in many stories. The character usually acts the same: Fairies are usually good, witches are usually evil, and kings and queens usually live in a castle.
2. Think about the fox in "The Gingerbread Man," "The Story of Chicken Little," or another familiar story.
   - What did you learn about foxes from listening to these stories? Possible answers: Foxes are tricky; foxes are hungry; foxes eat other animals.

Objectives

- Identify recurring characters in folk and fairy tales.
- Build vocabulary through listening, reading, and discussion.
- Use new vocabulary in written and spoken sentences.

Words to Know

Before reading "The Three Little Pigs,"

1. Have students say each word aloud.
2. Ask students if they know what each word means.
   - If students know a word's meaning, have them define it and use it in a sentence.
   - If students don't know a word's meaning, read them the definition and discuss the word with them.

brick – a hard block of baked clay that's used for building
chimney – a hollow pipe that takes smoke up and away from a fire in a fireplace
fortune – what the future holds
seek – to look or search for something
straw – yellow, dried stems of wheat

Read Aloud

Book Walk

Prepare students by taking them on a Book Walk of "The Three Little Pigs." Scan the story together, and ask students to make predictions.

1. Turn to the **table of contents**. Help students find the selection, and turn to that page.
2. Point to and read aloud the **title of the story**.
3. Have students look at the picture on the first page of the story. Answers to questions may vary.
   - Where do you think the story takes place?
   - What do you think might happen in the story?
   - What would you use to build a house? Why?

Objectives

- Make predictions based on title, illustrations, and/or context clues.
- Listen and respond to texts representing a variety of cultures, time periods, and traditions.

"The Three Little Pigs"

Now it's time to read "The Three Little Pigs." Have students sit next to you so that they can see the pictures and words while you read the story aloud.

Read aloud the entire story. Emphasize Words to Know as you come to them. To engage interest, **have students join in when you come to repeated lines**, such as "not by the hair of my chinny, chin, chin" and "I'll huff and I'll puff, and I'll blow your house in."

Check Your Reading

"The Three Little Pigs"

Have students retell the story in their own words to develop grammar, vocabulary, comprehension, and fluency skills. When finished, **ask students the following questions** to check their ability to identify recurring characters and repetitive text.

- Which character do you recognize from another story? the wolf
- Does the wolf in "The Three Little Pigs" act the way you expected? Answers will vary.
- How would describe the wolf? Possible answers: mean; a bully; scary; angry
- What does the wolf say to each pig when he knocks on its door? "Little pig, little pig, let me come in."
- What does each pig say back to the wolf? "No, no, not by the hair of my chinny, chin, chin."
- What does the wolf say when each pig won't let him in the house? "Then I'll huff and I'll puff, and I'll blow your house in!"

Objectives

- Identify recurring characters in folk and fairy tales.
- Identify repetitive text.
- Describe character(s).

Explore "The Three Little Pigs"

Lesson Overview

Offline	"The Three Little Pigs"	30 minutes
Get Ready	Characters: Their Problems and Solutions	
	Words to Know	
Read Aloud	Book Walk	
	"The Three Little Pigs"	
Check Your Reading	"The Three Little Pigs"	
Reading for Meaning	Problems and Solutions in "The Three Little Pigs"	

Materials

Supplied

- "The Three Little Pigs," *K[12] Read Aloud Treasury*, pp. 160–163

Keywords

character – a person or animal in a story

problem – an issue a character must solve in a story

setting – when and where a story takes place

solution – how a character solves a problem in a story

Advance Preparation

Before working with students, spend a few minutes reviewing Words to Know. Then review the Check Your Reading and Reading for Meaning activities to familiarize yourself with the questions and answers.

Big Ideas

Comprehension requires an understanding of story structure.

Offline 30 minutes

"The Three Little Pigs"

Work **together** with students to complete offline Get Ready, Read Aloud, Check Your Reading, and Reading for Meaning activities.

Get Ready

Characters: Their Problems and Solutions

Explore the story structure elements of character, problem, and solution.

1. Tell students that the people and animals in a story are called **characters**.
2. Explain that **a character usually needs to solve a problem**. There can be more than one character that needs to solve a problem in a story.
3. Have students recall the story of "The Honest Woodsman" to aid understanding of a character's problem and how it is solved.
   Say: Think about the story of "The Honest Woodsman." In that story, the woodsman's ax slides into a river.
   - What is the woodsman's problem? He needs to get his ax out of the river.
   - How does the woodsman solve his problem? The river fairy finds it for him.

TIP If students have not yet heard "The Honest Woodsman," use a familiar story that has an obvious problem and solution, such as "Sleeping Beauty" or "Little Red Riding Hood."

Objectives

- Identify story structure elements—problem and solution.
- Build vocabulary through listening, reading, and discussion.
- Use new vocabulary in written and spoken sentences.

Words to Know

Before reading "The Three Little Pigs,"

1. Have students say each word aloud.
2. Ask students if they know what each word means.
   - If students know a word's meaning, have them define it and use it in a sentence.
   - If students don't know a word's meaning, read them the definition and discuss the word with them.

brick – a hard block of baked clay that's used for building
chimney – a hollow pipe that takes smoke up and away from a fire in a fireplace
fortune – what the future holds
seek – to look or search for something
straw – yellow, dried stems of wheat

Read Aloud

Book Walk

Prepare students by taking them on a Book Walk of "The Three Little Pigs." Scan the story together to revisit the characters and events.

1. Turn to the selection. Point to and read aloud the **title of the story.**
2. Have students look at the **pictures** of the story.
   - Why doesn't the brick house fall down when the wolf blows on it? The bricks make the house strong.
   - Why do you think the wolf is able to blow in the straw house and the stick house? Straw and sticks make weak houses.

Objectives

- Listen and respond to texts representing a variety of cultures, time periods, and traditions.
- Activate prior knowledge by previewing text and/or discussing topic.

"The Three Little Pigs"

Now it's time to read "The Three Little Pigs." Have students sit next to you so that they can see the pictures and words while you read the story aloud.

Read aloud the entire story. Tell students to listen for the characters' problems and how they try to solve them.

Check Your Reading

"The Three Little Pigs"

Have students retell the story in their own words to develop grammar, vocabulary, comprehension, and fluency skills. When finished, **ask students the following questions** to check ability to identify parts of a story.

- Who are the characters in the story? the three little pigs; the wolf; Mother Pig
- Where does the story take place? at the houses of the three little pigs; in the woods
- What does Mother Pig tell her three little pigs to do? to go away and find their fortune
- What is the first thing each little pig does after leaving Mother Pig? build a house
- The wolf in this story is called the Big Bad Wolf. What does the wolf do that shows he's bad? He tells the pigs he'll blow their houses in if they don't let him inside; he blows down the house made of straw and the house made of sticks; he tells the pigs he wants to eat them.

Objectives

- Identify story structure elements—plot, setting, character(s).
- Describe character(s).

Reading for Meaning

Problems and Solutions in "The Three Little Pigs"

Remind students that stories have characters, and **characters have problems that they must solve**. Often, many of the events in a story are the things that characters do to try to solve their problem. **Ask students the following questions** to check their understanding of problem and solution.

- What problem does each little pig have after he builds his house? The wolf wants to come into his house and eat him.
- How does the first pig try to solve his problem? He doesn't let the wolf in when he knocks on the door. Does it work? No Why not? The wolf blows his house in. What does the first little pig do after his house is blown in? He runs away.
- How does the second pig try to solve his problem? He doesn't let the wolf in when he knocks on the door. Does it work? No Why not? The wolf blows his house in. What does the second little pig do after his house is blown in? He runs away.
- How does the third pig try to solve his problem? He doesn't let the wolf in when he knocks on the door. Does it work? Yes Why? His house is made of bricks, and the wolf can't blow it in.
- Why does the wolf climb down the chimney of the brick house? He wants to get inside and eat the third little pig.
- What happens when the wolf goes down the chimney? He falls into a pot of hot water. Does this finally solve the pigs' problem? Yes Why? The wolf runs away, and the pigs never see him again.

Objectives

- Identify story structure elements—problem and solution.
- Identify details that explain characters' actions.

Review "The Three Little Pigs"

Lesson Overview

Offline	"The Three Little Pigs"	30 minutes
Get Ready	Words to Know	
	Reread	
Reading for Meaning	Retell "The Three Little Pigs"	
Making Connections	Who, Where, What	
Beyond the Lesson	OPTIONAL: Role Reversal	

Big Ideas

- Comprehension requires an understanding of story structure.
- Comprehension requires the reader to self-monitor understanding.

Materials

Supplied

- "The Three Little Pigs," *K[12] Read Aloud Treasury*, pp. 160–163
- *K[12] Language Arts Activity Book*, p. LC 69

Keywords

graphic organizer – a visual tool used to show relationships between key concepts; formats include webs, diagrams, and charts

plot – what happens in a story

retelling – using your own words to tell a story that you have listened to or read

self-monitor – to notice if you do or do not understand what you are reading

story structure elements – components of a story; they include character, setting, plot, problem, and solution

Offline 30 minutes

"The Little Pigs"

Work **together** with students to complete offline Get Ready, Reading for Meaning, Making Connections, and Beyond the Lesson activities.

Get Ready

Words to Know

Ask students to define the following words and use them in a sentence:

brick
chimney
fortune
seek
straw

Correct any incorrect or vague definitions.

Objectives

- Build vocabulary through listening, reading, and discussion.
- Use new vocabulary in written and spoken sentences.

Reread

If you'd like to, reread the story to students. Otherwise, move on to the next activity.

Reading for Meaning

Retell "The Three Little Pigs"

Guide students to practice retelling.

Objectives

- Retell familiar stories.
- Sequence events from a text.

1. Remind students that one way readers can check their understanding of a story is by retelling it.
2. Remind students that **retelling means using your own words to tell what happens in a story** that you have listened to or read.
3. **When good readers retell a story, they tell the most important things that happen in the beginning, middle, and end of the story.** They mention the characters and the things that the characters do.
4. Ask the following questions to check students' ability to retell a story.
   - Retell the beginning of the story, the part about the first little pig. Example: The first little pig builds a straw house; when the Big, Bad Wolf knocks on his door, the pig won't let him in; the wolf blows the house in and the little pig runs away.
   - Retell the middle of the story, the part about the second little pig. Example: The second little pig builds a stick house; when the Big, Bad Wolf knocks on his door, the pig won't let him in; the wolf blows the house in and the little pig runs away.
   - Retell the ending of the story, the part about the third little pig. Example: The third little pig builds a brick house; the wolf can't blow the house in, so he goes down the chimney and falls into a pot of hot water; the wolf runs away, and the other pigs come to live with their brother.

Making Connections

Who, Where, What

Have students complete a graphic organizer called a *story map*. **They may dictate answers or draw pictures** for the story elements in each box.

1. On page LC 69 in *K[12] Language Arts Activity Book*, point to and read aloud the story title in the center of the story map.
2. Read aloud the label for the Characters box. Have students name the characters. Write the names, or have students draw the characters.
3. Repeat Step 2 for each box in the story map.

Objectives

- Demonstrate understanding through graphic organizers.
- Identify story structure elements—plot, setting, character(s).

Making Connections

Review "The Three Little Pigs"

Who, Where, What

Complete the story map.

Characters: Mother Pig; 1st little pig; 2nd little pig; 3rd little pig; Big Bad Wolf

Setting: the houses of the three little pigs; the woods

Title: "The Three Little Pigs"

Plot

Beginning of story: The 1st little pig builds a straw house that the wolf blows in, and the pig runs away.

Middle of story: The 2nd little pig builds a stick house that the wolf blows in, and the pig runs away.

End of story: The 3rd pig builds a brick house; the wolf can't blow it in, so he goes down the chimney and falls into a pot of hot water.

LANGUAGE ARTS BLUE LC 69

Beyond the Lesson

OPTIONAL: Role Reversal

This activity is intended for students who have extra time and would benefit from hearing an alternate version of the story. Feel free to skip this activity.

1. Go to a library, and look for a copy of *The Three Little Wolves and the Big Bad Pig* by Eugene Trivizas.
2. Lead a Book Walk, and then read aloud the story.
3. Have students tell how the stories are alike and different.
4. Ask them to tell which version is their favorite and why.

Objectives

- Compare and contrast two texts on the same topic.

Introduce "Hot and Cold"

Unit Overview

In this unit, students will explore the theme of *Hot and Cold* through the following reading selections:

- "Hot and Cold"
- "The Amazing Sahara"
- *The Snowy Day*

Lesson Overview

Offline	"Hot and Cold"	30 minutes
Get Ready	The Main Idea of an Article	
	Words to Know	
Read Aloud	Book Walk	
	"Hot and Cold"	
Check Your Reading	"Hot and Cold"	

Advance Preparation

Read "Hot and Cold" before beginning the Read Aloud activity, to locate Words to Know within the text.

Big Ideas

Comprehension entails an understanding of the organizational patterns of text.

Materials

Supplied

- "Hot and Cold," *Our Busy Bodies*, pp. 28–35

Article Synopsis

The world is full of opposites—light and dark, sweet and sour, hot and cold. We use at least one of our senses to tell the difference between pairs of opposites. When it comes to hot and cold, we use our *sense of touch.*

Keywords

fact – something that can be proven true

genre – a category for classifying literary works

main idea – the most important idea in a paragraph or text

nonfiction – writings about true things

Offline 30 minutes

"Hot and Cold"

Work **together** with students to complete offline Get Ready, Read Aloud, and Check Your Reading activities.

Get Ready

The Main Idea of an Article

Explore the idea that a nonfiction article has a main idea.

Objectives
- Identify the main idea.
- Increase concept and content vocabulary.
- Use new vocabulary in written and spoken sentences.

1. Tell students that a magazine article about real things, or **facts**, is called **nonfiction**. This is different from fiction writing, which is about made-up characters and events.
2. Explain that **an article has a main idea. This means it's mostly about one thing.** Good readers listen carefully so they can figure out what an article is mostly about.
3. Model how to determine the main idea.
   Read aloud: Water is interesting. When water gets really cold, it turns into ice. When water gets really hot, it turns into steam. When ice melts or steam cools off, it turns back into water.
   Say: This text mentions ice and steam, but both of these things are information about water. **The text is mostly about water.**
4. Have students practice figuring out the main idea.
   Read aloud: Ice can be used many ways. You can add ice to lemonade to keep it cold. You can put ice on a sprained ankle to make the swelling go down. Did you know that a snow cone is made out of crushed ice?
   - Which of the following tells the main idea, or what the text is mostly about? (a) Ice can be used in many ways; (b) You can put ice in lemonade; (c) You can make snow cones with ice. (a) Ice can be used in many ways. Why do you think answer (a) is correct? Answers will vary; guide students to recognize that each sentence gives information about how to use ice, so the text is mostly about how ice can be used in many ways.

Words to Know

Before reading "Hot and Cold,"

1. Have students say each word aloud.
2. Ask students if they know what each word means.
   - If students know a word's meaning, have them define it and use it in a sentence.
   - If students don't know a word's meaning, read them the definition and discuss the word with them.

opposite – a thing that is completely different from another; for example, big is the opposite of small
sense of touch – one of the five senses; the sense used to tell what something feels like
senses – the body's ability to see, smell, hear, touch, and taste

Read Aloud

Book Walk

Prepare students by taking them on a Book Walk of "Hot and Cold." Scan the magazine article together, and ask students to make predictions about the text. Answers to questions may vary.

1. Turn to the **table of contents**. Help students find the selection, and turn to that page.
2. Point to and read aloud the **title of the article**.
3. Have students look at the **pictures** in the article.
   - What do you think the article is about?
   - Name something that is hot.
   - Name something that is cold.
4. Point to and read aloud any **headers, captions,** or **other features** that stand out.
   - What do you think the article might say about how we can tell if something is hot or cold?

Objectives

- Make predictions based on title, illustrations, and/or context clues.
- Read and listen to a variety of texts for information and pleasure independently or as part of a group.

"Hot and Cold"

Now it's time to read "Hot and Cold." Have students sit next to you so that they can see the pictures and words while you read the article aloud.

Read aloud the entire article. Emphasize Words to Know as you come to them. If appropriate, use the pictures to help show what each word means. Tell students that **everything in the article is true** so it is **nonfiction**. Tell them to listen carefully to discover what the article is mostly about.

Check Your Reading

"Hot and Cold"

Have students retell "Hot and Cold" in their own words to develop grammar, vocabulary, comprehension, and fluency skills. When finished, **ask students the following questions** to check ability to identify the genre and main idea of the article, and to check general comprehension.

- How can you tell if a food is hot or cold? You use your sense of touch; you use your hands; you use your lips and tongue.
- Is a bowl of soup usually hot or cold? hot
- Is a bowl of ice cream hot or cold? cold
- What is this article mostly about? how we can feel hot and cold things with our sense of touch
- Is the article "Hot and Cold" about real or made-up things? real things
  How can you tell? It tells facts about how we feel things that are hot or cold.
- What do we call a text like this article, which is about how we use our sense of touch? nonfiction

Objectives

- Identify genre.
- Identify the main idea.

Explore "Hot and Cold"

Lesson Overview

Offline "Hot and Cold" 30 minutes

Get Ready	Facts in Nonfiction Articles
	Words to Know
Read Aloud	Book Walk
	"Hot and Cold"
Check Your Reading	"Hot and Cold"
Reading for Meaning	Facts in "Hot and Cold"

Materials

Supplied

- "Hot and Cold," *Our Busy Bodies*, pp. 28–35

Keywords

compare – to explain how two or more things are alike

contrast – to explain how two or more things are different

fact – something that can be proven true

Advance Preparation

Before working with students, spend a few minutes reviewing Words to Know. Then review the Check Your Reading and Reading for Meaning activities to familiarize yourself with the questions and answers.

Big Ideas

Comprehension entails an understanding of the organizational patterns of text.

Offline 30 minutes

"Hot and Cold"

Work **together** with students to complete offline Get Ready, Read Aloud, Check Your Reading, and Reading for Meaning activities.

Get Ready

Facts in Nonfiction Articles

Explore identifying facts.

1. Tell students that **nonfiction articles are filled with facts**. A fact is something that you can prove is true.
   - What day is it? Answers will vary.
     Say: The day is a fact. You can prove what day it is.
   - Where were you born? Answers will vary.
     Say: Your place of birth is a fact. You can prove where you were born.
   - Do some dogs bark? Yes
     Say: This is a fact. You can prove that some dogs bark.
2. Ask students to think of a nonfiction article that they have listened to.
   - Ask students to tell you a fact from that article.
   - If they cannot name a fact, show them a nonfiction article and help them find a fact.

Objectives

- Identify facts in informational text.
- Increase concept and content vocabulary.
- Use new vocabulary in written and spoken sentences.

Words to Know

Before reading "Hot and Cold,"

1. Have students say each word aloud.
2. Ask students if they know what each word means.
   - If students know a word's meaning, have them define it and use it in a sentence.
   - If students don't know a word's meaning, read them the definition and discuss the word with them.

opposite – a thing that is completely different from another; for example, big is the opposite of small
sense of touch – one of the five senses; the sense used to tell what something feels like
senses – the body's ability to see, smell, hear, touch, and taste

Read Aloud

Book Walk

Prepare students by taking them on a Book Walk of "Hot and Cold." Scan the magazine article together to revisit the text.

1. Turn to the selection.
2. Point to and read aloud the **title of the article**.
3. Have students look at the **pictures** in the article. Answers to questions may vary.
   - Have you ever put an ice cube in your mouth? What did it feel like?
   - Did you ever walk on hot sand or a hot sidewalk? How did it make your feet feel?

Objectives

- Read and listen to a variety of texts for information and pleasure independently or as part of a group.
- Activate prior knowledge by previewing text and/or discussing topic.

"Hot and Cold"

Now it's time to read "Hot and Cold." Have students sit next to you so that they can see the pictures and words while you read the article aloud.

Read aloud the entire article. Tell students to listen for facts, or things that are true, in the article.

Check Your Reading

"Hot and Cold"

Have students retell "Hot and Cold" in their own words to develop grammar, vocabulary, comprehension, and fluency skills. When finished, **ask students the following questions** to check ability to make comparisons.

1. Point to the picture of the dogs on page 28.
   - What do you notice about the dogs? One is big and one is small.
2. Point to the pictures of the fire and the girl in the snow on page 28.
   - How are fire and snow *different*? Fire is hot and snow is cold.
   - How are snow and a bowl of ice cream *alike*? They're both cold.
3. Point to the pictures of the girls eating soup and ice cream on page 32.
   - How are these two pictures the same? Both girls are eating something. How are they different? The soup is hot, and the ice cream is cold.
4. Point to the pictures page 35.
   - How are the pictures of drinks different? The drink in the mug is hot, and the drink in the pitcher is cold.

Objectives

- Compare and contrast elements within a text.

Reading for Meaning

Facts in "Hot and Cold"

Help students identify facts in "Hot and Cold."

Objectives

- Identify facts in informational text.

1. Remind students that "Hot and Cold" is a nonfiction article, so it has many **facts** in it.
2. **Ask students the following questions** to recall facts from the article.
   - Which of our five senses lets us feel things? the sense of touch
   - How can you use your sense of touch to tell if the food in a bowl is hot or cold? touch the outside of the bowl
   - What can you do to cool down a spoonful of hot soup? blow on it
   - What parts of your body can feel that ice cream is cold when you eat it? your lips and tongue
   - How does your face feel when the sun shines on it? warm or hot
   - How would jumping in cold water on a hot day make you feel? good; cool
   - Why would someone drink hot chocolate on a cold day? to feel warm inside

TIP If students have trouble answering a question, help them find the answer in the text and pictures of the article.

Review "Hot and Cold"

Lesson Overview

Offline	"Hot and Cold"	30 minutes
Get Ready	Words to Know	
	Reread or Retell	
Reading for Meaning	Visual Text Features in "Hot and Cold"	
Making Connections	How Do You Feel?	

Materials

Supplied

- Hot and Cold," *Our Busy Bodies*, pp. 28–35
- *K[12] Language Arts Activity Book*, p. LC 71

Also Needed

- glue stick
- scissors, round-end safety

Big Ideas

Comprehension is facilitated by an understanding of physical presentation (headings, subheads, graphics, and other features).

Keywords

graphic organizer – a visual tool used to show relationships between key concepts; formats include webs, diagrams, and charts

text feature – part of a text that helps a reader locate information and determine what is most important; examples include the title, table of contents, headings, pictures, and glossary

Offline 30 minutes

"Hot and Cold"

Work **together** with students to complete offline Get Ready, Reading for Meaning, and Making Connections activities.

Get Ready

Words to Know

Ask students to define the following words and use them in a sentence:

opposite **senses**
sense of touch

Correct any incorrect or vague definitions.

Objectives

- Use new vocabulary in written and spoken sentences.
- Increase concept and content vocabulary.

Reread or Retell

If you'd like to, reread the article to students. Otherwise, have students retell the article using the pictures as a guide, or move on to the next activity.

Reading for Meaning

Visual Text Features in "Hot and Cold"

Guide students to demonstrate the ability to identify and use visual text features such as titles, pictures, diagrams, and other graphic elements.

1. Point to the title of "Hot and Cold" on page 28.
   - Why is the word *Hot* written in red and why is *Cold* on a blue background? The color red looks hot, and the color blue looks cold.
2. Point to the boy and read the words around his head on page 29.
   - What do these words and lines tell us? the parts of our body that go with each of our five senses
3. Point to the picture of the girl holding the bowl of soup on page 31.
   - Why is there a thought bubble that shows the girl thinking about the beach? It shows how holding a bowl of hot soup on a cold day can make us think of something hot.
4. Point to the two pictures of children on page 33.
   - Why are the picture of the children on the beach on a red background, and the picture of the children in the water on a blue background? It's hot on the beach, and red makes us think of hot things; the water is cold, and blue makes us think of cold things.
   - What do you notice about the words *hot* and *cold* below the pictures? *Hot* is red and *cold* is blue; the colors of the words match the backgrounds.

Objectives

- Use visual text features to aid understanding of text.
- Identify the purpose of and information provided by illustrations, titles, charts, and graphs.
- Make inferences based on text and/or prior knowledge.

Making Connections

How Do You Feel?

Have students determine how they use their sense of touch and parts of their body to tell if something is hot or cold.

1. On page LC 71 in *K[12] Language Arts Activity Book*, point to the Venn diagram. **Say:** This is called a Venn diagram. We use it to show how things are alike and how they are different. Let's use it to show which parts of our body we're more likely to use to tell if something is hot or cold.
2. Read aloud the headings for the three categories of the diagram.
3. Have students cut out the pictures of hot and cold things.
4. For each picture, have students determine if they're more likely to use their hands and fingers or their lips and tongue—or both—to tell if the item is hot or cold. Have students place each item in the appropriate section. Answers will vary.
5. Have students justify their placement of each item. For example, some students may place the ice cream cone in the "Lips and Tongue" category because you eat ice cream. However, others may place it under "Both" because you can also touch the ice cream with your finger. Either placement would be correct as long as students can justify their answer.
6. Have students glue each picture in place.

Objectives

- Compare and contrast elements within a text.
- Demonstrate understanding through graphic organizers.

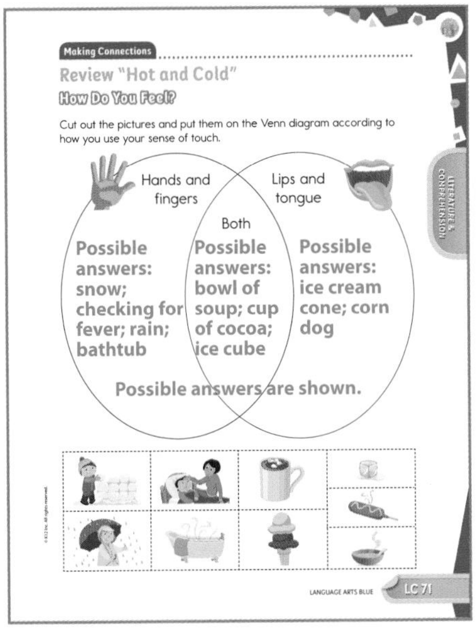
Making Connections
Review "Hot and Cold"
How Do You Feel?
Cut out the pictures and put them on the Venn diagram according to how you use your sense of touch.

LANGUAGE ARTS BLUE LC 71

Introduce "The Amazing Sahara"

Lesson Overview

Offline	"The Amazing Sahara"	30 minutes
Get Ready	The Purpose of an Article	
	Words to Know	
Read Aloud	Book Walk	
	"The Amazing Sahara"	
Check Your Reading	"The Amazing Sahara"	

Materials

Supplied

- "The Amazing Sahara," *Amazing Places*, pp. 20–29

Article Synopsis

Imagine that the entire United States was one vast desert—that's about the size of the Sahara. Although many people believe that this desert is a barren wasteland, there is actually life among the acres of giant sand dunes.

Keywords

author's purpose – the reason the author wrote a text: to entertain, to inform, to express an opinion, or to persuade

fact – something that can be proven true

nonfiction – writings about true things

Advance Preparation

Read "The Amazing Sahara" before beginning the Read Aloud activity, to locate Words to Know within the text.

Offline 30 minutes

"The Amazing Sahara"

Work **together** with students to complete offline Get Ready, Read Aloud, and Check Your Reading activities.

Get Ready

The Purpose of an Article

Explore the reasons why an author might write an article or story.

1. Explain that an author writes an article or story for a certain reason, or **purpose**. Good readers can figure out the purpose of a text by asking themselves, "Why did the author write this?"
   Say: Authors write articles and stories for one of the following reasons: to teach us something; to entertain us; to convince us of something; or to tell us what they think about something.
2. Read aloud information about a story, and model how to determine the author's purpose.
   Say: Listen as I read the title of a story and what it's about. In the story "Carlos, the Crazy Camel," the author tells a funny story about a camel named Carlos. This is a funny story, so I think the author wrote it to entertain us.
3. Have students practice naming the purpose of an article.
   Say: Listen as I read the title of an article and what it's about. In the article "Moving Sand," the author tells how sand dunes are always moving, like water in the ocean.
   - Why do you think the author wrote the article? to teach us about sand dunes

Objectives

- Identify the purpose of a text.
- Increase concept and content vocabulary.
- Use new vocabulary in written and spoken sentences.

Words to Know

Before reading "The Amazing Sahara,"

1. Have students say each word aloud.
2. Ask students if they know what each word means.
   - If students know a word's meaning, have them define it and use it in a sentence.
   - If students don't know a word's meaning, read them the definition and discuss the word with them.

desert – a large area of land where there is little water, rain, or plants
dune – a hill of loose sand, made by the wind blowing the sand
oasis – a place in the desert that has fresh water, where trees and plants grow
Sahara – the world's largest desert
spring – a place where water rises up from under the ground

TIP The word *oasis* is pronounced "oh-AY-sis."

Read Aloud

Book Walk

Prepare students by taking them on a Book Walk of "The Amazing Sahara." Scan the magazine article together, and ask students to make predictions about the text.

1. Turn to the **table of contents**. Help students find the selection, and turn to that page.
2. Point to and read aloud the **title of the article**.
3. Have students look at the **pictures** in the article. Answers to questions may vary.
   - What do you think the article is about?
   - What do you already know about deserts?
4. Point to and read aloud any **headers, captions,** or **other features** that stand out.
   - What do you think the article might tell us about the Sahara? Answers will vary.
   - Is the article about real or made-up things? real things

Objectives

- Make predictions based on title, illustrations, and/or context clues.
- Activate prior knowledge by previewing text and/or discussing topic.
- Read and listen to a variety of texts for information and pleasure independently or as part of a group.

"The Amazing Sahara"

Now it's time to read "The Amazing Sahara." Have students sit next to you so that they can see the pictures and words while you read the article aloud. Tell students to listen carefully so they can discover why the author wrote the article.

Read aloud the entire article. Emphasize Words to Know as you come to them. If appropriate, use the pictures to help show what each word means.

TIP The word *jerboa* is pronounced "juhr-BOH-uh."

Check Your Reading

"The Amazing Sahara"

Check students' comprehension of "The Amazing Sahara."

1. Remind students that an article about real things, or **facts**, is called *nonfiction*.
2. **Have students retell the article in their own words** to develop grammar, vocabulary, comprehension, and fluency skills. When finished, **ask students the following questions** to check general comprehension and their understanding of why the author wrote the article.
   - Is it true that the Sahara is the hottest place in the world? Yes
   - Where is the Sahara located? Africa
   - When does the Sahara get cold? at night
   - How long can a camel go without water? a week
   - There are many facts in this article. What do we call this kind of writing? nonfiction
   - Why do you think the author wrote this article? to teach us about the Sahara

Objectives

- Identify the purpose of a text.
- Identify different types of text.
- Answer questions requiring literal recall of details.

Explore "The Amazing Sahara"

Lesson Overview

Offline "The Amazing Sahara" **30 minutes**

Get Ready	Cause and Effect
	Words to Know
Read Aloud	Book Walk
	"The Amazing Sahara"
Check Your Reading	"The Amazing Sahara"
Reading for Meaning	Text Features in "The Amazing Sahara"

Materials

Supplied

- "The Amazing Sahara," *Amazing Places*, pp. 20–29

Keywords

cause – the reason why something happens

effect – the result of a cause

environmental print – words and symbols found in the world around us, such as those on signs, ads, and labels

text feature – part of a text that helps a reader locate information and determine what is most important; examples include the title, table of contents, headings, pictures, and glossary

Advance Preparation

Before working with students, spend a few minutes reviewing Words to Know. Then review the Check Your Reading and Reading for Meaning activities to familiarize yourself with the questions and answers.

Big Ideas

- Comprehension entails an understanding of the organizational patterns of text.
- Comprehension is facilitated by an understanding of physical presentation (headings, subheads, graphics, and other features).

Offline 30 minutes

"The Amazing Sahara"

Work **together** with students to complete offline Get Ready, Read Aloud, Check Your Reading, and Reading for Meaning activities.

Get Ready

Cause and Effect

Explore how one thing can cause another thing to happen.

1. Tell students that doing one thing can make another thing happen. The thing that you do is called the **cause**, and the thing that happens is called the **effect**. Examples of cause and effect are all around us.
   - **Cause:** The wind blows.
     Effect: A kite flies in the air.
   - **Cause:** You wave to a friend.
     Effect: Your friend waves back.
   - **Cause:** You flip a switch.
     Effect: The lights come on.
2. Have students practice identifying cause and effect.
   - What happens, or what is the effect, if you drop an egg? The egg cracks or breaks.

Objectives

- Describe cause-and-effect relationships in text.
- Increase concept and content vocabulary.
- Use new vocabulary in written and spoken sentences.

Words to Know

Before reading "The Amazing Sahara,"

1. Have students say each word aloud.
2. Ask students if they know what each word means.
   - If students know a word's meaning, have them define it and use it in a sentence.
   - If students don't know a word's meaning, read them the definition and discuss the word with them.

desert – a large area of land where there is little water, rain, or plants
dune – a hill of loose sand, made by the wind blowing the sand
oasis – a place in the desert that has fresh water, where trees and plants grow
Sahara – the world's largest desert
spring – a place where water rises up from under the ground

TIP The word *oasis* is pronounced "oh-AY-sis."

Read Aloud

Book Walk

Prepare students by taking them on a Book Walk of "The Amazing Sahara." Scan the magazine article together to revisit the text.

1. Turn to the selection.
2. Point to and read aloud the **title of the article**.
3. Have students look at the **pictures** in the article. Answers to questions may vary.
   - It can get very hot in the Sahara. What kind of clothes would you wear if you visited the Sahara?
   - What do you think it would be like to be in a sandstorm?
   - If you were in a sandstorm, what might you wear to protect your eyes and your body?

Objectives

- Read and listen to a variety of texts for information and pleasure independently or as part of a group.
- Make inferences based on text and/or prior knowledge.

"The Amazing Sahara"

Now it's time to read "The Amazing Sahara." Have students sit next to you so that they can see the pictures and words while you read the article aloud.

Read aloud the entire article. Tell students to listen carefully for things that cause other things to happen.

TIP The word *jerboa* is pronounced "juhr-BOH-uh."

Check Your Reading

"The Amazing Sahara"

Have students retell the article in their own words to develop grammar, vocabulary, comprehension, and fluency skills. When finished, **ask the following questions** to check understanding of cause and effect relationships.

- What causes sand dunes to form? strong winds
- What happens when strong winds blow at night in the Sahara? It gets chilly or cold.
- What happens if the wind blows *really* hard in the Sahara? It can cause a sandstorm.
- Why aren't there many plants or animals in the Sahara? It's too hot and dry.
- A camel has soft, wide feet. What does this help a camel do? walk across the sand
- Why does a jerboa dig under the sand during the hot day? to get to the cooler soil
- Why does a jerboa come out at night? It needs to look for food.

Objectives

- Describe cause-and-effect relationships in text.

Reading for Meaning

Text Features in "The Amazing Sahara"

Guide students to demonstrate understanding of the article's text features.

1. Point to the small world map on page 21.
   - What does this map show? where Africa is
2. Point to the large map of Africa on page 21.
   - What does the red part of the map of Africa show? where the Sahara is in Africa
3. Point to the thermometer on page 22.
   - Why is there a picture of a thermometer pointing to 130°F? to help you understand how hot it gets in the Sahara
4. Point to the white lines over the sand dunes on page 24.
   - What do the curly white lines on the picture of the sand dunes show you? how strong winds blow the sand and make big sand dunes
5. Point to the tree on page 25.
   - What does this picture of a single tree tell you? There aren't many plants in the Sahara because it's so hot and dry.
   - What else is on page 25 that lets you know that the Sahara is hot and dry? the drawing of the sun
6. Point to the camel-crossing sign on pages 26–27.
   - What is this object called? a sign
   - What is the picture on the sign? a camel
   - Why is this sign in the Sahara? It warns people to watch out for camels because they might be crossing the road.

Objectives

- Identify purpose of environmental print.
- Identify and comprehend environmental print.
- Identify the purpose of and information provided by illustrations, titles, charts, and graphs.

Review "The Amazing Sahara"

Lesson Overview

Offline	"The Amazing Sahara"	30 minutes
Get Ready	Words to Know	
	Reread or Retell	
Reading for Meaning	Visual Text Features in "The Amazing Sahara"	
Making Connections	One Cause, Three Effects	

Materials

Supplied

- "The Amazing Sahara," *Amazing Places*, pp. 20–29
- *K*[12] *Language Arts Activity Book*, p. LC 73

Also Needed

- crayons (optional)

Keywords

cause – the reason why something happens

effect – the result of a cause

text feature – part of a text that helps a reader locate information and determine what is most important; examples include the title, table of contents, headings, pictures, and glossary

Big Ideas

- Comprehension entails an understanding of the organizational patterns of text.
- Comprehension is facilitated by an understanding of physical presentation (headings, subheads, graphics, and other features).

Offline 30 minutes

"The Amazing Sahara"

Work **together** with students to complete offline Get Ready, Reading for Meaning, and Making Connections activities.

Get Ready

Words to Know

Ask students to define the following words and use them in a sentence:

desert **dune** **oasis** **Sahara** **spring**

Correct any incorrect or vague definitions.

Objectives

- Use new vocabulary in written and spoken sentences.
- Increase concept and content vocabulary.

Reread or Retell

If you'd like to, reread the article to students. Otherwise, have students retell the article using the pictures as a guide, or move on to the next activity.

Reading for Meaning

Visual Text Features in "The Amazing Sahara"

Have students demonstrate the ability to identify and use visual text features such as pictures and headings.

Objectives

- Use visual text features to aid understanding of text.
- Identify the purpose of and information provided by illustrations, titles, charts, and graphs.
- Make inferences based on text and/or prior knowledge.

1. Point to the frying pan and the puff of cold wind on pages 22 and 23.
   - Why is there a picture of a frying pan? to show that it gets really hot in the Sahara
   - Why is there a puff of wind blowing off the word *Cold*? to show that the Sahara is cold at night when the wind blows
   - Why is the frying pan on a red background and the cold wind on a blue background? The color red looks hot, and the color blue looks cold.
2. Point to the picture of the sandstorm on page 24.
   - What does this picture help the reader better understand? what a sandstorm looks like
3. Point to the caption next to the picture of the jerboa on page 27.
   - This sentence says that this animal is called a *jerboa*. How does the picture next to it help the reader better understand what a jerboa is? It shows that a jerboa looks like a kind of mouse.
4. Point to the picture of the people in the desert on page 29.
   - Why is this picture in the article? Possible answers: to show what it's like to live in the Sahara; to show that people can live in the Sahara even though it's so hot and dry

Making Connections

One Cause, Three Effects

Have students show how one cause can have multiple effects.

1. On page LC 73 in K^{12} *Language Arts Activity Book,* point to the cause-and-effect graphic organizer.
2. Point to and read aloud the word *Cause.*
3. Point to the box below it and read aloud the words inside.
   - Explain that strong winds in the Sahara *cause* things to happen.
4. Point to the arrows and the three boxes on the right.
   - Each arrow means that the cause leads to something else that happens—the effect.
   - Because the strong winds cause three things to happen, there are arrows that point to three boxes—one for each effect.
5. Ask students to name the three things that happen as a result of the strong winds, and write one in each box. chilly at night; sand dunes; sandstorms
6. If time allows, have students draw a picture on a separate piece of paper based on one of the effects of the strong winds in the Sahara.

Objectives

- Describe cause-and-effect relationships in text.
- Demonstrate understanding through graphic organizers

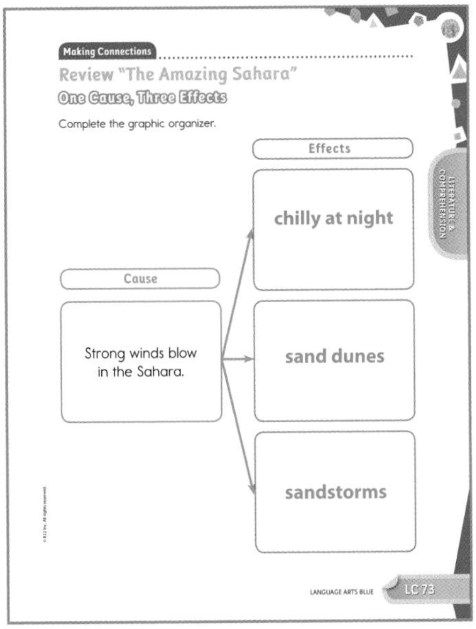
Making Connections

Review "The Amazing Sahara"

One Cause, Three Effects

Complete the graphic organizer.

Introduce *The Snowy Day*

Lesson Overview

Offline *The Snowy Day* — 30 minutes

Get Ready	Predictions
	Words to Know
Read Aloud	Book Walk
	The Snowy Day
Check Your Reading	*The Snowy Day*

Materials

Supplied

- *The Snowy Day* by Ezra Jack Keats

Story Synopsis

Overnight the city is transformed from an urban landscape into a snowy playground. What adventures await one small boy in this winter wonderland?

Keywords

prediction – a guess about what might happen that is based on information in a story and what you already know

prior knowledge – things you already know from past experience

Advance Preparation

Read *The Snowy Day* before beginning the Read Aloud activity, to locate Words to Know within the text.

Read the Read Aloud directions to be aware of stopping points in the story at which students will make predictions. Since this book has no page numbers, you should bookmark pages with stopping points.

Big Ideas

- Comprehension entails actively thinking about what is being read.
- Comprehension is facilitated when readers connect new information to information previously learned.

Offline 30 minutes

The Snowy Day

Work **together** with students to complete offline Get Ready, Read Aloud, and Check Your Reading activities.

Get Ready

Predictions

Explore making and revising predictions.

1. Tell students that **good readers make predictions**, or guesses, about what will happen in a story. We use **clues in the story and what we know from our own experiences** to predict what will happen next.
2. Good readers learn to change their predictions as they read more of a story and get more information.
3. Have students practice making and revising a prediction.
   Say: Roberto opened the closet door. He bent down and picked up a pair of old sneakers that were at the back of the closet.
   - What do you think will happen next? Answers will vary.
4. Have students revise their prediction.
   Say: Roberto sat down on his bed and took out a twenty-dollar bill that was hidden inside one of the sneakers. "Twenty dollars!" Roberto said out loud. "Just enough for that new video game!"
   - Now what do you think, or predict, will happen? Answers will vary but should involve Roberto going to the store and buying a new video game.
   - Did you change your prediction? If you did, what new clue made you change your guess? Roberto pulls out money; Roberto says twenty dollars is just enough to buy a new game.

TIP Do not describe a prediction as "wrong." This may discourage students from attempting to make predictions. Predictions are neither right nor wrong. We make the best prediction we can, based on the available information.

Objectives

- Make predictions before and during reading.
- Evaluate predictions.
- Build vocabulary through listening, reading, and discussion.
- Use new vocabulary in written and spoken sentences.

Words to Know

Before reading *The Snowy Day,*

1. Have students say each word aloud.
2. Ask students if they know what each word means.
   - If students know a word's meaning, have them define it and use it in a sentence.
   - If students don't know a word's meaning, read them the definition and discuss the word with them.

adventure – an exciting or dangerous experience
heaping – piled up
path – a trail for walking
smack – hit

Read Aloud

Book Walk

Prepare students by taking them on a Book Walk of *The Snowy Day*. Scan the beginning of the book together, and ask students to make predictions about the story.

1. Have students look at the picture on the cover. Point to and read aloud the **book title**.
2. Read aloud the name of the **author**.
3. Have students look at the picture on the first page of the story. Answers to questions may vary.
   - Where do you think the story takes place?
   - What do you think might happen in the story?
   - Have you ever played in the snow? If so, what did you do? If not, what would you like to do on a snowy day?

Objectives

- Make predictions based on title, illustrations, and/or context clues.
- Listen and respond to texts representing a variety of cultures, time periods, and traditions.
- Make predictions before and during reading.

The Snowy Day

Now it's time to read *The Snowy Day*. Have students sit next to you so that they can see the pictures and words while you read the story aloud.

Read aloud the entire story. Pause at the following points in the story to ask students what they predict will happen next. Jot down their predictions for later reference.

- After Peter wakes up and looks out the window
- After Peter finds a stick that's good for smacking a tree
- After Peter pretends he's a mountain climber and climbs up a hill
- After Peter puts the snowball in his pocket and goes inside the house
- After Peter and his friend go out together in the snow

Check Your Reading

The Snowy Day

Have students retell *The Snowy Day* in their own words to develop grammar, vocabulary, comprehension, and fluency skills. When finished, **ask students the following questions** to check their predictions. **Refer to the predictions you jotted down, as necessary.** Answers to questions may vary.

- What did you predict would happen after Peter wakes up and looks out the window?
- Were you surprised that snow falls on Peter's head when he smacks the tree with a stick? Why or why not?
- What did you predict would happen after Peter climbs up the hill? What really happens? He slides back down the hill.
- What did you predict would happen after Peter puts the snowball in his pocket and goes inside the house? What clues from the story or your own experiences did you use to make your prediction?
- What did you predict would happen after Peter and his friend go out together in the snow? What clues from the story or your own experiences did you use to make your prediction?

Objectives

- Evaluate predictions.

Explore *The Snowy Day*

Lesson Overview

Offline *The Snowy Day* — 30 minutes

Get Ready	How to Draw and Support a Conclusion
	Words to Know
Read Aloud	Book Walk
	The Snowy Day
Check Your Reading	*The Snowy Day*
Reading for Meaning	Draw Conclusions in *The Snowy Day*

Materials

Supplied

- *The Snowy Day* by Ezra Jack Keats

Keywords

draw a conclusion – to make a decision about something not stated directly in a text by considering information provided and what you know from past experience

sensory language – language that appeals to the five senses

Advance Preparation

Before working with students, spend a few minutes reviewing Words to Know. Then review the Check Your Reading and Reading for Meaning activities to familiarize yourself with the questions and answers.

Big Ideas

- Comprehension entails actively thinking about what is being read.
- Comprehension is facilitated when readers connect new information to information previously learned.
- Verbalizing your thoughts while modeling a reading strategy allows students to see what goes on inside the head of an effective reader; it makes visible the normally hidden process of comprehending text.

Offline 30 minutes

The Snowy Day

Work **together** with students to complete offline Get Ready, Read Aloud, Check Your Reading, and Reading for Meaning activities.

Get Ready

How to Draw and Support a Conclusion

Explore how to draw and support a conclusion.

1. Tell students that sometimes an author doesn't tell us everything in the words of a story. Good readers look for clues in the words and pictures to help them figure out things such as what a character is thinking or why a character is doing something.
2. Explain that, along with these clues, good readers think about what they know from personal experience. When readers do this, they **draw a conclusion**. A conclusion is based on what you read and pictures in the story, together with your knowledge learned from personal experience.
3. **Think aloud** while modeling how to draw and support a conclusion.
   Say: First, Han looked at the lions. Then he looked at the elephants. Next, he went to look at the polar bears.
4. Share your thoughts aloud so that students can understand the thought process of an effective reader.
   Say: I think that Hans is at the zoo, even though the paragraph doesn't say that. I can figure this out because people go to the zoo to see lions, elephants, and polar bears.
5. Help students draw and support a conclusion.
   Say: Sasha heard the booming thunder. He looked out the window and saw that everything was wet.
   - Why is everything outside wet? It's raining. How do you know this? When there's thunder, there's usually a rainstorm; when it rains, things get wet.
6. Remind students that sometimes an author will use words that help readers hear and imagine things in their mind as they read.
   - What words in the story about Sasha help you imagine what Sasha heard? booming thunder

Objectives

- Draw conclusions using text, illustrations, and/or prior knowledge.
- Support conclusions using text, illustrations, and/or prior knowledge.
- Build vocabulary through listening, reading, and discussion.
- Use new vocabulary in written and spoken sentences.

Words to Know

Before reading *The Snowy Day*,

1. Have students say each word aloud.

2. Ask students if they know what each word means.
   - If students know a word's meaning, have them define it and use it in a sentence.
   - If students don't know a word's meaning, read them the definition and discuss the word with them.

adventure – an exciting or dangerous experience
heaping – piled up
path – a trail for walking
smack – hit

Read Aloud

Book Walk

Prepare students by taking them on a Book Walk of *The Snowy Day*. Scan the story together to revisit the characters and events.

1. Read aloud the **book title**.
2. Have students locate the name of the **author**. Read the name of the author.
3. Look through the book. Have students describe what they see in the **pictures**. Answers to questions may vary.
   - Have you ever made tracks? How did you do it?
   - Have you ever touched snow? What was it like?

Objectives

- Listen and respond to texts representing a variety of cultures, time periods, and traditions.
- Activate prior knowledge by previewing text and/or discussing topic.

The Snowy Day

Now it's time to read *The Snowy Day*. Have students sit next to you so that they can see the pictures and words while you read the story aloud.

Read aloud the entire story. Remind students that both the words and the pictures give clues to help readers understand parts of the story that aren't directly stated by the author.

Check Your Reading

The Snowy Day

Have students retell *The Snowy Day* in their own words to develop grammar, vocabulary, comprehension, and fluency skills. When finished, remind students how an author will sometimes use words that help readers hear and see things in their mind. Then, **ask students the following questions** to check their ability to identify sensory language.

1. **Read aloud:** "Crunch, crunch, crunch, his feet sank into the snow."
   - Which words in the sentence do you hear more than once? *Crunch, crunch, crunch*
   - What do the words help you imagine? the sounds of Peter walking across the snow

Objectives

- Identify author's use of sensory language.

2. **Read aloud:** "It was a stick—a stick that was just right for smacking a snow-covered tree."
   - Which word in the sentence helps you imagine what Peter does with the stick? *smacking*
3. **Read aloud:** "Down fell the snow—plop!—on top of Peter's head."
   - What word helps you hear something? *plop*
4. **Read aloud:** "He climbed up a great big tall heaping mountain of snow . . . ."
   - Why does the author use so many words to describe the snow in this sentence? to help you imagine how big the pile of snow is

Reading for Meaning

Draw Conclusions in *The Snowy Day*

Help students draw and support conclusions about *The Snowy Day.*

1. Remind students that sometimes readers can figure out something the author doesn't state directly by using clues in the words and the pictures, along with thinking about their own experiences.
2. Have students look at what's outside the window in Peter's room on the first two pages of the story, and then have them study the next two pages where Peter first runs outside.
   - Does Peter live in the city or the country? the city   How can you tell? The big blocks of color are tall buildings like you would see in a city.
3. **Read aloud:** "He found something sticking out of the snow that made a new track. It was a stick—a stick that was just right for smacking a tree. Down fell the snow—plop!—on top of Peter's head."
   - What do you think Peter did with the stick? made a track and smacked a tree
   - What do you think made the snow plop on Peter's head? When he hit the tree with the stick, the snow fell down.
4. Have students look at the pages that show Peter sitting on the snow and the big boys having a snowball fight. Reread that page.
   - Share your thoughts on how you can figure out that Peter is too small to join in a snowball fight with the big boys. Guide students to think aloud. Possible thoughts: The white spot on Peter's snowsuit shows that he got knocked down by a snowball; the story says that Peter knew he wasn't old enough.
5. Have students look at the page that shows Peter making a snow angel.
   - How does Peter make a snow angel? He lies in the snow and moves his arms and legs up and down.
6. Have students look at the page that shows Peter looking for the snowball in his coat pocket.
   - What happened to the snowball Peter put in his pocket? It melted.
   - What clues from the story and your own experience helped you to figure it out? The story says that Peter goes in the warm house after he puts the snowball in his pocket; I know that snow melts when it gets warm.

Objectives

- Draw conclusions using text, illustrations, and/or prior knowledge.
- Support conclusions using text, illustrations, and/or prior knowledge.

Review *The Snowy Day*

Lesson Overview

Offline	*The Snowy Day*	30 minutes
Get Ready	Words to Know	
	Reread	
Reading for Meaning	Summarize *The Snowy Day*	
Making Connections	Recipe for a Snowy Day	
Beyond the Lesson	**OPTIONAL:** An Imaginary Snowy Day	

Materials

Supplied

- *The Snowy Day* by Ezra Jack Keats
- *K[12] Language Arts Activity Book*, p. LC 75

Also Needed

- glue stick
- scissors, round-end safety
- household objects – hat, scarf, mittens, jacket, sweater, boots (all optional)

Big Ideas

- Comprehension requires an understanding of story structure.
- Comprehension requires the reader to self-monitor understanding.

Keywords

self-monitor – to notice if you do or do not understand what you are reading

sequence – order

summarize – to tell the most important ideas or events of a text

summary – a short retelling that includes only the most important ideas or events of a text

Offline 30 minutes

The Snowy Day

Work **together** with students to complete offline Get Ready, Reading for Meaning, Making Connections, and Beyond the Lesson activities.

Get Ready

Words to Know

Ask students to define the following words and use each in a sentence:

adventure	**path**
heaping	**smack**

Correct any incorrect or vague definitions.

Objectives

- Use new vocabulary in written and spoken sentences.

Reread

If you'd like to, reread the story to students. Otherwise, move on to the next activity.

Reading for Meaning

Summarize *The Snowy Day*

Have students summarize *The Snowy Day*.

Objectives

- Summarize read-aloud stories.

1. Tell students that one way readers can check their own understanding of a story is by giving a summary.
2. Explain that a **summary** is a very short retelling that **includes only the most important things that happen in a story in the order that they happen.**
3. Point out that a summary is not the same as retelling a story because it does not include very many details.
4. Ask students to complete the following steps in order to summarize the story.
   - Tell what happens at the beginning of the story in one or two sentences. Example: Peter wakes up and sees snow outside his window; he puts on his snowsuit and goes outside.
   - Tell what happens in the middle of the story in one or two sentences. Example: Peter plays in the snow all day; he makes a snowball and puts it in his pocket just before he goes back inside his house.
   - Tell what happens at the end of the story in one or two sentences. Example: The snowball is gone when Peter looks for it after his bath; he goes to bed and dreams the sun melts all the snow, but it's still there when he wakes up.

Making Connections

Recipe for a Snowy Day

Have students practice their sequencing skills by ordering pictures that represent scenes from the story.

1. On page LC 75 in *K¹² Language Arts Activity Book,* have students cut out the pictures of scenes from the story.
2. Have students glue the pictures to a large sheet of paper to show the correct sequence of events.
   - Have students refer back to the book if they need help remembering the order of the story events.
3. Have them retell *The Snowy Day* using the sequenced pictures as a guide.

Making Connections

Review *The Snowy Day*

Recipe for a Snowy Day

Cut out the pictures. Glue them to a sheet of paper in the correct order. Retell the story when done.

3 6 5 2 1 4

LITERATURE & COMPREHENSION

LANGUAGE ARTS BLUE LC 75

Objectives

- Sequence events from a text.
- Retell a story using illustrations from the text as a guide.

Beyond the Lesson

OPTIONAL: An Imaginary Snowy Day

This activity is intended for students who have extra time and would benefit from pretending to be the character in the story. Feel free to skip this activity.

1. Have students put on winter clothing: hat, scarf, mittens, jacket, sweater, and boots.
2. As you read aloud *The Snowy Day,* have students reenact the scenes, pretending to be Peter and having his adventures in the snow.
   - No props are necessary; have students use their imagination.

Objectives

- Reenact a story in the correct sequence.
- Make connections with text: text-to-text, text-to-self, text-to-world.